Literary Dollars and Social Sense

Literary Dollars and Social Sense

A People's History of the Mass Market Book

Ronald J. Zboray and Mary Saracino Zboray

Routledge
New York • London

Published in 2005 by
Routledge
Taylor & Francis Group
270 Madison Avenue
New York, NY 10016
www.routledge-ny.com

10 9 8 7 6 5 4 3 2 1

Library of Congress Cataloging-in-Publication Data
Zboray, Ronald J.
   Literary dollars & social sense : a people's history of the mass market book / Ronald J. Zborary and Mary Saracino Zboray.
      p. cm.
   Includes bibliographical references.
   ISBN 0-415-94984-X (hb : alk. paper) — ISBN 0-415-97248-5 (pb : alk. paper) 1. Book Industries and trade—United States—History—19th century. 2. Books and reading—United States—History—19th century. 3. Books—United States—Marketing—History—19th century.
I. Title: Literary dollars and social sense. II. Zboray, Mary Saracino, 1953- III. Title.
   Z473.Z37 2005
   381'.45002'097309034—dc22   2004025135

CONTENTS

ACKNOWLEDGMENTS

We are grateful to many institutions and the people connected with them who were instrumental in bringing this book to fruition through generous support. Two grants from the National Endowment for the Humanities—an NEH–American Antiquarian Society six-month resident fellowship in 1992 and an NEH 1998–1999 Fellowship for University Teachers—provided generous support for research and writing and time off from university teaching duties. For awarding the 1992 fellowship we thank the American Antiquarian Society and its entire staff, but especially then director Marcus McCorison, along with Georgia Barnhill, Nancy Burkett, Joanne Chaison, John Hench, Tom Knoles, Marie Lamoreaux, Dennis Laurie, and Laura Wasowicz. We are also indebted to the Massachusetts Historical Society, which awarded the Benjamin F. Stevens Fellowship in 1993, and to its staff—particularly Ford Editor Conrad Edick Wright (director of the Center for New England Studies), librarian Peter Drummey, archivist Brenda Lawson, and former staff members Ed Hanson, Virginia Smith, Chris Steele, and Len Travers.

The Schlesinger Library at the former Radcliffe College (now a branch of Harvard University) provided a study grant in 1993, and later, for 1998–1999, dual honorary visiting fellowships. That institution, its then acting head Mary Maples Dunn, and its staff—particularly Jane Knowles, Anne Englehart, Marie-Hélène Gold, and former staff members Sylvia McDowell and Deirdre O'Neill—deserve our deepest thanks.

Georgia State University provided ample intramural support. It cost-shared the 1998–1999 NEH grant year, and it awarded Research Initiation Grants in 1994 and 1997, as well as a Quality Improvement Fund Award in 1994. In 1996 a Summer Faculty Research Grant and a College of Arts and Sciences Outstanding Junior Faculty Award supported summer travel to archives, as did yet another summer grant in 2000. The Interlibrary Loan Office there—and, above all, Margie Patterson—patiently filled our numerous requests. The History Department at GSU assisted in numerous ways. It granted research leave from teaching in Fall 1997, bestowed the 2001 Dale Alan Somers Memorial Award, and assigned a succession of excellent graduate research assistants: Steve Blankenship, Drew Brandon, Daniel Bronstein, Mike Brubaker, Robb Haberman, Chris Hawkins-Long, Bill Simson, and Dale Vanderhoerst.

More recently, new colleagues and staff at the University of Pittsburgh Department of Communication have offered much support for our work. As well, the university's Hillman Library interlibrary loan and circulation staff provided a steady stream of books, and we have benefitted by visiting the university's Darlington Memorial Library (presided over by the very helpful Marcia Grodsky) and the Foster Hall Collection at the American Music Center.

We owe inexpressible thanks to the staff members of the many archives we visited. They, including the above mentioned people at the American Antiquarian Society, the Massachusetts Historical Society, and the Schlesinger Library, generously gave us their time and attention. In addition to these helpful souls, several archivists whom we have not met in person graciously answered detailed written queries about their collections, and filled requests for photocopies and photographs. Many of these people went beyond the call of duty. Very special thanks go to Barbara Anderson and George Comtois (Lexington Historical Society) for opening their doors to us during off hours and holiday weekends in December 1995; Paul Carnahan (Vermont Historical Society) for giving us an electronic copy of Charles M. Cobb's diary; Darrol Pierson (Indiana State Library) for locating and inspecting the typeface of Charlotte Forten's long lost "To a Beloved Friend"; Rick Stattler (Rhode Island Historical Society) for directing us to important collections, sacrificing lunch hours to keep the manuscript room open, and proofreading our quotes; and Terri Tremblay (American Antiquarian Society) for patiently helping us locate illustrations.

Others who have immeasurably assisted us include Leanne Garland (Abraham Lincoln Library and Museum); Peg Hughes (Andover Historical Society); Robert Johnson-Lally (Archives of the Archdiocese of Boston); Robin D. Wear (Clifton Waller Barrett Library at the University of Virginia); Robert W. Lovett and Lorraine Muise (Beverly Historical Society and Museum); Giuseppi Bisaccia, Eugene Zepp, and Roberta Zonghi (Boston Public Library); Ronald D. Patkus (John J.

Burns Library at Boston College); Martha Mayo (Center for Lowell History at the University of Massachusetts at Lowell); Rev. Paul J. Nelligan, S.J., and Mark W. Savolis (College of the Holy Cross); Nancy Milnor and Martha H. Smart (Connecticut Historical Society); Mark Brown (John Hay Library at Brown University); Leslie A. Morris and Jennie Rathbun (Houghton Library at Harvard University); Alison Dinicola (Huntington Library); Cheryl Schnirring (Illinois State Historical Library); Stephen E. Novak (Augustus C. Long Health Sciences Library, Columbia University); Christine S. Albert, Bill Barry, and Nicholas Noyes (Maine Historical Society); Judy Huenneke and Sally A. Ulrich (Mary Baker Eddy Library); Joellen El Bashir (Moorland-Springarn Research Center at Howard University); Nicholas Graham (Massachusetts Historical Society); Jerry Anderson and Timothy Salls (New England Historic Genealogical Society); Bill Copley and Betsey Hamlin Morin (New Hampshire Historical Society); Elizabeth L. Plummer (Ohio Historical Society); Lisa Compton, Jane M. Hennedy, and Greta Smith (Old Colony Historical Society); Irene V. Axelrod, Christine Michelini, and Jane Ward (Peabody Essex Museum); and Susan Sanborn Barker, Susan Boone, Amy Hague, and Margaret R. Jessup (Sophia Smith Collection, Smith College).

Finally, we are grateful to the staffs at the American Textile History Museum, Lynn Museum, Marblehead Historical Society, Portland Public Library, South Carolina Historical Society, and the hundreds of archives and local historical societies scattered across the country to whom we have written letters of inquiry.

Acknowledging debts to professional colleagues is a difficult task for too many have been accrued on our decade-long journey that has brought us to so many places, whether sites of research or venues for delivering our work. A few among the many scholars to whom we owe thanks are Richard D. Brown, Lawrence Buell, Charles Capper, John Y. Cole, Phyllis Cole, Daniel A. Cohen, Cathy N. Davidson, Wayne Franklin, Janet Gabler-Hover, Philip F. Gura, Ellen Gruber Garvey, Mary Kelley, James Machor, Leo Marx, Marilyn Ferris Motz, Joel Myerson, Stephen Nissenbaum, Janice A. Radway, David S. Reynolds, Jonathan Rose, Robert Sattlemeyer, Alison Scott, Eleanor F. Shevlin, Lydia Schurman, Barbara Sicherman, Kenneth Silverman, Alan Trachtenberg, and Wayne Wiegand. Graduate students enrolled in Ronald J. Zboray's spring 2004 seminar in audience and reception history—Jasmine Cobb, Christine Feldman, Heather Fisher, Jessica Ghilani, Erika Molloseau, and Mark Porrovecchio—gave insightful comments on chapter 3.

At Routledge we owe former publishing director Karen A. Wolny our most heartfelt thanks for having faith in our manuscript and taking it on, and we deeply appreciate vice president William Germano's continuing enthusiasm for it. Thanks go also to Jaclyn Bergeron, Prudy Taylor Board, Gilad Foss, Kimberly Guinta, Fred Veith, and Daniel Webb. The careful reading and solid insights provided by our three specialist readers for Routledge have been invaluable.

We also thank editor J. Randolph Cox for granting permission to revise and greatly expand the original version of Ronald J. Zboray's "A Glimpse of Cheap Publishers in Antebellum Boston: John Townsend Trowbridge's *Martin Merrivale: His 'X' Mark*," (*Dime Novel Round-Up* 60, no. 5 [October 1991]: 78–83) in chapter 2. Apart from these few pages, the remainder of the content is entirely original to this book.

Last but not least we extend our gratitude backward over a century and a half to the many forgotten writers who bequeathed to a future generation records that often so eloquently describe encounters with the literary marketplace. We are deeply honored to be the remembrancers of both their everyday struggles and occasional triumphs.

INTRODUCTION

Social Authors and Disseminators in the Age of the Mass Market

Publication — is the Auction
Of the Mind of Man —
Poverty — be justifying
For so foul a thing

Possibly — ...
. . . .

In the Parcel — Be the Merchant
Of the Heavenly Grace —
But reduce no Human Spirit
To Disgrace of Price —

—Emily Dickinson, "Publication is the auction"
(poem 788)

While Emily Dickinson probably never intended it for the reading public, her 1863 poem might easily have resonated with contemporaries who witnessed the publishing industry's unprecedented surge during the three decades before the Civil War.[1] Once scarce, expensive, and limited in array, printed literature, fashioned by "the Mind of Man," had become an abundant, relatively cheap, and diversified mass-market commodity. Between 1850 and 1860 alone, the printing industry's product value increased by 168 percent, from nearly twelve to over thirty-one million dollars a year, an amount surpassed by only thirteen other branches of manufacturing. Large publishing establishments, such as Harper and Brothers, reaped enormous profits, but even the many smaller firms who collectively produced the bulk of output prospered. Although most authors fared less well, some could supplement an income or even subsist by writing. Clearly, by 1863, Dickinson's "Auction" was well underway with publishers, booksellers, and authors vying for "literary dollars."[2]

As print flooded the antebellum marketplace, "literary dollars" seemingly summoned everyone to the auction, including women, African Americans, and the working class. Commercial publishing houses and entrepreneurial printing establishments provided signal opportunities for aspiring litterateurs. The burgeoning periodical market tempted ambitious neophytes to submit poetry, short stories, novelettes, and sundry nonfiction pieces. Publishers lured traveling agents to open new, remote markets through subscriptions or direct sales. Literary entrepreneurs stimulated common readers' appetites by publicizing the authorial fame and affluence desired by many, but achieved by very few.

Although money and reputation beckoned, these were not easily earned. Rather than precipitating literary professionalism, the book trade meted out thankless tasks to most writers, editors, and disseminators. Periodical contributors were meagerly recompensed, if at all; untried book authors commonly shouldered some production costs. Urban booksellers typically survived just over a year at midcentury,[3] while upcountry subscription agents seldom garnered enough commissions to make ends meet. For most aspiring book tradespeople then, obscurity outweighed recognition and discouragement outflanked ambition.

Worse still, the market often strained the nexus between literary sensibilities and social sense. If, as in Jane Austen's *Sense and Sensibility* (1811), romantic "sensibility" was usually tempered by sober "sense," so too was the personal construction of literary selves in everyday life often anchored in social conventions and relations. Sociabilities nurtured literary culture, and vice versa. Profits could matter less than status in a society relishing literature and using it instrumentally to maintain social ties reconfigured by the "market revolution."[4] Writing and selling literature made "social sense," even if doing so yielded only cents, not literary dollars. But when social customs played within market contexts, both social sense and literary sensibility suffered. Suspicion greeted agents who came a-calling like neighborly visitors. Criticism awaited published authors expecting support from friends. Chastisement befell women writing for audiences beyond their families. Distrust attended editors altering submissions from acquaintances. What made "social sense" outside the literary marketplace only confused social relations emerging within it. It is no wonder that beginners seldom persisted.[5]

Literary Dollars and Social Sense not only captures popular disenchantment at "the Auction," it also recounts the triumph of social responsibilities over impersonal market forces. It is as if Dickinson's contemporaries had heeded her final exhortation: "But reduce no Human Spirit / To Disgrace of Price —." To negotiate fraying relationships, correspondents cast their favorite renowned authors as mediating friends. To bolster family members' fledgling periodicals, busy homemakers supplied original copy and proofread galleys. To ameliorate social woes through print, evangelicals and social reformers sacrificed time, effort, and money. To immortalize the deceased, mourners published elegies and genealogists, their family histories. But even the simplest motive of all—to be "fresher and brighter," as one authoress conceded—guaranteed some personal and social success that transcended the "Disgrace of Price."[6] *Literary Dollars and Social Sense* shows these people apprehending the marketplace through their reading and gossiping, addressing it through their writing and editing, and serving it through their vending and distributing.

This is a people's history in the truest sense, for it is based on a wide range of first-person accounts. Left by amateur and minor writers for the market, as well as by distributors working in the field, this material has largely remained unpublished and overlooked. In bringing it to light for the first time, *Literary Dollars and Social Sense* provides an unusual bottom-up view of publishing history. The book thus complements older top-down studies of famous authors and major publishers.[7] But it also revises the common portrayal of the antebellum literary market as far more advanced, organized, and publisher-controlled than it actually was.[8] A mass market for literature, served by multitudinous small operators, indeed had emerged *ahead* of extensive mass production and national distribution emanating from a few highly capitalized firms. Yet this precorporate literary system's vastness, complexity, and omnipresence necessarily eluded previous investigators who did not consult first-person materials. Only there, in the context of traditional local moral economies so vividly expressed in antebellum letters and diaries, do people's varied experiences of the market and its workings become apparent. As these people comment on their writing, publishing, editing, and selling—or lecturing, teaching, and otherwise performing literature for profit—they reveal their sometime opposition or acquiescence to literary commodification. Like the resistance narratives of subaltern groups vying against dominant powers offered in some previous "people's histories," the story here shows people pulling against unabashed literary entrepreneurialism.[9] The parallel may be clearest in the way some consumers challenged big-selling authors' publisher-driven celebrity claims, as we discuss later. In these pages, however, tensions between literary dollars and social sense were as likely to register within individuals themselves, as between conflicting social groups.

A "people's history of the mass-market book" perhaps could only have been written about the limited time period we consider in this study.[10] Before, most publishing was dominated by political, religious, and economic elites and it hardly addressed an actual national mass market; after, the emergent literary mass market was saturated via oligopolies of production and monopolies of distribution.[11] Postbellum corporate literary production crowded out the earlier hosts of amateur writers, petty publishers, and semi-independent distributors. In both periods, then, "a people's history" of publishing, aside from one based on consumption alone, would be virtually oxymoronic. What enabled, for the first time, such a history? In the early nineteenth-century industrial production and commercial distribution collided with longstanding social literary practices trickling down through a population increasingly able to read and more than willing to write—all within a landscape of vigorous national economic development.[12]

The antebellum period was thus a pivotal moment in the history of modern American mass-market publishing between its elite-driven past and its corporate-directed future. Accordingly, after we situate our work in prior scholarship, we briefly sketch authorship's and distribution's past in the early modern West before describing the popular prewar literary system. We wait until our conclusion to finish the story of how that system evolved into the twentieth century's familiar corporate-driven one. Instead, the rest of this introduction sets the stage for the many "informants" whose testimonies thread through the following chapters, as we discuss the book's scope and methods, present representative portraits of amateurs appearing throughout, and, finally, outline its organization.

AUTHORSHIP STUDY

American authorship study has been like a short tail wagging an enormous dog. Focus falls upon canonical writers, their coteries, and their publishers—a tiny group compared to the unsung armies contributing most copy to the press.[13] "In our literary world in this country, there is no lack in point of numbers of amateur authors," one magazine declared, recognizing their overwhelming presence. Learning more about canonized authors, not these publishing masses whom we hereafter dub "amateurs,"[14] has prompted studies of literary publishing, yet ever framed by the supposed antebellum emergence of professionalism.[15] This framing distorts the overall picture of literary production for print. After all, if a paying career marked success, nearly all writers failed miserably. Little room is left for more motivationally nuanced and temporary authorial engagements with the market, or for virtual collaborators who, by hatching ideas, offering encouragement, or disseminating writings fostered authors' literary development.

Still obscure, too, are the many writers producing literary manuscripts never intended for print—not only formal literary pieces, but correspondence, diaries, commonplace books, discourses, tracts, inscriptions, and fragments that have, apart from any functional uses, claims to being literature in their own right.[16] Scholars recently have explored how scribal culture, still vibrant centuries after Johannes Gutenberg, evoked the elective mode of "publishing"—that is, works circulated but not printed—called "social authorship." Social authors avoided print because it produced errors, corrupted authorial intentions, and froze a text in time; instead they valued the extended life a circulated manuscript text received. Also, they coveted manuscript production's often collaborative aspects and its benefits as an inexpensive "source of literary and intellectual capital."[17] Because scholars writing about the practice emphasize social participation, they invite reassessment of authorship as an expression of atomized individual intentions. By deliberately avoiding print, early modern social authors addressed networks of known readers who as collaborators commented upon and amended writings, and as disseminators read them aloud, conversed about them, or copied and mailed them. Manuscript literature circulated through correspondence, social calls, and messengers, at academic and literary club meetings, and in salons, coffeehouses, and taverns.[18] In this way, authors traded anonymous for select readerships and commercial for familiar distribution. Social authorship thus recasts printing as an alternative mode of publication, one not as revolutionary as commonly thought in connecting writers with audiences.[19]

Insofar as only a sliver of all manuscripts were printed and only a fraction of those were written by professionals, unpublished and amateur authorship is the rule against which writing for a living should be measured. As we will show, social authorship provided the creative pool from which amateurism emerged. Not surprisingly, market-oriented production more reflected these social origins than personal career aspirations. Similarly, amateurism contextualized professionalism. Indeed, both unpublished social authorship and published amateurism shaped the public's dawning perception that literary celebrities should serve rather than profit from the people.

FROM SCRIPTORIUM TO FACTORY

Social, amateur, and professional authorship and dissemination practices variably intersected over time. Within oral traditions predating script, specialized storytellers artfully performed compositions before often collaborating communities.[20] Later, with writing, ancient authors reached audiences via scrolls and codices sometimes handcopied by slaves; their medieval counterparts—monastic, cathedral, and lay university scriveners—multiplied textual reproductions, sometimes collectively in scriptoriums.[21] In late-fifteenth-century Europe, movable type and the hand-powered printing press spawned "print culture," distinct from the coexisting "scribal culture." Printing involved increasingly differentiated and specialized occupations (for example, pressmen, compositors, correctors, typefounders, and binders) and extensive distribution through booksellers, book fairs, and other sales venues—despite routine church or government censorship. Printing allowed greater and more standardized output while diminishing production time.[22] Yet variants (errors and corrections), often within a single run, seldom guaranteed exact replication of authors' manuscripts. Rampant plagiarism and piracy not only further corrupted texts, but could obscure original authorship.[23] Authors, however, remained largely pseudonymous or anonymous until the early modern era.[24] Expecting little or no money from publishing, they sought patrons or income from other sources.[25]

Early modern English print culture differed from the continent's. London, Oxford, and Cambridge, still entrenched in scribal practices, lagged behind continental publishing centers, including Venice, Paris, and Antwerp, which were larger and printed more and better quality imprints.[26] In England as nowhere else, early free trade in books and the influx of continental tradesmen gave way to protectionist licensing acts curtailing numbers of printers and foreign labor, and to government censorship, both enforced by the Stationers' Company, a trade guild chartered in 1557.[27] Despite the restrictive legacy, after 1710 authors fared better in England than elsewhere in that the Copyright Statute of that year, the first of its kind, granted authors final control of their literary property. The eventual rise of vernacular culture witnessed the construction of literary canons through biography and published collections. Grub Street hacks notwithstanding, authorial anonymity yielded to attribution, and obscurity to potential canonization.[28] All the while, social authorship flourished.

If England's overregulated publishing lagged, British North America's trailed even further. True, the printing press arrived in Massachusetts shortly after the 1630 Great Migration, but output there—and later, elsewhere—languished. Seventeenth-century publishing was less a trade than a sideline among sponsoring merchants who sometimes sold books. Business, governmental, and denominational job printing dominated. Shortages of skilled labor, cheap paper, and decent type stifled trade growth. English, Scottish, and Irish imports inundated the local trade, so the few reputable authors, mainly well-known ministers, sought overseas publication. With only gratis copies as rewards, some authors tried for more profits by assuming financial risks. But investors saw little return due to typically limited press runs; a run of five hundred copies was considered fairly large, though rare items, like Michael Wigglesworth's *Day of Doom* (1662, 1666) and Nathaniel Ames's eighteenth-century almanacs, did better. The success of almanacs was matched by that of newspapers. By 1765, they together accounted for an estimated 58.5 percent of all sheets printed in Boston. Though they signaled an increasingly secularized print culture presaging the American Revolution and offered opportunities for amateur writing, the two remained secondary to face-to-face encounters in the overall pattern of communication networks.[29]

Although the book trades and author-publisher relations changed only slowly from the mid-eighteenth to the early nineteenth centuries, a national literature nevertheless emerged. Worsening Anglo-American relations after 1765 coincided with a string of literary firsts. Inspired by *translatio studii*, or civilization's purported westward course, writers produced the first American novel, epic poem, and professionally acted play.[30] Independence brought countless calls for a national literature, answered haltingly by a few belles-lettrists, but more successfully by numerous schoolbook, geography, and dictionary authors.[31] Though a few best-selling postrevolutionary novelists like Susannah Rowson (*Charlotte Temple*, 1791) came and went, not until the 1820s did James Fenimore Cooper establish that an American writer could be renowned and well recompensed.[32] By then, the nation saw a "transportation revolution." Better roads and bridges, as well as new canal systems and river steamboats, stimulated print circulation, especially within entrepreneurial locales. Nevertheless, print production remained locally oriented and highly decentralized. Some of it addressed moral problems that Evangelicals attributed to the erosion of traditional ways of life caused by rapid economic development. More concerted efforts to Christianize the nation through mass religious publication logically followed: the American Bible Society (1817) and the American Tract Society (1823) would produce millions of items on the newly invented power presses.[33] Despite these innovations, the book trades before the 1830s remained backward compared with the general economic vibrancy.

Thereafter, American publishing progressed from a genteel, artisan trade supported by civic patronage, religious groups, and local businesses to a thriving, modern, cutthroat, profit-driven national industry. In this change, antebellum publishing stood on the cutting edge of business innovation. Firms like New York's Harper and Brothers and Boston's Frederick Gleason built integrated factories combining various processes under one roof, so that raw material came in one door and finished books and periodicals went out another. Competition sparked diversification; publishing led most mass-consumer industries in simultaneously marketing hundreds of different product "lines" over years. To create demand, publishers developed mass-marketing techniques through sales canvasses and national advertisements. To get the books out, they also bought bookstores or periodical depots in different cities to ensure their wares remained before the public—a form of vertical integration. More complex national distribution systems encompassed express companies, regional wholesalers, trade sales, and networks of correspondents. The industry pioneered modern managerial control through trade organizations that allowed publishers collectively to standardize practices and air grievances.[34] Overall, American publishing had reached industrial maturity during the antebellum years, while not yet reaching full corporate oligopolization.

Industrialization encouraged publishers to sustain some prominent authors' careers by keeping their works in print. Relatively permanent and reusable stereotype plates eliminated the cost of retypesetting future editions. The plates thus represented a long-term, large capital investment that did not always benefit authors. By making plates of British imprints, all unprotected by international copyright, an American publisher could literally capitalize upon the authors without paying them anything. So, apart from national pride, why invest in American authors at all? One answer is that federal copyright law afforded publishers exclusive control of their American properties, but not their piracies of foreign works. Moreover, with American authors, publishers could fine-tune, even commission, works for specific markets. There is little wonder that in 1856 Americans authored 80 percent of the titles published in the United States, up from only 30 percent in 1820.[35] Even greater opportunities opened through periodical publishers' need for steady streams of copy.[36]

Printing and publishing thus rode the crest of the huge economic surge coursing through (especially) the northeastern third of the nation, where in 1850 New York, Pennsylvania, and Massachusetts alone produced 81 percent of the industry's national product value—again, without significant monopolization. Indeed, as advanced firms flourished, they stimulated economic growth, from which more traditional artisan shops benefitted as well. Consequently, the overall number of firms dramatically increased; for example, Boston editorial offices grew from 113 during the 1820s to 665 during the 1840s.[37] Nearly every town with some commerce supported a weekly newspaper or two, and even midsized cities boasted several dailies or semiweeklies offering literary opportunities to local writers.[38]

ANTEBELLUM SOCIAL AUTHORSHIP

Despite the growing literary marketplace, social authorship practices persisted and evolved. Indeed, broadening literacy democratized literary aspirations. Diverse common people authored literary diaries, letters, poetry, and essays not intended for print. New forums for dissemination emerged, like the village lyceum and common school exhibitions, while exclusive coteries faded before more informal social exchanges. These developments aside, ordinary writers continued to produce manuscript literature for two symbiotically interacting reasons: for self-edification or self-improvement for social ends, and expressly for other people.[39]

Self-motivated production encompassed spontaneous, often therapeutic, but ever creative expressions prompted by amusing incidents, momentous occasions, unusual events, religious experience, natural settings, or everyday reading. Amid the swirl of inspiration, many youths became "addicted to the habit of writing stuff" as part of their literary socialization.[40] "Stuff" was mainly verse, but also short essays, songs, meditations, and even diaries, often themselves inherently literary, but also repositories of the other genres. Of course, adults wrote all of the above, but with more discrimination and purpose than children. What was written, however, matters less than why writing took place. Self-motivated writing in whatever form tempered emotions, focused attention, enhanced religious meditation, and quieted anxieties. It also memorialized fleeting events and passing scenes. Most of all, it assisted self-improvement by honing self-expression in a society valuing literary attainment.

By contrast, much literary writing was envisioned for certain recipients and answered distinct social invitations. Holidays, special occasions, farewells, and important life-cycle events called for poetic literary "gifts," like verse letters, book and album inscriptions, or notes accompanying presents. All these fulfilled social obligations, as did everyday correspondence that literarily conveyed personal news or enclosed pieces of original poetry. Even diaries, often "open books," could tailor their literary content for intended readers. Such private exchanges had their public counterparts, from students delivering their assigned compositions in classrooms and at community exhibitions to town lyceum members reading aloud their collectively written manuscript newspapers. Overall, these literary pieces were always produced with preconceived audiences in mind.

Such writings, however, often reached an unintended readership simply because of the circulation systems through which they passed. Once an author mailed, sent via page, hand-delivered, or recited a text to recipients, they became potential secondary disseminators who might transcribe it in letters, albums, and diaries, or verbally read or repeat it. They could even act as scribal publishers, making multiple copies from the original. Although unprecedented circulation was assured through emerging express companies, more frequent packet ships, and widening postal services, privacy was not, because intermediaries often read the mail or stole pieces of it.[41] In these ways authors lost control over their readership as their productions traveled through social networks and beyond. Worse still, readers sometimes "pirated" manuscript works for print without the author's knowledge.

There is little wonder that for some writers it seemed but a small step from social circulation in manuscript to publication in print. So why not take the plunge into print? After all, the small presses accounting for the bulk of production reached but a limited and predictable audience beyond intimate social circles. By reaching more people through print, authors could better propagate ideas, eulogize loved ones, or serve the public; and if a few dollars were made along the way, all the better. Having achieved social ends through print, some writers sought wider audiences via nationally oriented periodical and book publishers who were more likely to pay. A few authors writing for only money or fame shed the social motivations, but without entirely abandoning the wellspring of social inspiration.

VENUES AND AVENUES FOR PRINT

Writers seeking money had few options. Book publishing could be the most lucrative of these, but only in rare cases. Lucky authors might receive 10 percent of profits, but only after publishers deducted the edition's (usually overestimated) production cost from such profits. Little money was left for royalties unless the book was a rare "decided hit" with sales of around 10,000 copies. Indeed, most nonfiction books and pamphlets circulated in editions of a few hundred that were sponsored by religious, reform, or political organizations, leaving authors little or nothing. Despite fiction and verse publishers' often vigorous entrepreneurialism, only a few of their novelists or poets sustained any success. The vast majority of periodicals, especially organizationally affiliated ones, paid nothing or little. The many commissioned contributors to annuals and gift books, both expensive moneymaking serials, received only a small one-time payment, as did those writing for commercial monthlies offering one to three dollars per page. Famous writers received higher page rates from top monthlies, but not until the postbellum years could a viable living be made writing for them.[42]

Monthlies and newspapers shared characteristics with weeklies. Although formatted like large four-page newspapers with a banner, a masthead, and columns of tiny print, weeklies contained magazinelike fiction, poetry, and essays. Because the densely packed commercial "story weeklies" demanded an outpouring of original copy for each issue, they began to pay regular contributors. One late-1840s Boston weekly paid an unheard-of one hundred dollars for serialized novelettes, while the abolitionist weekly *National Era* serialized Harriet Beecher Stowe's *Uncle Tom's Cabin* (1851–1852) for four hundred dollars—slightly more than a skilled workingman's yearly wages, but hardly a middle-class income.[43] Another type of weekly targeting the vast market beyond major cities came in two varieties: (1) rural periodicals with news of local interest and original creative writing; and (2) country editions of urban dailies culled for items, often belles lettres, appealing to farm folk. Although they generally did not pay, these two venues could at least give amateurs a start.[44]

Finally, big cities supported dozens of newspapers needing copy. Competition drove publishers to offer more text for the price, by reducing type sizes and leading between lines, while increasing page size. Since there was seldom enough interesting news to fill the vast columns, urban newspapers became omnibuses of infotainment, mixing reportage and advertisements with editorials, fillers, jokes, speeches, anecdotes, sketches, vignettes, poems, fictional and historical pieces, anagrams, recipes, and bon mots. True, some of this was "borrowed" from other cities' papers; but because local competitors could clip the exact same material, editors sought original pieces to stand above the crowd. Numerous writers with ready pens eagerly filled dailies' and other publishing venues' needs.[45]

The industry's seemingly limitless productive capacity would have glutted the market were it not for petty retailers who acted as middlemen between publishers and consumers. The most traditional distribution outlets were printing offices and retail establishments like general country stores and stationers, but, increasingly, specialized bookstores and periodical depots served urban customers. Before the era's improved transportation enabled regional marketing, publishers frequently dumped inferior stock in the upcountry, making retailing there risky. Moreover, weather damage and poor handling could decrease a shipment's value upon its arrival to booksellers who had bought or bartered it at full price. Purchased inventory, damaged or not, languishing on the shelf represented money lost unless traded at high discount to settle accounts. Furthermore, slow and irregular transportation hindered urban-to-hinterland commercial communication. These problems discouraged selling premium goods on consignment, the system that evolved during the age of rail. Improved transportation lines more directly linked urban publishers to upcountry markets, reduced risk of damage, and facilitated business correspondence, all of which fostered trust between producers and distributors. Publishers now sent quality items without immediate financial obligation to the retailer, who stood to gain an approximately 25 percent "discount" of the list price; if retailers sold at list, they kept a quarter of the proceeds and remitted the rest to the publisher. However, if the book did not sell in a year, it went back to the publisher, who ate the shipping cost. As it required no up-front capital from booksellers, the system was well adapted to their characteristic financial instability. Only a few had the entrepreneurial talent to maintain a permanent customer base. For example, the average life span of a bookselling firm operating in Boston during the second decade of the 1800s was 10.83 years, but by the 1840s, it was 1.34 years.[46] Antebellum booksellers' temporary ventures thus resembled most speculating amateur writers' sporadic market engagements.

Similarly, itinerant distribution exhibited high rates of business entry and exit. Peddlers maintained colonial patterns, but their role in fueling a rural "village enlightenment" with urban products was fading. Instead, most now played the "aftermarket," picking up or bartering unwanted books to sell or trade elsewhere along their route—redistribution as much as distribution. For most peddlers, bookselling was but a sideline because they were constantly bested either by local retailers colluding with urban publishers or by aggressive publisher-sponsored subscription agents. Equipped only with a few samples, subscription sheets, and account books, traveling agents were freed from heavy stock loads, the ancient plight of peddlers. Agents had to inspire the prospective buyer's trust in an abstract transaction: a written promise to pay at a later date, for unseen goods that would arrive at some future time, after which the final collection of cash would take place. Some agents finagled payment beforehand, but too often poseurs ran off with money. Obviously, people entering the field needed good local reputations. Many agents thus traversed familiar locales among kin or neighbors, while some stayed put and let customers come to them. Publishers, of course, were not above authorizing several competitors for one territory; but because of high turnover, they increasingly granted exclusive territorial rights as an incentive. As public faith in the system grew at midcentury, so did anonymity, due to ever broader and distant franchises. This was nothing new, for "colporteurs" (agents of tract and Bible societies) had long disseminated free or cheap religious material to remote areas for little or no pay. Colporteurs seldom persisted, but other less systematic agents of urban benevolent organizations intermittently sold printed material and subscriptions over time. These varied distributors, however ephemeral, assured that the nation was well supplied with print.[47]

Alongside such publisher-driven distribution stood generally overlooked indirect dissemination, often by people who dispensed or loaned printed material as part of their profession. Clergymen's diaries and account books amply record gratis circulation of religious literature among parishioners and faraway colleagues. Lawyers constantly loaned law books and treatises to one another, while their offices were sites where visitors read newspapers. Librarians, in a time before open stacks were common, literally placed items into patrons' hands. Public, private, and Sunday school teachers themselves managed small institutional libraries, but played an even greater role in disseminating printed texts by reading them aloud in classroom exercises or hearing students do so.[48]

Literary dissemination also encompassed venues at which paid itinerant "readers" performed, including scripted panorama presentations, theatrical performances, public readings of classic plays, and lyceum and abolitionist lectures. These performances often had direct tie-ins with printed goods—say, programs sold at panoramas. But authors' performances also indirectly stimulated the market. After a lyceum presentation, attendees might buy the lecturer's books or the "audience-tested" text itself if it eventually appeared in print.[49] Attuned to listener response, author-performers took part in collaborative production reminiscent of social authorship's reliance upon input from dissemination networks.

Social authorship's manuscript dissemination mode had its counterpart, too, in the informal everyday circulation of print matter beyond publisher-controlled distribution systems. Familiar letters brimmed with periodical clippings. Private bundles, moved about by express companies or couriers, contained books and magazines as presents. Purchased newspapers were mailed at special low rates or given away during social calls to readerships beyond the point of sale. Indeed, one story-paper editor estimated in 1851 that for every issue received by subscription there were at least ten nonpaying readers.[50] Likewise, reading a book aloud to friends and neighbors, as was common, potentially satisfied their need to buy it.

In light of the above, social dissemination, determined by reciprocities of human relations, far outweighed market distribution. Given this predominance, for-profit amateurism necessarily bore social vestiges that clashed with the cash nexus. These disseminators looked less to literary dollars' dawn than to social sense's twilight. The sometime authors and disseminators for profit treated here thus often felt that the "logic" of the market made little sense in the face of social persistence, as people continued to employ literature to forge and maintain interpersonal bonds.

SCOPE AND METHODS

Discovering how writers, disseminators, and consumers experienced this tension between longstanding social uses of literature and the emerging literary marketplace poses severe challenges for researchers.[51] The mountain of print left by amateurs hardly conveys their thoughts or feelings about the market. Very few surviving publishers' records directly link the printed word with the amateurs largely responsible for writing and disseminating it.[52] Those that remain offer scant insight into attitudes toward the nascent literary economics because author-publisher correspondence tends to be straightforward and businesslike. Papers of canonical authors afford some glimpse of their early amateur phase, but leave open the question of their representativeness.

In view of these limitations, the present volume relies mainly upon quite different evidence: ordinary people's testaments to writing for print, disseminating literature, and contemplating authorial renown in the new literary marketplace. This testimony, mostly from manuscript diaries and letters, emerged out of our earlier regional study of everyday literary experience that was becoming common nationwide. Because the most intensive industrialization and commercialization occurred in the Northeast—especially, New England—and because it, too, nourished the celebrated Boston-centered literary renaissance and served as a major market for the New York and Philadelphia houses dominating publishing, our research drew upon over thirty archives throughout that region. We also gathered material from Charleston, Charlottesville, Indianapolis, Washington, D.C., and other places across the country. Thus, the many New England voices are joined by others from the West, the Middle Atlantic States, the South, and from Americans overseas.[53]

In seeking evidence of literary reception, consumption, and dissemination in nearly four thousand manuscript documents written by about 930 informants, we inevitably encountered many discussions of market-oriented authorship, publishing, and distribution. The comments of the 181 diarists and correspondents we cite in these pages emerged from our evidence as the most vocal, insightful, and socially representative among those who reported on amateur experiences and literary fame. The principles of selection thus mirror those of anthropologists who rely upon testimony from "key informants," those culturally positioned to speak most articulately to a specific research problem.[54]

The full set of informants comprises a diverse group. Less than a third of them resided in major or secondary publishing cities, while the rest came from a range of municipalities, including thriving agricultural county seats or college towns.[55] Demographically, the group contains roughly equal numbers of males and females of all ages over nine, with proportionally more younger folks—reflecting the population's overall youthfulness and short life expectancies.[56] While Protestants dominate the group as they did the population, there is testimony from Catholic and Jew alike, not to mention freethinkers and the irreligious. The Protestant denominations include African Methodist Episcopal, Baptist, Congregationalist (liberal and orthodox), Episcopalian, Methodist, Presbyterian, Quaker, Swedenborgian, Unitarian, and Universalist. Excepting some African Americans, the group's national origins are in northwestern or central Europe, including Ireland.

This was hardly a group solely composed of genteel amateurs, professionalized disseminators, and leisured literary consumers, as an occupational analysis reveals. This heterogeneity is partly attributable to a near-universal literacy in the North that engendered widespread reading—especially of newspapers. European travelogue writers marveled at American laborers and farmers reading papers, even on the job; so it is not surprising that at the bottom of the ladder we find dressmakers, farm laborers, ferrymen, leatherworkers, machine shop workers, mechanics, millworkers, peddlers, printers, seamen, stablekeepers, wagonmakers, and whalers. Lowly status was also shared by hardscrabble and other poor farmers. Somewhat above them are middling farmers; entry-level clerks or accountants in commercial banks, drygoods stores, shipping houses, or manufacturing firms; and minor civil servants like customs men or deeds officers. Also near the bottom are economically strapped students in common schools, state normal schools, academies, seminaries, and colleges. Many petty professionals like schoolteachers, music instructors, librarians, and some clergymen had low status and pay. Workingwomen had fewer occupational opportunities and made less than their male counterparts. Certainly, many if not most unmarried women and widows had to struggle, even if it meant writing for a mere pittance.[57]

Of course, our informants are drawn from higher status occupations, too. Some were marginal, but in the public eye, such as actors, auctioneers, lecturers, panorama showmen, and writers. The respectable petit bourgeoisie included booksellers, drug merchants, grain dealers, ship chandlers, and general shopkeepers. Better-paid professionals like editors, engineers, lawyers, physicians, and ministers with well-to-do congregations naturally appear. Top-of-the-ladder testimony comes from a few college or bank presidents, manufacturers, planters, politicians, publishers, and general businessmen with diversified investment portfolios, or the families of these uppercrust men. When the few on top are added to the many on the bottom, the general impression is that virtually anybody could write for print, distribute it, or interest him- or herself in authorial celebrity.

SKETCHES OF AMATEURS

We highlight throughout several amateur authors or distributors who typify our informant pool. Joshua Edwin Harris, born in Kennebunkport,

Maine, labored on a farm and in Biddeford and Lewiston mills before becoming first a traveling periodical agent for Boston editor Maturin Murray Ballou in May 1856 and then an amateur poet for Moses Dow's *Waverley* magazine in 1857. Harris combined writing, but evidently not always publishing, with factory labor until 1861 when he joined the Union Army.[58] Sarah P.E. Hale, sister of prominent politicos Alexander Hill Everett and Edward Everett and wife of newspaper editor Nathan Hale, began anonymously editing gift annuals for T.H. Carter after the Panic of 1837 threatened the family income. Versed in French and German, she reviewed foreign-language texts and translated pieces for periodicals or juvenile storybooks.[59] Writer Luella J.B. Case provided copy for her friend and editor of the annual *Rose of Sharon*, Sarah Edgarton. Despite her many household duties, Case also published prose and notices in her minister-husband's Unitarian periodical, *Star of Bethlehem*.[60]

Amateurs like Case provide insights into the literary marketplace through their observations, reading habits, and fandom. Cyrus Bradley, son of an unprosperous New Hampshire fur dealer and shopkeeper, attended Exeter Academy via a charity subscription and Dartmouth College while still in his early teens. Though sickly, he coedited a short-lived weekly literary paper from 1834 to 1835; later he published politician Isaac Hill's biography and toured Ohio and Michigan. There and at home he commented upon other editors, authors, booksellers, and librarians. John Park practiced medicine and edited a newspaper before establishing in 1811 a Boston women's academy, where he set Margaret Fuller and Frances Sargent Osgood on their paths toward authorship. We find him retired in Worcester, guiding his daughter, Louisa Park Hall, through the turbulent late-1830s literary market.[61] Seminary-educated Mary Pierce Poor, daughter of a Brookline, Massachusetts, liberal Congregationalist minister, fretted while writing her father's memoir in 1851, but enjoyed helping her husband Henry Varnum Poor edit, proofread, and illustrate his *Railroad Journal* after they moved to New York City. Her commentary on contemporary literary culture derived from prodigious reading. Like Poor, Ellen Wright, a twenty-year-old student from Auburn, New York, who attended Mrs. Sedgwick's Academy in the Berkshire Hills of Massachusetts, appraised popular authors of her day. An academic-year highlight was hearing a neighbor, the celebrated author and actress Fanny Kemble, read from the plays of William Shakespeare. Finally, Georgian James A. Healy, son of a slave and her Irish master, translated Jesuit works for a Catholic newspaper while enrolled at the College of the Holy Cross.

He read far and wide, but relished biographies and newspaper accounts of contemporary authors.[62]

Sometimes, amateur writers also disseminated their own or other people's literature, for a small income. The Congregationalist minister and farmer Seth Shaler Arnold of Westminster, Vermont, gave away, sold, bartered, or distributed his own printed texts, sometimes to booksellers. As a traveling agent, he sold religious, reform, and African Colonization Society periodical subscriptions. Mellen Chamberlain, born to a poor, westward-bound country shopkeeper, ascended the economic ladder to become a wealthy Cambridge-based lawyer. While studying law, however, he worked for a meager sum as a librarian, at an exhausting job of acquiring, circulating, and caring for books.[63] Whether disseminators, writers, or readers, each gives his or her own take upon the literary "auction."

ORGANIZATION

In this book, the records of these and many other persons give voice to common people's experiences with the literary marketplace. The first three chapters move from considerations of general amateurism, to specific cases of three minor writers at different critical career points, and then to public understanding of the authorial vocation. In chapter 1, "In and Out of Print," our informants show how and why social authors moved into the world of print. They describe various phases of publishing: inspiration, writing and revising, locating a publisher, copying and editing manuscripts, and proofreading and responding to the final product. Most amateurs found the process unsatisfying, for much of the social dimension of writing was lost to impersonal market forces. Consequently, they quickly passed "in and out" of the market. Chapter 2, "Textual Appearances," analyzes three persistent writers who achieved minor status: Philadelphian Charlotte Forten, Lowell-millgirl-turned-Illinois-teacher Lucy Larcom, and Upstate New Yorker John Townsend Trowbridge. We focus on events surrounding a single milestone publication from each of their long careers. We follow the paths taken to publish these pieces and note the fleeting success and ultimate disappointment attending their appearance. In each case, the intersection of personal biography, social influences, and market forces provides a unique perspective on the literary marketplace. Chapter 3, "From the Outside Looking In," reveals how social, amateur, and minor authors perceived other—often famous—authors. Insatiable curiosity about their lives, personalities, and even looks was satisfied by reading biographies, through gossip, and through face-to-face meetings at lyceums, parties, or public readings. Failing to meet the grandiose expectations, authors were ultimately depreciated by their admirers. Consequently, authors unwittingly provided a self-reflexive image of common folks' own alienation from the profession. Once "leveled," authors, including celebrity Charles Dickens, were admitted into a virtual social network of readers and sympathetic "scribblers." Having established the social sense of authorship in the first three chapters, we next inquire into the dissemination of publishers' products amid varying local communities. In chapter 4 we ask, Did ordinary Americans easily assume the role of literary consumers and did distributors fully imbibe market values? In pursuit of these questions, "Inside and Outside the Literary Marketplace" looks at sometime subscription agents, booksellers, librarians, teachers, and performative disseminators, and at their respective sites of transaction. Hardly compensated for their labors and alienated by the job's strain upon social relationships, most simply gave up. Hardier, idealistic distributors, however, endured, thus helping to sustain literary culture and the social world that nourished it.

In our conclusion we ponder authors who survived the antebellum marketplace and earned "The Privilege of Going On" into the late nineteenth century. What allowed some authors, especially Forten, Larcom, and Trowbridge, to go on? We then turn to now-canonized authors, as we view Emily Dickinson's, Henry David Thoreau's, and Ralph Waldo Emerson's writerly practices through the lens of contemporary social authorship and amateur experience. We also note changes in the industry that widened the gap between professional and amateur, while diminishing opportunities for the latter. We explore, too, a similar trend in literary dissemination: the publisher-directed professionalization of in-the-field literary distribution that virtually ended the regime of locally oriented distributors. We ponder the crystallization, at century's end, of authorial celebrity into images of demigods, which ultimately eroded the "social sense" that accompanied common people's pursuit of literary dollars. Finally, we assay the social costs of that erosion and, in a coda, reflect upon its meaning for American literary studies. Can the "Disgrace of Price" for published literature that Dickinson so presciently loathed as an "Auction / Of the Mind of Man" be ever dispelled?

1

IN AND OUT OF PRINT

While writing in his 1835 diary, whaler Moses Adams recalled a childhood acquaintance, Frederic S. Hill, with whom he had "exchanged … 'poetick effusions' & other 'productions' as 'keepsakes.'" Adams remembered that "before my going to sea" he packed a cherished few of his chum's poems in his oceanbound trunk. He assumed they would forever remain but tokens of youthful ambitions. Shortly after, he learned that Hill had gone from obscure poetaster to published poet. The seaman reminisced that Hill "had now become quite a literary character; writing much poetry, &c. for a newspaper … & felt a little ashamed of the less elegant productions of his *younger* days. He therefore requested me to return them, & promised me something new in their stead." Hill replaced his supposedly inferior manuscript creations with a story and some printed poems having titles like "Oh that I had wings like a dove" by "Alpheus" for "a new literary paper."[1] Through this transferral, Hill ritualistically elevated his printed pieces above his unpublished social authorship efforts.

Fearing that his writings, though published, yet lacked depth, Hill confessed to Adams: "they are rather of a still, quiet kind & make no more noize in the reader's heart, than a man in stockings does on a carpet." "To write *poetry*," he prescribed, "a man should be where you sometimes are—should see the wonders of the great deep." The conversion of pen and ink into print did not miraculously turn social authors into professionals. Nor did it transform amateurs' light, sentimental verse into high romantic poetry. After publishing a slim volume of

1

verse and two gift annuals that no more satisfied his aspirations than contributing to newspapers, Hill abandoned his dreams for editing, but "From bad calculations or mismanagement he failed." He finally found his métier on the Boston stage where, according to Adams, he "acquired a tenable credit as an actor & author" of two plays before his untimely death in 1851.[2]

Forgotten today, Frederic Hill navigated the rocky seas that only rarely led to professional authorship. Few aspirants completed the passage from writing as social authors for limited audiences to earning their daily bread through publications. Like Hill, many amateurs briefly saw their names in print but, to their chagrin, soon found that they could not sustain themselves through writing alone. Unable to break into national periodicals or be published by major houses, these sometime writers spent more time "out of print" than in it. When they did publish, it was only sporadically and usually in minor forums; otherwise, they made their living as actors, domestics, operatives, preachers, or in other vocations outside the book trades. Only the luckiest achieved fleeting local celebrity.[3]

Although some common scribblers tried, often futilely, to turn professional, most never dreamed of doing so, but simply welcomed both the chance to get into print and the occasional literary dollar or two that publishers might send them. Some writers merely created copy to help friends or family members in the industry. Others self-consciously sought edification, by propagating ideas, promoting their careers, serving their communities, practicing their writing, or simply amusing themselves. Some routes to print required little or no will on the part of authors, as when their purloined letters and private sympathy notes surfaced in news sheets, or when their sermons or speeches were cajoled from them by sponsoring congregations or political parties.

Yet, whatever their motives to write in whatever genre, amateurs walked a similar path from pen to print, first conceiving, developing, and placing material; then revising, copying, and proofing it; and finally seeing it in print, being remunerated for it, and acknowledging public praise or criticism of it.[4] To be sure, they hardly journeyed alone, for getting into print often meant relying upon other people along the way. Accordingly, most amateurs lacked the atomizing narcissism too often attributed to them ("[t]heir reputation is formed by an echo reverbrating [sic] their self praise," one observer cracked).[5] Intimates motivated authors, made suggestions, and peddled, copied, and proofread their work.[6] As manuscripts neared the typesetting stage, however, a host of strangers entered the picture. Publishers, editors, and the faceless reading public replaced friends, neighbors, and kinfolk as prime movers. The social relations surrounding literary production became increasingly unfamiliar and correspondingly abstract. The diminished sociability, along with the uneasy and sometime perilous market conditions, strongly discouraged many talented initiates and gave pause to veterans. Paradoxically, editors constantly complained of shortages of publishable copy when so many literate Americans could supply it, but simply did not want to do so.[7] Those who did inevitably found that, all in all, the transit from manuscript to printed page was not as pleasant, lucrative, or otherwise rewarding as it seemed from the outside looking in. This chapter analyzes amateurs' ambivalent market experience by first examining their motives, then following each subsequent step, from composing pieces to reflecting retrospectively upon the meaning of getting into print—or, possibly, out of the market altogether.

REASONS TO WRITE FOR PRINT

Because amateurs' contributions to midcentury literary production have been overlooked, their motivations remain unexamined as well. Knowing why they wrote is important because it helps position amateurs between social authorship and emerging literary professionalism. If they had fully embraced the market, one would expect to see them concentrating on moneymaking, career building, and grasping at celebrity. Instead, we see complex webs of motives that might include these among those with social origins. To untangle this nuanced web, we separate personal incentives from those of outside agents.

Self-Motivated Production

Writing that was not solicited by others was seldom entirely self-oriented, although the very idea of personal incentive would seem to point in that direction. As we will see, propagating ideas, attaining group prestige, and memorializing people were as much on amateurs' minds as self-edification and making money. Yet even economic impulses did not reduce to pure literary career ambition. In many cases, financial desperation drove amateurs to pick up the pen for a few extra dollars to fulfill immediate needs. It was, after all, a period of widespread economic insecurity, with frequent downturns and chronic unemployment. Sadly, among personal incentives, moneymaking was the most easily frustrated.

Pursuing Literary Dollars Many publishers rarely paid amateurs for copy, but rumors of significant earnings from top venues, which coursed through the social fabric of correspondence and conversation, inflated common expectations. "Frank Dalton dined here a few days since & was speaking of the immense number of subscribers to some of the periodicals," one Boston matron remarked in 1844. She, like others, automatically translated high circulations into literary dollars: "Graham's magazine had 30,000 [and] It is in the habit of paying its contributors 37 ½ cents a line for poetry," a generous amount in an age of the common dollar-a-day wage. One oft-repeated anecdote recounted how Harriet Beecher Stowe's popular novel *Uncle Tom's Cabin*, first serialized in the *National Era* in 1851 for four hundred dollars, reaped a fortune the following year in book form. "Mrs Stow [*sic*] has realized for the first 3 months of her book $10,000," one abolitionist exclaimed to her daughter in July 1852; "People say such success was never known in the annals of Literature."[8] Success stories like these suggested the path of periodical publishing was paved with gold.

It is no wonder that the impoverished and consumptive millworker Joshua Harris hoped against all odds to become a regular contributor to one of the many well-paying urban story papers. Having no entrée into the literary world, he fabricated a patron in popular Maine politician Hannibal Hamlin. Posing as "H. Hamlin," Harris solicited editor Maturin Murray Ballou in 1856: "A friend of mine wishes to know what you pay for articles such as apear weekly in the Flag [of Our Union] and Pictorial [Drawing Room Companion]." "Hamlin" also fibbed, quite transparently and with numerous spelling errors, about his protege's record: "My friend has written considerable for other publications and is a verry tallented writer of romance but comparitively a beginner." He wanted "to become a regular contributor to [Ballou's] valuable paper" to augment his meager pay in the mills—only about seventeen dollars a month—and to provide some security during bouts of unemployment and illness. In a later solicitation under his own name, he made no apologies for his pecuniary motives. "If your Original articles are all gratuitous," he posited with false superiority to another cheap-periodical editor, "I shall need no answer to this." Rebuffed, a disheartened Harris wrote again to Ballou, frankly pleading, "Heaven knows I need the money."[9]

The economic necessity occasioning Harris's writing was shared by many women with limited employment opportunities. "*[N]ecessity* compels me to try to publish it," Charlotte Forten confessed in her diary, while finishing a short story for New York's *Home Journal*. Illness had forced her recent resignation from a teaching position; wanting cash, she submitted her work and herself, as well, to the pangs of rejection: "Shall have little peace of mind till I know its fate." Financial need could even override deep conviction. "In the more pecuniary point of view, I can not afford to devote myself entirely to Anti-Slavery," a rural Pennsylvanian explained in 1844 to a goading advocate; "as a matter of necessity, I must vary my literary labors." A change in life circumstances, such as recent widowhood, might redirect literary output toward paying venues. For example, in her youth Mary Baker Eddy wrote for pleasure, with gratis pieces appearing in local newspapers; but when widowed in 1844, she also eyed national periodicals that might pay, like the *Covenant*, a Baltimore Odd Fellows organ, and the *Floral Wreath and Ladies' Monthly*, a genteel Charleston magazine, not to mention the ever popular *Godey's*. Not only widows but also estranged wives might suddenly seek money through writing. Rather than facing life in the mills after running away from a bad marriage, one Vermonter tried her hand at authorship. "Mary Gibson has left her husband at Lynn Mass. who is 68, rich & a poet," a neighbor recorded, adding, "She is now writing stories under the assumed name of Winnie Woodfern."[10] Beneath many a woman's pseudonyms lay tales of broken vows or deceased spouses.

Happily married women, too, might adopt pen names to supplement family income covertly through publishing. As Sarah P.E. Hale's family felt the Panic of 1837's dire effects, she produced her first works—illustrated children's books or, as she dubbed them, referring to her publisher, "little afairs I have made for [T. Harrington] Carter this season." Lest anyone read financial desperation, marital discontent, or unseemly ambition into her efforts, she veiled them, confiding to her brother, "My agency in the business is a great secret. ... I know you will be discreet." Only after years of quietly producing juveniles and gift annuals did she divulge her earnings. "The best part of my books, is that Carter has paid me today 170 dollars," she wrote in 1841; "So that I feel quite repaid for my labours." She relied upon her literary income so much that when it was jeopardized, she bitterly protested. "At the time I furnished the article in the Token for 1842 it was in the hope of receiving something in return," she sniped at publisher D.H. Williams, "but if the concern proved unfortunate, I sincerely regret it on account of others as well as myself."[11] The bottom line mattered more than the mere pleasure of seeing one's words in print.

Periodical editors were not immune to disappointment, either; in fact, the high risks involved virtually assured it. "This is the last no. of the first six months, & with it, I shall [end] my editorial career," Cyrus Bradley, the coeditor of Concord, New Hampshire's *Literary Gazette* declared in 1835. "It is hard to sustain one's zeal *without pay*," he observed, because "The publishers are too poor to pay the editors, & the editors are too poor to work for nothing." Bradley blamed his Concord readership, not himself, noting, "if the angel Gabriel should come from heaven and establish a literary paper here, he would be starved out in three months." Editors oblivious to hazard horrified skeptical loved ones. Maria White, for one, confided in 1842 to a friend about her fiancé, the then obscure lawyer but soon-to-be writer James Russell Lowell: "James said something to me ... about *editing a periodical*. ... [W]hen I think of the immense circulation that is necessary to make a thing of this kind profitable I cannot feel so sanguine." His foolish intention was bad enough, but the manic attitude that accompanied it was even worse. "If you could only see James clap his hands and say 'In *one* year, Maria we shall be married' you would not wonder at my anxiety," White explained, "even if it wholly succeeds [it] would wear on soul and body, but if he fails with such bright prospects as he proposes to himself I dread the revulsion." Such failure was more likely during economic downturns ensuing after the Panics of 1837 and 1857. For example, one aspiring Nininger, Minnesota, newspaper printer who had earlier left a Boston compositing job gave up and set out for Kansas in 1858 after his "Journal, for want of patronage ... at last quietly yielded up the Ghost." Willy Garrison laid out the conditions that drove his western sojourning brother, George Thompson Garrison, noting, "Business is almost unheard of ... stagnation is the only word that aptly describes the existing state of affairs."[12] Widespread retrenchment could send editors out of the trenches.

As if conventional publishing endeavors were not chancy enough, some gamblers sought quick returns from literary contests often devised as publicity ploys. "I will say that I have always enjoyed the lottery of the prize competitions," author-minister Edward Everett Hale recalled of the 1850s; "At a time when I was not troubled by having too much money, I received a prize offered by *Sartain's Magazine*." In February 1851 the magazine offered one hundred dollars to each of the ten best short prose pieces submitted, among which was Everett's "The Old and the New." That era's windfall prizes shocked former editor John Park, a Unitarian who winced at the "$300!!" awarded to Leonard Woods's Calvinistic 1835 *Essay on Native Depravity*. The money evidently went to promote religious orthodoxy as much as talent. Some auspiciously timed prizes aided career development, as in the case of John Park's daughter Louisa, who had in 1837 won "one of the highest prizes, fifty dollars" for best short story in the *New England Galaxy and Pearl* only days before her first book-length dramatic poem, *Miriam*, appeared. However, while Edward Everett Hale and Louisa Park took their prizes fair and square, many publishers fraudulently concocted such competitions to raise their papers' visibility, with little intention to part with much money. And when sponsoring editors awarded prizes to themselves writing under pen names, competitions devolved into shameless hoaxes. The *Flag of Our Union*'s Maturin Murray Ballou "won" that story paper's bogus prize—"the largest ever offered to writers"—year after year as "Captain Murray." These severe and often unfair practices cast in proper light the many heartbreakingly desperate people who hoped prizes would solve their financial woes. One pitiable example will suffice. "If you find any prizes offered any where I wish you to write me very particularly and I will have a piece ready speedily," one fifty-year-old Massachusetts widow in 1834 beseeched her son, a Virginia minister; "the fact is I am greatly in want of money and that would be my easiest way to get it."[13]

Propagating Ideas While most writers needing money assuredly risked disappointment, those propagating ideas through print fared better, for although earnings from advocacy pieces, if any, were small, their authors nonetheless immaterially profited because they simply wanted to spread information to a wider audience than could be reached with manuscripts. Yet, as we will see, vestiges of social authorship remained insofar as writers often targeted a limited, specialized, and identifiable readership, to which they themselves might distribute their work in person. Similarly, too, social authorship practices can be discerned in instances of collaborative production for social ends.

Seminarians, for example, looking to inspire faith or instill doctrine through print, at times saw a blurring of the boundaries between classroom group exercises and publication. Among everyday translation assignments in Latin and French at Holy Cross College, one led African American student James Healy and his classmates to publish their English-language version of the *Edifying Letters* in the *Catholic Observer*, a prominent sectarian newspaper. They thus made French Jesuit works available for the first time to the growing Catholic community. "My letter is now finished in this paper," Healy chronicled on March 8, 1849, with a realization that duty beckoned him onward; "I suppose there will soon be a call for another." There was, and so a week later Healy confirmed that "My letter is not yet finished. It will stand another publishing." Osmon Cleander Baker, a sixteen-year-old theology student at Wilbur Fisk's Wilbraham Wesleyan Academy, undertook a similar group writing mission in 1829. "It was proposed and carried that a short essay of theologickal subjects should be prepared for the New England [Christian] Herald a religious periodical under the patronage of the N. England Methodists," he declared after meeting with his theology classmates; "I was appointed by the class to prepare one subject viz The authenticity of the scriptures."[14] Advocacy publishing on the ministerial road fostered authorial camaraderie, but also foreshadowed future unsupervised individual production.

In propagating their faith, some minor clergymen, who published limited runs of sermons and other religious works at their own expense, were not so far removed from social authors producing for a familiar, restricted audience. Both eschewed publishers' investment in production, marketing, and distribution, and acted instead as their own "booksellers," forsaking profit making and far-flung audiences for self-determination. This is illustrated by the cases of Maine Swedenborgian Henry Worcester's 1837 Sermons and 1840 The Sabbath, both of which he paid Otis Clapp to print and have bound. Upon the author's death in 1841, his wife Olive managed the outstanding accounts with her "agent," Portland silversmith and Swedenborgian elder Oliver Gerrish. "I received Mr. Clapps Bill today," Gerrish shortly after informed Mrs. Worcester. "[B]y giving credit for Sermons & Sabbaths on hand his account nearly balances," he continued. The bookseller had evidently retained "3 or 400. Sabbaths folded in sheats" (unbound copies) and some bound Sermons as inventory—a form of credit against Worcester's printing bill. As long as Clapp could sell the books, the debt would eventually be paid without Olive Worcester immediately dipping into funds. Gerrish, however, reminded her that "the binder of the Sermons has a bill of $31.50 against the estate—The reason that it was not settled was, he bound the whole edition instead of part as ordered, and in consequence agreed to wait until the sales met the demand." But that might take a long time; Gerrish eventually worked out a deal whereby the binder's bill would be paid out of Clapp's sales. To boost sales—especially of the Sabbath, which were still sluggish by 1846 because of competition from a cheap Scottish edition—Gerrish recommended stitching the unbound copies "in stiff covers" rather than expensive leather, having Olive Worcester's brother "take all the books" and "giv[ing] the estate credit for $20.00 as books sold to him." All this meant that there would doubtless be little profit left to the widow in the end, even when the edition sold out.[15]

Rather than relying on such complex credit systems, other ministers paid some publishing costs out of pocket, as did rural Vermont Congregationalist Seth Shaler Arnold, who partly financed his domestic treatise

The Intellectual House-Keeper. He told his 1835 diary that the prominent Boston publisher "Mr. Odiorne is to print the House Keeper—to secure the Copy-Right for me—in my name—advertise and be at all the trouble—for the commission of 33 1/3 percent on the sale. I pay for printing paper and binding." He paid freight and binding costs for his other works, such as *The Family Choir*; these he mostly distributed himself, instead of using intermediaries.[16] By shouldering the financial burden, he, Worcester, and other proselytizers insured the spread of their ideas, if not the filling of their purses.

Social and political activists also furthered their causes through nonprofit publishing. Although "necessity" sometimes motivated her writing, Charlotte Forten frequently published for the abolitionist cause without fee. Similarly, one seventeen-year-old fishyard worker published gratis his "first Political article" (with others to follow) in the Newburyport *Herald*. He fashioned it as "an *appeal to the Whigs*, to arouse themselves, and make sure of preventing what might happen, if they remained inactive—*the election of Marcus Morton as Governor of the State.*" He later regretted that a "good measure of superlative pathos" marred its partisan fire. Sheets specializing in partisan essays burgeoned during election season, but vanished after votes were tallied. After all, these vehicles aimed for political rather than financial gain. "It is designed to last only till after the election & to counteract the influence of the Concord Patriot & the Courier," Cyrus Bradley noted of one ephemeral "whole hog Jackson" paper begun in January 1835. So quickly did these papers mushroom prior to elections that four days later he calculated, "We now have 14 papers in this little village (viz) Political." He not only followed the ebb and flow of political newspapers, but also used political periodicals to advance his viewpoints. One article "upon the present excitement against the Catholics" that he penned for the New Hampshire *Argus* in 1835, for example, counseled toleration for a group facing ever increasing bigotry, even after nativists burned a convent in Charlestown, Massachusetts, in 1834.[17] More than launching a paying writing career with this piece, he readied himself for adult political life.

Some advocates advanced knowledge while building professional careers in a manner reminiscent of manuscript authors who through scientific correspondence built reputations within select coteries.[18] After all, the period saw some of the earliest professional journals addressing emerging technologies and geared to a limited subscriber base.[19] One unpaid contributor was James Barnard Blake, a twenty-three-year-old Boston engineer who in March 1851 submitted an article to "Munn & Co New York Proprietors of the Scientific American" on "Illuminating Gas." Honored that the journal agreed to publish it, he also advanced a new lighting system. "I do not feel proud but still there is a feeling of satisfaction which pervades me," he beamed, "and which I hope will tend to cultivate scientific pursuits, rather than engender any flattering feelings." Eight months later, he submitted "a short article upon Coke, and left it at the Transcript office for publication." This served both his and his employer's professional goals: "My article on Coke appeared in the transcript and seemed to give satisfaction to those persons who are interested in the welfare of the company." Before technicians' academic credentialing, such scientific advocacy pieces were among the only ways to demonstrate one's expertise in areas of emerging knowledge.[20]

Attaining Authority If in some cases print more effectively propagated worthy ideas by spreading them further, in others it was the principal way to legitimate writings arousing skepticism. This was especially true for spiritualist publications that transferred purported messages from the "world of spirits" to the world of print. Nineteenth-century writing mediums frequently transcribed revelations from the afterlife. Simply by being printed, especially in major periodicals, messages attained greater authority and bolstered Spiritualist faith. African American editor William C. Nell remarked in 1851, "After reading the Tribune Correspondence from Hopedale = I felt ready to say that many now will be more likely to look favorably upon the Spiritual manifestations." In granting authority to the text, print likewise empowered mediums. Mary Poor noticed that Thomas Lake Harris's surge in popularity as a preacher in New York City coincided with the serial publication of some of his work (which included poems supposedly communicated from the hereafter). "Mr Harris he is over head & ears immersed in the spirits," Poor told her sister in 1852. "He preaches as they direct him to crowded houses," she explained, "& maintains that he constantly converses with angels."[21]

More cantankerous "spirits" accessing the printed word could provoke community conflict, especially if they challenged one another. Feuds could erupt as earthly channels jockeyed for positions of authority. Such was the case in Charles Cobb's Woodstock, Vermont, neighborhood, where in 1852 spirit manifestations inspired a few inhabitants to publish their communications. The resulting story of local turmoil, seen through the farm lad's eyes, is long and complex, but it repays telling for the insight it provides into the relationships among print, authority, and reputation.

The conflict emerged out of school politics, of all things. After farmer Isaac B. Hartwell began to receive otherworldly messages through fellow townsman Horace G. Wood, he determined in January 1852 to "make himself heard through the New York Tribune." Hartwell's piece not only elevated its author; its appearance coincided with medium Wood's conversion of the school district in which he taught. Wood had, however, coveted the better position on Woodstock Green. By February 26, 1852, "the principal part of the district wanted to hire Horace Wood to keep the school" there instead of the current teacher who was just suspiciously dismissed for whipping a student. Wood, characterized by the orthodox faction that controlled the district as "profane, intemperate and an infidel," did not get the job. Despite this setback, he furthered his reputation by conjuring a powerful ally from the grave. Around March 14, 1852, an address dictated to Wood by the ghost of George Washington was published in *Mystery*, a pamphlet compiled by fifty-two-year-old town matron and former Community Place communard Marenda B. Randall, a medium herself.[22]

With yet another published transcription to flaunt, Wood's spirits waged war against their local competition. In April of that year they declared medium George Grow to be a "humbug"; he in turn forged an anti-Wood alliance with Austin E. Simmons, a schoolteacher and district clerk from an old local family. Soon enough George Washington began speaking through Simmons, thus overriding Wood's transcription. The Simmons faction's vengeful spirits forthwith expelled Wood and Randall from Woodstock's Spiritualist Circle. With this, Wood became the victim of sexual innuendo—("putting it to Cynthia Woodward!!!!" according to Cobb)—and left town by September to preach in Auburn, New York. While there he was jailed, apparently for vagrancy. During his exile, Wood revamped his reputation by publishing a piece that October in the *Spiritual Telegraph* about Woodstock's Spiritualist community.[23]

With Wood safely out of the picture, Simmons became Woodstock's foremost Spiritualist preacher. Disapproving orthodox religious factions "appointed C[arlos] A. Pratt dist[rict] clerk, in the place of A.E. Simmons" in October 1852. Soon after, Simmons retaliated with a pamphlet of spiritual transcriptions "'written in 7 hours through my hand without ANY exertion on my part, of mind or will. So help me God.'" The pamphlet, of course, attacked "Carlos Pratt among other things." "He ought to be hit—the cuss," Charles Cobb commented of

Simmons. The feud ended only in March 1853 after elders interceded, asking Simmons to make up with Pratt and forbidding Spiritualist meetings in the town hall. By June 1853, villagers had all but forgotten their obsession with Spiritualism.[24]

This complex incident reveals yet another reason for publishing: to recruit print against opponents or to defend against attacks. Print allowed writers to place their case before more people than was possible with manuscripts alone. The act, moreover, suggested to readers that someone somewhere thought a large enough audience existed to justify its printing. Thus, when words were contested (as they were among Woodstock's Spiritualists), print was summoned to authenticate incorporeal messages, as speaking and transcribing alone could not. In this case, clashing messages undermined print's authority. The key question became not who triumphed, but whose reputation and livelihood suffered least. Had the antagonists not had recourse to print, one wonders if the outcome would have been so mutually destructive.[25]

Memorializing People If print could discredit people more effectively, it could also eulogize them more conspicuously. For those who wrote mourning verse, print became the ultimate way to pay tribute through words. An obituary poem's appearance in a newspaper meant that an anonymous readership could learn of the departed's virtues. These publications, often printed anonymously or signed with only initials, hardly publicized an author the way, say, a prize did. They seldom furthered literary careers, but could contribute to their writers' literary reputation within local circles. Because women often specialized more than men in newspaper mourning verse or obituaries, they had an unusual opportunity to earn the high regard of those they served.[26]

These writers' literary skills could be appreciated because obituaries meant so much to survivors. One father was so moved by Louisa Park's 1838 Worcester *Aegis* obituary of his daughter that he presented the author with a heartfelt thank-you note and personally charged mementos: the deceased's ring, ornate volumes of John Milton's poems, and a lock of hair. His gratitude continued months afterward, when he shipped Park an expensive writing desk to encourage her further efforts.[27] To achieve such authentic effect, Park summoned up intimate recollections of her father's former student. Meaningful mourning verse depended upon the effective deployment of this personal knowledge within romantic literary conventions. When Elizabeth Jocelyn from New Haven, Connecticut, drew upon shared childhood experiences to write her friend's March 1847 obituary for a local paper, she highlighted the former classmate's particular thrall with flowering streams encountered on springtime walks:

> She loved the streams that in silence wind
>   'Mid the haunts of the greenwood bowers,
> And the breeze that lulls itself to rest
>   In the heart of the summer flowers.
>
> Those streams will glide through their woodland home,
>   And the breeze 'mid the flow'rete play,
> But she who has loved them all, has gone,
>   From this world and its scenes away;
>
> To living streams in that world above,
>   Where flow'rs of immortal bloom
> Are fanned by the heavenly breeze that steal
>   Through the bowers of her blissful home.

So successful was Jocelyn at investing her mourning verse with personal meaning and making it accessible to an audience beyond survivors that one of her many other pieces found its way into the nationally oriented New York *Independent* in 1856, soon after she and her husband had moved to South Egremont, Massachusetts. "The Dark River," on a local tragedy, elegized people whom its readers would never have encountered in person: "3 persons in Egremont an old lady a young physician, & a child."[28] By commemorating the faceless dead, Jocelyn transcended personal grief and participated in an act of societal mourning.

Longer, more complex, and expensive to produce were other commemorative works like genealogies, memoirs, biographies, and local histories. These genres, requiring intensive research in libraries and private collections, customarily took years to prepare. Lawyer Augustus Dodge Rogers began his family genealogy sometime before 1846, but saw its completion in print only in 1859. Businessman Henry Wyles Cushman also toiled long and hard to complete his family record, but at great financial cost. In August 1855, he proudly announced, "The 'Cushman Genealogy'—a work in which I have been engaged for 5 or 6 years was first *published* today." He joked that its length seemed portentous: "It is a volume of 666 pages (see Revelations Chapter XIII, verse 18!!)." After his initial exuberance, he soberly accounted for what he felt was a costly but nevertheless worthy expenditure. "I have published an edition of 1000 copies which cost (including the engravings) about $2400," he affirmed.[29] The drive to serve their own families turned memorialists into virtual publishers.

Serving others without much self-expression, authors expended much time gathering relevant materials and faithfully transcribing, editing, and extracting the deceased's letters and diaries. Locating ample documentation was itself cause for celebration. "I am exceedingly happy to learn that you have found abundant materials for a memoir of Father [Sebastian] Rasles," an American Antiquarian Society librarian wrote to Boston Catholic Bishop Fenwick, who in 1833 sought documentation for an ill-fated biography of this martyred eighteenth-century missionary to the native Abenaki people. Beyond discovering sources, authors judiciously extracted and edited their subject's sometimes intimate words for print. A biographer was expected to quote the subject to such a degree that they together became virtual coauthors. Because this task was worrisome, New Yorker Mary Poor balked at editing her father's memoir and finished it only at great emotional cost. Her father, John Pierce, an important clergyman associated with Congregational liberalism, left candid and potentially damaging records of his colleagues. After designated biographer William Buell Sprague relinquished his duties to the reluctant Poor, she immediately saw the problems her predecessor envisioned. Pierce used his journal for "letting off the steam," she realized, and that put any compiler into a quandary between honesty and discretion:

> I am very much troubled about Father's memoirs. As I read them I find so much that is the most interesting of the whole that ought not to be published at present & so much ... that ought not to be done by one of his own family that I am afraid I should make but a tame thing of it & am tempted to give the whole up. A person who should take those volumes & without the slightest regard to the feelings of any party, publish all the interesting facts relative to the religious struggle of the first part of this century, would make an intensely interesting book. But I cannot & would not do this.

The published memoir did smooth out the rough edges of Pierce's life (and protected his contemporaries' reputations), as no doubt did several other posthumously published biographies that elided controversial issues with tactful editing.[30]

The passage of manuscript writings into print often resulted, as we have seen, from the author's agency. Diverse personal motivations, such as needing money, proliferating ideas, grasping for authority or vengeance, commemorating the deceased, and serving posterity, all prompted writers to publish. The motives we have discussed so far represent self-projections into a world in which known readers and strangers might mingle. In these cases, writers themselves self-consciously decided what to write and how to get it into print in order to capture this larger audience, but there were other roads to publication.

Publication via Others

Frequently, opportunities to publish materialized with little or no effort on the part of the author. Pieces emerged, for better or for worse, at another person's or organization's behest. At worst, opportunists confiscated private letters and published them without authors' permission. At best, editors supplicated writers to send them something while other interested parties—such as religious congregations—requested, funded, and published an author's writings. More commonly, family or friends in the publishing industry who needed quick and reliable copy for their publications asked for assistance. Whatever the circumstance, social intercession rather than personal drive brought about publication.[31]

Pirated Material Unwary correspondents, especially politicians and their families, were occasionally shocked when their personal letters appeared in newspapers. This deliberate transformation of letter writing from quasi-private communication to public performance led to bitter consequences. Freshman National Republican congressman John Davis learned in 1826 that a politico's written words were fair game for publishers, who were fed them by prying mail handlers. "My account of the fire returned to me in type very unexpectedly," he informed his wife concerning a December 1825 letter about the U.S. Capitol library burning. "Had I supposed it was destined to be this conspicuous I could have given it a little higher *finish*—it is however substantially correct," he observed, and jocularly concluded, "I expect next to see my account of '*New Years*'; & my letter to [three-year-old] John among the '*news paporials*.'" Even seasoned statesmen such as Democratic Congressman Charles Andrews, a ten-year veteran of Maine politics, were stung by piracy. "Hus. is disturbed … today by a private letter of his being published in the N. York Herald," his wife Persis recorded in 1851. Such theft, she noted, was "only one of the thorns of a political rose." Well-meaning correspondents sometimes submitted prominent family members' interesting letters to the press, as did Sarah P.E. Hale, sister of diplomat Alexander Hill Everett and wife of the Boston *Advertiser's* publisher. When she later learned of his disapproval, she repaired the breach in a letter to him, writing, "And before I go farther, I must apologize for having published in the Advertiser the letter about 'tea.' I had not received your letter, by the Paul Jones in which you make the request that none of yours should be published and as you had said nothing on the subject before, we concluded ... that there was no objection to printing the tea letter as it was altogether free from political remarks and on a subject of general interest and in fact it seemed to be too good to keep altogether to ourselves." Despite its seemingly apolitical message, his letter might have fueled partisan warfare, for he was serving under a Democratic administration and the *Advertiser* was a decidedly partisan Whig organ.[32]

Publication by Request If good intentions like Hale's backfired, most interventions helped authors—the best of circumstances alluded to above. The widespread practice of printing "by request" benefited many writers. The phrase *by request*, appearing on at least 3,847 American imprints published between 1830 and 1861, usually referred to the edition's institutionally sponsored production and advertised the author's nonmarket motives and modest ambitions. These represent but the tip of the iceberg of all requested printed material reported in the period's diaries and letters. To be sure, not all requests were so formal or disinterested. Even commercial publications, like magazines or gift annuals, contained much "requested" writing that more obliged the editor within amateurs' social networks than vaulted their literary careerism.[33]

Offers could be rebuffed—after all, they were not demands—but most people welcomed them. They were especially helpful to beginners like Charlotte Forten, who requited an invitation to publish an early poem delivered upon graduating from Salem Normal School in 1856. "At Dr. [Henry] Wheatland's request took him that poor, miserable poem," Forten wrote in her diary. Ever self-deprecating, she pleaded, "I wish he would not have it published. It is *not worth* it." Providence, Rhode Island, industrialist Zachariah Allen hinted at the formality of soliciting, noting that "the editors of the daily papers applied for the publication" of his 1860 address before the Rhode Island Historical Society; he reported that Roger Williams's recently exhumed body had been "eaten" by an apple tree's roots conforming to the shape of his skeleton "as if, indeed, moulded thereto by the powers of vegetable life." Most writers filled requests, even if it meant extra labor, such as copying or revising. One rural physician and postmaster who gave Democratic Party speeches proudly shouldered the task: "I have received this morning a very flattering letter from several gentlemen of Huntington, requesting me to write out my speech for publication—I have consented to do so."[34] Vigorous solicitation could nudge diffident or lazy writers.

Some authors worked particularly long and hard to fulfill mourners' requests for verses and obituaries. Pious Universalist versifier Eunice Cobb received several entreaties, some of them in person. "Had a call from Mrs. Cunningham of S. Boston," she recorded, "to see me in regard to writing an obituary for her deceased mother." As common were requests via mail. "Will you be so kind as to write for the Greenfield Democrat a short notice of sisters' death[?]" one man wrote in 1848, "By doing so you will oblidge [sic] Your cousin & Friend." When a defective obituary appeared, it became important for readers in the kinship network to know if the immediate family had authorized the writer. One upstate New Yorker, encountering a brother-in-law's obituary mysteriously lacking a death notice, asked her widowed sister about it. She replied, absolving herself, "You wished to know if I requested Br. C—to write Mr Beers obituary. I did not."[35] A family death could occasion a flurry of queries and commissions.

So could, curiously, the "birth" of a book in print precipitate requests to review it. Its author or other interested people blatantly asked friends to write these "notices," or, if obviously ingratiating, "puffs." One rural Methodist minister seemed unsurprised when he ran into a neighbor "on the green & was presented with his 'hand book'—with request that I should notice [it] in the Quar[terly] Review." Requests to puff could overwhelm editors; Sarah P.E. Hale declined to notice a recent edition of *The Simple Cobler of Aggawam in America* in her husband's newspaper, noting that "if you knew what lots of books we do have to puff now, you would not wonder that we have to stop to take a breath." In most cases, a book was expected to be puffed, not criticized. "When 'puffs' are not voluntary, the editor becomes a sort of literary recruiting-serjeant, [sic] and forces them into service," one commentator complained. Editors insured that only a writer who already—in the words of one choosing the reviewer of William Ellery Channing's *Poems*—"expressed great approbation" of the book "should be desired to puff it."[36]

Of course, editors invited other types of manuscripts, too, often through direct mail to prospective authors. Charlotte Forten, for example, "Received a prospectus of a magazine to which Mr. P ... R ... wishes me to contribute." "I may, occasionally," she averred. While solicitations were not promises, they were virtual guarantees from publishers needing copy, especially on timely topics. In this vein, a newspaperman pitched his brother an opportunity from the Lowell, Massachusetts, *Courier*'s editor during the 1844 presidential campaign: "If Charley has got any [Henry] Clay Songs Mr William Schouler would be in an exstacy to hear them." In their roles as editors, compilers of gift annuals begged acquaintances to send them something. Sarah Carter Edgarton, for one, hoped her friend Luella J.B. Case, ever-burdened with family duties, would contribute to her 1840 *The Rose of Sharon*. "I think I can venture to promise one article," Case responded in June 1839, "but it will not fill out the 50 pages now wanting." Nearly seven years later, Edgarton still counted on Case, who pledged, "I will endeavor to send you something—probably what comes easiest." Even though inside tracks gained authors access to print, they also kept periodicals running, for many editors depended upon a "stable" of contributors drawn from family and social circles. "I cannot ... understand the policy of the Publishers in taking the work out of his hands," Alexander Hill Everett remarked of his nephew's *Boston Miscellany* editorship. "They cannot help seeing that a large proportion of the contributors have been from his immediate personal friends." A magazine's success or failure often rested upon editors' bonds to authors.[37]

Unlike commercial publishers, organizational sponsors, such as churches and schools, pursued nonprofit objectives with their requests. Money for these projects was commonly raised by institutions. After Unitarian minister Alonzo Hill "consented to the publication of his sermon" on his predecessor Aaron Bancroft, congregants voted "to pay for the publishing." Industrious college organizations could finance the publication of sermons, too, sometimes through the age-old subscription method. On October 19, 1835 in the "President's woodshed," a clandestine "meeting was held of the friends of Anti slavery to devise ways and means to secure the publication of Rev. Mr [Henry] Wood's excellent antislavery sermon," Dartmouth's Cyrus Bradley declared of the college pastor, "A committee of one from each class was chosen to wait on Mr Wood with the request for a copy." Manuscript in hand, Bradley contacted a Concord publisher who estimated "that 1000 copies of Wood's sermon can be printed for 25 dollars." The same evening the news came back, "the faithful incendiaries came in, and in a few minutes, 1200 of the sermon were subscribed for. If we can get two thousand subscribed, they will probably come somewhat cheaper." After procuring seven hundred more promises the next day, he ordered two thousand copies, costing "a little more than two cents each," which began arriving by November 12, less than a month after the woodshed meeting.[38]

Although requested reviews, verse, speeches, and sermons demanded of their authors only small amounts of concentrated effort, and hence were numerous, solicited book-length manuscripts represented major commitments of money, time, and energy, and so were fewer. Most laborious were intensively researched local histories. Norridgewock, Maine, farmer William Allen began "preparing a historical sketch of this town at the request of our village Lyceum" in 1837. The amateur historian, who later wrote that he "amused" himself "during many years, collecting statistics and making sketches of the history of the towns in Maine in which I have lived," seemed pleased to "have had recourse to an original manuscript account of the battle written Aug 30 1724 now in my possession." It recounted the surprise attack by two hundred English colonists upon the Catholic-Indian settlement there and the slaughter of eighty or so inhabitants, including the aforementioned Father Rasle. Because it shed light on such controversies, Allen's edition of one thousand would sell out by the 1860s. News of a local history in progress might also attract aid. "Miss Electa Jones has been writing a history of Stockbridge & Mr Canning [a schoolmaster] takes charge of its publication," a minister's wife told her daughter in 1852. The book incorporated Mohican Hendrick Aupaumut's eighteenth-century manuscript, an oral history of his people. Publishing books by request could have charitable ends, to provide income for the author, while advancing a larger cause. The "friends" of emigré Peter Clarkin, who wrote *Reflections on Revelations* while in Ireland, "offered to pay for its being printed and give him the money the sale of them brought." One friend, particularly concerned about potato famine victims like Clarkin, "sold 24 at a dollar a piece, and hope[d] the money will do the poor man some good."[39] Books like these came into existence because of such benevolent souls.

Assisting Others Authors who sent manuscripts to friends or family members in the business often perceived of themselves as being assistants and not insiders; conversely, publishers felt grateful for this material—especially since demand for clean copy far outstripped supply. But most authors offering aid admitted they got something invaluable in return. Mellen Chamberlain, who wrote travel accounts for Brattleboro, Vermont's *Semi-weekly Eagle*, thought self-improvement came with accommodating requests. "I have consented to do this, chiefly, because they wish it," he admitted, "secondly, since it may mellow my style which is naturally stiff & heavy." Women particularly profited by this mutually beneficial arrangement. "I lent a hand in the way of translating a rather pleasant French novel, during the season when fill up matter is wanted," Sarah P.E. Hale explained of her work for her husband's Boston *Advertiser*. About writing for her son's *Boston Miscellany*, she claimed, "I have translated one of Mrs. Pichler[']s Novelettes from the German for my share." Hale occasionally acknowledged the literary self-gratification she enjoyed while helping, remarking once that "this gives variety to my occupations, and I think make[s] me fresher and brighter than if I were always hovering over my needle." Luella Case similarly balanced familial duty and self-expression. On the one hand, she complained that time spent assisting her newspaper editor husband was time stolen from correspondence: "But lately, Mr Case calls upon me so much for the 'Star' that I have little time for other writing." On the other hand, Case divulged personal motives: "I scribble for a more selfish reason, *'pour me amuser,'* and publish for the same." Mary Poor also blended work and pleasure in contributing to her husband's *American Railroad Journal*: "sometimes I draw for illustrations for the paper, & that is always pleasant to me." No doubt Eunice Cobb felt both useful and self-satisfied writing for her husband's Universalist periodical, the *Christian Freeman*.[40] In these ways women entered the public world of letters while remaining firmly ensconced in domestic roles, but even men were pulled along the path to print by social alliances.

PUBLISHING AND ITS CONSEQUENCES

The diverse motivations for publishing meant that manuscripts' geneses commensurately differed, but, due to common book trade practice, their fate as they moved toward print would become increasingly similar. Surprisingly, throughout the phases of publishing—composing, vetting, copying, submitting, editing, proofreading, and finally appearing in print—the social markedly intervened. If friends and family were so involved in getting into print, so too did they share in what authors got out of it, which was often less than anticipated. Together they balanced pride in the printed product with shame over its defects, gratification over positive reviews with disgruntlement over negative ones, and celebration of literary dollars with grief over payments withheld.

Getting Into Print

In contrast to the legendary solitary author scribbling away in a garret to make his or her way in the world at publishers' behest, the socially embedded amateur wrote from within lively domestic settings and interested communities that sometimes disparaged the writing impulse and, at others, through advice and assistance in manuscript preparation, encouraged it. Well-wishers helped, too, in submitting, editing, and proofreading material. Little wonder they could not help but see reflected on the printed page other people who had helped them along rather than merely their own hand.

Writing for Print Amateurs said little about the act of writing for publication other than its scheduling or drain upon time. Millworker Joshua Harris, for example, only left diary traces of his poetry in the making. Some pieces, such as "Impromptu," "I Wish I was Dead" (sure to offend contemporary sensibilities), and "Lines in Hattie Shute's Album," were evidently written in one sitting. Harris lavished time on the longer "Witches Sacrament" and "Dreamland Bridal," the latter begun in late August 1860 with "Strange is dreamlands marriage site." One month later Harris announced, "Have written a section for my poem of Dreamland Bridal tonight: 'Strange the Chapel whither led / I the maid. …'" He went on filling in lines at stolen moments: "'Saint not seraph on the wall / Miracle from Daemons fall'" or "'At the altar rose the priest / And with uplift symbols.'" Thus he continued through mid-December 1860. His other long-term project, "The Witches Sacrament," apparently begun in January 1860, survived his 1861 Union Army enlistment and continued until at least his 1863 mustering out. Before the war, he often wrote in evenings or on Sundays, when laid-off, or on sick leave. "Out with a lame arm today," Harris recorded in 1860, adding, "Have writen eight quartrains for a Poem entitled 'A Vision of Dissolution.'" Hard labor left energy only for sedentary writing: "Saw some wood and—Write some Poetry."[41] Amid sawdust and sweat, a poet's work was never done (see fig. 1.1).

As amateurs with jobs and families felt time pressing upon them, they devised strategies for completing work. Some stole time from other activities. "This afternoon I have spent in my library writing upon the subject of illuminating gas," engineer James Blake wrote one Sunday, "and I must say that I think I have received more benefit, than I should have had I attended church." Setting imaginary deadlines also worked. "Spent nearly all day in writing busily," Charlotte Forten wrote in her diary. "Determined to finish my story." Guilt

RECREATION FORMERLY.

Fig. 1.1 Like other laboring folk, Lowell Mill girls used their leisure time after hours for reading and writing, perhaps for publication in the *Lowell Offering. Source:* "Recreation Formerly," *HNMM* 22 (1861): 738. Courtesy of Cornell University Library, Making of America Digital Collection.

was an effective goad. One Methodist student confessed to dilatoriness concerning an essay in the works: "I have been preparing a communication for the press on the subjects of Baptism which ought to have been written weeks ago."[42] Amateurs waited upon sometimes sluggish muses.

The best solution was adherence to a predictable rhythm in which writing and everyday activities were woven together to yield mystifyingly high productivity. Sarah Edgarton elucidated the method for one astonished skeptic:

I rise about seven o'clock—eat breakfast, wipe dishes, sweep, make bed, sometimes churn, wash and iron—make toilet, then cloister myself in the study until dinner; when this is despatched, and the dishes are again in the cupboard I return to books and pen, and leave them not till night. Were she [the skeptic] to look in occasionally, she would see me sitting in my arm-chair, with a sheet before me, a happy countenance—sometimes frowning for a thought—a pile of books on the table in front, work-basket, unanswered letters, a dish of berries, flowers, scraps of poetry, etc. etc., all in fine disorder.

Sociable interruptions notwithstanding—"sometimes sisters come in, and we enjoy a fine laugh together"—her work progressed until "[t]he clock strikes twelve—a warning to close." With increasing publishing commitments, this fine machinery became "a treadmill of poetry"; she would "waste hours in vain struggles to acquit myself of duties that require instant execution." The resulting "weight of anxiety" led to burnout, with her "mind ... fettered and motionless."[43] Success ironically could defeat a proven literary routine.

Had Edgarton been married at the time, wifely duties would have caused additional anxiety. "[E]xperience has told me that the care of 'three good meals a day' is a formidable thing to any thing like fancy, or imagination," Luella Case observed after years of wedded life; "although," she stipulated, housework was "not absolutely incompatible with it." The balancing act, however, eventually took its toll: "What with scouring and scrubbing, and reading proof, and scribbling, (a variety you see) I had not a minute's time as my own." Sarah P.E. Hale likewise complained, "I have no time to read a word. [Daughter] Sarah requires almost constant attention and if I get a moment I am puffing at my Carter Books." So discrepant was marriage with women's authorship that its portent suggested career stoppage. Published poet Caroline Briggs's engagement set off alarms. "One of the young ladies in our family when told of yr. engagement," a friend told Briggs, "said quite mournfully— 'Oh I'm afraid she will write no more poetry'—I laughed outright and told her your life was all poetry now set to the sweetest music—'But,' still clinging to her fear, she replied 'we may never hear it.'" Briggs continued to write for periodicals, especially during the Civil War, thus defying predictions. Married women could be surprisingly resourceful in effectively managing time.[44]

To scoffers and gossips, married women writers who juggled chores seemed frivolous, selfish, and in violation of ordained roles. While Eliza Buckminster Lee worked on her *Life of Jean Paul Frederic Richter*, her friend Sarah P.E. Hale observed of her husband, "I suspect Mr. Lee's stiff notions may be a little nettled by her stepping so much out of the common court." Not all women's gossip was so supportive. Housewife Louisa Waterhouse, devoted to a demanding spouse, impugned married "scribbling women" in a spirited, perhaps fictionalized, conversation:

Lady.   Is Mrs. H.W. a very sensible woman?
Mrs.   Yes she is.
Lady.   Does she write much?
Mrs.   I should'nt think her a very sensible woman if she did; with her large family, her understanding is sufficiently manifested by her conversation & well regulated household, & I may add, by a very faithful discharge of the various duties of life.

Similarly, Harriet Hanson Robinson felt little compassion for one "orthodox minister[']s wife" more attentive to her writing than her neighbors. "[H]ad a note from Mrs Angier," Robinson recorded, "a sort of an apology for not calling sooner," and added, "she is [a] curious woman rather 'lack-a-daisycal.' a writer of verses." One wonders on which side—sympathizing or chastising—author Mary Baker Eddy stood regarding married women writers when she clipped "Female Authors" for her scrapbook: "'Do you really write for the press?' asked the captain of his fair neighbor. 'You need not look so alarmed,' answered she, laughing 'it is only a spiteful invention of the general, to damage my chances of getting married.'"[45] To court a writing woman was to hazard inattention when her muses called.

Unlike women, men seldom felt the sting of acid tongues railing against literary ambitions; however, they complained of a similar drain from time spent writing due to work or study. "I am overwhelmed with business," Cyrus Bradley asserted in the midst of his college semester. "Besides reading [William] Paley, with [Francis] Wayland, [Daniel] Dewar, & [John] Abercrombie, attending two Anatomical Lectures Daily & reading on the subject at home," the exhausted undergraduate disclosed, "I am engaged in putting [together] materials for a Biography." If college students' mental work crowded out writing time, manual laborers' physical exhaustion made the necessary concentration difficult. "I have spoiled a good deal of paper, and shed much ink," one "*scribbling*" fishyard worker griped, "but *produced* very little for so much material." Fears of squandering precious moments accompanied worries over dissipating health and wealth. The *New England Historical and Genealogical Register*'s editor grumbled that "It is a troublesome affair, & forces me so severely in labor that I must relinquish it soon, or I shall lose what little poor health I now have, & as to money—I have lost all that long ago." Overburdened men doubtless received more sympathy than women, but not without reservations. "[O]ur former Dixfield Minister ... is Reg., of Probate[,] Editor of two papers—preaches every sabbath & an unusual number of funeral sermons all over the

County," one Maine resident confided in her diary; "[h]is wife is entirely confined to a large family of little children even an infant of a few months." She pondered the inevitable effect: "How are they to find time to take care of the Public?"[46] A minister's wife was part of a public production duo.

Getting Advice Sympathetic friends and family members could also offer writers feedback, and even new ideas. "I think you had best come home this summer, it will make a deal of difference with my writing concerns," one widow implored her son; "I have finished my poem containing *5450* lines—and am now making out the notes perhaps 50 pages—Now if you could look it over and note the errors I could go right on and copy it." Most informal and face-to-face aid came as audience response to authors reading works in progress. "Louisa read me the two first chapters of a new story she is writing, on Joanna of Naples," John Park noted six months before it was published. He heartily approved, noting that "it appears to me a promising specimen of the performance." His daughter Louisa also read out loud "her first draught of a Review of Mrs Hughes's Memoir of Mrs Hemans."[47] In an era of widespread oral reading of published material, this method of audience testing could best predict a work's potential success.

To spare authors' feelings, friends and family often trod lightly. After all, affective relationships had to be preserved amid objective assessments of marketability. A friend deployed circumlocution when responding to draft poems: "This work ... will nev[er] have its due, from a great proportion of readers of the ord[inary] class ..., but with the literary class it will stand high." While some authors savored these wrought illusions, others suspected a bit of blarney in the sincerest compliments. "What would you think of me, if I were to tell you that your delicious flattery has tempted me to 'perpetrate' something like rhyme," Luella Case chastised Sarah Edgarton; "till *truth* came, and looked so cross in my face, that I finally agreed with her, that I had not the 'gift' of poetry." Charlotte Forten trusted her own distorted self-image more than the reflection others held up to her: "[F]inished my 'Lost Bride.' S.[arah] likes it much, but it seems to *me* silly and flat. I can't see any sense in it." For wary writers, getting candid opinions took some conniving. Elizabeth Jocelyn masked her authorial identity behind that of a less-talented sister in order to wrest criticism from her family: she "had quite a long conversation, on a piece of poetry, which I pretended was of Margarette's composition."[48] Objective criticism thus finagled could prove valuable in the marketplace.

Frank reviewers, however, faced being the bearers of bad news that could unintentionally stifle fledgling careers. The usually supportive John Park saw problems in his daughter Louisa's manuscript in progress about authors in George III's reign, which she called "Sketches of Eminent Women," noting, "She can make nothing of such tame subjects. Good people are very important in society, and ought to be honoured in remembrance; but mere goodness, without any extraordinary incidents of life, afford very limited scope for interesting biography. Should this work ever be printed, I am very certain Louisa's literary reputation would not stand so well as it does now, after the publication of Miriam, in poetry, and Joanna, in prose. Unpleasant as it is, I must give her my opinion on this subject." The next day Park's message took deadly effect: "This forenoon, I mentioned to Louisa the objections which seemed to me to dissuade from her persevering in her 'Biographical Sketches of distinguished Women.' She readily acquiesced, so far as to lay them aside for the present, and that is all I want." Louisa dropped the project and did not publish another book-length work while her father was alive.[49] In this way many a manuscript—indeed, entire careers—perished with a few well-intended words.

Copying If a manuscript survived the obstacles thrown its way—limited writing time, discouraging conditions, or harsh criticism—it usually was finalized by transcribing a copy for submission, a tiresome task. Many authors ritualistically recorded days spent in reaching this important stage of completion. This job demanded so much concentration that it could relieve woeful minds. After Sarah P.E. Hale's son Alexander died, she discovered that copying anesthetized her pain, writing that "the finishing [of] the copy I found I could do sometimes, when I could hardly fix my thoughts on any common occupation." Copying required sharp vision; thus, writers susceptible to eye strain called upon others to help. "I am and shall be, for some time, busily occupied in transcribing Louisa's Joanna of Naples," John Park commented, "her eyes not allowing to do it herself." He enjoyed the act of transcribing for its own sake: "Poor Louisa can go no where, but her pen is leading me briskly in Joanna. I am good for something; I can copy—thanks to my good father and mother, who took care that I should learn to write." The arduous completion of "above seventy pages of very close lines on long writing paper," took nearly two months.[50] These were literary labors of familial love.

How he thinks he would act—

How he would act—

If he should carry to a Publisher his Manuscript Novel, which he is sure is better than any thing of Dickens, and ought to bring him $50,000.

Fig. 1.2 This cartoon exaggerates authors' humiliating manuscript rejections at publishers' offices. *Source:* "How He Thinks He Would Act . . . ," *HNMM* 16 (1857): 142. Courtesy of Cornell University Library, Making of America Digital Collection.

Submitting Manuscripts Once they had a clean copy, authors were ready to submit to publishers. Writers who published by request or solicitation were, of course, spared blind manuscript submission. Though a hardy few called hat in hand upon urban publishers (see fig. 1.2), most authors sent either letters of interest or finished manuscripts. Unsolicited submissions elicited response more often than exploratory notes, as Joshua Harris discovered. After his many queries failed, he tried sending copies of his work. "I send you this package of manuscript which you can publish if you choose and if it is worth anything to you—send to me by mail anything or nothing," he wrote to the *Pictorial Drawing Room*'s editor. This failed, too, but a similar packet to the editor of the *Waverley* led to Harris's only known publications. Charlotte Forten also mailed publishers her finished work despite fears of finding "no one willing to publish such stuff." Knowing exactly to whom a manuscript should be directed was half the battle, and aspiring authors sometimes missed the mark. "I think your writings show a great deal of talent," *Godey's Lady's Book* editor Sara J. Clarke replied to a submitter, "But I unfortunately, am not the one to be of service to you." Clarke was "but a nominal editor of the 'Lady's Book'—have no control of it, whatever." In a time of silent partners and nominal editors, authors could never know if they merely encountered face-saving forms of rejection. To stave off refusal, some authors enclosed recommendation letters from prominent readers. "Having examined the Manuscript of considerable portions of a work on 'Morals & Manners,' prepared 'by a Lady,'" the Massachusetts state librarian declared in an endorsement, "I can heartily commend it as timely & valuable … [;] it is deemed by the undersigned, well adapted to its proposed end, & worthy of all encouragement."[51] The lack of standardized submission practices left room for diverse approaches.

Editors notified authors of acceptance or rejection in various ways. Some writers received a letter, perhaps with some feedback. Even solicited authors coveted letters of assessment. "Do not publish the vagaries I may send you if unfitted for the work," Luella Case requested of Sarah Edgarton, "but just give the reasons and if not too late, I will endeavor to send something else." Expecting no favors from her friend, Case added, "[D]o not be afraid to play the part of a *critic* in your capacity as Editress of the annual, and reject what is inappropriate, from whatever source it may come." Understanding that Edgarton played a traditionally male role in a world unsympathetic to professional women, Case spelled out her concern: "This to be sure is an unpleasant office, particularly for a lady, and I may possibly be the first to be condemned by my own suggestion, but if so—thus let it be."[52] Even disappointing letters advantaged aspiring amateurs craving editorial advice. Because correspondence expended editors' labor, they preferred more efficient ways to inform hopeful authors.

An easier alternative—and not coincidentally, a way to sell more issues to prospective authors—was notification through periodical columns. Sometimes submissions appeared in print without forewarning. "To my great astonishment," Charlotte Forten gasped, "see that my poor 'Glimpses' are published in the [National Anti-Slavery] Standard." Just as often, the targeted venue printed acceptance or rejection notices. "I see that the Scientific American says they shall commence a series of articles from an *able* correspondent upon Illuminating Gas next week," James Blake proudly recorded of his forthcoming piece. Joshua Harris also learned of his first acceptance in the *Waverley*'s pages: "Afternoon Went up town—bought a Waverly—A piece of Poetry which I sent to Mr Dow is accepted—will probably apear [*sic*] in a week or two—under my own name." Jubilant of his success, he confidently declared, "Guess I shall begin to apear Literary soon." Several more pieces by him were "accepted" in this manner, including "A wish & c," "'The dying stranger' by Ray Raymond" (a pseudonym), and "Lines to JEH"—the last apparently written anonymously to himself. The same magazine carried grim news of rejection: "Evening. Go up town Get my Pictorial[,] buy a Waverley—Poems from R[ay] R[aymond] are declined." Whatever the form of rebuke, waiting for a response could be excruciating. "Still no news of my poor story," Forten wrote two days after mailing the ill-fated "Lost Bride" to the *Home Journal*. "Though of course," she admitted, "'tis too soon."[53] Certainly, many authors with shaking hands scanned periodicals in search of their work—or its rejection notice.

Editorial Interventions Submissions that spontaneously appeared in print were usually edited, but without authors' input. In some cases, however, writers were put to the task. The worst form of editorial intervention meant reshaping submitted material beyond original conception. "Crosby was not willing to publish so few [hymns] but demanded 12 more & therefore as they cannot be written like a catalogue, but must wait for the right time, she has not yet been able to complete the number," one author's sister seethed; "Nine are done, & she hopes to get three more done before long, but you must see how much she has to take up her mind at present." Commercial demand outpaced creative supply. Disparity also could arise between what authors believed made a good book and what publishers thought could sell. After publishers delayed production of Ellen Hedge's anthology to target the holiday market, the author's mother revealed that "the addition, by their recommendation, of some Christmas and New Year's pieces spoiled the book, as Ellen thinks." Publishers also placed their mark upon the look of the book, at the risk of alienating the author. "I do not think the pictures in the books are so pretty as usual this year," Sarah P.E. Hale complained; "but with this part of the business I have nothing to do, I only write the stories and they fix them up as they please." One wonders what went through authors' minds when, after they expended so much effort in writing and copying to achieve a sense of completion, publishers treated their manuscripts as raw material for processing.[54]

Lest they disrupt social relations, amateur editors embedded in community life could not treat manuscripts as coolly as publishers playing the market. John Park, in charge of editing Alonzo Hill's "requested" sermon, argued with sponsoring cavilers who wanted to make changes he deemed unnecessary and injurious to his pastor: "Have a *deliberation* with Mr Burnside on Mr Hill's notes to his Funeral Sermon. A very unpleasant commission." As bearer of bad news after town magnate Samuel M'Gregore Burnside demanded changes, Park scoffed, "I was deputed to communicate a *recommendation* of several verbal alterations, and some considerable omissions! I went to Mr Hill's about eleven, and finished that disagreeable job."[55] The sermon appeared in print soon after, but not without hurt feelings and wounded pride—casualties of stepping into a world of print.

Proofreading After typesetting from edited copy was complete, there came yet another hurdle on the way to publishing: proofreading. At this last stage before final publication, mistakes might still be caught on "galley" sheets. Publishers increasingly hired in-house correctors, but much of the work fell to editors' voluntary proofreaders, usually women. Mary Poor, for example, "corrected proofs" for spouse Henry Varnum Poor's *American Railroad Journal* beginning in 1849. Likewise, Eunice Cobb "spent the evening, assisting husband in reading 'proof,'" for his *Christian Freeman*. Women's work habits and roles particularly suited them for the task. They were used to accurate and detailed work like sewing. Furthermore, it was but one step from women's traditional role, that of teaching children to read, to correcting copy. Within domestic rhythms, proofreading afforded leisure time away from physically taxing housework. "I help Willie all I can about the paper," Harriet Hanson Robinson claimed regarding her husband's short-lived *Lowell American*. "I have been reading proof. ... I hope to get so as to read it *well* soon," she remarked on a later occasion; "I can do it and plenty of housework and sewing besides."[56] That they were entrusted with such a technical, worldly, and, in other hands, professional responsibility suggests that women proofreaders could transcend domesticity.

Not only periodical editors' wives, but authors' female relatives participated in proofreading—that is, if the writer was lucky enough to receive galleys from the publisher, a practice that was by no means common or obligatory. Sarah P.E. Hale and her daughters corrected galleys for their uncle Alexander H. Everett, a high-powered literary figure associated with the elite *North American Review*. "[T]he girls read it carefully," Hale recorded of proofing copy for a book of his essays and poems. Women proofread not just because they felt duty-bound, but because it gave them a social sense of self-worth. Abigail Pierce prided herself that Reverend Pierce's fiftieth anniversary sermon was perfectly printed. "Father's address, the day of his jubilee, has come out in fine style," she beamed to her sister in 1847. "I feel amply repaid for all my labor in looking over proof sheets, to find but one small mistake in the whole book, and that is leaving out one letter in a word," she explained, adding that there was "[n]ot a single mistake in the numerous dates." While short books and articles required the same careful scrutiny as longer reference works, the latter more severely taxed the proofreader who strove for accuracy. With her husband's "new & *improved* edition of the Comprehensive Dictionary ... in press," Elizabeth Worcester apologized for not writing to her sister;

"I read the proofs, we are both *very* busy." For all of his wife's hard work, Joseph Worcester was grateful, especially in retrospect. After Elizabeth's health subsequently failed, he lamented, "When the Universal Dictionary was in the press, Eli[z]abeth was very helpful to me in reading the proofs; but she has not been able to do any thing of the kind, in relation to this work."[57] The stresses of going into print exacted an equally high price from both author and proofreader struggling to attain the impossible—a perfectly finished piece.

Proofreading was not only women's work, of course. The same social sense that motivated women compelled men to take up proofs for acquaintances and family. While on sick leave from school, Cyrus Bradley helped with "Dr. [John] Farmer['s] … great Documentary History." "I read the proof of his copies a little this afternoon," he recorded, "& at his request intend to employ myself in this manner some days." One did not need to be asked, for when proofs unexpectedly arrived loved ones might spring into action. When James Elliot Cabot's galleys appeared in his brother Edward's office, another sibling recounted the favor rendered: "Elliot has written a piece on acoustic architecture in Dwights Journal & with his accustomed mumness had not said a word to any body about it, so that when the proof sheets were brought to the office for correction, Edward did'nt know what to make of it, he corrected them however & they have appeared in yesterdays journal."[58] Through informal efforts like these, men and women volunteers insured quality within the publishing industry's products when few firms could afford proofreaders.

Appearing in Print The saga of publishing did not end with the correction of the galleys. Printed publication itself marked a special event in most authors' lives. "I did certainly feel very strangely at seeing myself, for the first time *in Print*," one neophyte recalled, "and read my articles, I can positively affirm *more than once*." A book's birth could be noted when it was first publicized; John Park proudly reported that his daughter Louisa's "'Joanna of Naples' [was] advertised in the Boston papers of this morning." Notices or prospectuses, if they appeared at all, occasionally and sometimes purposely miscalculated publication dates to garner advance orders. "I am sorry the publishers have given the public reason to expect the work will be finished so soon," an irked Joseph Worcester despaired of his dictionary. "It cannot be completed so soon, at the time named, by two or three months."[59] Misleading notices could only disappoint or confuse potential buyers. Moreover, there was always the chance that some catastrophe might prevent final publication.

Because only seeing was believing, most authors waited until they held the publication in their hands before declaring completion. When Henry Cushman announced to his diary that his genealogy was "first *published* today," he added the qualification, "that is, I received from the binders the first completed copy today." After purchasing an issue of the *Waverley* "up town," Joshua Harris registered the appearance of "'A friend' by J.E.H this week." Knowing that authors might savor this milestone of publication, Sarah P.E. Hale supplied a volume of her compiled gift books to those involved in its completion. "Contributors to an annual always have a copy sent them," Hale explained to her niece. Of one, Hale presumed, "she may like to see herself in print."[60] For a moment, the author's very identity became typographic.

Getting Out of Print

The initial excitement of seeing oneself in print, however, quickly wore thin. Despite the best intentions, mistakes crept into seemingly flawless galleys. Moreover, once brilliant ideas dulled with time, money did not come pouring in, and one's much anticipated mass readership never materialized. One author quickly descended from his castle in the air after celebrating his first newspaper article to sum up the chagrin that his counterparts experienced: "I query, if other readers averaged a *single* reading." "I thought the matter, then, vastly important," he reflected, "but before long, became sensible, of its not being momentous, and moreover of the faults of my style and argument."[61] As life went on and distance intervened between the text and the hand that produced it, authorial illusions faded.

Discovering Problems Errors in printing, grammar, spelling, and layout vexed authors as much if not more than any other blemish. Authors who neglected proofs had only themselves to blame for mistakes, but some were the publisher's fault. "There are divers pretty bad misprints in it, but I did not see the proof sheet," Sarah P.E. Hale rationalized of one of her translations. Even when authors scrutinized final drafts or proofs, panic-ridden last-minute changes could produce glitches. Luella Case confessed that fussing over one essay did more harm than good, admitting, "I was rather ashamed to find false grammar in it after it was published. The way it happened was this. Just before closing it for the mail, I read it to my brother, and he objected to the wording of the first part of the sentence, and I changed it, without reading the latter part to see if all was right then, and so made bad work with nouns and verbs." For journalists the pressures of weekly, daily, or hourly deadlines might cause errors. Newcomers were often startled to learn just how stressful it could be. "Looked at the Advertiser this morning & found three mistakes in almost as many lines," a recently hired newspaper court reporter wrote only a day after completing his first assignment. "I am shocked with my carelessness & shall hardly show my head out to day," he moaned, swearing, "Such another would ruin me and I should be obliged to relinquish my office. Heaven grant that no such consequences follow this instance." Editors, too, felt the pangs of imperfection, especially when trusty proofreaders were unavailable. "I am almost ashamed of its appearance at present," the *Railroad Journal's* Henry Varnum Poor confessed to his sojourning wife; "If you were here we could prepare the articles together. I depend much upon your aid in the work."[62] The fear of error could be eased by sharing responsibility.

Editors and journalists, of course, could redeem themselves as new, more polished numbers appeared and old errors were forgotten, whereas book authors seldom had another immediate opportunity. Errors loomed much larger and seemed written in stone. "You will see that there is a mistake in the arrangement of the two last chapters of the little book," a distracted Sarah Worcester scratched using careless script and spelling: "The rany day should have gone last." She sighed in resignation, "I am sorry but I cannot heop it now." Second chances sometimes came with second editions. Only six months after *Miriam* first appeared, Louisa Park had a "corrected copy ... with an additional preface, by Deacon Butman" ready for reprinting. For authors not anticipating new editions, tipped-in errata sheets (printed slips identifying and correcting textual errors) could salvage some typos. For example, three weeks after Seth Arnold saw the publication of his congregation's *Confession of Faith*, he had errata pages ready for insertion. "[G]ot the corrected errors to the confession and covenant, and paid $1.50 to Mr. Moor," he wrote, peevishly calculating the book's cost: "making in all expense $30.60 besides my time."[63] Backpedaling was not only embarrassing, it drained money and took effort.

Typographical perfection mattered less to some authors looking back upon their work than tone and overall quality or presentation. Somehow seeing pieces in print could make authors regret ever writing them. "Aunt Margaretta ... asks if I wrote the lines to 'W.L.G.' in the Liberator," a mortified Charlotte Forten diarized; "If ever I write doggerel again I shall be careful not to sign my own initials." Women in particular shared their doubts with one another over their writing's merit. After publishing in the *Rose of Sharon*, Luella Case told editor

Sarah Edgarton, "I cease to wonder that you importune *mediocre* writers like myself, to help fill up its pages." In return, Edgarton herself admitted that she felt "too conscious of my infirmities" to aim for "a more open and elevated literary field" than Universalist publishing alone, as advocated by Case. On another occasion, Edgarton pled "personally guilty to" the charge of "throwing ... thoughts carelessly to the press, without study or revision." Other negative self-judgments with little apologia became devastatingly summary. Sarah Worcester, besides regretting the mistaken reversal of her book's two final chapters, thought it was, overall, "rather lifeless." Likewise, one mother was convinced that last-minute additions to her daughter's gift annual "destroy[ed] the unity of it." For some women, confidence born of experience never filled the empty spaces carved out by self-doubt. After years of translating for periodicals, Sarah P.E. Hale judged her own work as harshly as a novice would. "I have made a translation ... for the paper, which I suppose you will see," Hale informed her brother; "I thought it pleasant when I read it, but the process of translation makes me so tired of a thing, that it always seems dull."[64] As an editor's wife, her "insider's" perspective alerted her to self-criticism's omnipresence.

Critical Reception Self-reproach was not always the worst enemy of self-esteem, for adversarial commentators could deflate any vestiges of pride that escaped personal rebuke. In one case, a close friend of Charlotte Forten irrationally attacked her essay, "Glimpses of New England," two months after it appeared in the *National Anti-Slavery Standard*. "Miss S.[arah] P.R.[emond] I hear has burst out most venomously upon my poor 'Glimpses'—accusing them of being pro-slavery and heaven knows what all," Forten was shocked to learn. "I *pity* her," she concluded. Clearly, getting into print could break down the most trustful social ties. Even editors of scandal sheets that printed vicious gossip about locals could corrode relations among victims. After "Edwin S. Teller," pseudonymous editor of the *Adder* out of Middletown, Connecticut, attacked the town's "old sinners" in his debut paper, he derided resulting letters of complaint in his next: "Ajax," Teller sneered at one protester, "You talk rather loud; but if you want to flog us, come on, we are open." The paper's masthead, a snake with the motto "'Tread on Me and I'll Bite,'" speaks for itself (see fig. 1.3). This same edition, with its insipid cliff-hanger, "The Hunchback of the Wyoming," and a racist parody of a school integration sermon entitled "*Belubed Bredren*," drove one reader to despair. As Philip Sage, the

THE ADDER.

"TREAD ON ME AND I'LL BITE."

Vol 1. Middletown, March 14, 1849. No. 2.

A SPLENDID ORIGINAL ROMANCE,

WRITTEN EXPRESSLY FOR THE ADDER,

THE HUNCHBACK

OF THE WYOMING,

OR,

THE STRANGER OF THE SUSQUEHANNAH.

A TALE OF THE OLDEN TIME.

BY THE BOY IN BOOTS.

CHAPTER III.

A Change of Scene.

A few miles north of London there lived a man and his child. The mother of the child had been called away while it was yet an infant. Near, in front of the house a bubbling brook ran murmuring past, while in the rear the hill rose abrupt and steep, covered with thick dense brushes and towering trees.

One pleasant afternoon while the child played around in the pleasant sunshine or the cooling shade, a faint cry was heard, the father rushed to the door but nothing could be seen of his Son, and the search which he immediately caused to be made, and which was continued thro' the night and the next day, proved fruitless and the old man turned to his home. Elan, that was the name of his son, was marked by an anchor which stretched across the smooth fair skin, and the old man said "I will not despair, hope whispers in my ear that I shall see Elan again."

Eleven times the Earth had travelled around the sun—Near three hundred times the moon had waxed and waned again since Elan had been gone.

The busy rattling rumbling noise of this world of London had in some degree subsided; but still the lights that shone from the gaudy windows shone with undiminished radiance. Above—

The pale cold moon was well nigh hidden in the sable clouds.

Yet the giddy youth in the Queens Coffee House took no note of the time, but the wine flowed and the jest sparkled in all the hilarity of bacchanalian glee.

CHAPTER IV.

Death.

Two pedestrians stopped before the door gazed a moment upon the scene within and entered—

One an old and withered crone, whose very face was a glaring index of the blackest heart within; her companion—

A stunted piece of deformity, with an enormous hunch upon his back, his dark eyes sparkling from beneath his shaggy brow, while the coarse red hair was mattered over his brazen forehead.

And as they entered, every eye was fixed upon them; the glasses were set upon the table with the ruby wine sparkling in the radiant light—the merry jest had ceased for all were intent upon the strangers, whose frightful look bespoke forth many ejaculations of wonder and surprise,— "Bill"—

One at length spoke.

"—ill" said he "we were just raking you about your dulcinea, and lo! she stands before you with your successful rival."

This was received by the company with boisterous laughter while the person addressed joined in the mirth.

"By G—d, Jim, that's too bad on a fellow but too good to be lost. Give the boys some good wine Jenkins—more wine, you see its on me fairly. Come stir you old devil, don't you see the boys are waiting! But hold, perhaps my fair friend, and as Jim says, her accept-

ed lover,' would like something as well as ourselves. What say you, my dear," said Bill, addressing the old woman, "what say you, my dear, will you take some wine?"

The old crone cast a look of withering scorn upon the speaker, which gradually changed to a satisfied smile.

"No wine, but some brandy for me, what ye say, eh? Sammy?

"I don't want no brandy; but drink some rum, or not, I don't keer which."

"He's a pretty specimen of mankind, at least, don't you think so, Bill?"

"Well, Jim, it's my opinion that he's an opera singer—perhaps a Lion among the ladies—see what a beautiful figure."

A roar of laughter followed this display...ion stood aloof with evident marks of dissatisfaction.

"A Lion among the ladies! why, Bill, you must be deserving a straight jacket, or else old Jenkins' wine finds store-room in the garret, where your brains should be A Lion indeed! Why, I should think him more of a Camel—look at his back once, a Lion with a Camel's back!".

Another deafening peal of laughter followed this; and while the merry forget a moment the object of their mirth, we will take a look at them.

The crone and Sammy converse silently a moment—

And as the panther approaches his prey, with steps as stealthy and noiseless did they approach the table, with the upturned glasses to their lips—

With a sudden spring they clutched the two who had made their jokes at their expense, and held them by their throats till the blood had ceased to circulate, and their faces wore a pallid hue.

And did their comrades raise no hand for their defence?

The others were frozen to their chairs with involuntary terror, for the movement was so sudden and unexpected they could not raise a hand or strike a blow in their defence.

Jenkins returned. The first glance showed him the state of affairs. Dropping his wine, he rushed to the Hunchback and forced him to quit his hold.— This was sufficient to arouse the energies of the party. Rising from their seats, they encompassed the crone and her com-

---

Fig. 1.3 Insipid fiction and vile gossip characterized this Middletown, Connecticut, scandal sheet that drove one resident to despair. *Source: Adder* 1, no. 2 (1849): 1; Connecticut Historical Society, Hartford, Connecticut.

outgoing U.S. Customs collector wrongly accused by neighbors of being the spiteful "Teller," vented in his diary,

> I have been much amused to day to hear the opinions of different individuals in regard to the Editor or Editors; Mr. Gleason said he did not think much of the romances on the first page if Mr. Sage did write it ... and Miss Rand Summer said the Negro sermon was written by Sage, you can see his expressions in every line. Oh! ye Solomons why does not the people appreciate your talents, you are the only redeeming point in this city. *I begin to think I am a Sonambulist and Edit the paper while in a trance.* ... They cannot injure me, if so, I will leave town and hide myself among the caves of California.

Sage's frantic response to the rumors unveiled a deeper dejection—a dampening of spirits over his imperiled political career that left him contemplating suicide the next day. Sage received criticism for pieces he did not write, of course, but it only reflected the low literary reputation he had locally.[65]

Conflicts of this sort were not confined to face-to-face relations, but were frequently fought out in the impersonal arena of print. The week after engineer James Blake's article on "Illuminating Gas" appeared in the *Scientific American,* he sensed an adversary's ominous approach: "I see quite a spirited article from the pen of that great humbug Mr Paine; in which he states that I in my last article after casting a slur upon 'New Lights,['] *assume* that carbon is the base of all illuminating gasses." Blake shuddered as he hastily scrawled, making mistakes in his penmanship and grammar, "he says he [will] show the falseness of [it] in his next article next week." What was only foreshadowed on April 11, 1851, arrived eight days later: "Mr Paine I see has written to me in the Sci American, quite a pugnacious piece." A stoic Blake resolved, "I shall not notice it, however." He then braced himself for the next storm: "Another of the series of articles appears in the Sci American today," he recorded on April 25; "I hope they will not bring discredit upon me." Although turbulent, his first passage through the world of print eventually brought him to safe shores. He rejoiced on July 10 that "a highly complimentary paragraph by the editor," concluded the "series of articles on gas."[66] In the face of such printed salvos, some overwrought authors simply removed themselves from the emotional battlefield of publishing and reverted to social authorship. Restricted circulation simply and effectively avoided unsolicited criticism.

Not all authors took foes' words to heart. Those who wrote out of ideology received printed rebuttals more coolly; no matter how deleterious, these seldom penetrated authors' emotional armor. "I find I have been attacked pretty sharply in the State of Maine, on the report of [the] investigating Committee," one Portland lawyer blandly observed of a newspaper parry against his account of the city government's role in the violent 1855 rum riot there, "but the writer Mr. Poor deals in declamative & violent denunciatory language without argument which can have little effect & therefore I let it pass." He then accentuated the positive, observing, "The report has a wide circulation & a good affect." Cyrus Bradley, in his role as antislavery warrior, also resisted verbal slings and arrows: "The second number of the Abolitionist appeared with two communications of mine; one on the duty of Abolitionists to appeal to the ballot-box & elect to Congress such as will vote for the Abol.[ition] of Slavery in the ten miles [i.e., Washington, D.C.]. To this, the publisher in his editorial remarks, does not seem to assent." Some levelheaded authors got even instead of angry. "Two protestant papers of Boston have accused of falsehood some passages of the life of the Cardinal de Cheverus," his biographer André Jean Marie Hamon wrote in defense of himself to Boston's Roman Catholic Bishop Fenwick. "Can I dare, My Lord, to beseech your Lordship to acquaint me with the modifications, the changings, the additions or suppositions which truth and prudence could require in the second edition which the author is about to deliver to the public[?]" he solicited.[67] Enlisting powerful supporters in rebuttal exchanges was a good strategy.

If rebuke could fluster an author, conversely, positive response seldom went to a writer's head. Few gloated about reviewers' admiration, for most understood the difference between bald-faced flattery and disinterested response within the impersonal world of publishing. Always ready to come to terms with the industry for what it was, Sarah P.E. Hale saw through "good reviews." She wrote with frankness, but also sarcasm, about the reception of her gift annuals: "My little books for the season are out, and have received the usual quantity of puffs from Newspaper Editors who have not apparently read them." As she understood it, these fawning colleagues wanted to keep in her husband's good graces; friends in the trade also depended upon her rare abilities as a translator to keep them well supplied. John Park, once himself an editor, knew how to spot sincere praise among the deception. While admitting that a friend's review of his daughter Louisa's *Miriam* was "very complimentary," he looked beneath the surface to find that thought, time, and care went into it; "what is better," he concluded, was that it was a "well written notice of *Miriam*."[68] To Park, a puff was thoughtless; a good review was deliberated and conscientious.

Payment Just as puffs represented airy confections, reimbursement was often less than substantial. Indeed, a dollar per piece or page was considered generous in periodical publication, while book royalties, often ten or fifteen cents per copy, depended upon profits after production costs were met. If scant fees encouraged rookies used to nothing, then that went double for the lucky few making much more. "[T]he carmaster, brought Louisa a check from Mr Goodrich for fifty dollars," John Park noted, "for some contributions with which she had furnished him for the 'Token' for 1839." Park recognized that his daughter's flair with words could prove lucrative: "this is doing very well." Olive Worcester, who owned the copyright to her deceased husband Henry's *Sermons*, eventually collected unexpected profits that he did not live long enough to see, but which hardly repaid costs: "Wrote to Mr Gerrish this eve acknowledging the receipt of $100 dollars for the sale of books written by my dear husband." But the amount of money earned was relative to the task at hand. The astute Sarah P.E. Hale balanced the scales carefully. "They are no great affairs," she said of her first gift annuals, "but the pay was small and I did not think it worth while to exert myself to a *terrible* degree upon the occasion." With shrewd insight she concluded, "I believe they are quite as good as the man expected for his money and perhaps as good as he could have got elsewhere."[69] In the world of commercial publishing, authorial responsibility stopped at the bottom line.

Some authors were happy to receive as payment only free copies of their publications. When schoolteacher Lucy Larcom published poetry in the *National Era*, she received "in return" only a free copy of the paper. "Nothing further was asked or expected," she later declared. Democrat partisan Thaddeus DeWolf noted in his diary that he "received 15 copies of the [Hampden *Statesman*] daily Extra of this morning" containing his political speech. For James Blake, some complimentary issues of the magazine in which he published both gratified and surprised him: "Rec'd a package of Sci Americans from the editors, also my manuscript, and am pleased to think they send me no bill for the papers."[70] The mysteries of publishing obviously left amateurs confused and wondering about credits and debits.

But for everyone involved—the keen as well as the naive—collecting payment was not always easy. When Louisa Park won a prize of fifty dollars for her "Caroline Gray" on April 8, 1837, her father, savvy to publishers' tricks, remained skeptical that his daughter would ever see the money; given the instability of publishers' lot during the panic year, he soberly assessed the situation, noting, "This is flattering news, but not quite so gratifying as would be the *receipt* of the awarded premium—the pecuniary responsibility of the Editor being rather problematical." As he followed dire reports that month—"The news from Boston, as to failures, worse and worse"—he launched a campaign to collect Louisa's just due. On May 20, he "wrote to the Editors of the Galaxy respecting the Prize Premium due from them to Louisa, for 'Caroline Gray'; wrote likewise to my son [John], enclosing the above." Sixty days later Park "Receive[d] a letter from John, stating his unsuccessful applications to the editor of the Galaxy, for Louisa's Premium, so long due, and no prospect yet of payment." Only on September 22, after five months of badgering, could Park breath a sigh of relief: "I send a letter to John, acknowledging the receipt of $50 for Louisa, for her story ... , from the publishers of the Galaxy; so that, at last, is settled."[71] Publishers promised, but did not always readily deliver.

Some of this is because, financial panic or not, publishers always seemed poised on the brink of ruin. Lydia Maria Child, the famous abolitionist author, once remarked of a Boston publisher, "as for Colman, he fails about four times a year." Samuel Colman was not unlike others of his trade, but rumors of failures often proved too true. Colman would indeed eventually go bankrupt, much to the disconcertion of his star author, Henry Wadsworth Longfellow, who would be left with nothing but a golden handshake for his efforts. A worried Sarah P.E. Hale reported of another teetering publishing house in 1841, "Marsh & Capen have for some weeks been in hot water, it is said they have not actually failed & that they will go on again with their business, but it is pretty much at a stand now, and I have my fears." She fretted to her brother that the firm promised "to pay ten percent on all the copies printed of two volumes, one payable in March, the other April, but I do not depend much upon it. I regret now that I took the book out of Carter's hands, but I did what I thought was for the best at the time." The hearsay proved untenable, and Hale was relieved to learn that "Marsh & Capen have not altogether failed ... and have actually paid me, the half they owed me (175$) and promise the rest next month. I am almost ashamed of such a gossiping letter."[72] Actually getting paid her due in the aftermath of the worst panic the city had sustained surprised Hale almost as much as the survival of her friends Bela Marsh and Nahum Capen.

CONCLUSION

Although Sarah P.E. Hale was lucky enough to earn some kind of reward from publishing—money, amusement, and a sense of worth in helping her family—many other amateur writers did not feel so well compensated. What they got out of publishing seldom matched what they put into it. If money motivated them, they soon found that dollars earned were few and far between. If idealism had moved them to write, then the economic reality of limited distribution determined that their printed words could never change the world. Any vanity in seeing one's efforts in print quickly faded with each newly found error that jumped off the page and with every ill-conceived line that haunted memory. Both the brusque reviewer and the laudatory "puffer" gave little satisfaction to authors who expected more respectful or serious engagement with their work. Clicking tongues admonished married women who supposedly wasted time in writing for publication. Furthermore, publications did not elevate a writer to the status of litterateur; nor did publishing always break the silences that surrounded pages left in manuscript form. One author, as we have seen, realized he was fortunate "if other readers averaged a *single* reading" of his essays.[73] Diary keepers and especially letter writers might or might not conceivably draw in larger audiences, but certainly those readers would engage the text more closely and would better understand the context in which it was created. Thus, the relationship between amateurs and their printed pages (as opposed to social authors and their manuscripts) was an uneasy one indeed—rather cold, restrictive, dissatisfying, and even disappointing.

But face-to-face social connections intervened in the troubled alliance, warming it as best they could with human involvement. Family and friends offered encouragement as well as candid advice about works in progress. They suggested avenues for publishing as well, wresting a piece out of an author's hands to carry off to an editor. Helpful assistants offered their labor and mental keenness in editing and reading proof pages for a time-constrained author. By copying lengthy manuscripts, intercedents volunteered their time and sharp vision in the quest for publication. Interested individuals, political constituencies, lyceum groups, or congregations made requests to publish an author's manuscript. At times these interested parties funded and distributed the finished products as well. Memories of the deceased inspired mourning verse that reached the public world of letters. In these ways, the publication process became imbued with the same social networks that fostered personal writings such as diaries, letters, and manuscript verse and prose. Although the end product took a printed form and the audience extended to the impersonal and faceless public, these published writings necessarily bore the imprint of the author's social life.

The serendipity of living in a certain time and place, however, staged the author's social world. The romance of the sea that inspired whaler Moses Adams also stole him away from society and its opportunities for publishing, and eventually, in February 1837, took his life; landlubbing, conversely, allowed his friend Frederic S. Hill to market his creations. Yet a writer with more tenable links to the publishing industry, such as Sarah P.E. Hale, would have entrées that escaped Hill. She was literally married to the industry, and she bore children who would graduate from writing school newspapers as playthings to editing profitable Boston dailies and some literary monthlies. But many other amateur writers were not so fortunate. Outsiders like Joshua Harris fended for themselves. The luck of being well-positioned also played a role for those who received requests to publish. Just being an active and wealthy congregation's pastor, like Alonzo Hill of Worcester's Second Parish, or a zealous abolitionist college student, like Cyrus Bradley, could bring about unexpected opportunity. Having time to spare induced an every-day writer to publish as much as did the need for money. And certainly scholarly attainment was a boon to writers who hoped to gain influence through the printed word. Death, however, could seize the most promising of scholars, including Dartmouth graduate Bradley, who in 1838 at age nineteen, seems to have succumbed to the era's dreaded disease—consumption.[74]

The Vermont farmer (and witness to Woodstock's 1852 Spiritualist infighting) Charles Cobb, who, by the outbreak of the Civil War found himself playing fiddle in traveling bands and working at odd jobs, pondered in 1853 his own fragile destiny as an author in terms of the odds set for him by life. "I never can live by labor—," he asserted after hauling with his father "13 loads of manure" on a spring day, but added, "I never can have a chance to educate myself—I have no mechanical ingenuity, and I must live by what I'm now doing." Cobb then turned his attention to his favorite author, a celebrated poet born into quite different circumstances. "I must pen something or die. If I'd bee[n] in Lord Byron's place—," the impoverished lad imagined, "I should have done exactly what he did no doubt—I shall as 'tis on a miserable scale." Despite a seemingly cruel fate that endowed one man with wealth, brilliance, talent, and fame, and another with but acres of someone else's land to till, Cobb summoned up his wit to level the playing field. Comparing himself favorably to the author whose indiscrete lifestyle bred scandal, Cobb confided, "only I must say I'm cautious as the Devil. If C.M. Cobb committed a roguery he never would be detected—never."[75] Had he appeared in and out of print as did so many of his antebellum contemporaries, he, like they, might still not be, either.

2

TEXTUAL APPEARANCES

"Greatly to my surprise received a note full of kind thanks, and a dollar from Bishop P.[ayne] for my simple contribution," Charlotte Forten confided in her diary in May 1858 regarding her poem, "To a Beloved Friend." Thrown upon relatives' charity by an illness that temporarily forced her out of schoolteaching, the twenty-year-old rejoiced over "[t]he first money I've ever made by *writing*."[1] With her first literary dollar in hand, Forten, who had only published gratis, could now number herself among paid authors and even envision a modest literary career to augment and, perhaps, someday, replace her meager grammar-school income. The limited publication opportunities available then for African American writers made her first taste of literary professionalism that much sweeter. Her newfound status became a wellspring of pride from which she would draw creative energy.[2]

The arrival of the dollar precipitated a prolific period. One day later she finished an essay, "Glimpses of New England," which would appear in the *National Anti-Slavery Standard* in June 1858. In July, she produced a poem, "The Angel's Visit," that came out in November 1858 in the *Repository of Religion and Literature*, the same journal that first purchased her work. From 1859 to 1860 she published four more poems, "The Two Voices," "The Wind among the Poplars," "The Slave Girl's Prayer," and "In the Country," two of which were reprinted. She might have maintained her stride had not a serious respiratory illness in 1860 broken her will and spirit, already wounded by bigotry and a haunting "sense of intellectual inadequacy" that gave her precious little peace of mind. Given her low self-esteem and an evident submission rejection of "The Lost Bride," by a mainstream magazine, the unexpected appearance of "To a Beloved Friend" was a transformative experience. Like the once promising African American magazine in which it appeared, however, it has remained buried until its appearance here (see appendix 1).[3]

Such has been the fate of so many early pieces by minor writers who achieved some antebellum success and even more later public recognition. Their works have gone out of print or been relegated to dusty library shelves along with evidentiary fragments that tell the story of their "textual appearances." So, too, have these minor authors been buried beneath the shadow of prominent and more talented ones receiving most scholarly attention. Regardless of their productions' intrinsic merit, amateurs like Forten who persevered within the industry long after the exhilaration of the "first dollar" wore thin, reveal the mechanisms jump-starting and guiding lesser, and, indeed, some major careers.[4]

This chapter will explore three minor authors—Charlotte Forten, Lucy Larcom, and John Townsend Trowbridge—as case studies of mid-century authorship on the borderline between amateurism and professionalism. By concentrating upon only a few writers, we can map more precisely than in the last chapter the intersections among biography, the literary marketplace, authorship, and publication. The focus falls on events surrounding a single milestone publication on the rocky road to professionalization. For the furthest to travel, Forten, it was the moment of first payment; for Larcom at midjourney, it was her first appearance in book form; for Trowbridge reaching the end, it was the "serious," intricately plotted novel he hoped would make his international reputation and secure a full-time living as a litterateur.

We first consider Charlotte Forten's "To a Beloved Friend," conceived in the vein of social authorship as a thank you note for a spring flower gift bouquet. That the black community and its publishers shepherded her poem into print becomes evident, as we trace its transit from letter paper to a page in a periodical conducted and authored solely by African Americans. With this publication and a subsequent one, Forten was invited to become a regular contributor to the *Repository*.[5] The poem's history also reveals some antebellum vestiges of social authorship and thus challenges the individualism traditionally attributed to the period's canonical authors.[6] Yet, because African American writers had little access to white literary patronage beyond that of abolitionists, this poem's story suggests the type of black community resources upon which they could draw. Alongside the insights it offers into amateurism and African American authorship, "To a Beloved Friend" provides a window into the creative process and its everyday influences.

After Forten, we pick up Lucy Larcom's story well after she had gotten her first dollars. She had already contributed many pieces to periodicals before and after she moved west in 1846. The story centers on her first book, *Similitudes, from the Ocean and the Prairie* (1854), a collection of essays published shortly after she returned disappointed from Illinois to Massachusetts.[7] Like Forten, Larcom was compelled to write by incidents of everyday life and natural settings—many of them western. Through some of the pieces that had previously appeared in the Lowell, Massachusetts, millworkers' *New England Offering* she maintained continuity with her working-class readers, more than a few of whom, like she, had moved on to schoolteaching or awakening opportunities in the near-Midwest. As a whole, however, the book aimed higher and wider, as Larcom attempted to establish herself as an emerging litterateur. In much the same manner as "To a Beloved Friend," *Similitudes* benefited by social and professional patronage; in this case it was that of the popular poet John Greenleaf Whittier, her friend and informal "agent," who also came to Charlotte Forten's aid on different occasions (indeed, Forten and Larcom once met at Whittier's home).[8] Yet, as we will see, Larcom had difficulty breaking out of the limited Boston children's market, much as Forten in vain pursued publication in general periodicals beyond her abolitionist and African Methodist Episcopal Church circles. Despite some national recognition for her magazine poem, "Hannah Binding Shoes" (1857), Larcom produced during the antebellum years only three more short books, all for children. Only four years after she became an editor of the juvenile magazine *Our Young Folks* in 1865 did her first volume of verse for a general readership appear, followed by several more. The career promise of *Similitudes* would be deferred for more than fifteen years, much of which she spent painfully teaching at Wheaton Seminary in order to make a living.

The chapter concludes with a glimpse at Larcom's future coeditor at *Our Young Folks*, John Townsend Trowbridge, and his 1854 novel *Martin Merrivale: His X Mark*, published at a more advanced career stage than were Forten's "To a Beloved Friend" and Larcom's *Similitudes*.[9] Like Forten and Larcom, he taught school while penning imaginative pieces and, like the latter, he traveled to Illinois and back. After a time in New York City, he entered Boston's literary scene, first as a hack writer and occasional editor for story papers, and then as a well-known children's book author, a status to which Larcom only aspired in the decade after *Similitudes*. His own frustrating experiences among local book people spurred him to write the scathing industry exposé *Martin Merrivale*. This semiautobiographical novel, published in parts, sheds important light upon the conflicted relationships between publisher and author, marketplace and inspiration, profit making and personal integrity—in essence, literary dollars and social sense—for someone on the cusp of professionalization. We follow him as he turns from optimism over his recent success in the children's market with *Father Brighthopes* to disappointment over the tepid notices *Merrivale* received. He finally adopted a dogged professional persona that would make him a prolific, if minor, figure in postbellum literature. Trowbridge had little foresight that *Merrivale*'s very critical edge would doom it. Despite this failure, the experience transformed him: he began as a literary dreamer within village social relations, and became a pen-for-hire realist in the rough-and-tumble urban publishing scene's "Auction / Of the Mind."

While these three writers eventually attained a modicum of recognition eluding most of the amateurs discussed in chapter 1, all shared similar trials and tribulations in starting off. As we follow these three signal pieces through press, we emphasize the social influences at work upon literary inspiration and production. In fact, we see these writers bringing social feeling to bear upon their writing, as they infuse literary conventions, like poetic bouquet tributes, Teutonic moral sketches, and man-on-the-make urban narratives, with personal meaning. Not surprisingly, tensions between the market and older ways make their own "textual appearances" in these pieces' contents. Even after the author's disappointment in the marketplace, the social sense that often begot writing would return as a source of succor and further inspiration. In all, the literary market proved a heavy taskmaster. In the alternation between the hope of literary dollars and the reassertion of social sense, we see these writers slowly, painfully, and inevitably acquiring the values of literary professionalism quite at odds with the social authorship milieu from which their early effusions emerged.

CHARLOTTE FORTEN'S FIRST DOLLAR

Prior to earning her first dollar, Charlotte Forten (see fig. 2.1) mostly wrote for a listening audience and published gratis. Audiences heard

Fig. 2.1 Studio portrait of Charlotte L. Forten Grimké c. 1870s. Carte-de-visite Collection, photographer: C.M. Bell, courtesy Photographs and Prints Division, Schomburg Center for Research in Black Culture, New York Public Library, Astor, Lenox and Tilden Foundations.

her poems read aloud at her two graduation commencements in March 1855 and July 1856. At the latter Salem Normal School event, Forten delivered the stirring antislavery lines foreshadowing her later contrastive use of flowers in her first-dollar poem:

> They boast of Freedom in this land of ours;
> Yet every breeze that comes from Southern bow'rs,
> Laden with the rich fragrance of bright flow'rs,
> Brings us the captive's cry of deep despair,
> His bitter moan, his agonizing prayer.

Later, attendees at a March 1858 "Commemorative Festival" listened to her equally scathing "Parody on 'Red, White and Blue'" sung by a quartet:

> My country, Oh! when wilt thou triumph
> Over Slavery, that terrible sin?
> Till freed from this curse, thou canst never
> Hope blessings from Heaven to win.

This event, organized by abolitionist William C. Nell and other black community leaders, both honored Boston Massacre martyr Crispus Attucks along with his fellow African American compatriots and mourned the first anniversary of the Dred Scott decision. The song and her Salem Normal School graduation poem were both printed, reaching an even still wider audience. Besides these pieces, her story "The Lost Bride" was probably written expressly for the *Home Journal*'s national readership. Edited by celebrity poet and essayist Nathaniel Parker Willis in New York, this weekly's circulation reached well over 16,000 before the Civil War.[10] Even though the magazine rejected her story, Forten clearly had her eyes set on entering the public literary world.

Although it was published in a literary journal, "To a Beloved Friend" began as a private social manuscript, a thank you note for a gift. The inspiration for this ostensibly romantic poem with critical underpinnings traces to a commonplace social exchange suggested in the subtitle, "On Receiving a Tiny Bouquet of Wild Flowers from the Hills of Our Dear New England." The "tiny bouquet" was sent in late April 1858 by Sarah Cassey Smith, the twenty-five-year-old daughter of Amy (Cassey) Remond, who with her husband, abolitionist lecturer Charles Lenox Remond, acted as Forten's guardians while she was attending Higginson Grammar School and the Normal School in Salem, Massachusetts, between 1853 and 1856. While Forten was living with the Remonds, Smith, whose husband had gone off to California and left her a widow in May 1855, deepened a friendship with her begun in childhood in Philadelphia where they lived in the same neighborhood. The bond in Salem grew so strong that when Forten temporarily moved to Philadelphia to restore her health in March 1858, the two kept in close contact through writing and gift exchange.[11]

Smith well knew how much Forten loved flowers, because they frequently accompanied each other on nature walks, sometimes to gather springtime's bounty. In other ways, Forten's passion for flowers must have been evident to Smith, who witnessed her pleasure in giving and receiving May baskets and spring nosegays. In the midst of summer's verdant splendor, and upon accepting a bouquet from her teacher Mary Shepard, Forten averred to her diary an almost religious reverence for them. "Truly 'your voiceless lips, oh flowers! are living preachers'"—so she quoted poet Horatio Smith's "Hymn to the Flowers" to voice her own awe. "Many a noble and beautiful sermon ye preach for us," she added in imitation of Smith. Whatever simple pleasures or sacred blessings Forten intuitively received from flowers was akin to a transcendentalist's perception of religion and nature. A true romantic at heart, she was also a rare contemporary admirer of Emerson's writings.[12]

Forten's affinity for flowers not only demonstrated a spiritual appreciation of nature, but symbolized her profound attachment to New England's countryside and, conversely, her disdain of urban settings, particularly her birthplace, Philadelphia. In April 1858, shortly after she arrived there on her convalescent visit, she disclosed in her diary imaginative flights sweeping her back up north, writing, "Went to Independence Square, and sat there a long time, watching the graceful little squirrels as they bounded so lightly over the green grass—as green now—almost as if it were summer, and tried to imagine that I was in dear Old Salem, far away from the crowd and tumult of a great city. But it needed only to turn from the trees, the grass, and the squirrels, and look out upon the busy street, to dispel the illusion." At another time, she cried out as if in exile, "Dear Salem! I wish I could see thee!" This Salem-Philadelphia, country-city dichotomy reflected her conviction that African Americans were relatively freer in New England. Upon being "*refused* at two ice cream saloons" in the City of Brotherly Love, Forten exclaimed, "Oh, how terribly I felt! … I cannot stay in such a place. I long for N.[ew] E.[ngland]." A week later she angrily complained, "Refused again in a salon. This place is totally hateful to me."[13] When Smith mailed her bouquet, then, she was sending Forten a palpable bit of New England to hold in her hands along with a large dose of a less tangible substance—toleration.

The bouquet, redolent with associations of freedom, cherished friends, and the landscape Forten had grown to love, could not have arrived in Philadelphia at a better time on May 1, 1858; the night before, she had felt overwhelmed by her environment. "[T]he air is now very oppressive, and weighs me down," she penned; "I feel *miserably* both in mind and body." The next day she took a long shopping trip leaving her remorseful she had "lost this bright, beautiful May day."

That evening, she received "a little billet from dear S.[arah] containing a tiny bouquet of May flowers, violets, and a columbine." Within the Victorian language of flowers the gift sent a distinct message: it symbolized welcome (mayflowers) to the temporary home and a friend's constant regard (violets) in the face of separation (the columbine). "She [Smith] gathered them on the dear old hills *expressly* for me," Forten exclaimed; "I shall always prize them *very* highly." That she so esteemed this token of affection, reminiscent of New England "Maying" gifts, yet singular in its specific social meaning, is evidenced by the immediate summoning of her muses to immortalize it and the personal bond it represented.[14] The result was "To a Beloved Friend."

Forten began her poem the day after getting the floral bundle. "[T]ried, in some verses to express to S.[arah] my thanks for her dear little flowers," she recorded on May 2, 1858. In mailing this verse in a letter, she followed the contemporary literary custom of composing epistolary poems as greetings, birthday presents, or valentines—all social gestures wrapped in literary packaging. These same social authors sometimes avowed that reading a striking piece of writing kindled creative emulation. Forten had just finished reading aloud the "'Maniac,' a scene from [William Shakespeare's] 'Julius Caesar,' and some of [John Greenleaf] Whittier's spirited A.[nti] S.[lavery] poems" before sitting down to write. However, "To a Beloved Friend" does not imitate, either in substance or style, any of them. The poem instead reflects a general romantic sensibility this prodigious reader acquired by savoring—and sometimes even committing to memory—the works of Elizabeth Barrett Browning; Lord Byron; William Cowper; Henry Wadsworth Longfellow; Alfred, Lord Tennyson; and William Wordsworth.[15] The poem also transforms her quotidian prose into poetic lines that echo her journal's persistent themes: loving flowers, missing Salem, and disdaining Philadelphia's intolerance.

At first glance, the poem, about her dismal May Day shopping trip and the subsequent welcomed arrival of the bouquet, seems tritely imitative of nature poetry. But a closer reading reveals the poem's subtle theme of racial oppression embedded in the country-city (Salem-Philadelphia) binaries symbolized by spring flowers. It is, of course, only one of a number of ways in which this deceptively simple poem may be read. It is also a heartfelt thank you note, a tribute to steadfast friendship, and an exploration of the therapeutics of remembrance. But given her earlier poems' antislavery themes and her later Reconstruction-era piece, "Flower-Fairies' Reception" (1874), an "allegory of the nation" (in which flowers again signify New England and the South, and country and city values), it becomes plausible that "To a Beloved Friend" also addresses larger issues involving racism and slavery. Forten cleverly masked her poem's subversive allusion perhaps because she worried it would be intercepted in the mail. For whatever reasons she may have veiled her meaning, the poem reflects her diary entries' loathing of Philadelphia and the racial hatred she experienced there. Indeed, in it, Philadelphia becomes a metaphor for Southern racial prejudice (that is, south of New England and worsening by degrees from there toward Southern enslavement). The North-South, freedom-slavery dichotomy complicates her equation of New England with the country and Philadelphia with the archetypal city.[16]

In the first three stanzas (see appendix 1), Forten clearly juxtaposes the city and the country to express her own conflicted relationship with her native Philadelphia and her longing for her adoptive New England home.[17] The repetition of the word *weary* places the reader on a poetic treadmill that replicates Forten's own mired experiences and her impatience with the "noisy throng" of passing city folk who represent a constant drone of bigotry. She transforms urban facades into prisonlike "high, thick walls" and introduces with italicized emphasis what will become a leitmotif: "glimpses"—the all-too-painfully short moments of freedom experienced by someone in confinement. The sense of persecution is suffocating her.

The next five stanzas develop these themes and demonstrate the bouquet's therapeutic effects. In the fourth she underscores her fevered asphyxiation ("And I longed to breathe again, love") with a strategically placed address of endearment—*love*—that doubles the meaning of the word *breathe*: the inability to respire, and, the desire to inhale "Northern air" or freedom. She then in the fifth stanza picks up on the "warm"/"cooling" duality she introduced in the first verse and animates the very air she longs to breathe (and that will help her breathe again) with healing properties. Though in reality she is in Philadelphia because she is ill, she here represents that she is soul sick precisely because she is in Philadelphia. Having declared in verse four her alienation from there by the possessive "our hill-sides," here she longs for the palliating, "cooling breezes" to be felt upon them. The personification of the breezes that kiss and speak (both romantic clichés) suggest here a thinly veiled human referencing that plays throughout the rest of the poem: a conflation of remembered me, thee, and nature as symbolized by the bouquet. In the sixth, seventh, and eighth stanzas, the bouquet, also personified (Forten goes so far as to equate it with a "lover" that "thrilled my heart with

[p]leasure") begins to work its magic in delivering Forten from her oppressive environment.[18]

The remaining stanzas describe Forten's deliverance—the unexpected bouquet's beneficent effect upon her ailing mood as memories of Salem and Smith herself flood in. Simply looking at the flowers instantly evokes soothing recollections of Salem's sights, sounds, and sense, such that she relives past social experience with her friend. That mental transportation of herself through time and space becomes essential to her liberation from Philadelphia's oppression. Indeed, Forten identified so much with Smith that during her deepest reverie, she relinquishes the first personal singular "I" for the plural "we." Forten reanimates the world around her, as lively imagery suddenly displaces allusions to stifled action (imprisonment, asphyxiation, exhaustion) and impenetrability (high walls, pavement). She writes of "pleasant rambles" and "roaming." She envisions "wild waves" dashing the shore as if they were battering rams. The sense of liberation is overwhelming.

In the last three stanzas, she returns to the present, where—with spirits renewed—she is able to thank Smith "for these glimpses. ..." By repeating this keyword, she then reprises the themes of confinement and the therapeutics of remembrance. The "*Glimpses* of sky" that only peeked out between city buildings at the beginning of the poem can flood Forten's imaginary landscape with rays of hope. Because the poem represents the two friends' social experience and collectively produced meaning as much as Forten's personal feelings, these glimpses of "home" have broader significance: when speaking of her "loved and distant home" in the fourteenth stanza she no longer refers to contemporary Salem, but to a temporal space "when" she and Smith "no longer ... may roam." It is a future United States, free for all African Americans. This metaphor, however, is tightly concealed by Forten's double meaning of "home"—superficially Salem, but more likely heaven; it is a future place of rest, or, not roaming. But just as heaven in slave spirituals frequently stands for the North (and freedom), Forten's heavenly "home" may signify the longed-for abolition of slavery.[19] The seemingly simple gift of spring flowers carries a distinct social message about renewal and hope for emancipation. By poem's end, Forten thoroughly imbues the flowers with Smith's presence such that it virtually materializes in the bouquet, a veritable crystal ball. With this transferal, Smith's symbolic rescue of her friend via the flowers was finally achieved. Emancipation for all African Americans awaited the future.

Forten probably sent "To a Beloved Friend" to Smith shortly after completion, but it was not destined to remain in her hands alone. On May 16, 1858, Forten submitted it, perhaps edited, to African Methodist Episcopal Bishop Daniel Alexander Payne for publication. It was hardly anonymous; Payne himself had solicited Forten's work during an evidently coincidental meeting at a mutual Philadelphia friend's home on May 14, 1858. He was in town to address the annual Philadelphia Conferences, held there four days later. During this eventful social call Forten prayed and chatted with Payne, whom she considered "a singular person, but very kind hearted." During their conversation he asked her "to contribute to a magazine of which he is editor" and Forten "promised to *try*."[20]

This foray into publishing emerged from the same kind of sociabilities that nurtured most amateurs. While publishers sometimes accepted unsolicited submissions, authors could, as we have seen in chapter 1, circumvent this often frustrating step by drawing upon sponsors within local networks. Heartened by these patrons' encouragements, solicitations, vending, or financial backing, amateur authors escaped the potential impersonality of book-trade transactions. So, too, some publishing houses and professional editors, albeit with much heftier financial backing, provided security for their own "stable" of authors. One need only recall *Boston Miscellany* editor Nathan Hale Jr., who relied upon "his immediate personal friends" to contribute in "large proportion" to his magazine.[21] A middle-class partisan editor's son, Hale socialized with mainly high Unitarian, Whiggish, and white elites.

Forten was unable to benefit from such social circles. As a free African American woman, she faced a pathway to publishing necessarily complicated by gender, race, and class, the latter due to her father's rapid financial decline between 1855 and 1858 and her consequent need to make her own way. Like many women authors, she was obliged to write for money. Like her white counterparts, however, she was constrained by the era's proscriptions against stepping onto authorship's "public stage." The discouragements were greater still for African American authors, whether male or female, for they had few publishing possibilities available to them outside of abolitionist venues. Black publishing houses and presses were relatively rare, short-lived, and had limited circulation. Social networks that provided entrées to publishers were less extensive for African Americans than for whites. Snubbed by white society, Forten generally fraternized within "Black Salem," with family and black neighbors in Philadelphia and nearby Byberry, and with white and black abolitionists. If these groupings were "elite" it was only by standards relative to the masses of impoverished free blacks, for most of the people in her circles were of the lower middle class: schoolteachers, shopkeepers, and providers of personal services, like hairdressers. Still, however much her social activities were circumscribed—more so than those of her white counterparts—she benefited through the few small-time literary patrons who traversed her social circles: African American businessman Joseph Putnam, who placed her "Glimpses of New England"; white Salem physician Henry Wheatland, who requested to have her poem for Normal School graduation exercises published; black abolitionist William C. Nell, who solicited her "Parody on 'Red, White and Blue'"; and, of course, Daniel A. Payne.[22]

On May 16, Forten made good on her promise and, under the pen name of Lottie, "[s]ent my simple verses about the flowers to Bishop P.[ayne]." "He is such a critic," she worried, "that I don't believe he'll think them worth publishing." She had some reason to fear Payne's judgment, for he was not only an eminent church leader, scholar, and founder of Wilberforce University, but a historian, editor, and author who had published in various periodicals and produced *The Pleasures and Other Miscellaneous Poems* in 1850. Needing money, Forten subjected her epistolary poem to editorial review. Whether she sent her poem to Payne at the *Repository* office in Indianapolis, where he acted as titular head, or to Wilberforce University remains unclear. Once it was in Payne's hands, however, he ushered it into print. He may have conceivably put it before another African Methodist Episcopal periodical, the *Christian Recorder* (as has been surmised), before finally settling on the *Repository*, but that seems unlikely. The *Recorder* had been undergoing financial difficulties since 1854 and it only irregularly issued scattered numbers between that year and 1868. Conversely, the *Repository*, a periodical that was recently initiated by two literary societies at the African Methodist Episcopal Church's 1857 Indiana Conference, rested upon a firmer foundation; having acquired a modest but respectable subscription list of five hundred people, the magazine turned a profit after its first year. Moreover, because it published young unknown black writers, many of whom were women, it was ideally suited to Forten's profile.[23]

Although Forten fretted over her poem's fate, she actually had little to fear. "To a Beloved Friend" accorded with Payne's romantic taste; his own versifying about the transcendent qualities of nature made him a kindred spirit. Poetic preferences aside, he fostered her talents, in part because he felt personally responsible for her welfare. In 1840 Payne had met Forten in Philadelphia, unbeknownst to her at the time, when she was not yet three years old and soon to be left motherless by the consumptive Mary Virginia Forten. Payne probably became acquainted with the Forten family in the fall of 1839 after he had moved to the city, where he would open a grammar school in early 1840. By that time, Mary Forten had "the premonitory symptoms" of tuberculosis that would eventually take her life on July 10, 1840. While Payne was attending to her deathbed in Philadelphia, he witnessed a touching scene enacted by her and Charlotte. His 1858 *Repository* article recounted the vignette: "They brought her infant [Charlotte] to the bed,—she said, '*I have kissed my babe, put her away, the Lord will have mercy upon her. He has promised to be a friend to the orphan and the fatherless children.*'" Because of this episode, Payne took special interest in the daughter's spiritual and material well-being. "Eighteen years have passed away, since I saw and heard this dying mother *commit* her infant daughter to the care of the Eternal," Payne explained in his article. "Has God betrayed the confidence which was then put in him?"[24] Inextricably tied to Charlotte's welfare through fate, Payne acted as her literary patron.

This he did not once, but twice: first when he published "To a Beloved Friend," and again when he printed her poem "The Angel's Visit" with his *Repository* essay on "Mrs. Mary Virginia Forten." "Hear her in the Poetic effusions of her noble soul," he offered by way of introduction. The eulogy was probably printed less for the deceased's sake than for Charlotte's benefit. Indeed, the last three paragraphs are a tribute to the young poet. "The tender hearted Cowper has not written any thing more beautiful and touching than these lines of the gifted Miss Charlotte Forten," he proclaimed.[25]

In "The Angel's Visit" Forten encounters her mother once again. This occurred on June 18, 1858, the same happy day she discovered her "Glimpses of New England" in the *National Anti-Slavery Standard*, thanks to the efforts of Joseph Putnam, a Salem hair salon proprietor who took Forten under his wing after Amy Cassey Remond died. That evening, she suddenly felt the mother's spirit manifestation in the summer breezes and rains, writing, "Such nights as these it seems to me that the spirits of the dear, departed ones are nearer to us. Spirit vows seem breathing in my ear;—spirit influences, calm and deep and holy, seem twining themselves around my weary heart.—My mother! my loved lost mother! Thou are hovering near me now! Oh! bless and lead aright thy erring child, and let it not be very long ere thou claimest her again for thine own!" Many lines in "Angel's Visit" rephrase this diary entry. "'Twas on a glorious summer eve, / A lovely eve in June," the poem begins, with an indication of a timing similar to that of the "apparition." In another stanza, Forten almost directly paraphrases from her diary entry: "'On such a night as this,' methought, / 'Angelic forms are near.'" She continues to reflect the poetic language of her diary: "['] Oh mother, loved and lost!' I cried / 'Methinks thou'rt near me now.'" By the end of the poem, Forten claims that "from my heart the weary pain / Forever more had flown."[26] The revelation underscored Forten's sense of security, due to her good fortune in publishing "To a Beloved Friend" and "Glimpses."

About a month after she encountered her mother's spiritual presence, Forten reported that she "[w]rote a little poem—'The Angel's Visit,' for Bishop P.[ayne]'s Magazine." Always self-critical, she commented, "but tis a poor little concern, fear tis not worth publishing." Payne, of course, deemed it worthy for prominent placement within the "Mother's Department." Whether Forten earned yet another dollar is uncertain, but if she did it probably came with Payne's letter sent in late November 1858, the month of publication. What was more important than the second dollar was that Payne admitted Forten into his circle of authors. "We trust that every one of our issues shall be enriched by some beautiful thoughts from the gifted pen of 'LOTTIE!'" he announced in his introduction to "The Angel's Visit."[27] Forten now could contribute as a regular to an African American literary magazine in addition to antislavery newspapers.

As Payne was writing his laudatory introduction, Forten was succumbing to yet another debilitating infirmity. "Should Miss Forten's life be spared, and her health restored, I have no doubt but that she will yet distinguish herself as a Poetess," Payne presumed. Her health was indeed restored, but by that time, the Civil War had erupted and Forten temporarily channeled her energies into teaching South Carolina's freedmen and -women. Unlike Forten, the *Repository* did not survive the war's end; by April 1864, it perished, like many other small, denominational periodicals before it. Highly financed, secular national magazines, such as the *Atlantic Monthly* and *Harpers*, flourished to the benefit of their own stables of often prestigious, well-paid contributors. Of course, as we will discuss in this volume's conclusion, Forten went on to publish her essay "Life on the Sea Islands" in the *Atlantic Monthly* in 1864, her translation of *Madame Thérèse* in 1869, and several other pieces; but in the highly competitive postbellum industry, Forten's social circles, of which John Greenleaf Whittier and

Thomas Wentworth Higginson were the most supportive members, failed to help her break through with enough force to become a well-known national author. Whittier and Higginson themselves lacked the patronage they enjoyed before the war and they went the way of the very New England Renaissance that nurtured them, into a quick decline after decades of literary flourishing.[28]

Although hardly of amateur quality, Forten was relegated to the ranks of those who published only periodically, and received a few dollars here and there, in part because her opportunities were narrow. If her contemporaries withheld remunerative avenues of publication, they also failed to recompense her with their esteem. She was denied, then and perhaps even now, renown for her talents. "Were she white," author William Wells Brown explained in 1863, "America would recognize her as one of its brightest gems." Brown's words still ring true. But his allusion to valuable jewels, apt as it was, could only be matched by a floral metaphor—one of which Forten herself might approve: were she white, America would recognize her, in her own words, as the most "bright and graceful columbine" within its literary bouquet.[29] Forten might have savored the irony, for within the white Victorian language of flowers, columbines meant nothing less than desertion.

LUCY LARCOM'S LITTLE "'LUCRE'"

Unlike Charlotte Forten, whose growing reputation was hampered by racism, poor health, and lack of publishing opportunities, Lucy Larcom (see fig. 2.2) could, by 1863—the year Brown celebrated Forten—leave a full-time teaching position at Wheaton Seminary for a life of literary dollars. By then she had published several pieces in genteel or high-paying popular literary periodicals, including *Sartain's*, which provided her first five dollars in 1849, the *Knickerbocker*, the *Crayon*, and the *Atlantic Monthly*, which paid ten dollars and more for poems. After winning a prize for her widely published song *Call to Kansas* (1855), she became a regular, paid contributor to the *Congregationalist*. The second printing in 1857 of her "trademark" poem "Hannah Binding Shoes"—a moving portrait of an Essex County shoebinder's perpetual waiting for her fisherman husband to return from sea—only enhanced her fame.[30] Her four-volume *Similitudes* series (1854–61) reached a fairly wide audience. By 1863, then, Larcom looked back upon a sizable body of work keeping her in the public eye.

Ten years earlier, Larcom had reached a turning point on the path from amateurism to professionalism with the appearance of her first

Fig. 2.2 Lucy Larcom [14.725], photograph courtesy Peabody Essex Museum.

book of "prose poems," or moral essays, *Similitudes, from the Ocean and the Prairie*, copublished by the major firms John P. Jewett and Company in Boston and Jewett, Proctor, and Worthington in Cleveland, Ohio. But earnings from its sales hardly matched the increasing value of her literary repute. "Writing gets a poor remuneration in 'lucre,' unless one can create a sensation by some sudden flash," she confessed only months after her first book appeared. Social approbation also eluded her debut as a book author. "Now I do not feel the destiny of authorship upon me yet," she told her literary mentor, John Greenleaf Whittier, in a letter filled with mixed emotions about her book: gratification in her sisters' pride; skepticism of the many printed puffs; and chagrin over some "old acquaintances[']" criticism that it was not a volume of poetry.[31] Ever sober about her ambitions, Larcom now questioned her simple equation of book authorship with a leap in literary renown. At the same time, she experienced the fragility of the potential social power vested in publishing.

Long before she published *Similitudes*, Larcom's childhood literary experiences were framed by the language of poetry and the customs of social authorship that provided an appreciative, familiar audience for her effusions. Of her early poetic imagination, she remarked in her autobiography, "I am sincerely grateful that it was given to me, from childhood, to see life from this point of view." At age seven she first committed one of her lyrical visions to paper, with her brother John doing his best beside her, in their home's garret in Beverly, Massachusetts, on a rainy day. After later producing illustrated manuscript volumes of ballads, she received social invitations to inscribe a neighbor's album and orally "publish" her poetry to an encouraging aunt. Moving in 1835 to Lowell, where her mother would keep a boardinghouse, Larcom continued to write and win social commendation while working in the textile mills there. "It seemed strange to me that people should notice them," she admitted, "or should think my writing verses anything peculiar; for I supposed that they were in everybody's mind, just as they were in mine, and that anybody could write them who chose." While in Lowell, Emeline Larcom disciplined her younger sister's talents by starting a literary club composed of boardinghouse girls who published a short-lived manuscript literary sheet called "The Diving Bell." The two Larcom sisters also joined a neighborhood writing and discussion group, The Improvement Circle, predecessor to the larger coterie that would publish in the *Lowell Offering*.[32]

Larcom's earliest printed publications were in Lowell-based periodicals. Her first piece appeared in the *Operative's Magazine*, a product of her Congregational church's literary society, which was edited by two millworker-teachers. In September 1841 Emeline Larcom urged her sister, on a break from millwork, "to improve the time and write for the next" issue of that magazine. After it merged with the Universalist Church's *Lowell Offering*, in 1842, Larcom sent her writings to the new publication. When a Philadelphia paper reprinted one *Offering* poem, Larcom "felt for the first time that there might be such a thing as public opinion worth caring for, in addition to doing one's best for its own sake."[33] She had acquired a trait distinguishing resolute social authors and incurable amateurs from more pliable protoprofessionals—an eagerness to conform to a national reading public's expectations.

This willingness can be seen in her 1846 decision to join the mass migration west to where she would receive poetic inspiration from the plains and prairies. In the spring, Larcom left Massachusetts with her sister Emeline, her husband, his brother, and a friend from the mills, for St. Clair County, Illinois, where Larcom conducted a district school. She later taught in the Alton and Woodburn area farther west, and attended Monticello Seminary in Godfrey in September 1849 before coming back home to Beverly in the summer of 1852. All the while she continued to write pieces, many of which had distinctive western settings and themes. "The Pioneer's Vision," published in 1849, brought her the aforementioned first five dollars from *Sartain's*. Probably most of the other pieces printed during her western sojourn were recompensed with free copies or subscriptions rather than money. However, as she sent her work far and wide—to *Sartain's* in Philadelphia, the *Salem Register*, the *New England Offering* (the successor to the *Lowell Offering*), sundry papers in St. Louis, and the *National Era* in Washington, D.C.—she became ever more nationally oriented. It is impossible to know just how many pieces were reprinted in an even wider web of newspapers. Oddly enough, however, it was "those little short 'Similitudes' that [she] used to write at the West," several of which were originally published in the *New England Offering* between 1846 and 1850, that became the foundation for her first book, compiled, edited, and printed shortly after her 1852 return to Massachusetts.[34]

In *Similitudes, from the Ocean and the Prairie*, a collection of forty short moral essays, Larcom attempted to locate the similarities between the New England of her childhood and the Midwest of her early adulthood so as to bridge her disjunctive cross-regional experiences. Massachusetts life seemed relatively carefree compared to harsh Illinois prairie conditions: living in a crude, crowded cabin and teaching in even cruder ones, surviving an outbreak of malaria, watching her sisters' babies die, enduring dust and inclement weather, while laboring constantly at domestic chores. Even though she escaped the pioneer's deprivations by enrolling in Monticello Seminary, she could not elude homesickness. "It is strange that the spot of earth where we were born should make such a difference to us," she observed years later in her memoir. "People can live and grow anywhere, but people as well as plants have their *habitat*,—the place where they belong, and where they find their happiest, because their most natural life. If I had opened my eyes upon this planet elsewhere than in this northeastern corner of Massachusetts, elsewhere than on this green, rocky strip of shore between Beverly Bridge and the Misery Islands, it seems to me as if I must have been somebody else, and not myself." She was an uprooted plant, struggling to thrive in an unsuitable environment.[35]

Similar natural imagery infused *Similitudes*. Each essay concerned an aspect of nature that is either universal, such as "raindrops," "flowers," and "the moon," or specific to place, such as "The Missouri" and "prairie violet." In these Larcom often endowed nature with human qualities. She was probably inspired by Johann Gottfried Herder's essays or Friedrich Wilhelm Krummacher's works, which she had translated years earlier. She and several other Lowell millwomen had taken private evening German lessons from a native-speaking music professor. Exactly what she read and translated of the German romantics is not clear from her memoir. She does mention there her early attempts to translate Jean Paul Richter's "New Year's Night of an Unhappy Man"; she tentatively credits him with the idea of prose poems. Herder's religious children's stories certainly shared with hers an animated portrayal of nature which offered easily comprehended moral lessons; Krummacher's *Elisha, the Tishbite* or his parables, like *Similitudes*, taught trust in God's master plan. Many of Larcom's similitudes concern wise decision making, crossroads in life, ethical dilemmas, and, ultimately, submission to divine will—themes pertinent to her Western years. After all, it was there and then that she had to choose between going to Monticello Seminary or remaining with her sister, moving to California to be wed or staying single in Illinois, and, ultimately, continuing on there or moving back home. Most of all, the Calvinist in Larcom wanted to fulfill her life's purpose, but she was as yet uncertain what that was.[36]

Given the equivocalness swirling around her, it is not surprising that the essays with western settings tend toward adult characters or mature themes. One in particular, "Mississippi and Missouri" (see appendix 2) illustrates a clash of disparate elements battling it out—perhaps a reflection of her own divided life. Larcom highlights the two rivers' different origins, one in the far West, and the other, relatively farther east. That they merge on the western border of Illinois, the very state in which she was living was probably not lost on the author. The Mississippi, "pure and a peaceful stream" representative of both Larcom's eastern past and childhood innocence, emerges "from pellucid lakes" and "verdant bluffs." Like Forten in "To a Beloved Friend," Larcom invests the flowers and trees that inhabit the river's banks with symbolic meaning. The brilliant red or orange trumpet flower, the bright foliage of the cottonwood, the fruit-bearing willow twig and pawpaw suggest brighter, happier, and more productive days in the Northeast. Though most of these plants may have been unfamiliar to the young Larcom in her native "habitat," here, she like Forten though more subtly, employs luxuriant foliage to represent her New England past.

Western settings by contrast seemed alien, even threatening. The muddy Missouri flows "from the north-west," she writes, "bringing sand, earth, and upturned roots." The barren—indeed, deathly—imagery of uprooted trees and loose dirt makes the verdant life associated with the Mississippi all that much more vibrant. That the Missouri passed by "many wigwams and unburied tomahawks" furthers the theme of rootlessness. Although that imagery probably appealed to Westerners' fear of attacks by Native Americans, the "unburied tomahawks," or warfare, might be read as a byproduct of their violent displacement due to territorial expansion. For in another similitude, "The Steam Whistle," Larcom mocks so-called progress: "Down with your wigwams, Chippewas and Sioux! they are right in the path of the iron horse [railroad]; but he will condescend to use them for provender."[37] The tragic uprooting of Native Americans from their lands evidently struck a sympathetic chord with Larcom withering in her new environment.

Seen another way, the muddy Missouri symbolized for Larcom the soul tainted by earthly desire. The West's tantalizing possibilities for a better life had lured her away from old social ties and acceptance of her lot. Like the two rivers that "meet ... unwillingly" in "one dark, powerful river," her past and present melded in a pool of confusion, doubt, and spiritual stagnation. Alluding to the hasty decision to go west, Larcom presents the moral of the story: "Impetuous as human passion, the great river of the west ... suggests to the thoughtful traveller ... the mingling of good and evil in his own nature." With this internal moral ambiguity established, she ends by contemplating the tragedy of compromising social sense with ambitious self-serving. "How came the strong current within so deeply stained? ... And is there any ocean broad and deep enough to absorb from his being the pollutions of the earth?"[38] Writing about her western misadventure atoned for her abandoning her roots in search of greener pastures.

With such literary therapy gradually dripping from her pen, Larcom while in Illinois published some of her similitudes in the *New England Offering*, with some reprinted in the *National Era* and perhaps other newspapers. Yet, without John Greenleaf Whittier's social patronage, they may never have found a larger audience. Years before the book's publication, Larcom had established ties with the antislavery activist, editor, and poet. She met him, then editor of Lowell's *Middlesex Standard*, a Liberty Party sheet, at one of the Improvement Circle's 1844 meetings to which the *Offering*'s Harriet Farley invited him. Larcom renewed her acquaintance when she submitted an antislavery poem, "The Burning Prairie," to him as the *National Era*'s corresponding editor. Eight months prior to its May 25, 1848 appearance, Whittier introduced *Era* readers to Larcom's *New England Offering* pieces. He puffed them as "a series of fables, or 'Prose Poems,' by Lucy Larcom, who has recently left her loom at Lowell, for the comparative freedom of a school teacher in the West." A reprint of "The Prairie Violets," which he compared to the "parables of Krummacher and Lessing," followed on the page. About a year later, he reprinted a "passage of great beauty" from her *Offering* poem, "Elisha and the Angels." Perhaps his greatest boon was placing his biographical sketch of her in Rufus Griswold's famed *Female Poets of America*. Although Larcom felt her inclusion was "no great distinction, however, since there were a hundred names or so, besides," Whittier realized it enhanced her status as a national "poet" above "verse writers" of local distinction. The anthology's biographical information unveiled anonymous or obscure authorial personae before the public eye to reveal the writer as social being—a crucial step in building a reputation as a litterateur. Without much initiative on Larcom's part, Whittier embarked upon a lifelong patronage of the up-and-coming author.[39]

After Larcom moved back to Beverly in 1852 she was but a short distance away from Whittier in Amesbury, Massachusetts. In such close communion, she and her literary advocate went for leisurely drives or chatted together at her home. In the spring of 1853 they discussed publishing her similitudes in book form. Whittier's earlier praise of her *Offering* essays suggests the project may have been brewing for some time, yet he impulsively pried the work from her hands, as he apologized in Quaker locution for "carrying off thy MS. in so unceremonious a manner." Whatever its initial condition—a fully edited, neatly copied, and well-conceived collection or a disorderly heap of *Offering* clippings and a few hastily written additions—Whittier certainly had a book manuscript with five illustrations by Larcom herself in his hands by early July 1853.[40]

Shortly after obtaining it, Whittier used whatever influence he had in the literary marketplace to find a publisher. On July 8 he sent it to his own (and that of Henry Wadsworth Longfellow and Nathaniel Hawthorne), James T. Fields, with a letter that cleverly pitched essentially reprinted essays as original material. To counter the "this-has-been-printed-before" criticism, he reminded Fields that American publishers routinely reprinted British texts: "I am quite sure that if it was an *English* book of equal merit and beauty, it w[oul]d not lack republication here at once." He then pointed out the prose's foreign flavor and its distinctive Germanic accents: "The little prose poems, are unlike anything in our literature, and remind one of the German writer, Lessing." Whittier realized the sketches filled a gap in the market for German literature, much of which remained untranslated. With another nod to marketing, Whittier noted, "They are equally adapted to young and old," or virtually any reader. Including illustrations was a good strategy, but Larcom's were amateurish; "in the hands of an Engraver," Whittier insisted, they "wd. make effective pictures." In order perhaps to mask Larcom's unconventionally ardent career aspirations, he avowed her feminine diffidence. She "is a novice in writing and bookmaking, and with no ambition to appear in print," he fibbed, while making a personal plea. "[W]ere I not perfectly certain that her little collection is worthy of type," he confidently endorsed, "I would be the last to encourage her to take even this small step to publicity." Knowing publishers were strapped for reading time, Whittier suggested that a "leisure hour" would suffice for four essays he highlighted.[41] The letter, however persuasive, failed to convince Fields.

Within days of the rebuff, Whittier convinced none other than Boston's John P. Jewett (of Harriet Beecher Stowe's *Uncle Tom's Cabin* fame) to publish it. Whittier had recently written lyrics for a hit tie-in song, *Little Eva: Uncle Tom's Guardian Angel*, and Stowe's novel had first been serialized in his *National Era*. Indebted to the Quaker poet Whittier, Jewett took a chance on a newcomer who had not already established herself as a juvenile writer, as had John H. Amory and Joseph Banvard before her. After Whittier informed Larcom of the good news on July 28, 1853, matters proceeded rapidly toward November publication.[42]

In Whittier's opinion, the manuscript was incomplete. He asked Larcom for "a *'few more of the same sort'*"—probably previously written essays. "[I]t wd. be well to add them," he advised, "as the book will otherwise be rather small." Other editorial changes were made, for titles mentioned in the Fields letter were either dropped or reworked. For example, "The Steam-Boat and Niagara" most likely became "Maid of the Mist," while "My Father's House," was retitled "Our Father's House." Whether Larcom herself had much input remains unclear; certainly Whittier would edit her work, sometimes "ruthlessly." Larcom only told friends that "J.G. Whittier … has been helping me about it." Whatever their editorial history, Larcom's *Offering* essays had clearly undergone changes for *Similitudes*. Mainly, her prose was truncated, for length and tedium were perennial concerns to publishers, especially for books aiming partly for a juvenile readership. Long paragraphs were broken up, short sentences were combined, and cumbersome lines (or clauses) eliminated altogether. Redundancies and vagaries were addressed; grammar and punctuation were tightened. Larcom and Whittier were unable to tinker too much after July, however, since Jewett was "ready to commence it, at once."[43]

By September 1853, Whittier and his protégée were confident that *Similitudes* was in press, but uncertain of its future. "I am anxious to see thy little book in print," he admitted to Larcom on September 3, and cautiously added, "Whatever may be its fate with the public at large, I feel quite sure it will give thee a place in the best minds and hearts." It was "The best kind of fame, after all." Larcom, who as a child felt "that anybody who had written a book would have a right to feel very proud" was thrilled. "I'm going to have a book published! this fall," she bragged to western friends on September 28, but like Whittier she expressed some doubts. "I dont know whether it will be a losing affair to the publisher, or not," she worried, and ventured a marketing scheme: "Do you suppose it would be a good plan to send some to any bookstore in St. Louis?" She feared both limited distribution and sales. If sales did not cover costs, Jewett would forfeit his investment and though Larcom would suffer no loss, she might not gain, either. "There were two thousand copies printed, and if they should all sell, I suppose I should have a little something from the profits; but the expenses of publishing are considerable," she later realized, "and of course, the publishers would see that they were paid themselves, before they could give me a share."[44] The harsher realities of book publishing were setting in.

By November 17 Larcom was distributing copies to well-wishers, or promising to do so, while hoping for the best. Her fears about distribution were now quelled. Because Jewett's copublishing branch in Cleveland "would attend to sending them West," she was heartened that *Similitudes* "may be in some of the bookstores in St. Louis now" for acquaintances there to purchase. That western outlet, opened only in November 1851, quickly became a tried-and-true one for Jewett's books, not only because of *Uncle Tom's Cabin's* outstanding success in the west, but also because it supplied the region with conservative, yet reformist Congregationalist or Presbyterian imprints in demand there. These included two volumes by Lyman Beecher, known less for being Harriet Beecher Stowe's father than for his efforts at winning the west for Protestantism and his help in founding the "benevolent empire" of antebellum reform.[45] Larcom's elixir of Congregationalism and German Romanticism, her theme of migrant displacement, and her regional scenes doubtless made it a good shot for a western market.

The book's deftly timed release and fine appearance also inspired hope against the odds. "I do not anticipate a great sale for it, as there is nothing very wonderful in it," she explained; "It makes a very pretty little gift-book, however. And I should think might go very well during the holidays." Whittier, to whom she sent a copy, agreed: "The Book is beautifully got up, as it ought to be, for it is highly creditable to its author." *Similitudes* was well designed as a "small, neat volume," 6 1/2 by 4 3/8 inches for easy hand cradling, even by children, yet it was by no means a toy book. It was about an inch or so smaller in both dimensions than a typical duodecimo volume targeted at adult readers. It featured visually appealing red, blue, or green cloth bindings, blind-stamped front and back with a triple rule frame and floral ornament; the centered gold-stamped cartouche enclosed the title.[46]

The volume's illustrations were a key selling point. The title page's delicate engraving was executed by Boston's Baker, Smith, and Andrew, who did the first fully illustrated edition of *Uncle Tom's Cabin* but who otherwise specialized in children's books. To garner children's visual interest, they rendered on *Similitude's* title page (see fig. 2.3) an attractive sylvan riverine setting vertically anchored by two evergreen trees, one thriving and straight, the other denuded and leaning— an obvious reference to the Manichean dualisms treated within. Emerging from between the firs was a doe traipsing down the river-bank. Curiously, the scene features neither ocean nor prairie, as in the book's subtitle, but rather a mountainous or hilly region, with water or flat land only in the distant background. The obvious disjuncture between subtitle and illustration may account for only the short title *Similitudes* and publisher information appearing on the page. *Similitudes, from the Ocean and the Prairie* instead appears on the previous unadorned "bastard" page that conventionally truncated full titles.

Fig. 2.3 Title page engraving showing neither ocean nor prairie, from Lucy Larcom's first book. *Source: Similitudes: From the Ocean and the Prairie* (Boston: John P. Jewett/Cleveland, Ohio: Jewett, Proctor, and Worthington, 1854), courtesy American Antiquarian Society.

Whether the title page's illustration or the six others lacing through the book were based on Larcom's original sketches cannot be discerned. If her drawings were used, the overall execution suggests considerable refinement of them. Thus, with its fine binding, convenient format, and imaginatively detailed illustrations, the book's features alone could tempt buyers.[47]

That it was "noticed everywhere with favor," as Whittier reported, must have brightened Larcom's spirits if only because puffs boosted sales. Ever attentive to his client, Whittier penned some of his own for the *Era*. "Another writer for the *Era*–Lucy Larcom–has in the press of J.P. Jewett & Co., of Boston, a unique and altogether original little volume," he declared in his endorsement, "entitled 'Similitudes from the Sea-side [*sic*] and the Prairie' a series of prose poems, evincing delicate fancy and great beauty of thought and expression." As part of his publicity campaign, he published at least three of her poems in the *Era* between November 17 and December 1, 1853.[48]

By May 1854, however, the book's sales had only provided the aforementioned "poor remuneration in 'lucre.'" Perhaps the elegant little volume's price was too low. For a gift book which usually could run more than a few dollars, it was a bargain: fifty cents for a copy with plain edges, and only a few cents more for a copy with gilt edges.[49] Very many books would have to sell before Larcom saw any sorely needed money. Around that time Whittier insisted Larcom should write a novel for cash. "Whenever I take up 'Similitudes', or read a letter of thine, I am impressed with the notion that thou shouldst write a story of sufficient length for a book by itself," he suggested on May 14, 1854. "It vexes me to see such a work as the Lamplighter having such a run, when you cannot remember a single sentence or idea in it after reading it," he fumed, referring to yet another Jewett hit. "I am sure thee could do better—give pleasure to thy old friends, & make a thousand new ones—and 'put money in thy purse' if I may be permitted to speak after the manner of a Yankee." Larcom did indeed begin writing a book around this time. By September she was becoming desperate for literary dollars or other remuneration. "Dont think I'm in trouble. Not a bit!" Larcom explained to a western friend, "But one cant live without coppers, in Yankee-land or anywhere." Meanwhile, Whittier badgered her. "Can I do anything for thee on thy new Book!—If so, let me know of it," he queried in October. "I like thy plan of the book as far as developed in thy letter," he continued and gave advice on the characters. Bogged down with teaching at Wheaton Female Seminary, Larcom by January 1855 was still determined to write the novel, "resolving to be very industrious, with the new year," even if she had "to steal time o'nights." To goad her on, Whittier published a notice of the forthcoming book in the *Era*. In a blurb for recently published books by the paper's contributors, including William Elder, Martha Russell, Grace Greenwood, Alice Cary, and William Henry Hurlburt, Whittier proclaimed that "John P. Jewett & Co., of Boston … will issue during the present year a story of American life from the pen of Lucy Larcom." He opined, "Judging from some sheets of the manuscript, which we have seen, we predict for it a large popularity." After seeing the notice for her yet unfinished manuscript, an alarmed Larcom confided to a western friend, "I have begun the story, but fear I cannot finish it, while teaching." "What shall I do?" she wondered, explaining, "I should never have thought I could write a story at all, if he had not suggested it." She even worried about a "'breach of promise'" should she not finish it. Whittier tried to allay her panic by declaring, "The announcement can do no harm, even if circumstances should prevent thee from writing it this year. Don't hurry the matter."[50] She apparently never finished her novel. Whittier's plan for literary celebrity on par with Maria Susanna Cummins or Harriet Beecher Stowe backfired. Instead of swimming when thrown into water, Larcom sank.

With her unfinished novel went a possible literary windfall, but Larcom nevertheless eventually achieved repute as a minor author, after all. *Similitudes*, it turns out, had a longer life than expected, as it gradually moved through its first edition during the 1850s. It was even reprinted, probably sometime around 1860, by Boston's Henry Hoyt from the original plates. Her developing career helped keep the book afloat. After the "Hannah Binding Shoes" fanfare in 1857, she was able to interest publishers in three more "similitudes" collections: *Lottie's Thought-Book* (1858), *Ships in the Mist, and Other Stories* (1860), and *Leila among the Mountains* (1861). The house of Jewett, hit hard by the Panic of 1857, did not survive to handle these books. Despite mounting acclaim, Larcom's literary milestone came in 1861: "So far as successful publication goes, perhaps the first I considered so came when a poem of mine was accepted by the 'Atlantic Monthly.'" With "The Rose Enthroned," Larcom joined James T. Fields's coterie, after which several *Atlantic* pieces followed. More importantly, in 1864 Fields gave her an editorship for *Our Young Folks* that carried a salary of fifty dollars a month, a living wage then. Relocating close enough to the Boston and New York marketplace to feel its pulse had finally paid off. Social sense had driven her back to old ties and friendly relations but also to literary networks directly connecting her with the marketplace. Although the three might not together form a happy family—*Similitudes* was after all something of a disappointment, as would be her conflicted relations with her *Our Young Folks* coeditors—Larcom, literary dollars, and social sense, could at least peacefully coexist.[51]

JOHN TOWNSEND TROWBRIDGE'S "X" MARK

Beyond the quickly maturing children's book market that Larcom's *Similitudes* addressed were other rapidly growing areas, like story-paper fiction, which could advance mainstream writing careers. Boston's story weeklies, with nationalistic titles like *Star Spangled Banner, Uncle Sam, True Flag, Flag of Our Union,* and *Universal Yankee Nation,* made an unprecedented commitment to publishing fiction titles by Americans. They found substantial readerships: average weekly circulations amounted to tens of thousands in the 1840s and a few exceeded 100,000 in the mid-1850s. They gave a generation of young American writers—including Timothy Shay Arthur, Joseph Holt Ingraham, and Sylvanus Cobb—a chance to hone their skills. Yet, very few documents testify to the inner workings of the publishing houses that produced story weeklies. The three major publishers, Frederick Gleason, the Williams Brothers, and Justin Jones left no business records or other papers.[52] Local genteel publishers—John P. Jewett, Ticknor and Fields, and Phillips, Sampson, to name a few—felt themselves above story papers that catered to wider tastes. Many authors who became prominent understandably played down their early work in the cheap fiction trade.

One notable exception was John Townsend Trowbridge (see fig. 2.4), who commonly wrote as "Paul Creyton." Born in 1827 in Ogden, on the Erie Canal in upstate New York's Burnt-Over District, he was in youth bit by the writing bug. Like most amateurs, he wrote for himself or his social circles long before attempting to publish. As a youngster, his polished productions met with skepticism. "I began to write verses when I was thirteen," he recalled in his autobiography, "but I was accused by some of my mates of copying them out of books, until I composed an acrostic on the name of one of them." When he was sixteen, an anonymous patron placed one verse in the *Rochester Republican*—Trowbridge's first publication. It was even reprinted in faraway Chicago. These happy experiences set him on a lifelong course toward a literary career.[53]

Trowbridge thereafter published some verse in other local papers, taught school while working as a farmhand and, for a fruitless short

Fig. 2.4 Carte-de-visite of John Townsend Trowbridge, J.T. Trowbridge Papers, pfMS Am 2019 (340), by permission of the Houghton Library, Harvard University.

time, farmed in frontier Naperville, Illinois. In 1847, at nineteen, he came to New York to seek his authorial fortune. With the encouragement of editor and publisher Mordecai Noah, he wrote short pieces for the New York press, while falling back on a Jersey City pencil-case-engraving factory job. In 1848, Trowbridge visited Boston at the height of the story-paper mania to secure literary contacts. "I found the latitude of Boston so hospitable to those light literary ventures," he reminisced, "that I prolonged my stay … [into] a permanent residence." Demand outstripped supply: "I found the Boston weeklies ready to accept about everything I had to offer, and set gleefully to work to furnish the sort of contributions most in demand. 'Stories, give us stories!' said they all; and stories they had from me from that time forth."[54]

While laboring in the cheap fiction trade from 1847 to the mid-1850s, he usually received from fifty cents to a dollar for a column in periodicals. He contributed to the *Olive Branch*, the *Mirror of the Fair* (for which he wrote "almost the entire contents"), the *American Sentinel*, the *Carpet Bag*, the *Yankee Blade*, and *Union Jack*. He read of his submissions' acceptance in the *Flag of Our Union* and probably other papers, much as Joshua Harris had in the *Waverley* magazine (see chapter 1). "'Florence Darnley, or the Outlaw Reclaimed,' a prose sketch by Paul Creyton, is accepted for next week," the *Flag* announced on December 16, 1848. Payment was too small for a living wage, so he patched together miscellaneous paying tasks. For six months in late 1849 he became the editor of *Yankee Nation*, anonymously bankrolled by a periodical dealer, Hotchkiss and Company, and probably by Frederick Gleason, the publisher of the competing *Flag of Our Union*. As editor, Trowbridge enjoyed "always having my contributions accepted," but still desired serious regard, long-term stability, and higher pay. "If I could rise in my profession, as I think I ought to rise, or make any advance in worldly prosperity, there would certainly be something to cheer me," he confessed to author Charles Graham Halpine in 1852; "but on this d[amne]d level of existence, I come to a stand still, & lie down in despair." These "fits of despondency" accompanied "feeble health," as well as "ennui & disgust with" what he called "this stupid life."[55] Though acquiring a name in the trade, he could only get pamphlets of about one hundred pages published.

Like that of Lucy Larcom, Trowbridge's breakthrough into publishing in longer, more permanent form (with hard covers) came with a series of modest volumes, aimed at the emerging children's literature market. In 1853 one story paper editor, *Yankee Blade*'s William Mathews, made connections necessary to have *Father Brighthopes; or, An Old Clergyman's Vacation*, published by Phillips, Sampson, a mainstream general trade house. This short religious and domestic novel published in May 1853 rode the wake of Harriet Beecher Stowe's *Uncle Tom's Cabin*'s success the previous year. Young readers and their families took to *Brighthopes* immediately, apparently for its "practical Christianity." "Brighthopes so successful," Trowbridge wrote in his diary on June 8, 1853, "that he [Phillips] means to follow it up with another volume, at once." In response, Trowbridge immediately began work on *Hearts and Faces; or Home-Life Unveiled*, corrected the "last proof sheets" on July 2, 1853, and saw it in print by September. With his books—including

Deserted Family; or, Wanderings of an Outcast, published around
the same time as *Brighthopes*—selling rapidly, Trowbridge purchased
lavish gifts for his family. "Wordsworth gilt to Mother, penciling gold to
Ruila & Martha, & a $5 pin to Maria," he recorded bestowing in August
of that year. By the end of October, *Father Brighthopes,* at fifty cents in
muslin and seventy-five cents in gilt, had sold over 4,500 copies. Its
author was able to draw out "$165.62," an amount he deemed "good for
a five month sale of a new book"—on average, just over three-and-a-
half cents a copy. Trowbridge was undergoing a "spiritual illumination,"
enjoying better health, and beginning yet another book, *Burrcliff:
Its Sunshine and Its Clouds.* He was dissatisfied, however, that his literary
productions were all simple children's novels under three hundred
pages. Trowbridge longed for the reputation of a Charles Dickens or
a William Makepeace Thackeray, who employed lengthier formats
addressed to adult audiences.[56]

Trowbridge's publishing forays, he thought, were but a lowly
apprenticeship to celebrated authorship. It was time to graduate into
the big league. Having once unsuccessfully beseeched Phillips, Sampson to let him try an intricately plotted novel, he now found they were
willing to comply with a "full-fledged work of fiction ... issued in
monthly parts." It was an unusual publication mode for an American
author; as chapters were completed, they would appear as pamphlets
while the author continued work. On January 27, 1854, he went home
with Charles Sampson and "made arrangements to write 'Martin
Merrivale.'" It was immediately noticed in the press before Trowbridge
had written a word, much like Whittier's notice of Larcom's abortive
novel. Trowbridge sailed through the first three chapters, completed by
March 19, with high hopes, reporting "health fair, imagination & c. ...
Have grown much spiritually." Perhaps confident he could support a
spouse, at this time he also began courting, but his "Ellen L" evidently
promised herself to another man. "There is soul in her which interests
me deeply, & which I have power over: but she is in fetters, which she
thinks she cannot break," he remarked in his March 23, 1854, diary
entry. "What will come of it, I do not know," he added a few days
later.[57] So, it was with general optimism for the future, tempered
only by wariness attending courtship, that Trowbridge began *Martin
Merrivale: His X Mark,* based loosely on his life as a writer.

In this book Trowbridge drew upon his experiences as a migrant
from agricultural towns to industrializing cities, and, consequently, as
a cheap fiction writer and editor. Like Trowbridge, the novel's hero,
Martin Merrivale, dreamed of literary dollars at his old homestead and

ventured forth to realize them. According to Trowbridge's later description, the story concerned "a young writer from a rural village going to Boston to find a publisher for his great romance, The Beggar of Bagdad." Merrivale's "adventures among publishers, editors, and 'brother authors ... ' were among the best things in it," Trowbridge averred. He admitted, however, that "the romantic and sentimental parts were the poorest."[58] Indeed, one encounters such stereotypical characters as Caleb Thorne, the inebriate beggar; Thorne's daughter Alice, a blind, visionary Little Eva clone who weeps incessantly and converts the hardhearted with the mere touch of her hand; Chesebro' Dabney, a fifteen-year-old country bumpkin and village runaway, physically abused by his mother and destined to become a solid clerk in a merchant house; a confusing array of women with ruined reputations; a saintly village minister; and an army of minor characters such as quaint boardinghouse residents with Dickensian names like Wormlett and Toplink. Merrivale, who at times seems to vanish without trace, is a bastard child of the wealthy Colonel Merrivale. The colonel covers up the secret of Martin's parentage with the lie that the young man is an orphan nephew. Martin's eventual discovery of his true past and the prospect of his future inheritance from his father forms the weak climax of the story.

This formulaic plot aside, *Merrivale* provides a rare glimpse of Boston's cheap publishing, one of the only surviving insider accounts of the trade. The cheap press of the period acknowledged this verisimilitude. For example, Maturin Murray Ballou (a.k.a. Lieutenant Murray) wrote in his *Pictorial Drawing Room Companion* in 1857: Merrivale's frequent "interviews with the publishers and his subsequent slavery as a newspaper contributor are most feelingly yet comically portrayed. Any man who has been obliged to depend on his pen in this city for his livelihood, will pronounce the pictures in this book unequalled."[59] Of course, the narrative was self-serving for Trowbridge and this bias must be taken into account. He was desperately trying to establish himself as a genteel author and naturally wished to put distance between himself and the scheming, money-grubbing publishers he sketches. Ironically, Merrivale, who plays the victim, hardly reflects Trowbridge's own involvement in management.

But still, the vexations he registers, however overdrawn, reflected common experiences among many fiction hacks of the time. Martin's dreams that the *Beggar of Bagdad* would be snapped up by respectable publishers collapses during his second day in Boston. Trowbridge's own experience with bringing a volume before Phillips, Sampson, parallels the novel's sketch of initial manuscript submission to a genteel book publisher,[60] in which we read, "With a palpitating heart, the ambitious author opened his immortal manuscript on the desk of the mighty man of books. He felt that it was a great moment in his life; the ship of fame was launched upon the wide ocean of his future, to invite its favoring gales, and to brave its storms; and glowing, flushed, exalted with the inspiration of hope, he made a rather incoherent address, in which the idea conveyed was, that he had chosen the said bookseller, before all others, to honor and enrich his house with the publication of the great Romance" (79).[61] The publisher blinks his eyes and tells him to leave the romance until the next week for in-house evaluation. Martin returns to find that the manuscript has been rejected because the style was "'too fine.'" The publisher officiously explains, "'At the present time ... high-wrought fictions are not in very great demand. The popular taste is for simple, natural pictures of life'" (153).

Martin goes home "[c]rushed in spirit, deserted by fortune," to his blind boarding housemate Alice (156). After learning of his failure, she recounts a hallucination she had of him carrying a cross up a mountain and stopping to build a flimsy house only to have it blown down before he reached the summit. After hearing this, he resolves to pitch the manuscript not to the flames, but to the *Streamer of the Free*, a story paper. The editor eyes the chapter headings, including "How the Seven Robbers Were Outwitted; and What Became of the Supposed Idiot Who Outwitted Them" and pronounces them "'Capital!'" but says he has enough material for six months (162). He, however, encourages Martin to submit shorter pieces. Martin tries three other publishers, the last of whom reluctantly agrees to look over the manuscript but refuses to pay an advance.

Desperate for money, Martin returns to his boardinghouse to pen a romantic poem of lost love á là Edgar Allan Poe. The next day he brings it to the *Streamer*'s publisher, Mr. Drove. Partially blind, he misreads Martin's sublime opening line, "In this grand old leafy palace, / Deep within the lonely grove" (166) as "'In this grand old *leaky* palace / Deep whitening the ... comely grove.'" Drove ironically calls the manuscript "'blind,'" but offers to publish it with no compensation (175). Martin withdraws his poem but promises some short prose at a dollar a column.

Martin then visits the *Portfolio*'s offices and receives a similar rebuff, although the editor (named Killings, and based upon the Boston comic Ossian E. Dodge) invites Martin to write song lyrics for his local panorama. Panoramas, popular forms of nineteenth-century entertainment, as we will discuss in chapter 4, comprised a large painted canvas, sometimes slowly unrolled and lit from behind. Its exotic locations, historical sites, and natural wonders were often explained in scripted lectures. In *Merrivale*, the character Killings not only lectures, but occasionally breaks into songs that appear in published form in the *Portfolio*—an early case of entertainment product tie-ins. In real life, the comic Dodge often took credit in his *Literary Museum* (on which the *Portfolio* is based) for writing these sentimental songs, such as "We are Growing Very Old, Kate" and "Mary O'Shane; A Ballad." "He called himself a song-writer," Trowbridge testified in his memoir. "I wrote the words of one of these," he declared, "and I had reason to believe that all the songs he claimed as his own were produced in this vicarious manner."[62]

Like the character Killings, Dodge depended upon a stable of writers to reinvent his mundane life as something extraordinary. Thanks to them, Dodge could assume various guises; he was "[t]he wag, the wit, the composer of music, and one of the best singers in the world," according to a self-commissioned promotion. He was made larger than life in another, which touted him as a brilliant inventor:

> By the way, speaking of Dodge's invention, we might as well mention a whistle he once made of a *pig's tail*[.] He made serial keys to it and played on it with accuracy and precision, the song—
> 'The last link is broken
> That bound me to thee.'
> Mozart once got music out of hogs by selecting sixty, and arraying them according to their voices. ... But if the great German composer *led the van*, by producing music out of *a hog's head*—the Yankee prince of comic singers *brought up the rear* by producing music out of a *pig's tail.*

Dubious promotions like these reveal Dodge for the confidence man that he was, exploiting his authors' labor and audiences' trust. There is little wonder that Frederick Douglass described him as "shrewd," if "humorous, and laughable." Dodge's sacrifice of social sense for entertainment dollars bore a price. One sympathetic contemporary who knew him well, sometime Universalist preacher and women's medical lecturer Eunice Cobb, interpreted his deceptive behavior as savvy entrepreneurialism. "But few know the true character of our dear friend," she commented sympathetically, after her daughter's death terminated their engagement. "His position ... and his business has prevented him from being known, as he really is," the mother confided in her diary in

1853. "But, to *know him*, is to love him," she averred, "and I hope that I may long enjoy his pleasant and profitable society."[63] While refashioning himself into a popular icon, Dodge became socially isolated beneath his own literary ruse.

In this sense, the fictional Killings closely mirrors the real Dodge. In order to drum up business for his comic routine, Killings offers Martin money for songs and outrageous fictitious stories about the *"Great Killings"* for newspaper placement (181–83). After his *Portfolio* visit, Martin goes home with several writing assignments, and hopes for literary dollars. He prepares a sketch, "White Hairs and Auburn Tresses; or, The Old Man and His Youthful Bride" for the *Streamer* and, after seeing Killing's panorama, writes some song lyrics (185–87). When he returns to see Killings with his lyrics and asks payment, the comic holds out for yet another song and a piece for the *Portfolio* (189).

A few days later, Martin revisits the *Streamer* to learn of his story's fate. The editor, Quintus Quill-driver, who may be based on literary entrepreneur Justin Jones, is having a lost weekend. The publisher remarks, "'Drunk or sober, it don't make any difference, apparently; though I often think he does his best when he is a good deal over the bay'" (220). The publisher asks Martin to write a leader column, On the "Tyranny of Capital," because a rival paper has published a series on the topic. Drove proposes, "'[S]upposing you write a scathing and fiery article, blowing up the rich and siding with the laboring classes?'" (221). Then he offers Martin the chance to write "puffs" for other papers; he gives as an example "'[t]he *Streamer of the Free*, for this week, is, by all odds, the best number of that best of papers we have ever seen.'" The publisher declares "'puff-writing is an art by itself,—d'ye know it? You have to make your paragraphs terse and pointed, 'cause they have to be paid for at so much a line'" (221-22). Martin tries a few obnoxious puffs for a joke, but Drove calls one "'the best puff we have had in a month'" (224). Martin wonders why Drove does not write his own puffs, to which he replies, "'I have my reasons.'" Martin "having glanced unconsciously at a letter Mr. Drove was writing, and discovered certain inaccuracies of orthography and construction ..., did not question the validity of those 'reasons'" (223). Functional illiteracy was clearly no bar for aspirants in the publishing game.[64]

At this point, the besotted editor staggers to his feet and accompanies Martin to meet Killings at the *Portfolio*. Along the way they encounter a Ned Redwort (based perhaps upon the notorious blood-and-thunder novelist Ned Buntline) who says he writes each day, eighty pages of foolscap, or large fifteen-by-twelve-inch sheets. He affirms that his tales of derring-do are based on his own experiences and shows his scars to prove it. Like Killings, he melts his personality into his literary personae. Eventually, they reach Killings and demand payment, but he forces Martin to beg for it (see appendix 3). First, the comic says he does not have small change to pay the writer his two-and-a-half dollars. He then offers Martin a tenspot, or "X" (one meaning of the subtitle's peculiar phrase, "His X Mark"), asking the empty-pocketed author to break it, which he obviously cannot.[65] Killings next scavenges around, instead, for devalued New England coin, thereby contrasting the author's literary merit with the market's devaluation of his talent. It is the first literary remuneration Martin receives, though worth even less than Charlotte Forten's first dollar. Killings humiliatingly places the coins atop Martin's hat instead of in his hand. Martin redeems the situation by playing along in the farce: he tips the coins off his hat into his handkerchief, ties them in a ball, and bangs them against his knee to hear the "musical chink." Playing the fool, he exits the *Portfolio* office to the jangle of his meager earnings.

This darkly humorous scene from chapter 16 was probably written shortly after the first number of *Martin Merrivale* appeared before an indifferent reading public on May 1, 1854. "Martin Merrivale, no 1 has been out one week—M.M. in numbers [i.e., three-chapter parts] is a real failure," Trowbridge despaired on May 7, 1854, "may the dead have a resurrection—in book form." He had "want[ed] the first number to have a good start" knowing that sluggish sales in the first week would predict dismal sales for the fourteen subsequent numbers; if an audience was not hooked from the start, why would they read the rest? Trowbridge knew he was finishing what would be a flop. "Am writing the 15th number," he penned on the same day he learned the terrible news. "Am *not* satisfied with it at all," he concluded. The same day he noted he even lost interest in love. "'Ellen L' went home on Friday," he could write, much to his own surprise, "I saw her for the last time with perfect indifference!"[66] Trowbridge felt about her as the reading public felt about *Martin Merrivale.*

Merrivale's failure may account for Trowbridge's scathing portrayal of Killings in the hat-tipping scene. "Killings, I here confess, was frankly intended as a portrait of [Ossian] Dodge, whose charlatanism and love of notoriety I then believed (I am not quite so sure now) made him legitimate game for my satire, after some unfairness in his treatment of me had caused a rupture between us," he recollected in his autobiography. "Dodge, ... insisted on paying his small debts with them [fourpences]," he continued, "a practice I recalled when, in writing Martin Merrivale, I described Killings, in his dealings with the hero, opening a leather pouch, counting out forty smooth-worn fourpences, and tendering them to Martin on the crown of his hat." He explained that at the time, "banks would take them only at a discount."[67] Fifteen chapters deep into a failed book, Trowbridge naturally recalled his previous fallout with Dodge over payment and made it the arresting finale of chapter sixteen.

Besides striking back at Dodge, the scene inadvertently targets an even earlier instance of publisher conniving, when Trowbridge was but a teenager in upstate New York. The *Niagara Courier*'s editor very reluctantly awarded a prize to Trowbridge's poem, A "New Year's Address," that he printed on January 1, 1845. Trowbridge was supposed to be given an expensive "bound copy of Griswold's Poets of America," but the promised book never materialized. Frustrated, he trudged down to the *Courier* office to inquire after it. "To my chagrin I was informed that it had not yet been purchased," he painfully remembered, "but that if I would call again in a couple of days it would be ready for me." Returning to the office only to find there was "[s]till no book," Trowbridge spouted some angry words and marched off in a huff. Only then did the editor, like Killings, devise an embarrassing way of compensating the author. "As I was going out of the office," Trowbridge recounted, "he called me back, and taking out his pocket-book, offered me in settlement of my claim a dollar and a half. As the edition specified would have cost twice as much, I felt that I had been circumvented." The hard won money left its own "X mark"—an emotional scar. "I had determined never again to subject myself to the humiliation of seeming to beg for what rightfully belonged to me," Trowbridge avowed. "Thus the triumph of receiving my first compensation for literary effort ... had its dash of unpleasantness," he concluded. Like Merrivale's forty fourpence pieces, Trowbridge's first money earned by writing came at great cost to his dignity. The edition, however, of which he "was exceedingly desirous of possessing," was worth more to him than the three dollars it drew on the market. Rufus Griswold's 1842 *Poets and Poetry of America* was important in establishing a native pantheon of poets; withholding it was tantamount to denying Trowbridge's own literary merit. He found little left to admire about his "Address." "Even what remained to me of my self-complacency on this occasion was extinguished a little later, when I reëxamined my New Year's Address with a sickening doubt, an appalling apprehension, that it might be—that it *was* ... mere bosh," he wrote, reflecting the self-effacement.

It was the same X-ing that ensued after Martin's hopes are crushed in the book, and as Trowbridge's were, due to the unfolding novel's poor reception.[68] Yet Trowbridge slogged on to finish *Merrivale*.

With the discounted fourpences jingling around in Martin's handkerchief hardly mollifying his dire need for cash, he rescues his "Beggar of Bagdad" from its procrastinating publisher and submits it to the *Streamer of the Free* for serialization. That paper's publisher then recommends cutting it by half: "'You see, our readers want everything condensed, rapid, dramatic. Take any ordinary novel, and cut it down one-half, and it'll be twice as good as it was before'" (247). The publisher advises him to cut his many florid descriptions.[69] Merrivale is finally offered a few more suggestions: "'Call it "Alphiddi, the Disguised Prince," or something of that kind,—startling, you know. ... "The Disguised Prince: or, The Mysteries of Venice,"—how's that?'"—to which Martin politely points out that the story is set in Bagdad. The publisher retorts: "'You can change it to Venice easy, enough. ... All you'll have to do will be to alter the word Bagdad to Venice, and the what-do-you-call-it river to the something-or-other sea'" (250). Martin agrees to the mutilation, for fifteen dollars; he had expected at least one hundred. *Merrivale*'s narrator sums up the episode: "Such was the fate of the 'Beggar of Bagdad.' The great Oriental Romance dwindled into an insignificant novelette; the author's fame reached never beyond the circulation of the *Streamer of the Free*; and the wealth which had filled the fertile future, in his imaginative brain ... became at last a tangible paltry sum, insufficient to pay two months' board" (252). A sadder but wiser Martin begins a steady round of hack pieces for the cheap story papers, even though "the task of writing and selling short articles was attended with circumstances exceedingly painful and perplexing to a mind so sensitive" as Martin's (255). Still, he "found himself one of the most popular of the young writers" of his day and eked out a meager living from his pen (493); "he wrote an article, sold it, received his pay, and that was the last of it" (494). He learned a key lesson of the emerging literary marketplace—quality goes begging, while quantity is rewarded.

Martin's aesthetics had undergone a not-so-subtle transformation that speaks volumes about the writer's stance in a world of intensifying capitalism. When, toward the end of the novel, the *True Standard*'s editor reintroduces Martin to the genteel book publisher who had first rejected the *Beggar of Bagdad*, the author is, of course, a changed man. Martin's brief explanation of his authorial strategy catches the hardened book publisher's ear: "'I think literature should not be frivolous. It should be made to meet the needs of society. ... With so much evil in the world to be overcome with the good,—with so much ignorance, wrong and slavery of every kind to be combated, even in this land of boasted light and liberty,—a writer should not trifle'" (496). Using the same rationale that later writers like William Dean Howells employed in their fight to counter "pernicious fiction" with realism, Martin calls the *Beggar of Bagdad*, "mere trash" (497).[70] Even the book he eventually writes for the publisher displeases him. "I am almost ashamed of the whole affair," he claims (525–26), and he is glad that he used a pseudonym.

This same self-effacement reemerges at the story's climax, when Martin regains his patrimony. Yet here the "X" mark of the title turns out to be, tellingly, a gold cross that his father gave his unfortunate mother immediately before their break (see fig. 2.5, center). The same "cross" is supernaturally reproduced as a "hieroglyph of destiny," a birthmark on Martin's neck (549). The mark thus symbolizes disruption of personal relations on several levels: between Martin's father and mother, himself and his patrimony, and, in the larger sense, himself and Boston's publishers. The disruption extends even to Trowbridge vengefully caricaturing his once close colleague Ossian Dodge because of a monetary dispute—literary dollars at war with social sense. Because of the failure that became abundantly clear about midway through writing the novel, the "X" takes on an unintended, ironic meaning: the "X" can be interpreted as Trowbridge's sign repudiating his own creation and the ambitions that had inspired it.

Nonetheless, Trowbridge ultimately saves his hero from total despair. Martin finds redemption through the saintly woman he is destined to marry—Margaret, the local minister's sister. She provides a lesson to Martin (and Trowbridge) in audience building when she encounters an orphan crying wildly because of his schoolmates. "'The boys plagued me—cause they said my mother an't my mother—she found me in a poor-house,'" the boy whimpers. Margaret tells each of the offenders "how sorry she was to hear what they had done"—she weeps and they all, out of shame, join her. For Martin, the "incident ... was of dearer account than the story of his country's freedom"—an implicit rejection of the Boston story papers's flag-waving bombast. Martin resolves to "'labor in the fields of humanity. ... No fear of prejudice, no low ambition, no tempting bait of luxury, shall turn me from my purpose ... and this work will be sweeter to my soul than the joys of princes or the dreams of lovers!'" (551–53). The literary dollars of high romance give way to the social sense of self-sacrificing realism.

Now enabled like Margaret to defang the sinner's bite, Martin soon after meets up with his newly discovered father as a haughty politician

Fig. 2.5 Each number's cover for the serialized version of *Martin Merrivale* bore this engraving showing the many manifestations of X's found throughout the novel. *Source:* Paul Creyton, *Martin Merrivale: His X Mark* (Boston: Phillips, Sampson/New York: J.C. Derby, 1854), copy in the library of Ronald and Mary Zboray.

passes by. Martin's father introduces him as his son—upon which the visitor smiles salaciously but when met with Martin's own smile performed "serenely," changes his tune: "Mr. C—grasped [Martin's] hand with unfeigned admiration." For Martin, "the incident was symbolical and prophetic. Thus the world received our hero: first with a smile of derision, then with genuine and cordial esteem. And thus Martin met the world: first with a blush, then with the serenity of conscious truth" (556). At the close of a book that otherwise ends happily, Trowbridge interjects a despondent note. After declaring the final page the "most welcome leaf of all," he bids "Farewell! Ah, could the reader know with what emotions that word comes from the heart of him who hath written a book, not for fame, still less for fortune, but all for love" (558).

Readers could not have known just how heavily that "farewell" would weigh upon Trowbridge, for with it his six months' labor and all hopes for the novel ended. "The work appears to me to be a miserable failure," he confided in his diary shortly after he put down his pen. "Was I ever so sick of any work?" he asked himself at the end of the summer that he felt was "misspent" on writing it. To make matters worse, four days after completing the novel his courtship with "Ellen L." was broken off. It would take some time before Trowbridge came to terms with *Martin Merrivale*. The fruits of his labor eventually paid off in book form. "[I]t was not until the volume had time to make its way with the public, as it did but slowly," he recalled, "that I received any substantial returns for my steady half-year's labor."[71] Apparently, the story had meant something to audiences, after all—especially to Martin Merrivale's real-life counterparts, who, while passing "in and out" of the marketplace, realigned their dreams with reality. It also said what they dared not say to publishers shattering those dreams.

Like Margaret with her mission to the savage schoolboys, Trowbridge had told those abusing him as a struggling young author how sorry he was that they had done so—that somehow by exposing the nascent entrepreneurialism pitting all against all in the selfish drive for literary dollars, thoughtless people would come to their social senses. In this regard, Merrivale stands near the head of a long line of survivors changed by their encounters with literary entrepreneurship whose mission becomes redeeming their oppressors and their audiences. These two may be identical, of course, as only the more darkly perceptive American writers have discerned. In his *Confidence Man* (1857), Herman Melville expressed this message in the gilt-edge barber's pasteboard on his ship of fools, the Fidèle. The sign that appeared consistently throughout a book in which deceit is ubiquitous, read simply, "No Trust."[72]

Trowbridge and many popular writers after him—whether out of self-delusion, self-interest, or self-centeredness—would beyond all reason continue to trust a system injurious to the integrity of their original vision, however naive it may have been. At age seventy-five, the once would-be Great American Author looked back on his life and reiterated a poem he offered to the world on his fiftieth birthday. "I keep some portion of my early dream; / Brokenly bright," he disclosed, "like moonbeams on a river." In a more prosaic mood, he concluded: "Not that I would ever have divorced myself from the Muse; but I would have kept her the mistress of the ménage, not the maid."[73] Literary dollars came at a high price to one's literary sensibility.

CONCLUSION

All three of the authors considered here survived (to varying degrees) the antebellum publishing industry to compete in the cut throat postbellum market. They "won," as we will see in this book's conclusion, what Larcom dubbed the "privilege of going on."[74] What did they learn that allowed them to go on? All three aimed, if not always successfully, for the largest, well-paying periodicals and fell back upon smaller ones when necessary. Their drive to publish sprang from moneymaking and not, primarily, from ideology, though it played a role. All were persistent and resilient to setbacks and disappointment. They all also learned to take advantage of patronage, swallowing their pride if necessary to get an inside track. As the three also tried to address a national market, they compromised their artistic or other values, when expedient. Most of all, these authors came to accept that market values inevitably intruded into their social worlds: socioprofessional contacts were both happily forged and painfully broken in the publishing industry; the dividing line between friend and literary agent was usually blurry; socially charged communication and everyday social inspiration could be turned into profit. These were the very traits helping these authors to "go on" well after the Civil War ended.

The literary marketplace seemingly exacted more from Trowbridge than the other two authors presented here, precisely because he achieved more status and money than they did. It was one of the ironies of professionalism with which he grappled and finally understood: to earn a living by writing, he would necessarily compromise his literary vision. So, too, did he forsake his notion that the marketplace was fertile ground for social relationships with "brother authors" and paternalistic publishers all striving for the same end—disinterested literary attainment. His professional affiliations yielded little more than "social cents," worth less even than Martin's devalued coin. The deprivation of both a book trade's "family" and a place within the nineteenth-century literary canon seemed all the greater simply because he coveted them and felt entitled to them. These losses were casualties of the unabashed professional ambition common to many of the period's male authors.

Of course, the female authors considered here concealed their deepest ambitions (and disappointments) within the rhetoric of domesticity, and, indeed, may have convinced themselves that they wanted no more than just recompense for their efforts and their families' and friends' love. They rarely took X marks for granted or expected warm reception from publishers, patrons, and critics. Even an old family friend like Bishop Payne was treated by Forten with reserve, and a fond acquaintance like Whittier was admonished by Larcom for being too protective. "Why should I always write with you holding my hand?" Larcom chided her mentor, "My conscience and my pride rebel."[75] But these women honed their "social sense" outside of the marketplace, and they kept the two—intimate relations and authorship—distinct while cleverly translating their everyday experiences into literary dollars. Perhaps they lusted less after fame than Trowbridge. Invariably, though, the flame of ambition flared up. "Oh! that I could become suddenly inspired and write as only great poets can write," Charlotte Forten agonized while trying to pen lines for her 1856 commencement poem; "or that I might write a beautiful poem of two hundred lines in my sleep as Coleridge did."[76] It was Coleridge who represented the unattainable ideal in authorship.

Calling on some celebrity lore, Forten imagined that what was hard work for her was effortless dreaming for others. Had she somehow been able to communicate with the dead poet, he doubtless would have informed her otherwise. "I have given time, pains, every thing to this," Coleridge once wrote when he submitted manuscript material to a publisher.[77] Forten was not alone among her contemporaries in constructing a self-reflexive mirror out of another author's image. Wondering about other authors, as we will see in chapter 3, allowed the full range of writers—social, amateur, minor, up to the most fully professionalized major ones—to fashion an imaginary literary community that included others with the same writerly sensibilities. But social sense rather than literary dollars held this virtual community together through the everyday interactions between readers and texts, and fans and celebrities, that transcended marketplace value.

3

FROM THE OUTSIDE LOOKING IN

"Concord is a sort of mecca to me," Lucy Larcom declared in a December 1854 letter to her friend Harriet Robinson. "I don't know that I should dare to meet any of the 'Celebrities,' though," the Wheaton Seminary teacher demurred. Concord, Massachusetts, resident Robinson had invited Larcom to make the short pilgrimage there from Norton in the same state, but she feared meeting the famous locals, Transcendentalist authors Ralph Waldo Emerson and Henry David Thoreau. Yet Larcom's fascination with the men who produced *Nature* and *Walden* compelled her, like a strong magnet, toward this literary shrine. "I'd like to peep in at their sitting room windows some dark night when they wouldn't see me," she proposed as an alternative to a face-to-face encounter that Robinson wanted to arrange.[1] Although as we have seen, Larcom had published literature of her own, including *Similitudes, from the Ocean and the Prairie* and poetry in the *Offering*, she regarded Emerson and Thoreau as larger than life, unapproachable "celebrities" inhabiting a different world upon which she could only gaze from a distance. Still, she wanted to know about them as fellow human beings, how they lived in the everyday world, what their homes were like, what they did at night while she, an unseen voyeur, intruded upon their private, quotidian spaces. She at once venerated and leveled the authors to a plane of existence shared by all.

No matter where literate Americans stood vis à vis the industry—social authors completely outside of it, like Charles Cobb; amateurs "in and out of print," like Joshua Harris; or minor authors more in it than out, like Lucy Larcom—they took the perspective of curious outsiders looking in when they focused upon other authors. They did this even with lowly ones, but especially with litterateurs, those who had achieved some renown. Outsiders wanted to know about the person behind the publication and, consequently, they constructed a rough image from bits and pieces of printed and oral information. They read about writers in newspapers, biographies, and memoirs. They also formed opinions about authors from scrutinizing their novels, poems, and essays—as if intimate traits revealed themselves on the printed page. Word-of-mouth gossip and material artifacts filled in details about litterateurs. Travelers, for example, visited favorite authors' dwellings and gravestones to imbibe the ambience; other folks studied engraved or painted portraits for clues to authorial character.[2]

Some observers, discontent with piecemeal evidence and shadowy images, struggled to glimpse literary producers in the flesh. Keen lyceum auditors surveyed speakers, many of them well-known authors. As audiences watched these lecturers, they created mental snapshots to treasure for years to come. Passengers briefly crossed paths with writers who availed themselves of ever-increasing opportunities for travel by carriage, sail, steamship, or train. Lucky spectators might even chance to shake hands and converse with litterateurs in more congenial atmospheres, such as at dinner parties, picnics, and behind stage after performances. Bolder fans cajoled autographs or other souvenirs. The most fortunate outsiders, including Lucy Larcom, who summoned up her courage to journey to Concord in 1856, actually beheld litterateurs going about their everyday lives.

This chapter explores the fascination with authors of varying status, from obscure local writers known only by initials signed to their periodical verse or prose, to international celebrities, living or dead.[3] That popular interest encompassed a range of expression, from reading and thinking about writers, to contemplating their statues and portraits, to seeing authors in person. Outsiders looking in longed to ferret out human details about the person who authored printed materials. Their interest even extended, albeit in a more limited way, to other literary players such as publishers and booksellers. As everyday writers peeked in upon their fellow producers, the often coldly mechanical marketplace of literary dollars acquired social sense. As the worthiness of these literary "worthies" was weighed on local social scales, producers for profit became like family or neighbors.[4]

We frame the analysis here as if such encounters between outsiders and industry insiders proceeded from the virtual (such as through reading) to the actual, for the ultimate experience was person to person. First, we look at ways people traced authors' lives through their reading of newspapers, memoirs, and biographies. Writers of all sorts might try to tap into an author's presence by closely perusing his or her literary production, as they called upon their experience of penning their own verse and prose to appraise the writing style. We then turn to orally delivered information—impressions and hearsay, from scuttle-butt to encomiums. From there we analyze responses to material shad-ows of authorial existence—their houses or graves, or their visages rendered in paint or ink. Finally, we consider face-to-face engagements with authors in the lecture hall, at school, during travel, and at parties. We end with a brief coda in which we see how all these manifestations of author-interest worked together in the case of Charles Dickens, who caused a stir in 1842 when he voyaged from England to tour first the Northeast and then the rest of the country.

READING ABOUT AUTHORS

One of the easiest and most economical ways to learn about contempo-rary authors was through periodicals featuring information contributed by distant correspondents or cribbed from incoming "exchange" papers.[5] The electromagnetic telegraph, established during the early 1840s, also brought news about authors for local papers or magazines to print. Anecdotes accumulated from these accounts often wound up as short, journalistic statements in diaries. These various media announced myriad events, from authors' whereabouts to the release of their latest publications to news about their families.

Above all, though, newspaper and magazine readers focused upon obituaries. They recorded beloved authors' deaths in the same manner they noted family and friends passing away: they saved news clippings, entered dates of death, or transcribed newspaper lines directly into their diaries. Reports from abroad about European literary luminaries, such as Thomas Moore, Walter Scott, and Eugene Sue, touched scribblers who immortalized these authors in diaries and scrapbooks. Obituaries of American writers might prompt readers to commemorate native-born talent. Readers honored authors' deaths in various ways. A simple declaration of fact lifted from the papers often sufficed. One rural music teacher merely recorded in July 1860, "The celebrated novelist G.P.R. James died recently at Venice." A grocer's wife, who chronicled the decease of kings, presidents, and other statesmen, gave special regard to one renowned transcendentalist in 1850: "Ship Elizabeth from

Gibralter wrecked on Fire Island 4 miles from Long Island Light-house—Margaret Fuller Ossoli perished with her husband & child." An author's demise could be anticipated, too: "Tom Moore the poet[,] from a softening of the brain[,] has completely lost his memory & must soon die," African American seminarian James Healy journalized in June 1849 in his room at Holy Cross College. Occasionally, even a bookseller's death garnered notice. "B.B. Muss[e]y the publisher died to-day," a schoolboy scrawled on January 12, 1857. Obituaries cut from newspapers sometimes took the place of these factual transcriptions. When the author of one of Americans' favorite poems, *Lalla Rookh*, died in 1852, Mary Baker Eddy pasted a Boston *Post* obituary of Thomas Moore, of Irish melodies' fame, in her scrapbook and nestled it among mementos of her own family members.[6] These terse snippets symbolized profounder sentiment among lamenting readers.

Often readers sorrowfully expounded upon short news reports. "The papers announce the death of Eugene Sue and Thomas Dick L.L.D, each having exercised a marked influence among their respective class of readers," a disabled clerk declared in his diary on August 30, 1857, comparing the racy novelist with a prominent theologian known for eschatologically reconciling science and religion. He appended his own farewell to Sue, whose works stirred the masses in nineteenth-century Paris, writing, "His characters still live in the remembrance of those with whom he dwelt." A wealthy diplomat's daughter, who read in London of Thomas Moore's death, sighed, "What a sad fate. He says in one of his songs that the appreciation of love and friendship is above all to be desired, and 'When these are departed I care not to live.' He little thought what an example he would be of this very fact." Like those who mourned for authors they never met, one young woman grieved for Walter Scott, who died in September 1832, and pondered her loss in a lengthy diary entry: "It is no doubt selfish to wish he could have lived longer, for I trust he is far happier in receiving the reward of a well-spent life." When Cyrus Bradley, too, read of Scott's death, he remarked, "All I can say is, Peace be to his ashes! Who will not say Amen!!" Two days later he pasted an engraving of Scott into his diary. Even the death of an author's spouse anguished readers, as if they were all afflicted family members. A stablekeeper's wife reading "intelligence of the death of the wife of N.P. Willis" composed a eulogy of Mary Leighton Stace Willis, who succumbed to scarlet fever:

She is spoken of as being a very lovely and attractive woman. How I have wished to see her because she was the choice of Willis! but now my desire will never be gratified in this world. I sympathize with the bereaved husband deeply for I think he would appreciate a good and lovable wife as he seems to have much reverence for all that is fine and beautiful in woman. His love and respect for his mother is beautifully shown in many of his poems and the man who has proper reverence and affection for his mother can generally be trusted with another woman's happiness.[7]

For this young woman, Mrs. Willis was proof that her husband revered all women, even those among his anonymous audience.

It did not take such solemn news stories to move readers; in fact, trivia could wind up as part of a day's entry. While the initiation of a small, local newspaper such as "the Vergennes Citizen" sometimes merited but a diary line or two, the marriage, financial ruin, trial, or the scandalous deeds of people in the publishing industry received more notice. Elizabeth Jocelyn, for example, noted that amateur author "Mr William [Thompson] Bacon poet, and minister, was married last evening, to E[lizabeth Ann] Knight." That "Alex Dumas the celebrated novel writer has become insolvent" became diary material for James Healy perhaps because he felt an affinity with fellow progeny of black slaves and white masters. One ferryman followed the 1822 trial of publisher "Joseph T. Buckingham, editor of the galaxy, Boston [who] was prosecuted before the Municipal Court in Boston last week for publishing a libel on John N. Maffitt a celebrated Methodist preacher. [T]he Jury's verdict 'Not Guilty.'" The large sums of money passing between authors and publishers astounded one farm wife who noted, in a rare acknowledgment of literary dollars, that Harpers once offered English novelist William Makepeace Thackeray "$800 for 3 Lectures in Providence ..., [$]1000 for copy right, when he is weary of reading these Lectures to the public." Intelligence, perhaps even the forgoing, was not always accurate. One abolitionist condemned disturbing slander against black activist Frederick Douglass, white antislavery author Mattie Griffith, and her sister. "Last week ... they were attacked by a *low, paltry* newspaper to be sure, but one which has extensive circulation, in the most grossly *indecent* manner," he complained in 1849 to an English friend; "a coarse wood-cut was paraded representing them as contending with each other for the caresses of the 'Nigger Douglass,' whose face and attitude, also, were of the same filthy cast."[8] Newspapers commonly claiming to be authoritative did not necessarily guarantee verity. Furthermore, they only skimmed the surface of the lives of authors—and mainly living ones at that.

To gain deeper—and plausibly, more accurate—ideas of authors both living and dead, readers turned to biography. After finishing the *Memoirs* of Andrew Fuller, a prolific writer and Baptist theologian, one pious spinster explained why "Biography is my favorite subject for reading." "[E]ach new character of excellences," she continued, "seems to add to my list of friends." Numerous biographies, autobiographies, and memoirs offered readers such intimate acquaintance with writers that they could become "friends."[9] Although these accounts appeared in sundry forms, from essay-length vignettes to highly interpretive narratives wrought by a biographer or autobiographer, to compiled hodgepodges of an author's transcribed letters and diary entries, readers often conflated the range into one genre. Life writings could account for as much as a third of nonfiction book titles read by Americans. They relished lives of novelists and poets, chiefly Walter Scott and Byron, but also of prose writers, such as William Ellery Channing, François de Salignac de La Mothe Fénelon, and Margaret Fuller. Readers favored lives of prominent writers, but they enjoyed biographies of minor ones, too.[10]

Lengthy biographies gratified a craving for in-depth knowledge about authors' personalities, religious sentiments, or personal relationships. John Gibson Lockhart's *Memoirs of the Life of Sir Walter Scott*, published in seven volumes beginning in 1837, stands as a good example. Bostonian clerk Daniel Child devoted four diary pages to facts about Scott after reading it. When he finished the last volume on April 26, 1841, "after having the work in hand about a year," he began his extensive account, writing, "In this work is found a rich fund of instruction and amusement—a treasury of matter for useful reflection to the grave and the gay, the wise and the simple, the virtuous and the vicious. Sir Walter Scott possessed a mind of gigantic powers of imagination, and of deep reflection—a promptness of decision, a readiness of execution, and a strength of endurance which discover the origin of his unparalleled success in delighting the civilized world by his literary labors." A Boston Custom House worker from rural Maine enjoyed Lockhart's life for its insight into Scott's literary production: "It gives very interesting accts. of the circumstances under which his works were written, The Lady of the Lake, Marmion, Lord of the Isles etc. etc." The book was so interesting that readers could not put it down. "Just Xv pupils at school to day and the time has hung heavily on my hands," one teacher sighed after a hard day in the classroom. "But the evenings pass on Lockhart's Scott to which I must give a second reading," he continued. "It is so entertaining that it is quite impossible for me to examine it with that leisure[d] care which I would exercise on a less exciting work," he explained, concluding that "Scot[t]'s life was a romance not less exciting than anything which he has written."[11] This exhausted reader valued Lockhart's skillful presentation of a real-life story in a delightfully novelistic fashion.

Wanting to be as enthralled by biography as fiction, readers nonetheless insisted upon verisimilitude. This thirst for authenticity accompanied hunger for the subject's own words. "In reading biographies I always get a better idea of the person's real character through some unpremeditated, spontaneous letter, than through the tedious estimates of the author," a bank teller wrote. "The letter may be ten lines or ten pages," he continued, "but it is the key that gives us free admission to the man's heart, and we behold the purpose & symmetry of the life at once." A Methodist divinity student concurred, writing,

> A great fault is committed by many biographers in not giving the language of the subject itself in its original state. The biographer may use a better style and write with a greater degree of rhetorical accuracy than the subject yet he cannot make us acquain[ted] with the person of whom he writes and show us his true character in such a lucid manner as the subjects own writings will show him. The Journal or Diary of most pious persons is a transcript of their minds. They write as they think and speak as they feel. A Biographer in his own language cannot express the breathings of their soul and the desires of their hearts.[12]

Discursive biographers were, consequently, often taken with a grain of salt.

If readers wanted authorial biography to simulate reality, they also desired something essentially uplifting. To achieve that often illusory end, biographers carefully selected, elided, and arranged material to underscore noble traits and lofty ambitions. A classic example of strategic scissoring for inspirational effect was *Memoirs of Margaret Fuller Ossoli* (1852); one woman, who "took it up prejudiced against it," was persuaded after reading it that Fuller "was truly a wonderful creature and had some of the noblest elements of character." Most biographers did not have to work so hard to convince skeptical readers. "I have ... been reading a life of Coleridge in which I have been delighted," one factory-town woman announced to a rural cousin. "[A]nd [I] am very happy to be by it confirmd in the belief that he was a truly *good* as well as great man," she concluded. Judgments of authors' moral character extended to that of biographers themselves. Cyrus Bradley savored in

1835 Washington Irving's "sketches of Abbotsford," because it revealed the virtues of both biographer and subject: "It contains many interesting traits of the private character of Sir Walter Scott. He [Irving] is certainly a true Christian, who like Scott, repined not at the dispensations of Providence, was always cheerful and always doing good." Yet subjects did not have to be saints. Religious biographies that ferreted out minor character flaws ironically allowed readers to further identify with the subject. "Have been reading in [William Ellery] Channing's Memoirs," a schoolteacher reported in 1854. "How much I admire the serene beauty of his character," she mused, "Yet it was not made so entirely without struggles with himself." From this, she drew the lesson, "If *he* could overcome an inherited irritability, may I not in a great degree overcome an acquired one. I *will* endeavor."[13] The mastery of small imperfections at once humanized authors and made them models for self-improvement.

Although readers may have assumed that a great writer was a good person as well, they could not always make an easy case. They nonetheless tried to rationalize discrepancies between the idealized author and the real one. Some authorial biographies particularly tested readers' religious toleration. "The character of that man was very excellent although a Catholic," one nativist accountant conceded after completing a memoir of the eighteenth-century literary critic and classicist Bishop François Fénelon. Such forbearance of religious difference had its moral counterpart. Readers often glossed moral weaknesses by weighing them against writerly quality. In this way, a retired physician tipped the scales in favor of English novelist Laurence Sterne. "Sterne with all his talent, urbanity, & gravity (& every other avity), was a bad man, a bad husband, & a bad Father," he admitted to his wife. Still, "Sterne was a fine but very laborious writer (but there was great labour)."[14]

In Lord Byron's case, fans took pains either to ignore or forgive his licentious behavior. A social author, affectionately dubbed "Byrona," plainly said in 1833 that with which her contemporaries would agree, "Say what you will of Byron he could write Poetry." Charlotte Forten agreed. After reading Thomas Moore's *Life of Lord Byron*, she admitted that "One almost forgets the faults of the great poet in admiration of his wonderful genius, and his many noble traits of character." Refusing to let facts compromise his admiration, a devout seaman wrote in his diary, "I have employed myself reading the writings of Lord Byron, his private letters while he was in Italy and the south of Europe, his Amours with the ladies there." "I must say I think he was a mad Brained, rash man," he declared, "yet I think he was drove to it, he had a loving heart could it have been cultured right." He blamed the poet's spouse. "I think Lady Byron his wife was destitute of the strength of love of which he manifested for her," he concluded in this diary at sea, kept for his own wife. A fifteen-year-old schoolboy instead indicted Byron's mother. "I found much in his character to admire, & that was noble," he noted after reading the "early life of ...Byron." "And I cannot but think that much of the passionate nature," he continued, "was fashioned & cherished by the injudicious treatment & government of his Mother." After naming the alleged instigator of Byron's moral downfall, the boy celebrated the poet's creative genius: "But with all his virtues if they can be so called, & his many vices, the spirit of Poetry reigned supreme, & it is a sad pity his most extraordinary talents have been so badly employed."[15] Regarding Byron, art trumped morality.

Life stories could leave dark and unshakable impressions upon readers who learned of authors' miseries. Just as news of their death caused grief, so, too, sorrowful episodes induced melancholy. "I have just been reading Montagu's account of the fall and disgrace of Lord Bacon," one schoolteacher declared, "I always read this with sadness, the Lord Chancellor displays such a noble grief, such a broken heart and so great a soul." John Park detected a similar strain in Scott's life. "I finished the 7th and last volume of Lockhart's Life of Sir Walter Scott," Park began; "nothing in Romance was ever more affecting than this sad reality. ... [I]n Romance, we have but to shut the book, & however distressed our feelings, our sympathies soon cease, because we know they are excited by a phantom of imagination; but the close of Sir Walter's Life is a pathetic narrative, embracing *facts* which remain fixed in the memory. The minute circumstances detailed by Lockhart, simply as they occurred, make a deep and painful impression, which reflection does not relieve, but rather increases." Even Mellen Chamberlain, who read Lockhart's life for pleasure, succumbed to its depressing finale: "have been reading the seventh volume ...; this is the most gloomy period of his whole history—poor man, poor Walter Scott." Even fictionalized life stories left emotional scars. After scanning white abolitionist Mattie Griffith's *Autobiography of a Female Slave*, Charlotte Forten recoiled. "Some parts of it almost too horrible to be believed, did we not know that they cannot exceed the terrible reality," she wrote. Applying the pseudo-autobiography's lessons to abolitionist struggles, she continued, "It is *dreadful, dreadful* that *such* scenes can be daily and hourly enacted in this enlightened age, and *most* enlightened republic. How long, Oh Lord, how long, wilt thou delay thy vengeance?"[16] Readers' empathy with life-story subjects, imagined or real, thus could generalize to broader ethical or social issues.

However much an author's life might affect readers, they sometimes looked beyond biographies to examine the literary oeuvre itself. A biography often whetted the reader's appetite for the subject's books. After a young bonnet-factory hand took up a sketch of French proto-Romantic novelist Madame Anne-Louise-Germaine de Staël, she determined to "commence reading her *Corinne.*" Many readers thought they could know writers best through their unique legacy of productions. These readers often spoke of the author's presence virtually emanating from the printed page. On it they located a range of traits, both admirable and despicable. Emerson's erudite friend, Sarah Ripley, for one, concluded that a German writer was noble after reading "His poem on Werther's Charlotte with others." They were enough "proof that the man had an apprehension of pure love and the dignity of virtue." Pointing to Voltaire's "inscriptions, pictures, last verses &c &c" for "proofs," a Connecticut schoolmaster deemed the philosophe "to have been one of the vainest men of any age." Through reading, women particularly communed with authors as if they were present, conversing and listening. "I think I never read any book where the communication between writer & reader seemed to me so direct," one housewife wrote to her sister of Florence Nightingale's *Notes on Nursing*; "It is like talking to her, asking her questions & hearing all the results of her experience." So profound were these imaginary dialogues that some readers offered their friendship, even their love. "Have you read the 'Western Captive' by Mrs Seba Smith?" Luella Case asked Sarah Edgarton. "I am more than 'half in love' with 'Mrs Seba' Smith from the reading of it," Case gushed, supposing that the authoress "must have a beautiful soul, for none other could have drawn 'Margaret.[']" Similarly, a Brookline minister's daughter came to love Mary Howitt and dreamed of having her as a friend after reading her poetry. "Her 'birds and flowers and other country things' is full of gems, she has such a loving heart such childlike simplicity and such a sympathy with every thing that lives and grows that I cannot help loving her," the young woman divulged to her fiancé; "I cannot help thinking while I read th[em] how much she would enjoy Brookline and our woods and hills." Even anonymous authors were cherished. "Reading that article once completely won my best regards & respects to the quaint writer," a young farmer journalized one cold December night after finishing "Night Sketches beneath an Umbrella." "I wish I knew who he be. I know not farther than three little letters will tell me. And these are slipped my memory." It was none other than Nathaniel Hawthorne.[17] In these ways, the printed word told more than a story; it established between writer and reader a relationship transcending the limits of time and space.

Of course, literary productions could also repulse readers by eliciting disapproval, even hatred. Sarah P.E. Hale deciphered one German novelist's unfavorable traits: "I have finished the last of Hahn Hahn and ... I have made up my mind that the author is not a good woman." After reading *Refugee in America*, one sojourner impugned author Frances Trollope's virtues: "I should like to know who this said Mrs. Trollope may be. I do not believe it is a *lady*." One reader even issued a death sentence. "Finished 'Woman as she was & as she should be,' a work written by Mrs. Seba Smith," a rural Vermonter hissed; "all together the meanest book I ever read, the author should live to write one more & then die."[18] These violent reactions belie stereotypes of Victorian prudence.

If readers presumed to know an author by simply reading his or her work, they also ventured critical assessments of published writing. As social and amateur producers themselves, the highly self-critical writers boldly scrutinized professional style. They were hardly passive and fawning receptacles for authorial sway. "Read Dickens Christmas Carols [*sic*]. Tolerably good, much in his usual style of exaggeration," a Boston matron opined, before limning a domestic dispute; "my husband says he has described a character of which there are very few in the world," against which she snidely countered, "I do not believe Dickens is destined to live forever." After plowing through one of Thomas Carlyle's biographical essays, seminary student Ellen Wright sniped at his abstruse prose: "Done up Cromwell. & thankful for it. [S]uch queer snappy fragmentary style." Bias could lurk beneath more extensive analyses. Unitarian Cyrus Bradley lambasted Baptist theologian Francis Wayland, writing, "Read a sermon in Dr Wayland's discourses, on the Abuse of Imagination. Its style is hasty, clumsy, & his ideas would exclude everything like an exalted aim." Bradley concluded that people smart enough to write books would not subscribe to Wayland's persuasion: "I am confident, neither he nor any man who has executed even such a literary enterprise as the publication of an octavo volume, ever adhered to his precepts." Some readers not content with summary judgments delved deeper to understand stylistic peculiarities. Mary Pierce Poor applied the rudimentary German she acquired from female neighbors to criticize Margaret Fuller's translation of Johann Peter Eckermann's *Conversations with Goethe*. Poor nevertheless understood some problems of translating, including the quest for freshness: "It is written in a very animated and easy style though at times it seems to be a close imitation of Carlisle—perhaps this is owing to the fact that both have translated Goethe's writings and may have acquired that similarity by intimate acquaintance with the same author."[19] These evaluations of authors' precision, clarity, and elegance not only reflected readers' own grappling with the craft of writing, but their antideferential stance toward professional expertise.

Of course, readers could produce their own puffs. One teenager pronounced without qualification that "Emelia Wyndham, [is] a very powerfully written story." Upon finishing Washington Irving's *Life of Washington*, a young clerk from Greenbush, New York, lauded it: "I like the stile [*sic*] very much, he is not so prosey and moralizes less than a good many historians." Henry Varnum Poor more unequivocally praised Charles Dickens's style in *Nicholas Nickleby*. "[I] am completely astonished with the power of the writer," he revealed to his fiancée (who did not share his opinion); "except [for] Shakespeare, I do not believe there ever existed such a delineator of human nature."[20] As readers found kindred authorial spirits among professionals, the latter rose in the former's estimation.

Thus, when people turned to printed works to learn more about the author, they did so as fellow producers and inhabitants of a virtual social world in which writers and readers mingled. Because they were nearly all social or amateur authors who regularly penned diaries and letters, as well as more conventional literary genres, they naturally became sensitive to other writers' styles. Struggling to express their most heartfelt selves on paper, they could easily think professional authors did the same in print. Authors, therefore, could turn into virtual friends or lovers. Even biographies and memoirs could leave such sharp impressions that readers empathized with deceased writers' woes and joys. Finally, news stories that informed readers of an author's death elicited deeply felt grief for persons never seen, but who had become, nonetheless, part of the family.

HEARING ABOUT AUTHORS

Gossip augmented that which was gleaned from print with unique insights on literary personality. It made authors part of the everyday conversational fabric and testified greatly to the familiarity some authors enjoyed. A powerful engine for social cohesion and, occasionally, of course, victimage, gossip betrays an intense community interest and requires a willingness to spread the word and listen to it. At stake is usually more than the subject's reputation, but rather the formation or maintenance of attitudes shared among gossipers. As people spoke about authors, they bound themselves together. Social sense converged upon literary celebrity, and wrested it from its marketplace origins.[21]

Gossip about authors commonly arose from cities in which authors lived, traveled, and did business, the same places where a strong literary sensibility was cultivated within even middling social circles. But gossip seldom confined itself to neighborhood authors; it pursued writers living outside local gossip networks. Streams of sojourners passing through publishing centers or by authors' homes acquired informative tidbits. Some literary gossip was mere rumor, of course, but some made verifiable claims, collected as it was from people with firsthand dealings with authors and publishers. Within Boston's or Philadelphia's relatively small and tight-knit social cliques, news spread rapidly, at dinner parties and during social calls. Outside the main urban networks, gossip spread through letters and diaries, which in turn spawned on-the-ground chatter.[22]

Gossip about authors ranged from good to bad, much like that about friends, neighbors, and kin. It sometimes merely reflected innocuous musings shared with others. One Bostonian defended Louisa Park's literary prospects against charges "that perhaps Miss P. like many ladies had put all that she had into one book," by insisting that her *Joanna of Naples* "shows that she has some power left." Sometimes gossipers situated authors' literary dollar making in domestic scenes of social sense. "I am told the young lady authoress, who lives in Dorchester wrote it for her sister's children, & read it to them in manuscript, one chapter at a time, little thinking how popular it would be when printed," one woman wrote to her sister of Maria Cummins's recently published bestseller, *The Lamplighter*. "The first bookseller who examined the manuscript offered her 500 dollars for the copy right," she added, reckoning with an amateur's admiration, "besides ten per cent of the profits of the sale." Such glowing accounts only enhanced the aura of celebrity.[23]

By contrast, negative remarks could turn celebrity into notoriety. "I hear much said against Mrs [Harriet] Martineau," a Northampton schoolgirl reported about the British author who was touring the United States in 1837; "her book it seems does not do much credit to the manner in which she requites hospitality & kind offices," the student snipped, referring to the author's *Society in America*. Another bit of scuttlebutt centered upon author-actress Fanny Kemble, who like Martineau and other British-born celebrities, was accused of snubbing Americans. "Strange stories are afloat concerning her encounters with clerks &c. at the dry goods stores," a Salem matron informed her daughter while Kemble was in Boston reading Shakespearean drama to crowded houses. "I know not how much truth is in them," she continued, "but hope wherever she displays her tyrannical spirit, she will meet with those, who will have courage enough to let her know that the American People have a sense of justice and know what belongs to good manners." Upon hearing damaging rumors, faithful fans demurred. Correspondence from England about the scandal surrounding John Ruskin's marriage annulment elicited the following confession: "It really makes my heart-ache to be obliged to believe such unsatisfactory things about Ruskin." Apparently, people privy to besmirching comments arising from social or personal networks were less likely than biography readers to forgive a favorite writer's flaws.[24]

Gossipers with access to trustworthy informants gained credibility. Elizabeth Cary Agassiz related news straight from William Makepeace Thackeray's mouth while he was lecturing in Charleston alternately with her husband, Louis Agassiz, writing, "I heard ... the other day, something interesting of [the author of] Jane Eyre. ... It seems that he [Thackeray] knows a good deal about her & takes an interest in her. Her real name is Charlotte Brontey (don't know how to spell it) but she lives in great retirement, and indeed is kept almost a prisoner by her father, who is excessively jealous of her literary reputation; doesn't like it to be spoken of before him, and will not allow her to go into society, where it might bring her into notice." In a letter some years later that picked up the thread of gossip, Sarah Cary confirmed her sister's dismal characterization of Brontë's father when on a trip to Rome she saw a "lithograph of some of Currer Bell's manuscripts," written in "microscopic" script. Cary assumed the reason was that the "father was so stingy that she was obliged to economize his paper." In this case, seeing was believing, as it was for many who weighed evidence about authors. Even first person testimony from strangers carried significance. "A lady from Hartford Conn. rode on the seat with me ...," a sojourning farmer wrote in his diary. "She told me, that she was intimately acquainted with Mrs. [Lydia Howard] Sigourney, and she was a very excellent, worthy woman, and she thought her age was about 70."[25] Information acquired from common folk who met authors outvalued vague hearsay, as shown in the amount of space diarists accorded the intelligence.

Gossip about face-to-face encounters predictably elicited references to mannerisms, age, and appearance, as people made them puzzle pieces for visual reconstructions. Future author Martha Reade Nash Lamb visualized William Cullen Bryant from his childhood classmate, her father. "I had asked so many questions about how he looked in his youth and what he said and did," she recalled many years later, "that I almost fancied I had actually seen him write 'Thanatopsis.'" The lines of visual reconstruction could become complex, yet that did not stop them from being repeated. In one, a mother heard a verbal sketch of Nathaniel Hawthorne from her daughter at school, who heard it from her teacher, who heard it during a conversation with a famous boarder, Swedish author Fredrika Bremer. "[H]ow exceedingly diffident is Mr. H! and what a wretched evening they spent—'brilliant flashes of silences' occurring often," the student reported her teacher recollecting of this chat. "'But' Miss Bremer s[ai]d. 'those eyes! were more than a conversation, more than many conversations!'"[26] Elaborate gossip networks allowed authorial charisma to enchant even at second or third remove.

Another hearsay account of Hawthorne's magnetic visage gave lawyer Henry Varnum Poor ample bait for enticing his fiancée and hints at the erotic play an attractive author could inspire among readers—yet another indication of the intimacy accorded writers. "Mr Upham tells me that I bear a striking resemblance to Nathl Hawthorne, Author of the 'Twice Told Tales,' so strong that he took me for him the first time he saw me go into church," Poor boasted, with mock vanity from Bangor, Maine, to Mary Pierce in Brookline, Massachusetts. "[Q]uite a flattering compliment is it not?" he asked. He continued the epistolary seduction with sexual innuendo, referring perhaps to his own intimate relationship with Pierce. "Hawthorne is now in the Custom House in Boston," Poor informed her, but warned, "Should you see this *likeness* of myself you are at liberty to scrutinize it as closely as you please but I shall protest against your making any *other appropriation of it.*" Pierce coyly evaded the lure with her own wit and charm. "I never had the pleasure of seeing the author of the 'Twice told tales,'" she admitted, "but am now very desirous of making his acquaintance, and judging for myself. I am curious to know whether I should agree in opinion with Mr Upham, persons differ so much in seeing likenesses." She ended by matching Poor's suggestive remark with one of her own: "and then you know I ought to be better acquainted with your appearance than he."[27] There was seemingly no limit to which readers would go in identifying with authors.

Physical traits were sometimes best left to the imagination, however. African American dramatist Mary Webb's description of Anna Jameson, famed author of *Sacred and Legendary Art*, disillusioned Charlotte Forten. "[M]y *ideal* writer, who, I imagined, must be a spiritual beauty,"

Forten began and quoted Webb, "is a 'great, fat woman, who comes into a room puffing and blowing!'" Forten's blunt reaction was, "Horrible! Horrible!" Male celebrities were not spared. Lucy Larcom had some second thoughts about seeing Henry David Thoreau after reading Harriet Robinson's description. "I dont think I shall 'fall in love' with him, certainly not, if he looks to me as he does to you," she assured her friend and posited, "Perhaps he caught the resemblance to the birds you speak of, from living out in the woods, like 'Jeminy Jed.'" One reason readers might not want a negative visual image of a favorite author is that it might be indelible and ever-present when reading. While studying law at Harvard University, Mellen Chamberlain read Henry Brougham much less frequently and with less relish, after hearing from a professor over dinner that "Lord Brougham swears like pirate, is low and undignified, has no respect, is dissolute in his habits and ugly in his persons, without influence &c. &c."[28] Such, for better or ill, was the power of literary gossip.

SEEING MATERIAL REPRESENTATIONS

Instead of collecting word-of-mouth depictions of authors to transcribe into their diaries, some fans gathered images themselves. Short of meeting authors, the traveler could at least visit their haunts. The antebellum years saw a slew of books and magazines with illustrations of William Shakespeare's Stratford-on-Avon, Walter Scott's Abbotsford, or Washington Irving's Sunny Side, which whetted readers' appetites to see these literary sites. The well-to-do could voyage abroad to Europe to gaze upon Lord Byron's or Johann Wolfgang von Goethe's homes, while people of more modest means, like Lucy Larcom, might "peep in" at the "sitting room windows" of native-born notables. Literary enthusiasts who could not travel to these places might dream about them. "[W]ho that has read the glowing descriptions of Scott and Burns," Charlotte Forten wondered, "would not wish to visit their beloved home, the land which they have immortalized …?"[29]

When Americans traveled abroad, they frequently scheduled a visit to sites associated with authors. Travelers' steps can be traced in correspondence home and in diary entries. "[H]ave visited the home of Shakspeare [sic], Walter Scott, & today we are on a pilgrimage to Burns's home," one such letter relayed. Tersely written diaries gave similar impressions of quantity over quality in travel experiences. Brevity implied efficient use of writing time during a busy itinerary, not necessarily shallow impressions. Along with countless stops at famed cathedrals, ancient ruins, and medieval castles, a Connecticut school-teacher recorded that he "Visited Shakespeare's home," saw at Havre "the birthplace of Bernadine St. Pierre author of Paul and Virginia," and, at Marseilles, glimpsed "the residence of Madam Sevigné, from which she wrote some of her celebrated letters." A prosperous drygoods dealer "[s]aw ... the houses where Luther, Goethe ... were born," but in England his traveling "companion could not get up any interest or enthusiasm at Stratford on Avon ... [and] expressed a wish that we had not gone there & was quite impatient to be off to Kenilworth." It was, according to another visitor, "a place of great interest to all readers of Scott's Novels, and Lovers of history." Guidebooks might help tourists locate such literary houses. Some of these were purchased before embarking and helped while away the hours at sea. One passenger reported that he "Spent considerable time reading" them. While in London, a traveler headed straightaway "to two Bookstores to get our Passports bound, and to furnish ourselves with Guidebooks" before making her way to Lake Geneva, where she "passed the situations of Madame de Stael—Byron, and Gibbon." Just as literature was becoming part of Americans' mental map at home, abroad they could engage in actual literary tourism.[30]

Unexpected sightings of litterateurs' homes during nontourist travel were marked as special events. While visiting her father's Boston family, a Vermonter did some sightseeing during a shopping spree. "[W]e passed through Cambridge," she recorded, "& saw Washington's old quarters now the residence of Henry Wadsworth Longfellow the poet." The eighteenth-century house on Brattle Street impressed an out-of-town teenager, who casually noted she "passed the residence of 'H. W. Longfellow' also 'Washington's tree.'" Although Longfellow and his house were well known to poetry lovers, minor writers' homes could seem significant. When lawyer Mellen Chamberlain traveled to Maine on business, he seemed as pleased to have "[p]assed by the Cottage of [Sylvester] Judd—author of Margrett [sic]" as to have seen the capitol city's "State House[,] Insane Asylum & the U.S. Arsenal." Mere proximity sometimes enhanced the overall excitement of traveling. A New Hampshire tract-society collector journeying to a Philadelphia convention characterized cities and towns he passed through by their literary residents. "[A]bout one hours' ride brought us to Hartford, one of the most handsome, and pleasant cities of our happy New-England," he wrote while riding a train, "and the residence of Mrs. Lydia Huntley Sigourney, the Queen Poetess of N. England, if not the United States." Five days later on a Hudson River steamboat, he glided by Tarrytown and recalled "'*Sunny-side*,' the beautiful residence of Washington Irving."[31] A popular sense of American literary geography was slowly emerging, as literary celebrity contributed to the public images of places and so familiarized them with readers.

Sketches of homes by those venturing a closer look brimmed with social meaning. Visitors summoned up ghosts of those once inhabiting the hallowed rooms. "We were introduced to the kitchen ... after the sitting room—a large old fashioned fireplace occupies one entire side of the kitchen—in one corner is a bacon closet," a Stratford-on-Avon visitor began her diary entry. "In the other [corner of the kitchen] is a niche where I presume Shakespeare has been seated many times. ... [We] found ourselves in the chamber where the Immortal Shakespeare was born ... every part covered with names of individuals who have visited the place—among them are Byron, William Pitt, and other distinguished persons—Scott's name is written upon one of the panes of glass of the only window in the room. ..." She not only populated each nook and cranny with "distinguished persons," but tried as well to revive the bard's literary muses. "I had the audacity to seat myself in the same spot," the housewife confessed, "—(but I did not receive the least poetic inspiration)." Like her, Harriet Robinson invested her description of a literary pilgrimage with social significance, as she named those accompanying her. "Lucy [Larcom], Mary and I went to 'Walden' and hunted up the site of H D [T]horeaus house 'the hermit of Walden woods,'" Robinson recorded, but the journey proved almost fruitless: "There is nothing left of it but the cellar, which is not over a foot deep." She then retraced the domicile's human history with little concern for unflattering episodes. "[H]e lived there three years in the woods by the pond much to the wonder of his townsmen and more to the wonder of the townswomen probably," she joked before challenging his integrity: "He pretended to live on three or four cents a day but we have good authority for believing that his closet was often replenished from his mothers larders which he made no account of." In this way, Robinson could imagine a lively social life out of simple ruins.[32]

History and contemporary life could collide in literary sites. Charlotte Forten's summation of "Longfellow's house, once the headquarters of Washington" included the human dimension as well; she chided the inhabitant for disrespecting the house's colonial roots. "It has not the antiquated appearance which I had hoped to see," Forten wrote, disappointed. "How could the poet have had it renewed[?]" Few besides Forten so reverentially expected high standards of historical preservation. Some visitors thought that change enlivened tradition and even understood that life went on in these historical houses. While reading Lockhart's life of Scott, John Park received a call from a visitor to the novelist's home, Abbotsford. "Sir Walter's study has been kept by his son, the present Sir Walter Scott, precisely as it was left by the illustrious poet," Park learned; "the cane, hat, coat &c which he wore when walking out on his grounds, all remain where he placed them." Park interested himself more in the current residents and their present circumstances: "I was glad to hear that the son, though inheriting none of the literary eminence of his father, is much esteemed in the neighbourhood, as a worthy and amiable gentleman, sustaining his rank with liberality, free from extravagance." Much to Park's disappointment, his guest never met Scott's son, as "the proprietor was out hunting."[33] Literary fame descended within the author's family.

Most litterateurs' houses, like Scott's, remained in private hands, but already on the horizon of literary dollar making was Shakespeare's birthplace. After 1847, when the Shakespeare Birthday Committee acquired the house to prevent its shipment to the United States by P. T. Barnum, the site featured formal public access via, at first, optional donations and eventually fixed admissions, along with souvenir vending. Evidence that the spirit of capitalism had invaded the site bemused a sardonic 1855 pilgrim writing home on mass-produced stationery emblazoned with an engraving not of the actual birth site, but of the nearby childhood home of the Bard's wife, Anne Hathaway (see fig. 3.1). "I send the above picture as proof of our having been in Shakspear's [sic] native place," he told his sister, "it having been bought at a little table in the room where he is supposed to have been born." The age of the literary souvenir was at hand.[34]

Beyond houses, the most important literary destinations were monuments. Employing the same shorthand for statues as houses, travelers probably masked their more complex critical assessments. Edinburgh's soaring Walter Scott monument astounded a sojourning second mate, who noted, "[It] was I should think some hundreds of feet high, with a statue of him some thirty feet high on the top of it." Elevation alone did not make a monument worthy, however, for another American in Scotland deemed Robert Burns's equally dominating monument emphatically "*not good.*" Because statues symbolized the personal bond between the author and the audience, they had to fulfill lofty expectations of how a litterateur should be immortalized in stone. Yet a dash of whimsy, if appropriate to the author, also appealed to viewers' tastes. The fanciful statuary group of Walter Scott and his character "Old Mortality," enshrined side by side in Philadelphia's Laurel Hill Cemetery (see fig. 3.2),

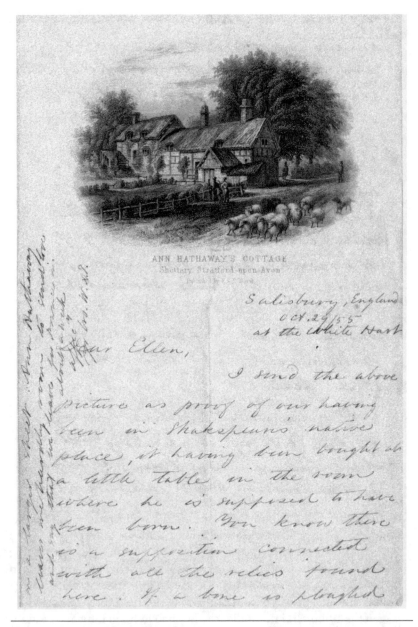

Fig. 3.1 This piece of stationery with an engraving of Anne Hathaway's cottage was purchased at William Shakespeare's birthplace by one traveler. *Source:* William A. Tappan to Ellen Tappan, October 29, 1855, Sturgis–Tappan–Prout Collection, courtesy Sophia Smith Collection, Smith College.

Fig. 3.2 Visitors to Laurel Hill Cemetery were usually delighted with the "Old Mortality" statue inspired by Walter Scott's novel of the same name. *Source:* Plate between 128 and 129 in *Guide to Laurel Hill Cemetery, Near Philadelphia* (Philadelphia: Laurel Hill Cemetery/C. Sherman, 1847).

satisfied at least two viewers' anticipations of how the pair should be depicted. One called it "a wonderful piece of Statuary," while another thought it "truly worth a visit to the Grounds to see."[35] Literary statuary stimulated the imagination, even though viewers seldom did more than record their delight.

If readers could not visit monuments, two-dimensional representations could be more easily accessed. Not surprisingly, these elicited more comments. While minor characters like "Old Mortality" were fair game for creative interpretation, major authors were not. Viewers could easily compare one portrait with another or they could liken a depiction to the writer's visage. And they did not have to travel to museums to see cheaply reproduced engravings and prints. At an agricultural exhibition, one farmer who happened upon a painting of his former classmate and Democratic editor-author Chandler E. Potter recorded, "it was an excellent one, & looked just like Chandler[.] He is now a city judge of Manchester N.H." A Providence housewife also admired an artist's rendition of her favorite author appearing in the popular *Graham's Magazine*: "It has a portrait of N.P. Willis. Said to be a good likeness and we think it is although I have seen him but once." The two images, one mental and the other printed, were compatible. Always frozen in time, portraits begged comparison with real, aging persons. Fanny Kemble's portrait stayed young and "beautiful," according to Ellen Wright, while the author's looks mellowed with the years. After visiting Kemble's home near school, Wright marked the difference with an irreverent litotes: "it doesn't look unlike her at the present date—and tho' far from handsome now, she looks like the remains of a genius." She conceded that Kemble still "has a fire in her eye." Dead authors fared better because their portraits took on an ageless transcendence. Cyrus Bradley, for example, studied the engraving of the eighteenth-century African American poet Phillis Wheatley for its timeless qualities (see fig. 3.3). After reading her poems and contemplating her tragic enslavement, Bradley called upon pseudoscience to decipher the "handsome portrait" of an author whose intellect defied all constraints put upon it: "Who could look at that high forehead ... without believing what Phrenology teaches, that mental cultivation will promote the development of that part of the skull[?]"[36] Literary endeavors left facial traces, according to him.

Response to visual imagery often emerged within a sociable atmosphere. When groups of people simultaneously shared in viewing, they incorporated the author's likeness into a social world. Some viewers formed their reactions during calls to homes. For Mellen Chamberlain, apprehending "a fine head of Tennyson the poet" became a social event—part of an 1846 visit to future editor Thomas Wentworth Higginson's residence. Likewise, Charlotte Forten examined two portraits of Nathaniel Hawthorne when she called at his sister's in Salem. Pleasantly surprised that "there is in his countenance no trace of that gloom which pervades some of his writings," Forten admitted, "I had pictured the author to myself as very dark and gloomy-looking. But I was agreeably disappointed." Whisperings among friends about paintings of authors in galleries invariably influenced reception. "I met Miss Foley at the Atheneaum, who [took] me round to see the artists and pictures," Lucy Larcom reported in 1859. "There I saw crayon heads of Emerson and Whittier. By Rowse and Barry." Even lone viewers might implicate another person in their reception. John Park, a Virgil enthusiast, was in his former student's thoughts when she beheld the poet's grave: "Louisa ... Brought me from my good ... pupil, Mrs Rogers, a beautiful sprig of Fern, plucked by her own fair hand from the Tomb of Virgil, near Naples, 'expressly for me.'" Travelers might recruit their literary tourism

Fig. 3.3 One New Hampshire reader of Phillis Wheatley's poetry greatly admired this frontispiece portrait in her book, *Poems. Source:* Phillis Wheatley, *Poems on Various Subjects, Religious and Moral* (London: A. Bell, 1773), courtesy American Antiquarian Society.

for navigating courtship, as in the case of one whose letter elicited his fiancée's reflections upon his pious character, writing, "His soul seems on fire as he attempts to convey an idea to me of the emotions awakened within him on visiting some of the shrines and ruins sacred to the memory of great men whose names will outlive the domes erected to commemorate their ashes. And as he stood before the tomb of Shakespear[e], Dryden, [Henry] Howard[,] [Issac] Watts &c. he was forced to exclaim, 'And is this all of earth?'" His religious awakening in turn inspired her to contemplate her future role as a wife: "If I am to go through the journey of life with him I will endeavor to give him a full, free, and peaceful heart, disencumbered of all useless and baneful attachments."[37] The shared meditation on life's vanity, awakened by the contemplation of immortal authors, acted as a bond between the two, who would soon marry. In diverse and sometimes surprising ways, visual representations of authors were instrumental to forging social ties.

SEEING AUTHORS

Nothing short of face-to-face engagement satisfied deeply curious fans. They could at last see, hear, and even touch the human being behind the text, whom they had heretofore only mentally pictured. Even obscure figures, like textbook authors or fiction hacks, roused a sense of familiarity that beckoned visualization. Of the minor novelist Hannah Gardner Creamer, Charlotte Forten declared, "I had read a book which she wrote and had felt a desire to see her." Rendezvous could be planned; people called upon literary neighbors or met authors at private parties, in churches, or at lecture halls. Other encounters, however, resulted from accidents. Noted writers and speakers crossed paths with common readers in railcars, carriages, boardinghouses, hotels, and bookstores. Those keeping records of these sightings remarked upon the circumstances under which meetings took place, as well as the author's appearance, mannerisms, and sociability.[38]

For urban dwellers or residents of literary towns like Concord, Massachusetts, authors emerged as real figures within a landscape of everyday life. Writers appeared in the same social circles, local churches, and city streets and parks as did common residents. Many downtown bookstores were magnets for authors conducting business, sharing ideas, and promoting publications. One young clerk in Boston's Old Corner Bookshop was "continually associating with such men as [Edward] Everett, Longfellow[,] [George Stillman] Hillard *et it more genus* who congregate daily at T[icknor] & F[ield]'s store."

Libraries were also places to rub elbows with celebrities. While doing local library research, genealogist Augustus Dodge Rogers ran into *The Scarlet Letter*'s author, a fellow Salemite: "at Atheneum a few minutes see N. Hawthorne there." Even authors' kin could excite fans. "There is a relative of Margaret Fuller's at Mr. Agassiz['s] school Margie F.," Ellen Wright wrote home while visiting Cambridge, "—The college boys call her the *Agony*! She is very attractive, with brilliant cheeks, & talks pretty well."[39] Such were the halo effects of local literary renown.

Social calls from authors were always possible for locals. One Cambridge schoolgirl met "Proffessor Longfellow" and another author visiting him from the South, the cheap-fiction hack, "Proffessor [Joseph Holt] Ingraham," when they both "came up" one afternoon. So present were litterateurs among some cities' elites that author visits became unremarkable, resulting in terse diary entries like, "The usual Saturday evening—the Sturgis girls, Nellie Hooper, & Mr Ralph W. Emerson." Likewise, when Mary Poor took tea at her transcendentalist brother-in-law Frederick Henry Hedge's home, she casually penned only the line, "Waldo Emerson was there." Emerson and Thoreau, of course, dropped in upon people with little connection to transcendentalism other than proximity to Concord. Harriet Hanson Robinson, who shared a sewing circle with Emerson's wife Lidian, received visits from both. While she enjoyed Thoreau's company, Emerson impressed her far more: "H.D. Thoreau called, he was quite eloquent. He is considered to resemble Mr Emerson, but I do not think he does. Mr E. is a god by the side of him." Robinson returned the calls sensing that she was not just visiting neighbors, but entering unusual, if not eccentric personalties' homes; to the Emerson household she went "expecting the parrot to talk 'transcendentally'" in imitation of its keeper.[40] Nothing apparently would surprise her.

For Charlotte Forten, however, a visit from abolitionist poet John Greenleaf Whittier, who lived a short train ride away, was a tremendous surprise. She hardly expected him to show up at her door after sending him a fan letter. She breathlessly wrote in her journal, "I scarcely know myself tonight;—a great and sudden joy has completely dazzled—overpowered me. This evening Miss R.[emond] sent for me in haste saying a gentleman wished to see me. I went wondering who it *could* be, and found—[John Greenleaf] Whittier! one of the few men whom I truly reverence for their great minds and greater hearts. I cannot *say* all that I *felt*—even to *thee*, my Journal! I stood like one bewildered before the noble poet, whose kindly, earnest greeting *could* not increase my love and admiration for him." After discussing everything "from *agriculture* to *spiritualism*," Whittier invited Forten to repay the call, as was customary. "God bless him!" she exclaimed, "This is a day to be marked with a white stone."[41] A visit from a renowned local author sharing one's deepest political commitments was an unforgettable event.

During sojourns abroad, people in certain elite circles naturally crossed litterateurs' paths, so they seldom expressed Forten's awe. An ambassador's daughter, acting as her father's informal deputy, recorded that she met "Mr. Herman Melville author of Typee, Omoo, etc.," and "Lady Georgiana Fullerton, authoress of 'Ellen Middleton' and 'Grantley Manor' at Lord Carlisle's." Her impressions, typical of those collecting food for gossip, included a physical profile. "I saw Martin Farquhar Tupper coming out of Church who flew up and made a great fuss over Papa," the young woman wrote of this well-known poet, and added, "He is a vulgar-looking man." She conceded in 1851 that the vain Alexander Baillie Cochrane, author of *Young Italy* (1850), was "a nice looking person" but also "clever, and well aware of the fact." However, occasionally even cosmopolitan travelers were dumbstruck by renowned authors, as happened to one seated with historian Thomas Babbington Macaulay at dinner. With her "ears pinned *very far back*," she "listened to the most agreeable conversation, I ever heard, by far," but apparently said little herself.[42]

One did not have to travel in such exalted circles to see literary lions in their native habitat. For example, an Episcopalian missionary on his way home to Connecticut from the west stopped by New York and "entered the Tribune office ostensibly to purchase a Whigs Almanac but really to get a sight of the eccentric but talented Horace Greeley." He was not disappointed: "While looking over the Almanac, as fortune would have it, the gentleman came in"; he drank in enough to write a lengthy description of the famed editor. Another traveler, a farm woman from Bangor, Maine, who was visiting her Bostonian brother-in-law, went to the 1842 Harvard University commencement, in which "the only son of a particular friend" took part. The acquaintance gave her entrée to "a very handsome collation at his room"—a reception with food and drink—"where we saw many of the *Literati* and fashionables from Boston."[43] Even poor upcountry farmfolk, as they went a-visiting, sometimes rubbed elbows with professional authors.

People who stayed put still encountered authors traveling for health, business, or pleasure. For some well-to-do boardinghouse dwellers, such as John Park, sociabilities with authors were more than likely. "There is now in our house Mrs. S.H. DeKroyft, with a book to sell," he entered in his diary, "of which I bought one, at one dollar." He went on to describe the blind New Yorker peddling her autobiographical *A Place in Thy Memory,* noting, "The history of the woman is interesting. She was engaged to a young man, who was taken sick. She attended him sedulously; but he grew worse, and being like[ly] to die he wished to be married. It was consumated, and he died. The lady who became a 'bride, widow and blind' within a month, wrote several letters to her friends, which she afterwards, by the advice of friends collected, and published in a volume." The homage carried Park through a spirited reading of the book. Brief fortuitous meetings between visiting authors and locals usually registered only as thumbnail sketches. For example, Mellen Chamberlain passed by a sauntering Longellow, who was taking the water cure in Brattleboro, Vermont, and jotted down, "Longfellow ... does not look the Poet—rather dressy." Expecting a more romantic-looking, perhaps Bohemian type, Chamberlain could only express his disenchantment.[44] The people's favorite did not have to dress like the masses who loved him.

Sometimes authors and readers in transit bumped into one another to varying effect. One such propitious coincidence seemed ordained from on high for a spiritualist dabbler reading through *Principles of Nature,* delivered in a trance to an amanuensis. On a westbound train, his brother by luck sat next to the book's author, an event occasioning amazement: "You had Andrew Jackson Davis for a traveling companion home. What is the effect of such companionship upon you? I am making progress in the book with good results. By it my convictions are strengthened that the 'Great Positive Mind is the perfection of inconceivable purity.'" Not all serendipitous traveling experiences generated such excitement, for literary celebrities were not automatically lionized. On finally meeting antislavery author Mattie Griffith by chance on a riverboat, Charlotte Forten could only describe her as "a plain and unpretending young lady; but she is pleasant and I like her much." Big authors might be so repulsive that they provoked insults. After sharing an uncomfortable stagecoach ride with "Mr. Phelps and Lady, formerly Mrs. Lincoln, authoress" of popular science textbooks, Mellen Chamberlain decried her "insolent questions" and "disgusting egotism." He then ridiculed her girth, commenting that "she is truly a great woman, for it was only with immense squeezing that she got into the coach." At times witnesses scarcely recognized their brush with fame. For example, one Shaker remembered meeting, but hardly identifying, a notable black abolitionist author-lecturer who stopped by her Enfield, Connecticut, community. She recorded that "A slave calling her name Sojourner Truth paid us a visit"—a misunderstanding

of Truth's free status. A member of a sect disapproving of secular reading, the Shaker likely played down Truth's career as an author, or was
unaware of it.[45] The authorial publicity machine was not yet
all pervasive.

A key component of authorial publicity was public speaking, which
often went beyond watching performances to socializing. Listeners
welcomed the prospect of shaking hands or making small talk with the
author-performers, such as "cold water warrior" John B. Gough. "This
has been a great day with us," a temperance advocate wrote with excitement after a locally sponsored picnic for the cause. "There were a
number of speakers all very good but the saving grace was Mr Gough
with whom I had the pleasure of speaking before returning from the
ground." At a Democratic Young Men's convention, a Hartford
businessman chanced to dine with the distinguished historian and
politico who spoke: "Geo. Bancroft adressed the meeting. Mr Bancroft
with Genl. Hinnman & S.B. Grant dined with me. Turtle soup. Boiled
Turkey. Roast Beef. Pudding mince pies & dessert constituted the
dinner in the main." Clearly, in the partisan's account, the repast
competed with Bancroft's notoriously vague conversation and won.[46]

For lyceum organizers, like John Park or Portland lawyer William
Willis, the chance for a postperformance tête à tête with a speaker was
greatly increased; indeed, etiquette demanded extensive sociabilities.
Willis tried to schedule an evening with British novelist G.P.R. James on
the day he lectured at the Portland Lyceum, but was rebuffed. "Invited
him to day," Willis told his diary, "but he declined." Willis's impression
of James's lecture—"dull ... & badly delivered, with excessive inspira-
tions of snuff"—may have reflected the snub. John Park entertained
speakers in his boardinghouse after lecture night, and he had better luck
than Willis with James. "[A]sked him and his son to go into our parlor,
where they remained until about nine. Mr James is a great talker," Park
complained, "but pleasant company." Earlier that year, Park and his wife
also hobnobbed with English actress and author Fanny Kemble.
Through her Shakespeare readings and book *A Year of Consolation*, she
achieved a popularity exceeding that of most performers (see fig. 3.4).
On the evening Kemble read *Richard III* to a full house at Worcester's
Flagg Hall, Park scratched in his diary, "the Revd Mr [Edward Everett]
Hale politely offered to introduce me to her" after "she had retired to
her recess [i.e., dressing room]." Park's wife demurred, though: "Mrs
Park had hesitated when invited to be introduced, but when I came
forth with a favorable report, she returned with me to the recess." Her
shyness conquered, Agnes Major Park realized that she had much in

Fig. 3.4 Though depicting Fanny Kemble's 1850 London engagement, this set-up with chair and table was similar to the one she used on her American tours. *Source:* "Mrs. Fanny Kemble's 'Readings' in London," *International Magazine of Literature, Art, and Science* 1 (1850): 310, courtesy of Cornell University Library, Making of America Digital Collection.

common with Kemble; he noted that "when in the course of conversation, Mrs Park mentioned having seen her Uncle John Kemble, her aunt, Mrs Siddons, and her own mother frequently upon the London stage, Mrs Kemble asked with much animation— 'Are you English?'—'I am—I was born in London.' Mrs Kemble grasped both her hands, and the short interview closed with utmost cordiality." The interaction continued at the boardinghouse where the Parks lived and Kemble stayed:

"Having both been introduced to Mrs Kemble civility required that we should call upon her …—so after *our* dinner, but long before Mrs Kemble's dinner hour we were announced and admitted." Etiquette once again decreed that Kemble return the call, which she did the next afternoon. After some time spent "in animated, fluent and interesting conversation," Agnes Park requested and received an autograph.[47] The distance between celebrity and fan was closed through conventions of everyday sociability.

Upon closer inspection, such relationships were seldom one-on-one, but involved wider networks of kin and friends. After all, the conversation between Agnes Park and Kemble was filled with references to family members and past experiences. "Interpretive communities" held together through conversation and correspondence could also actively shape celebrity reception. In this manner, Ellen Wright's reception of Fanny Kemble was negotiated through letters to her sisters and her mother, women's rights advocate and abolitionist Martha Coffin Wright, and chats with classmates she recorded to send to her. Before hearing a schoolroom Shakespeare reading by her famous Berkshire Hills neighbor, Wright was starstruck. "What do you think! Mrs. Kemble has just passed thro' this apartment!" she excitedly wrote to her mother in December 1860; "She came in her sleigh, and got out at our door, instead of at the front door, so we let her in, and we stared at her for about five minutes." All the while Wright apparently little thought about the disjuncture between her family's feminism and Kemble's more conservative stance. Soon enough, Wright and her classmates were invited to Kemble's home. Wright lavished praise upon both the traces of Kemble's literary dollars—her ornate furnishings, huge piano, and abundance of books—and her social sense, seen in portraits of her family and mementos. So taken was she with these celebrity trappings that upon later hearing that "Mrs. Kemble *reads* to us!" Wright seemed ecstatic: "Think of that—I will tell you about it on Sunday, if I survive the pleasure."[48]

Clearly, as Wright had to address her activist family in her letters, she could only increasingly present Kemble more equivocally, if not disdainfully, as social sense struggled with the dazzle of literary celebrity. She did "survive" Kemble's reading to form a picture that was not as flattering as she had expected. "On Friday," she noted, "Mrs. Kemble read to us, two parts of Henry VIII. & would have read the death & c. but her coachman came, and being more punctual in leaving, than in arriving, we lost the famous finale. … One can never tire, hearing her—It is all fine acting—She sat thro' it all, but it was superb! Have you heard her? I dont think she is one to inspire love at first sight—she is too formal—*aiming* at the *queenly. ...*" Into the praise was woven acknowledgment of various social sins: tardiness, abrupt departure, being seated while delivering a formal address, and dismissive formality. To these Wright added in another letter Kemble's reliance upon so many servants, seven in all. Worse still was Kemble's haughty disregard for schoolmistress Sedgwick's slavish devotion. "[S]he *snubs* (vulgar but expressive) Mrs. S.[edgwick] to a painful degree," Wright complained. She concluded, ambiguously, "What then! she is a genius." Was Kemble, like Byron, forgiven flaws because she was gifted, or was she being blamed for using genius as an excuse for them?[49]

When fans saw their favorite authors, they often experienced, like Wright, mixed feelings. When confronted with reality, fantastic images of greatness came tumbling down. Readers somehow expected authors to be above the norm—in intelligence, in mannerism, and even in appearance. Phelps's huge body, Longfellow's conservative dress, or Tupper's oddity annoyed them, as did James's chatty manner or Kemble's imperiousness. Observers penetrating authorial façades seemed surprised to find genuine human beings beneath with all their flaws. Like Agnes Park and Fanny Kemble, or Charlotte Forten and John Greenleaf Whittier, pairs of authors and readers sometimes discovered, to their surprise, that they had much in common. Beyond these special relationships many, perhaps most, readers came to see through direct encounters with an author that she or he was but part of, but not above, a larger humanity. Authors and readers all shared an understanding of the dynamics of production, whether it be summoning inspiration, preparing submissions, keeping a regular diary, or crafting a good letter—production at different levels and within varying senses of the word, but production, nonetheless. Being on the outside looking in was, thus, in the eye of the beholder; a world of literary dollars that distinguished professionals from amateurs, celebrities from lesser lights, could only be illusory in a world of social sense.

"WHEN DICKENS WAS HERE"

Charles Dickens surprised many Americans during his 1842 visit for his ability to make them feel as if he was only human. Probably no living larger-than-life figure existed for American readers, who devoured his works with as much relish as they did those of Lord Byron, Walter Scott, and the classics. But while touring the Northeast after stopping first at Boston, Worcester, and Hartford, Dickens touched the lives of his fans to a degree that was surprising even to them. He warmly engaged them in conversations at parties, apologized profusely for missing engagements, devoted attention to his wife despite the whirlwind activities, and possessed unassuming, even humble, mannerisms. Even his "average" looks seemed appropriate for his personality. Although people fussed over Dickens, he somehow broke through the show, and turned the tables of celebrity upon readers: they began to sympathize with his confinement within the walls of fame.[50]

From the moment Dickens arrived in Boston in January 1842, crowds closed in around him in a hearty but suffocating tribute. Even the working classes loved Dickens and joined the hoopla. "The town has been thrown into great commotion by the arrival of Dickens," Sarah P.E. Hale wrote to her brother in London. "His books have been universally read here you know, and admired by all classes of people." Even modern cabbies' forerunners caught the fever: "On the arrival of the steamer, the hackmen all called out for the privilege of taking 'Boz for nothing.'" The excitement spilled out into the streets, Hale noted, and "people were flocking every hour of the day to the Tremont House to see him." In Worcester the same kind of broad-based Dickens mania manifested itself, even in churches. "Our church was unusually full—many from other societies," John Park grumbled, "—for what?—to hear the preaching?—Oh no;—to get a glance at Boz!! who was expected to be present—but he did not come."[51] Literary lions, even in absentia, could fill the pews.

For those outside of Dickens's orbit, newspapers, engravings, and gossip allowed them to partake of the fun. A young schoolteacher from Lexington, Massachusetts, a town Dickens did not tour, devoted part of an evening filled with chores to "reading an account of the Dinner given in Honor of Charles Dickens at the Papanti's Hall" in the *Saturday Evening Gazette*. About the same time, a New York French student vicariously involved herself through news accounts of Boz's dinner in her hometown, Hartford, and in New York, where she recorded a toast he made: "'The Literature of America: She well knows how to do honor to her own Literature, & to that of other lands.'" Up in Gardiner, Maine, a woman received from her brother a Boston paper containing an amusing "account of the dinner given to Mr. Dickens." The next morning, with her baby son present, she reported back that "I read at the breakfast table the song by Mr. Field, which amused Henry so much that we finally laughed to see him laugh & he laughed at first to see us laugh." That this happened at mealtime was appropriate, given the lines predicting the American public's devouring of the lion:

> They'll eat you, Boz, in Boston! and
> They'll eat you in New York!
> Whenever caught, they'll play a bles-
> Sed game of knife and fork.

Other people hoped for an autograph or an engraving of their beloved Dickens. One man wondered if a distant relative did not have the same yearnings for a pictorial glimpse of Dickens: "Have you not longed to see this public benefactor? I have not had the privilege, but hope to see his likeness." Finally, for those out of the "loop hole" of excitement, like one Yankee woman residing in Louisiana while Dickens conquered the Northeast, partaking of the event could simply mean parsing the author's name and memorializing it—if only by assigning it to one's livestock. "We are quite amused in this loop hole," she noted, "to see the excitement that Dickens is producing in the North. He seems to be making quite a triumphant tour through the land. I wish that he had a better name. It is one we always thought we could swear by without sinning—What the Dickens! and the Dickens he did! are too familiar phrases to feel any great respect for the name. I have two pigs that I shall call one great Dickens, and the other little Dickens in humble imitation of great Pepper & little Pepper."[52] No animal was too lowly to be graced with a great author's moniker.

For socially distinguished folks "in the loop," however, a night at Dickens's feasts and balls was a distinct possibility. Some were huge galas, like that thrown at Papanti's Hall by the "Young Men of Boston" or the banquet at Hartford's City Hotel with upwards of seven hundred guests; others were "little evening part[ies]," like that sponsored for the manufacturing elite, hosted by the George Bancrofts, or the private dinner given by the governor of Massachusetts at his Worcester home. The grander affairs effectively excluded many attendees by charging high admission fees, as much as fifteen dollars per person or the equivalent of about three week's wages for a skilled worker. One traveling businessman who declined to pay the ten-dollar admission to a St. Louis Dickens Ball explained to his wife that the sum "would feed the babies for some time." The smaller New England dinner parties, according to Boz himself, differed little from London affairs, except that the former began at a "more rational hour," were stocked with plenty of oysters, and were "a little louder and more cheerful."[53] Literary sociability reigned supreme.

Dickens graciously withheld comment about the young guests who dressed up like his fictional creations—potentially nightmarish Yankee renditions of characters from *Nicholas Nickleby* or *Oliver Twist* riding the cars or stalking the crooked streets at night to attend a Boston fete in his honor. One young man from Marblehead described his and his friends' plans to dress up for the Great Boz dinner: "I shall probably be up next Tuesday to see Mr Dickens and if you want to see him you may go with me. 'Pan' is going up as Mrs. Squeers, and Bill as Charlie Bates; Sarah Dana wants for to go as Mrs Nickleby senior." Nor did Dickens mention the ill-fated dinner sponsored by transcendentalist writer Elizabeth Peabody, at which the fatigued author did not show. This particular dinner party of about sixty guests—"the grand beings," according to Sarah P.E. Hale—was scheduled during one of Peabody's "Wednesday evening Symposiums." "Dickens promised to go," Hale gossiped to her brother, but "sad to relate instead of the lion came a *note* stating that he was too unwell to come. It was the night after his great dinner, and he [had] been so dragged round and carried from one thing to another that he was obliged to give up. The party were all on the tip toe of expectation, and formed themselves into a sort of pla-toon and Miss Peabody walked up and down reading the fatal note. The party hardly recovered from the disappointment the rest of the evening." The bemused brother dryly jibed at the literati there: "What a pity ... that Boz should have lost the transcendental Sympo-sium"—rather than the other way around.[54]

What did guests at a Dickens event think of the novelist? Most were surprised that he was warmer than other British visitors like Frances Trollope, Harriet Martineau, or Fanny Kemble. Dickens, especially on the New England leg of his tour, instead earnestly attempted to be affa-ble. Sarah P.E. Hale, who poked fun at Elizabeth Peabody's pretensions, saw in Dickens the opposite sort of character. "Dickens has been very much liked here," she claimed; "The young folks think he is a perfect beauty." After spending time with Dickens at the Bancrofts, she concluded, "he is certainly very unpretending and agreeable in his manners" and "appeared very simple and unaffected ..., really touched at the interest people manifested in his works." In a gesture toward social sense, Dickens conversed with Hale about her brother, then U.S. minister to Britain—"a good subject of talk for us," Hale thought. A twenty-seven-year-old fan who attended Mrs. William Lawrence's Dickens party also "had a delightful talk with Dickens" about

"Washington Irving, sculpture, etc." She admitted, "I stopped and drew back several times to give him an opportunity to leave me if he chose but he very kindly continued to resume the conversation, until someone took me away to dance—after that he spoke to me twice again, entirely voluntarily on his part, and gave me a gripe at parting, the effects of which I think I still feel in my fingers." Not everyone got close to Dickens, even at small gatherings. A textile manufacturer's daughter invited to the Bancrofts complained, "He was still so followed that though I was presented I had little or no opportunity to see him." Expecting a magnetic presence, she was "wofuly disappointed at the first peep" and deduced that "his face is one that must improve upon acquaintance." In a time when facial planes and head bumps were read to discern character, the drive to reconcile the inner and outer person was not entirely shallow.[55]

As favorable gossip about Dickens spread, people who declined invitations rued it. The businessman who was loath to "'fork up'" ten dollars to see Dickens in St. Louis confessed that "I now almost regret that I did not attend the Ball last evening having had a number of invitations but being a stranger I thought I should feel awkward." Nevertheless, he secured "an autograph of Dickens," for his son, who "should have it for his cabinet." John Park had similar second thoughts after turning down a party invitation: "Before evening, Mrs Park and I began to hesitate about going to Governour Davis's, to see the lion, though specially invited—and finally concluded to stay at home and finish our letters to Louisa." He tersely explained, "I dislike such show visits." As fate would have it, however, Park bumped into Dickens departing the next morning at the Worcester transportation station: "From the few minutes conversation I had with him," Park conceded, "he appeared to me a frank, unassuming animated character—much at his ease, but far from supercilious." With newfound admiration, that evening Park inscribed Dickens's birthdate in his diary and later confessed in a letter to a friend that Dickens's "animation … appeared natural, habitual, and honestly hearty." He seemed so down to earth that Park found in the famous author "some resemblance" to his correspondent's "much esteemed son." "To say it was striking would certainly be far from a compliment to the latter," Park waffled, venturing that "It was perhaps only his far famed *Frankness*; and why should there not lie in that, a certain degree of similarity." Her son's name was Frank, so Park could pun on Dickens's famed forthrightness. Ironically, Park's estimation of Dickens grew higher even as he leveled the celebrity to the status of an everyday acquaintance. The "show visit" Park had feared never transpired, for Dickens, the man, managed to break through the facade of Dickens, the author.[56]

Dickens's visit to the United States summoned up, in microcosm, all the permutations of celebrity worship, and its opposite, celebrity toppling. In their role of "outsiders looking in," ordinary folks scrutinized this famed author's comings and goings and assessed his every move. Most people spied upon "the lion" from a safe distance, by following the news coverage about him, hearing morsels of information in conversation and letters, and collecting autographs or portraits. A few fortunate people had the chance to meet, converse, and socialize with the author; they formed opinions about Dickens's appearance, manners, and character. But within these assessments, sharp judgments that burst the bubble of celebrity seldom escaped mention. The wealthy young woman who expected to be dazzled by Dickens at the Bancrofts' was instead struck by his lackluster comportment. The Louisianian thought the name "Dickens" fit only for swearing and pigs. And John Park feared that likening someone's face to Dickens's would be insulting. Yet because these observers stripped the author of suprahuman qualities to invest him with all of the hallmarks of mediocrity, the famous Boz was permitted to join the everyday community of people who read, laughed, gossiped about him, and fondly remembered the time "when Dickens was here."[57]

"I am in a hurry to have Dickens go home that he may write some more, are not you?" Mary Poor asked her sister in April 1842. She conveyed the strong bond between author and audience that defied physical separation: literary production. Even after Dickens sailed back home, he remained among Americans in spirit who confronted him through his writings. "Dickens' work on this country is out by the Gr[eat] Western," an industrialist wrote in his diary when *American Notes* appeared shortly after the author's tour ended; "a fine print, everybody reading it, to the straining of their eyes." Through his travel account that treated Yankees kindly, but savaged their neighbors to the South and West, Dickens continued to participate in Americans' literary social world: people bought, lent, borrowed, and made gift presentations of copies of the book. John Park received *Notes* as a present from his neighbor the day it came out and began "forthwith to read them." Other people talked to one another about it, imagining how it was being received. "Have you read Dicken's 'Notes,' and what think you of them?" Luella Case asked Sarah Edgarton; "I think the Americans are generally too cross with him ... we have no right to blame him if he tells no intentional falsehoods." Years after its publication,

Ellen Wright, a baby "when Dickens was here," nevertheless wanted to read about the tour with her teacher and classmates during evening "reading hour": "I suggested Dickens Notes on America—but Mad. shook her head—I consider it my bounden duty to get that book read, whenever I can, it is so vilified by stupid people who cant take a joke."[58] The book retained its power to deflate prodigious American self-regard.

Along with *Notes*, fans used Dickens's other works as instruments for maintaining social ties and generational connections. In January 1844, Sarah P.E. Hale received a New Year's present from her brother in London, "Dickens' last book a 'Christmas Carol' in press," two months before it reached Boston bookstores. A gift distinctive for its timeliness, it also held special meaning as a token of sibling affection and remembrance in the face of separation. But Dickens's works made social sense beyond gift giving. In 1857, a pregnant newlywed from Bangor consulted both Dickens and her sister, about what to call her expectant arrival. After listing a few names such as "Alice," "Margaret," "Lenora," and "Bessie," the mother fastened upon "Agnes." "This last, Dickens has made me love," she explained, referring to Agnes Wickfield, *David Copperfield*'s heroine. One Bostonian also wove Dickens into her family life in 1851, when she performed needlework for her sister's child: "I amused myself by knitting on baby's jacket and reading Dickens' sketches in Italy." For a millworker, Dickens provided social glue during a visit with a friend in 1859: "I had commenced reading Dicken's [*sic*] 'Hard Times'—and either Mrs. Lawrence and myself read aloud alternately almost all day—it is an interesting interesting story." Like her, a locomotive clerk invited Dickens into his social circle when in March 1844 he "commenced reading, aloud, Charles Dickens' 'Christmas Carol'" to his family. Dickens helped bridge the distance between two sisters and their uncle and cousin traveling abroad. "We have played many games at backgammon and are reading Dickens book about Italy," one sister wrote in a letter to Venice; "we shall know almost as much about it [Italy] as you and Posy, when you come home."[59] Reading a travel account by a skilled literary delineator was nearly as good as being there.

Dickens held a special place in the hearts of ordinary Americans enacting their social life, but other writers played a similar role in the same communal drama in which literature was put to social ends. Litterateurs' words for sale were harnessed by readers to give and take, to mold and utilize, in the maintenance of priceless human relations. In these relations litterateurs were seldom seen as men and women out for the main economic chance—not even Dickens, who after all came in part to counter American piracy of his works, a theft of his literary dollars. What literature *should* mean was far too social for that.[60] Rather, by disseminating authors' ideas—through conversing, lending a book, gift giving, reading out loud, or by naming a child after a fictional character—people not only spread literary culture, they also united with one another over shared encounters with texts. As texts passed through one then another doorway, the beloved author became like a relative who visited one family's household after another, binding their residents together through common literary experiences. But there were other ways to distribute texts besides by social sense alone, and that was for profit or by profession. Dreams of literary dollars filled the heads of many go-betweens who in order to sell their wares passed from the marketplace of print into the social circuits of local realities. What they would find, sometimes much to their chagrin and despite their earnest efforts at gain, as we will see, was that their market-oriented initiatives at distribution would be often transformed into socially constructive acts of dissemination.

4

INSIDE AND OUTSIDE THE LITERARY
MARKETPLACE

In May 1856, months before Joshua Harris, the Saco, Maine, mill-worker with Byronic aspirations, solicited publishers for his verse, he pursued another literary vocation, that of traveling agent. As a southeastern Maine sales representative for Boston publisher Maturin Murray Ballou, he knocked on doors in Alfred, Newfield, Springdale, and Kennebunkport to sell magazine subscriptions. A typical day was tiresome enough, but one Friday in July 1856 was so bad that he vented his frustrations in his diary:

> I rap at the front door—Neat looking lady appears—Good morning!
> Good morning! responds the lady—Would you like to subscribe for
> a Newspaper or Magazine[?]—I have Ballou[']s Dollar Monthly
> Magazine[,] Flag of our Union and Ballou[']s Pictorials. I should
> not.... [M]eet gent at the gate—ask him if he would like to sub-
> scribe—he says I have no time to read—I go on—2nd house—Lady
> opens asks me in—take a seat—lady enquires where I am
> from—how long I have been in this business &c[.] Dont subscribe.
> ... 3d Two ladys in the yard—old and young lady—young lady buys
> one sheet of I[mpression] P[aper] 4th Old lady invites me
> in—don[']t trade any....

After thirty or so other visits with nothing to show but the sale of a sheet of copy paper, he called it a day. After only four months on the road suffering through days like these, he quit his sales job to seek millwork again in Saco.[1] He had awoken, for the time being at least, from his dreams of literary dollars.

Unsuccessful solicitations were but one vexation of literary agents. Travel was difficult; in rural areas most roads were little more than dirt (sometimes mud) paths frequently interrupted by rivers spanned by unstable, creaking bridges or irregular ferry service. Harris probably plodded such byways, but other agents moved along them on horseback. Developed areas were little better, with their ever-changing, unreliable transportation routes. Rail lines, steamboats or coastal packets, and stage coaches seldom put passengers' comfort or convenience first. As agents bumped along from town to town, week after week, the indifference or hostility they met with could provoke chronic homesickness. Life on the road seemed hardly worth the meager pay less costs of travel, meals, and lodging. Most agents relied on commissions that came only when patrons were willing to buy.

Because would-be purchasers viewed the reading materials being hawked as relative luxuries or superfluities, agents used all their wiles to make their wares seem like necessities. Thus, sales depended upon the agent's effective interpersonal communication, which was commonly worn thin by the job's stresses—successive doors shut in one's face and annoyed, vacant, or even angry expressions of intractable people. But even benign or affable interactions could erode salespeople's confidence, for these human connections were ultimately bound to monetary transactions instead of to kinship or friendship. The human intercourse Harris described wore an amiable face—"Good morning!" and "take a seat"—but was actually fleeting, curt, dismissive, and even cold at times, especially to the agent whose motive, after all, was to make the sale. For agents the only good customer was a paying one, but for many townsfolk the only good literary experience was a sociable one, unsullied by the cash nexus. The collision of desperate sellers with sociable readers bred relationships neither entirely disingenuous nor familiar, yet tied with economic strings to literary dissemination. Thus, tension between the market and the social often emerged in these relationships. For the reader, a long conversation with an agent about books that did not result in a sale could itself be a gratifying encounter; for the agent, it might only be a grating waste of time and effort.[2]

This chapter explores that uneasy relationship of social sense to the literary marketplace from the perspective of ordinary folk, who, like Harris, were at some time in their life paid for their work as distributors or disseminators of literature. Sometimes in and sometimes out of the market, they provide keener insight into the meaning of the cash nexus for the social relations of literature than do professionals who more fully imbibed the values of literary commercialization. The distributors considered here, most of whom were not long committed to a career in the publishing industry, include both amateurs and short-term professionals. Some handled books, pamphlets, or periodicals: tract agents, peddlers, amateur authors selling their own works, and, of course, publishers' agents, who, like Harris, heard the baneful phrase, "I should not," etched upon their memory.[3] Paid disseminators discussed herein include librarians, schoolteachers, and performers from panorama men to lyceum lecturers. Librarians were just emerging out of volunteer social service to employment, but not yet fully into professional social service. Some of these disseminators dispersed texts orally or visually: district schoolteachers reading publications aloud in the classroom, panorama showmen reciting scripts in the exhibition hall, and lecturers reading from their manuscripts at lyceums. Of course, a few amateurs found the work satisfying and made substantial profits. But like would-be authors, many were called and few were chosen, and after being chosen, some of these no longer wanted to be. Indeed, most who plied the trade did so temporarily, and consequently stepped back into a literary social world less compromised by market demands.

While inside the literary marketplace, however, distributors experienced the disparities, but also the commonalities between gratis dissemination embedded in social practices and marketplace distribution wedded to monetary gain. In this sense, distribution needs to be distinguished from social dissemination. Social dissemination began with "consumers" who lent or gave away literature for social ends, while market distribution started with publishers who directed their wares outward through agents for monetary ends. Between gratis dissemination and market distribution were paid disseminators, like librarians and teachers, whose institutionalized positions emerged from everyday practices but who did not sell goods. In social dissemination, literature often coursed through groups of recipients who added their own interpersonal meaning as texts passed from hand to hand or were read aloud; as literature circulated in this fashion, it gained in social value. In market distribution, the seller targeted a specific purchaser whose only contribution was to place cash in the hands of the middleman whose mission was to make the sale regardless of whether the item was ever read after that. Yet even in money-driven relationships, sociability did not entirely erode because distributors adopted everyday social practices for their trade. For example, as agents came a-calling, the resulting personal conversations in homes sometimes drowned out the jargon of trade. Bookstore clerks and librarians overheard or engaged in literary conversations with patrons. Paid teachers and lecturers not only performed a job involving oral reading, but a humanistic service, as did meagerly recompensed librarians. Ministers offered a spiritual service in which social—indeed, communal—ties were forged while undertaking professional duties that included distributing texts. Indeed, it was difficult to distribute literature without also disseminating it, because distributing depended on interpersonal communication, and hence fell under the sway of local social sense.[4]

Unlike authorship, in which the social nexus between writer and reader was usually an abstract one enacted through print with only rare person-to-person encounters, distribution and paid dissemination were almost always tangible and localized products of them. No one thought of leveling agents, librarians, and teachers because unlike litterateurs they seldom attained celebrity status, unless they also became well-known authors, politicos, or lecturers. There was little drive, say, to peep into booksellers' homes as Lucy Larcom wished to do to the Concord, Massachusetts, transcendentalists. Sites of literary dissemination itself, however, could arouse interest, but more for the social value or intellectual investment than the economic power they represented. Americans valued the interior social life of bookstores and they treated venerable booksellers as old friends but scarcely inquired about the state of business. They also treasured and made pilgrimages to great repositories such as New York City's Astor Library, the Library of Congress, and the Boston Public Library, but only very rarely wondered at institutional financial bases. Prestigious libraries stood for literary achievement and dissemination on a majestic scale, but not capitalization. Americans' persistence in framing even these institutions in social terms affords yet another opportunity to ponder the relationship between dreams of literary dollars and realities of social sense.

The chapter unfolds on three concurrent levels as it moves from profit-seeking distribution to remunerated dissemination, from people who deliver literary goods to those who serve society or perform for the public's edification and entertainment, and from the printed to the oral word. We begin with what would seem to be the purest entrepreneurial activities of all: in-the-field solicitations by book and periodical agents.

Yet even here, as we discuss, social sense complicated their selling tactics, as well as those of retailers like booksellers. Outside the book trades, people profiting by private sales or auctions sought to avoid the "Disgrace of Price." Since social feeling often accompanied books and periodicals changing hands for cash, we next inquire into whether sites of distribution, like bookstores, were accordingly seen more as marketplaces than sites for socializing and conducting nonliterary business. We then contrast these public perceptions with those of libraries, sites mostly outside the literary marketplace per se, to find attitudes toward them similar to those surrounding bookstores. From reports of visitors to distribution and dissemination sites, we turn to custodians of the latter institutions, the salaried librarians who disseminated books, to sketch out their occupational experiences. What demands were placed upon them by their jobs and their patrons? What ethics informed librarians' actions as they served their clientele? After venturing answers to these questions, we go one step further, to consider an already professionalizing group of salaried literary disseminators, primary and secondary schoolteachers reading book excerpts and articles aloud. For both teachers and librarians alike, the combination of a poorly paid yet highly demanding job and the need to render effectively services that were once usually provided in much more private and informal social settings engendered widespread occupational dissatisfaction. Nor were public oral disseminators, performers of the word before paying audiences, free from similar tensions between literary dollars and social sense. We conclude the chapter by delineating the social demands upon two groups of profit-driven itinerants, panorama men and lecturers. Ironically, for these, the social nature of dissemination necessarily moderated the money-getting aura surrounding distributors. Throughout, as we weigh the differences between distribution and dissemination among these varied cases, we will see the often subtle ways that the market sometimes served or subverted the social relations of literature.

THE WORLD OF DISTRIBUTORS

Paid literary distributors like agents and booksellers faced enormous difficulties. People generally expected literature to circulate as "naturally" as social feeling within a system of interpersonal exchange outside of the market. Books and periodicals came into their hands far more frequently through these exchanges than through the relatively few bookstores, subscription agents, and other commercial outlets nationwide. True, many imprints had to be bought before entering this exchange system. But each purchase potentially led to several subsequent dissemination acts—for instance, gift giving or borrowing and lending—with no cash transaction involved. Dissemination beyond the market occurred during face-to-face interactions, such as social calls and family gatherings, and via long-distance delivery systems such as the postal service, express companies, or private couriers. A very common practice was mailing purchased newspapers to distant friends or family. These papers, signaling that all was well, and sometimes unlawfully inscribed with messages, substituted for letters, which were more expensive to send. Papers received could be sent again like chain letters. An even more common extramarket form of dissemination was reading aloud one's printed matter to various listeners in sociable settings. Such oral performances could account for about half of the occasions someone read. With so much literature in gratis circulation, why pay for that which one could usually get for free?[5]

Distribution for profit only supplemented this interpersonal dissemination and so had to adjust to it. Communities were so steeped in literary sociabilities surrounding dissemination that they had trouble understanding commercial distribution—an attitude that distributors wanting to make sales had to take into account. The hard sell could disbalance the delicate give-and-take of literary sociability. Blatant attempts at moneymaking could signal self-serving, avarice, or lack of sociability. Distributors were in a bind: they had to sell to a customer base generally unwilling to buy while not coming off like they were trying to. This dilemma affected agents most directly, as we will see, but also shaped the lives of petty booksellers and other amateur distributors. As long as Americans greatly cherished the practices of literary dissemination outside the marketplace, distributors could scarcely expect easy sales.

Agents

Agents faced the task of coaxing a reader's interest in a current or future title in a publisher's literary inventory, usually through subscription. Trade publishers employed agents to secure sales, especially in rural areas with few bookstores. But tract agents and abolitionists acting mainly out of ideology also sold subscriptions and maybe had some payment for their services. Agents of all stripes had to hone their skills as salespersons while setting aside any distaste for interacting with people primarily over money. Customers' greatest defense against sales pitches was lack of means. "All would buy if they had the money,"

Harris once complained. Seth Arnold, an agent for the American Colonization Society's *African Repository*, similarly observed, "Called on not less than a dozen distinguished individuals, all approving of Colonization, and not one would give a cent, or subscribe." A subscription might cost "too much," or "it was above my mark." Widespread dread of agents only added to their frustration. "Fell on to a Book agent, Thompson," schoolteacher Mellen Chamberlain moaned; "God save us." The first thought occurring to John Park when a stranger showed up at his door was, "I shall be beset to subscribe for some literary work."[6]

The occasional charlatan made matters worse. "A very 'stout gentleman' called upon me, as an agent of [Phillips & Sampson] to solicit my subscription for their edition of Shakespeare," a diplomat explained to his nephew. "He represented it (in terms I dare say unauthorized by them) as a very expensive & meritorious work which they were getting up," he continued, confessing, "I subscribed to the tune of I think 30 dollars…. I have not yet received it, nor seen any specimen of it." Such scams, duping even the most prominent and worldly citizens, only lowered trust in agents. Rogues gave agency such a bad name that some nonprofit volunteers felt tainted, describing their subscription selling as "a begging expedition," or "an irksome, ungracious, ungentlemanly business." Subscription obviously demanded that the agent be able to inspire trust in the subscriber that the book or periodical would eventually materialize. Despite these problems, publishers and authors embraced subscription because it assured them of a ready-made audience.[7]

Magazine subscriptions, still the most familiar form of this type of selling, then depended upon agents themselves buying back issues in order to sell future ones. This unwillingness to finance sample copies testified to publishers' lack of trust in agents. Haverhill's Cyrus Farnham, an agent for Weeks, Jordan, was given "specimen nos. of our principal works [e.g., *Lady's Book*] which are charged to you at the prices in the bill in sale, & are to be exhibited to procure subscribers for the current vols of the works." Joshua Harris also "bought some sample papers" before commencing his agency for Ballou. By showing his customers current or back numbers, Harris gave them, at his own expense and for the publisher's gain, a taste of what was to come.[8]

That foreshadowing was much more difficult for agents armed only with prospectuses, printed sheets describing a forthcoming text and its material features. After all, this meant selling only an idea of a future property based on the sheet's description and the agent's word. For instance, David Plumer, a rural New Hampshire agent for Boston-based antiquarian bookseller Samuel G. Drake, was given in 1833 "two of the prospectuses" for Drake's forthcoming *Indians of North America*, criticizing the Pilgrims' treatment of Native Americans. The prospectuses spelled out the terms of sale, which Drake promised his representative "shall be *more than complied with*." His prospectuses probably also denoted the book's dimensions and summarized its contents: "a full account of the Late War in the west, with the lives of the chiefs engaged in it." Some prospectuses, such as that for the 1844 Democratic campaign newspaper *Whip and Spur*, featured, along with terms of twenty-five cents a copy (of which five cents went to the agent), detailed cartoons and quotations aimed at partisans (see fig. 4.1). This one damned opposition candidate Henry Clay with his own words on slavery, while pictorially waving in the margins "The Working Man's Banner." A prospectus could feature eye-catching material to satisfy anyone who might "feel some curiosity to see it."[9]

More than simply enticing purchasers, prospectuses often were instruments of commitment to the project because they contained blank spaces for signatures—public pledges to buy. When passed around a social network within a town, such sheets were sometimes called "circular advertisements." These were particularly effective with agents having local social standing. "It appears to us if you would have a circular advertisement printed & circulated in yr. village you might collect a large number of subscribers who now send to Boston or subscribe to travelling agts.," Weeks, Jordan, advised their agent. Here, agents could deftly deploy social feeling, for when subscribers added their signatures they joined in the symbolic community of names appearing on the list. First among the six Bernardstown, Massachusetts, signatories of the aforementioned *Whip and Spur* prospectus, for example, was local real estate magnate and railroad director Henry Wyles Cushman.[10] Thus, subscription became a visible act of affiliation with the social group supporting future publication, and this was one reason why bigwigs were often solicited first or even saw their names appear without their knowledge in order to induce "lesser" folk to subscribe.

Even though prospectuses could collect signatures, they were only one way to obtain pledges to buy forthcoming or newly published works. Samuel G. Drake simply asked Plumer to devise his own method: "You can either stick on a piece of paper at the bottom of the proposals or put it into a small book." Some agents jotted notes in their diaries to replace or supplement lists, as Seth Arnold did while collecting subscribers for the *African Repository*: "Mrs. Goodwilley paid

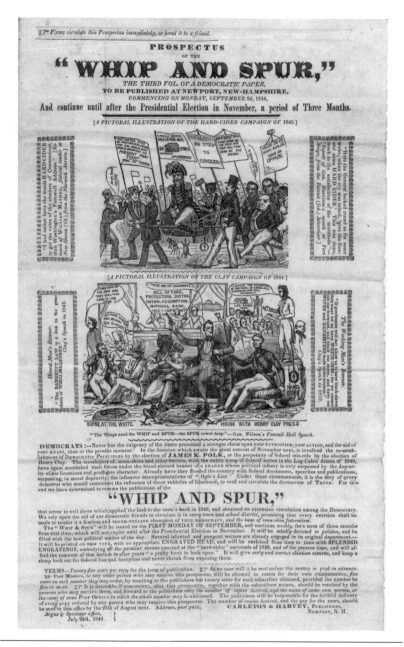

Fig. 4.1 This prospectus for an 1844 Democratic campaign paper contained many eye-catching features. *Source:* Prospectus of *Whip and Spur* (Newport, N.H.: Carleton and Harvey, 1844), Special Collections, 11 C 7, box 14, folder 40, courtesy New England Historic Genealogical Society.

her subscription 1 do[llar.] After leaving the hospitible [*sic*] roof of Rev. Mr. Pringle—called on Mr. Cowls. He gave me a dollar to pay for 2 numbers of the Repository already received 25 cts & the remainder 75 cts a donation. Mr James Smith paid me for the Repository another year. $1.50." Arnold apparently kept a separate "account book" as well, with a more systematic list of names, credits, debits, and nonfungible donations, for he not only collected signatures, but often money, too, and therefore needed more complex records.[11]

Commissions, expenses, and other transactions had to be calculated within publishers' guidelines. To discourage competitive discounting or agents overcharging, publishers tried to set fixed prices and commissions. For example, one story-paper publisher instructed Joshua Harris to "'send any number of subscribers you please with the money as follows, Flag $1.50. Pictorial $2. and the Magazine.80¢'[;] the regular prices for these are $2—$3. and $1." Upon receiving this letter, he did the simple math, "leaving me a commission of .50. 1.00. and [.]20. for one subscriber of each." The same commission rate also applied to Cyrus Farnham of Weeks, Jordan. "The subscription price of each is upon the work & may be found in our Catalogue of which we send you a few for circulation," his employer explained. "Our commission to you upon those prices will be 25%." Samuel G. Drake paid agent David Plumer more, a maximum 33 percent on sales of *Indians of North America*; "I give the persons employed half a dollar a piece for every book disposed of—none to be disposed of for less than $1.50," he explained.[12]

Straight commissions were not the only form of payment, for sometimes agents received a salary and, possibly, money for travel expenses, while others got only outright bounties on each subscription. In the late 1820s Samuel G. Drake offered a combination of flat salary and reimbursement for costs incurred on the road while selling Benjamin Church's *King Philip's War*. To one agent, he promised, "I will give you 20 dollars a month and bear your expenses if you will go over your town and neighboring towns through." He probably abandoned this strategy in favor of commissions because it gave agents little incentive to clinch the sale. There were other ways to encourage agents. For example, a Universalist minister who in 1836 acted as agent for the *Gospel Sun* received his pay based on numbers of subscriptions. He reported that the editor "is to pay me a shilling per year for every subscriber to the paper, payments to be made semi-annually." Any new subscribers he obtained meant more money for him.[13]

Most agents funded traveling expenses out of pocket or had to find creative ways to evade them. "[P]aid out .62 1/2 for expenses," twenty-six-year-old Almon Benson jotted in his diary while hitting the trail for the *Sunday School Advocate*. Although he "got several signers" that day, that money was dear to the sometime farm laborer. In addition to paying for transportation and food, agents, of course, had to find their own lodgings—not always easy given the ill-developed state of American hostelry, especially in rural towns. "Had to travel till after eight o'clock before I could get put up," Harris griped one night in 1856; "found quarters at last with somebody—don[']t know who." Agents on long and circuitous routes constantly fell upon the mercy of strangers. To avoid room and board charges, these hard-traveling agents might depend upon townspeople to put them up for free or next to nothing. In May 1837, Almon Benson, for example, set off from Gilmanton, New Hampshire, and rode on horseback to Barnstead, and then to Pittsfield, back to Barnstead to head for Barrington, and then on to Rochester, Great Falls, Summersworth, Dover, Durham, Nero Market, Exeter, Kingston, Nottingham, and Northwood; he finally arrived home after more than three weeks away. Over that period he was ever grateful for the beneficence of other people who extended to him the sociabilities granted to any poor traveler. In this way, sociability served the needs of the distributor by saving on immediate expenses. Even when, occasionally, Benson offered money to his hosts, it seemed to be part of a social dynamic priming the pump for sales: "rainy put up at night with Mr Isac Jacobs paid him .25—obtained 7 Subscribers." At other times, he felt lucky to get a meager meal: "in Milton got 7 names—staied over night with a mizer ... appeared to have but 1 spoon in his house—for the same that I ate my supper with was in the meat plate the next morning—and that 1 was a very poor one." Despite the hardships, he persevered; nearing the end of his sojourns, he noted, "arose much worn down with fatigue, but felt it good to thank God for His favor especially that He had been with me in the midst of strangers and had supplied all my wants." But hardship and dislocation were nothing new to Benson who summed up his twenty-sixth year: "for the last year I have travelled about 400 miles; have earned about $140.00; Studied about 7 months Since June 25 1836, have written 14 letters home; taught school 14 weeks, spent 3 weeks for the Advocate; have troddled about 50 towns have [been] remarkably blest in my endeavors to get an education, my health has been good, have wanted for nothing."[14] On the scales of life, personal benefits far outweighed the little money he earned.

For some agents, social sense seamlessly blended with selling. "At Union village called on John Lord and sons—He fed me and horse very hospitably & paid me $1.50 for the [African] Repository one year," clergyman Seth Arnold recorded while gathering subscriptions. A week later his spirits were still high: "My heart cheered with very kind and hospitable treatment in Brot. M's family." On another occasion he was "hospitably entertained" by host "A.H. Gilmore Esq." in Fairlee, Vermont. If sociability lightened traveling agents' burden, it could also intrude upon sales and overwhelm the discussion. "[C]all at Mr Ds first—he enquires about [my brother] William," Joshua Harris explained; "does not patronize me any." He at times took friendly banter for nosiness—and perhaps rightly so, given the popular mistrust of agents: "A man asked me where was [I] going—told him to Kennebunk—he asked where I came from—told him from Shapleigh—he asked if I had been at work there—I said yes—he wanted to know what I had been doing—told him making shoes—for—I think it is none of his business what my business is." Of course, the man purchased no subscription. Benson and Arnold experienced warmer reception probably because they were clerics, while Harris, a lay salesman, was often suspect. No amount of chatting relieved his sense of isolation. "Never was so hom[e]sick in all my life," Harris moaned shortly before he gave up his traveling agency altogether.[15]

Once subscriptions were collected and sent to the publisher along with any advance money, traveling did not necessarily end. Some agents delivered promised items; even magazines might be sent to agents to distribute. "You can have the nos. [of the *Lady's Book*] sent thro the P.O. or may have a parcel made up & sent you monthly," Weeks, Jordan offered their agent. While a few publishers used express companies to deliver books to subscribers, agents more likely distributed them. Whatever trust the publisher placed in the agent was tested at this point. "The person who gets the subscribers must deliver the books, & hence you see the propriety of having men that can be depended upon," Samuel G. Drake informed his cousin, kin in whom he felt particularly confident.[16]

At this point in the transaction, book buyers often placed money in agents' hands. The time lapse between selling and collecting encouraged sociability at the start of the agent-customer relationship while leaving the pecuniary stigma to the end. What was gained in sociability, however, was often lost in tardy payment. When just before Christmas 1847 Seth Arnold distributed temperance manuals to his Papermill Village family subscribers, he had to wait until the end of January for all of them to finally pay up. It was particularly painful for him because he himself had financed over a hundred copies. Not surprisingly, his congregation of dirt farmers and papermill workers only reluctantly parted with what little money they had, even for a good cause.[17]

Peddlers, like agents distributing materials, also traveled about with goods on hand. The difference was that peddlers owned their motley stock and carried all of it with them to be sold or bartered as they went along. Although few peddlers specialized in bookselling by the 1830s, some still included almanacs and other pieces of literature among their wares. Purchasers confused peddlers with agents; one leatherworker scribbled in his diary that the "'History of the World' book peddler was round last week," when the man was probably a subscription agent. Agents carrying along extra cargo to sell deemed themselves peddlers. Joshua Harris, for example, sold original printed recipes for "*Wart Killer*" and "for washing," "at one dollar per copy," along with ink and copy paper made from his own "Magic Duplicative Material." When he encountered a man selling "oil cloths and indelible ink," he could only dub him "A brother pedlar." Other salespersons alternated peddling with agency, overlapping some days of combined work. While Seth Arnold was returning home after collecting subscriptions to the *African Repository*, he "[t]ook bibles of Mr. A. Kingsbury, and testaments, to the value of $30.32 1/2, to be sold—given to the poor or returned" and proceeded to sell them on the road. Given the hardship and loneliness of a traveling life, peddlers, like agents, succumbed to homesickness. "Depressed in spirit and with sad memories of home, I sit gloomily at the fireplace," one peddler, who probably sold a few literary items among his "various articles," wrote in his diary. While holed up in a farmhouse during a blizzard, he reported, "The farmer's wife, a former schoolmistress, realized my state of mind and admonished me." After this confrontation, he realized, "I have my health and what I want to eat and drink; good shelter protects me from wind and weather" and asked "Why must I worry?" He concluded by drawing a line between dollars and sense: "No, gold shall not drive me to misery. May the devil have the banknotes and let me have a book to read that I may be of good cheer!"[18] Juxtaposing banknotes and books, the peddler forgot that the book comforting him may have been sold to the family by a fellow traveling salesman. One man's diversion was another man's commodity.

In agents' account books and business correspondence, literature naturally reduced to a commodity. In most cases, keeping track of business was fairly simple—a matter of "sending the List of Subscribers for Periodicals," as one rural minister did, along with any money he collected. But often the record keeping became more complex. Deadbeat subscribers required special notation, as did barter transactions. Seth Arnold, for example, used a volume of "missionary maps" (plotting their worldwide activities) worth seventy-five cents as partial payment of a farmer's $6.76 bill for potatoes, milk, and a cash loan: "Settled with Mr. Cragin, & paid him for 4 1/4 bushels of potatoes $1.46 and 82 1/2 quarts of milk at 4 cts $3.30 = $4.76 & cash $2.00 = $6.76. I gave recei[p]t... for $6.00 and crossed subscriptions for maps 75 cts = $6.75." Larger scale bartering, of course, meant multiple accounts. One agent called at several rural Vermont schools "To exchange the Primary [*Smith's First Book in Geography*] for Mitchels [competing atlas] by receiving 15 cts. for the difference, and the geography and atlas [*The Geography of the Heavens*] by receiving 30 cts." The books were normally priced at thirty and sixty cents, respectively. If the agent succeeded, he would not only remit to his employers the surplus cash, but would also help them obtain a monopoly on the local geography textbook market. The school district might be likely to order future new editions of *Smith's First Book* at full price. But, at this stage, the publishers seemed more concerned with flushing out the old copies, for they instructed the agent that "if they have the last edition of Mitchel's not much soiled" he should "exchange eve[n]."[19] Agents' everyday transactions in the field could intervene between the publisher's list price and the eventual net gain.

At times recordkeepers were overwhelmed. This was especially true for people involved in larger, far-flung enterprises, such as the Massachusetts Anti-Slavery Society. Samuel May Jr., himself an agent in charge of various other agents at home and overseas, found himself awash in paper:

> It is a pretty intricate matter to keep all these little accounts straight and we cannot be too exact & particular. It is far the most puzzling thing *I* have ever undertaken in the shape of money-accounts. So many different concerns—Bazaar, Standard, Liberator, Bugle, Una, Tract Fund, Books & Pictures for one & another,—& payments coming for this year, & next year, & back years,—all mixed together, and all to be separated,—the date to which subscriptions are paid to be noted & preserved, &c. &c. make the work a rather difficult one, at best, I am always doubtful how I shall come through it, and always wish I were a practiced book-keeper, when the thing has to be done.[20]

The welter of paper communications made it difficult to keep an eye on the bottom line.

Other Sales

Bookkeeping was just as difficult for amateur authors hawking their writing. While some amateurs or their families enlisted agents to sell their works and handle all the bookkeeping—as we have seen in chapter 1, Olive Worcester sold her late husband's sermons through one—some pursued their own sales. Seth Arnold, for example, helped distribute his *Family Choir.* While waiting for eight hundred copies to be bound, he finalized arrangements with one informal "wholesaler" (and cocompiler): "Rev. Mr. Colman is to take one hundred at cost viz. $8.39 Mr. C[olman] will send 100 copies to Boston." After returning home from the binder with fifty copies of his book in hand, he "Left 19 copies with Mr. Kingsbury for sale, and left 12 copies for the Rev. Mr. Burnham, to be sent to him" by Kingsbury. Arnold had the same arrangement for his first book, *Intellectual Housekeeper.* While the printer advertised and apparently distributed the book locally, he left bundles with neighbors: "12 copies of the In. House K. at Mr. Ansel Glover's ... 3 D[itt]o. with Maj. Warner—3 D[itt]o. with Mrs. Doct. Hatch." Due to sluggish sales, he also "Took back 6 Intellectual House Keepers from Bellows Falls Book Store."[21] Overall, Arnold had to track how many copies remained on the market, where they were at any given moment, and whether he or some middleman had placed them there.

Amateurs like Arnold were joined by authors of greater repute concerned with selling and publicizing their books. "The celebrated Mr Audubon called to solicit my subscription to his Octavo Edition of his Ornithology—... the price being a *hundred dollars* for the work!" John Park winced, concerning a reduced-sized version of *Birds of America.* And there were those authors who, no matter how much their publishers did to distribute their works, always had to put in their two cents. "Munroe did not seem to me to be doing quite so much as he might to get my book into circulation," author and politician Alexander Hill Everett griped to his nephew. He went on to recommend an advertising ploy: "Would it not be well to have some placards placed at the windows of the shops, where it is sold, and perhaps have it advertised a little more freely? I should like to get rid of these as soon as possible and prepare for another enlarged edition in two volumes."[22] Thus, authors could exert much effort and worry to help market their publications.

Unlike marketing by authors or agents who saw their books as commodities, informal sales by book owners often meant parting with long-held, cherished possessions. This made setting prices difficult, especially given market fluctuations. A valued and beloved book could be virtually worthless on the open market. To buffer themselves from such market realities, some folks enlisted professional auctioneers, but public auctions connoted private need of cash and, perhaps, a life of squandering. "The late Wm. Holmes' library & plate sold to day at auction" because his "estate is insolvent," one lawyer grimaced, adding that "he offered to young people a striking example of the injudiciousness of neglecting their regular profession for political life." Perhaps fear of exposure explains why a financially strapped John Park quietly arranged for a private sale of his magazine collection, but not before asking a bookseller's estimate of its worth. "I write to Messrs Little and Brown, to ascertain the market price of the Edinburgh Review, which Mr [D]owley talks of buying of me," he recorded. Had Park not gone armed with the estimate into negotiating the sale, social sense may have blinded the parties to the fair market price. With copies of the *Edinburgh*, added to his run of copies of the Washington *Globe*, fetching 150 dollars from Dowley, an emotionally wrought Park weighed the pros and cons: "I feel very unwilling to part with [the *Edinburgh Reviews*]; but my dividends have been so much curtailed by the mismanagement of Banks, that I must raise the wind, somehow, the approaching season, to meet my unavoidable disbursements." Embarrassing "Disgrace of Price" thus mingled with a sense of irrecoverable loss. Estate sales could be particularly trying for survivors seeing traces of loved ones in their books. "[A] most painful day—clothing all sold except books," one destitute widow wrote. The next morning the auction resumed: "I was very busy until the sale commenced—at 10, of the Books." With these last mementos of her loved one gone, she finally realized her home was empty, seeing "a desolate house which for many years has been associated with every thing delightful to me, only 5 weeks to day since our dear friend was laid in his last resting place." The departure of the books they shared signaled the cessation of intimate ties. For one industrialist the quick, cheap sale of remaining copies of his own *Philosophy of the Mechanics of Nature* to its New York printer-bookseller symbolized his financial calamity after the Panic of 1857. "This will close the account of printing this book," he penned resignedly, "with a loss of about $150 besides years of laborious research."[23] By his reckoning, he lost more in years spent than in dollars and cents.

Of course, not all sales grew from deprivation, for ephemeral reading material could quickly pile up in useless, troublesome heaps. In her move from Lowell to Concord, Harriet Robinson disposed of some periodicals through a former fellow millworker. "Harriet Curtis was over the other day[;] she has sold Gody & Grahams Magazine for me for four dollars," Robinson explained, observing, "I had rather sell those magazines we dont care to keep for the money than to have a house full of old trash it is so difficult to move." Like her, Moses Adams retained little sentimental value for the "lot of old newspapers, found in the garret" that he sold in adolescence "to procure raisors & shave myself." And one editor recalled that in his youth in rural Connecticut, he gladly parted with his *Book of Common Prayer* which "had no credit in our family, or in any other family in the town"; it was "exchanged with a peddler for two pamphlets,—Addison's Cato, and a New-Year's Sermon."[24]

Personal sellers balanced the scales between emotional attachment and economic gain, using their own life stories as a counterpoise— stories that ultimately determined the value of the literature they owned, kept, or determined to sell. Keenly aware of these stories, purchasers likewise weighed heavily the cost to sellers. "Received a note from Dr [Linus Pierpont] Brockett asking me to call his boarding place for some books which he had laid out for me in payment of a bill in part," a Hartford businessman reported of a failing local editor. "I complied with his request but almost regretted that I had done so when I saw the distress of Mrs. Brockett who had just seen McKennedy the keeper of the jail to which her husband had just been consigned for want of bail," the purchaser went on; "I took his books & saying what I could to comfort Mrs. B."[25] Bartering away books, in this case, hardly cleared Brockett of his poverty or freed him from prison, but it certainly indicted this creditor as an unwitting agent in a human tragedy involving the "sale" of precious possessions.

Far rarer than the many sad or desperate circumstances that made people temporary agents of distribution were instances of would-be businessmen as literary retailers. Relatively few folks ventured beyond barter or amateur sales into specialized literary shopkeeping (books and periodicals, of course, were then sold in general stores or as sidelines). After all, there were only 1,720 booksellers among the 23 million Americans the 1850 U.S. census counted. Booksellers moved in and out of the business more rapidly than perhaps even amateur authors, for owning a bookstore was an exceedingly risky venture. As we have noted in the book's introduction, Boston bookstores in the 1840s lasted on average only over a year, whereas three decades earlier the expected duration was nearly eleven years; in the 1830s, it was just over four. With diminishing odds like these, those who gambled knew well what they were in for. In order to keep afloat, booksellers had to move more and more merchandise, as industry-wide profit margins narrowed due to increased production. Having to sell ever more was difficult because of the sociabilities—not necessarily of the kind yielding sales—that bookstores traditionally encouraged. There is little wonder that when one accountant "entered into the Book business with brothers Albert and Charles" he did so with eyes open. "I do not expect to reap much pecuniary advantage from this arrangement myself," he explained of a store in tiny Sharon, Massachusetts, "but if it will make a profitable business for A.[lbert] H.[ixon] I am content." Nearly three weeks later the brothers were leaving "cases of books" in Boston "in a commission store for sale"—a bad sign indicating an insufficient local market for their inventory. Eventually Hixon and his brothers gave up bookselling for the shoe business.[26]

Regardless of their chances for success, some booksellers were simply happy to pass time among an abundance of books and to greet the local celebrities and amateur literati discussing publishing trends and contemporary issues. Such were the aspirations of many young men attracted to the trade. One of these was Amos Armsby, a sickly, weak-eyed youth, but an avid reader and library patron, who longed against all odds to work in a major bookselling center. "I have some hope of getting a chance in a Book store in Boston 79 Cornhill," he averred. Those who did get such positions often performed physical labor rather than intellectual work much to their chagrin. "I did not accomplish very much to day[;] opened boxes from Philadelphia containing libraries and miscellaneous works," a clerk complained after an evening in his father's shop.[27] For lowly clerks, at least, bookselling became enough like any other business that the pleasure of laboring among great literary works quickly faded.

Thus far print distribution has been considered from the viewpoint of people roaming through the literary marketplace as temporary agents, sometime salespersons, and short-term bookshop proprietors. People outside the trade often confronted the same issues as their employed counterparts, such as when selling literary possessions under pressing circumstances. For distributors, low pay, often frustrating bookkeeping, and physically burdensome travel or labor were the most obvious liabilities. Although other occupations had similar—indeed, greater—problems, none perhaps were as irascible as those generated by an industry proffering timelessly valuable literary products, but that itself was one of the most unstable and highly capitalized.[28] Despite its contradictions, the local literary marketplace retained a semblance of social sense, and at best, it nourished social intercourse within the distribution networks established between agent and subscriber, salesperson and purchaser. But did people outside the trade view sites of literary distribution and dissemination through the lens of literary dollars or social sense?

VISITING PLACES OF DISTRIBUTION AND DISSEMINATION

The brisk circulation of literature can be most clearly glimpsed in bookstores, popular periodical depots, and libraries where books, pamphlets, and magazines went from shelves to readers' hands at an often frenetic pace. Perhaps no sites were greater expressions of the marketplace, for both the commercial outlets and the libraries showcased the wide variety of goods available due to publishing's industrialization. In fact, visitors to different literary centers were often so fascinated by mechanized production and its fruits that they toured publishing factories.[29] As we will see, however, few diarists and letter writers celebrated literary venues as palaces of consumption, but instead managed to view them as extensions of friendship, kinship, and community networks.

Bookstores

When Elizabeth Pierce, a minister's daughter, traveled from Brookline, Massachusetts, to Concord, New Hampshire, she unexpectedly passed a minor monument to distribution, a bookshop she had seen only in an illustration. "We reached the hotel in Concord ... at 11 A.M.," she told her diary, "on looking from the window recognized immediately the bookstore of John F. Brown, with wh. I had long been familiar, as engraven upon the cover of my pocket Almanack" (see fig. 4.2). She duly noted the reunion: "It seemed like an old friend, & the state-house near it, as represented in the print."[30] Seen every time she used her almanac, the bookstore's two-dimensional image had come to life in three dimensions, as an "old friend" inhabiting her social networks.

Bookstores clearly were more than establishments of selling. Although customers might rate each shop's range, scope, or unusual holdings, they emphasized social aspects over purchases. Bookstore shopping hardly filled even a line or two in most diaries or letters. More likely, record keepers mentioned reading in these venues—not

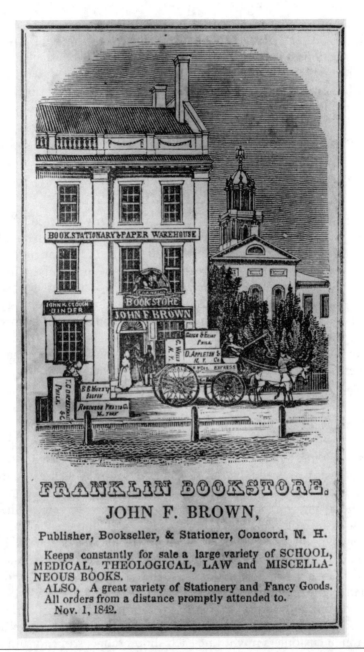

Fig. 4.2 One minister's daughter cherished this almanac cover engraving and the bookstore it represented. *Source:* Engraving of "Franklin Bookstore," *Brown's Almanack, Pocket Memorandum and Account Book, 1844* (Concord, N.H.: J.F. Brown, 1843), courtesy American Antiquarian Society.

always as a prelude to buying—or looking at portraits on the walls. Merely visiting a bookstore might mark a return to normal social circulation after seclusion. "For the first time in a long while," John Park noted with relief after a long disability, "I walk out as far as Tucker's, the bookseller's." One might even get inoculated against smallpox at rural bookstores. Some stores housed circulating libraries that spawned longstanding relationships between borrowers and shopkeepers. Bookstores were places where bundles sent by loved ones at a distance might be picked up; familial and social associations filled shops through the very packages sent and the conversations retrieving them elicited. Bookstores' myriad social connotations gave diarists and correspondents ample food for rumination.[31]

If just seeing bookstores conjured good feelings, as it did for Park and Pierce, then there is little wonder that many visitors sketched in diaries and letters the amiable interactions occurring in them. Retail outlets could serve by accident or intention as meeting grounds leading to subsequent social activity. "[O]n my way home went into Orrins shop to get some ink," a schoolteacher reported one evening after work, having spotted her fiancé "B[.] there." He "went home with me and I read awhile aloud," she continued. At bookstores, public as well as social spaces, one might expect to bump into acquaintances. Accordingly, perhaps, diarists recorded bookstore rendezvous in more detail than their purchases. A Lowell clerk, for one, bought a periodical containing the popular poem "Nothing to Wear" and "saw Miss Nichols at Walkins Book Store." A grain dealer "Met Henry [T]erry & Mr E R Root at [G]eers Book store" in Hartford while purchasing a volume on the politician and lawyer Rufus Choate. A widow took her son out for an evening of social calling that began in a Cambridge bookstore: "At home 'till 4 oclk, then Henry & I went to Mr Arnold's bookstore met Aunt Mary W. and I went into Jacob's. [A]fter that to G'pa Edes."[32] These meetings were immortalized in diaries alongside the titles bought as if both activities were one and the same.

Beyond these casual encounters, students, lawyers, and book tradespeople habituated bookstores to talk about professional issues, authorship, or other literary matters, further backgrounding book buying. Indeed, they often prearranged meetings with colleagues there, though they also chanced running into acquaintances. As a law student, Mellen Chamberlain arranged to converse "with Joseph Walker a student from this town" Hanover, New Hampshire, "at Mr Brown's Bookstore." After he moved to Cambridge, his routine bookstore-hopping in downtown Boston connected him with colleagues and professors. Likewise, Salem lawyer Augustus Dodge Rogers came upon acquaintances at various local venues; "stop in at F. Putnam's Book Store," a characteristic entry read, "chat with H.[enry] Wheatland," a local physician. Rogers fortuitously met strangers sharing similar interests. "Talking this eve.g., with a Mr. Wallis of Beverly at Mr. Whipples bookstore about Dr. Fisher's wife Rebecca Stanford," he remarked on one such occasion. The encounter helped Rogers gather information about his family for his genealogy in progress. Of course, professional sociabilities could be guarded insofar as a competitive spirit pervaded them. "Was with Harris at the Bookstores this morning & had considerable conversation with him about antiquities, autographs &c. &c.," Mellen Chamberlain, a diehard autograph hound noted. "He has made some acquisitions of late," he continued, "but seems inclined to keep his knowledge to himself, which is well enough among collectors." Yet the conversation remained, after all, "considerable."[33] By these lights, professional activity buzzed within bookstores, where the business of buying and selling provided a mere backdrop for forging and maintaining relationships.

Customers' sociable discussion could entertain eavesdroppers. Augustus Rogers described hearing a conversation at Whipples: "F. Peabody comes in talks with Dr. Robinson, concerning Prof. [Benjamin] Peirce's discovery at Cambridge, that the planet supposed to have been discovered by [Urbain] le Verrier is not the one he took it for but was discovered by accident. [T]his was the paper read before the Am. Acad. of Arts & Sciences." Chats about professional squabbles, literary issues, and legendary figures could be overshadowed by sensational newspaper stories. In December 1849 Rogers tapped into ongoing buzz at Putnam's about the slaying in Boston of Dr. George Parkman allegedly by Professor John White Webster. "Stop at Dr. F. Eben Putnam, S.G. Wheatland there &c. talking over murder, all absorbing topic!" the lawyer penned with perhaps more interest in the story as a cultural phenomenon than as a legal one, for the trial was a frequently recorded news item in a wide array of local letters and diaries.[34]

Such storytelling extended even to booksellers, who regaled (or assailed) visitors having time to spare and a willing ear to lend. Cyrus Bradley, sojourning in Baltimore, Maryland, "walked to the Book Store of Jos. Cushing & Sons," and listened to "shop talk" by the former "publisher of the... Farmer's Cabinet, at Amherst, N.H." The man held forth on topics ranging from publication and sales of Henry Marie Brackenridge's history of the War of 1812, to tittle-tattle about Parson Weems, the famous peddler and author of the life of George Washington. As Bradley paraphrased what he heard, "Seeing the old gentleman

[Weems] in his store one day, searching among his small books and pamphlets, he asked him what he wanted. 'Oh, I want some anecdotes.' 'Anecdotes! what do you want of anecdotes?' 'Oh sir, I am writing a Life and I want to get some anecdotes for it.' 'But do you publish these anecdotes as matters of fact?' 'Oh yes sir, if you only work 'em in right, they'll do just as well.'"[35] A tall story told on a long afternoon made the day pass pleasantly for this shopkeeper and his customer.

Diarists also jotted down visits to new, unusual, or foreign bookstores as important stops along their road through life. "We took a peep into Sabins new building—a new bookstore," a Rhode Islander noted, adding that her sister "Sarah bought a new Bible yesterday." "At Mr. Drake's Antiquarian Bookstore," Cyrus Bradley recorded while in Boston, "I saw great quantities of curious, valuable & antique books." One lawyer's daughter visiting Philadelphia confessed that, despite her disapproval of "browsing," she "spent as much as an hour in a most fascinating German and French book store."[36] It was the novelty that elicited comment, not the briskness of trade or the availability of titles just asking to be purchased.

Rarer than records of bookstore visits were those of book tradespeople yet even these brimmed with interpersonal associations. An entry in an 1851 Dublin travel diary reads, "We went into Mr. McGlashan's, the bookseller … , who has made Papa so many presents." In the same diarist's 1849 volume even a book agent received special mention: "Mr. Davis came in. … He brought in Mr. Stevens, a cousin of Nat Hubbard's[,] who lives abroad, and purchases books for American libraries." Of course, traveling booksellers called upon local writers. One literary entrepreneur passing through Portland went to see its well-known historian, who shared a passion for rare books and who later described the visit, writing, "C[harles] B. Norton the historical & antiquarian bookseller in New York called on me: took him to the Athenaeum &c & to ride." On their day together, the two, like so many contemporaries, created social bonds while visiting a literary site, where the cash nexus could easily slip out of mind.[37]

Libraries

It is not surprising that the two men visited the Portland Athenaeum, one of the city's most prestigious institutions. Libraries naturally aroused deep curiosity among bookmen like Norton, but also among common travelers. Even more than bookstores as distribution points, unusual or renowned libraries as sites of dissemination captured sojourners' attention. If they received special introductions, they could stroll through reading rooms and, rarely, the stacks—easy public library access and self-retrievals for the most part awaited the future. When a Wesleyan University student, for example, "[v]isited Washington Colle[ge]" in Hartford, he recorded that he was "introduced into the Library-Cabinet and Society Rooms." The impressions that visitors registered upon seeing libraries ranged from mere mentions to more complex description of holdings or of social interactions with librarians or other visitors. But both the terse note and the elaboration reflected similar degrees of engrossment. For one poor itinerant minister, the "view of m[i]nerals, ...paintings and libraries" he took in while on a trip to Dartmouth College was a special, perhaps once-in-a-lifetime event, although marked by few words. Lengthier descriptions could reveal livelier scenes, as in one farm woman's account of her visit to the Maine State Capitol and Library with an elderly new acquaintance: "found my companion very bookish, & of my own taste. We soon forgot our company in a Vol. of English History reading to each other alternately & making comments." "[W]e soon again forgot everything but Burns—each pointing out favorite passages & a most delightful time we had," she continued, concluding, "It was well that he is an old grey headed man with a family, for we were getting quite smitten."[38] For every complex entry like this there are doubtless dozens of terse ones that only hint at libraries' rich social life.

Travelers too busy to write account for many of the short entries. Yet they reveal that certain famous libraries were on sightseers' mental maps of literary sites. A trip to New York, for example, cried out for at least a stop at the grandiose Astor Library or Clinton Hall, the preferred site of one newlywed Congregationalist minister who went into "the various departments of Sub[scriptio]n Room—Library—Reading Room & Athenaeum." In Providence "the Atheneum" caught Mellen Chamberlain's attention on a business trip; he wrote that while there "a student kindly showed me the society libraries." The Boston Public Library, novel for its time "in that you can get the books free gratus," in the words of a contemporary, was on many tourists' lists. Native pride in another fine repository moved a Bostonian to introduce a visiting Englishman "at the Boston Athenæum, the best Library in New England next to that of Harvard College, having a complete Reading Room attached"—few libraries had these rooms as of yet. To see the Library of Congress "into which none are admitted without an introduction," one fourteen-year-old Hartfordite probably had to summon her uncle's acquaintance with Kentucky Senator Henry Clay. Worcester visitors with local connections might trek down to the American Antiquarian Society which was, according to one Bostonian's diary, "well worth visiting." John Park, a member, took guests from Providence to "every room" of Antiquarian Hall, an unusual privilege for outsiders. Curiously, visitors remarked upon "this beautiful town," or its "pure" air, as well as the library's "numberless ancient things" or its "collection of newspapers ... the most valuable probably in the country."[39] This meant use value rather than monetary worth, for runs of old newspapers then brought exceedingly low prices.

Tourists gravitated to great libraries just to be near the vast and precious collections, and even sometimes to peruse their volumes. A new addition to the "very valuable collection" at the Harvard College Library "recently selected in Europe" impressed John Park, who also called "the binding of the books, splendid." Alongside *splendid*, the term *curious* was regularly applied to library collections, for they commonly housed unusual objects other than books. One Oxford traveler pointed out the "very curious things, among others some specimens of the Indian paper painting from Mexico," at the Bodleian Library. A Bostonian reported seeing while at the American Antiquarian Society a collection of state historical and financial "manuscripts, many of wh. are very curious." An amble through the Library of Congress resulted in the following entry: "We saw here a great many curiosities—consisting of portraits, medals, coins, books, & c." Similarly, Cyrus Bradley at the "rooms of the Mass. Hist. Society," wondered at the "great & valuable collection of curiosities... relating to the history of New England," including "[t]he department of Indian implements [which] is particularly valuable."[40] Again, such items had little market value, though there was abundant social capital in seeing them.

Besides exulting in curiosities, visitors were awed with plentitude. At the Maine State Library, a rural schoolteacher and his father "enjoy[ed] a rich treat from gazing at the engravings which we found there in abundance." Of course, unimaginable numbers of volumes also contributed to an overwhelming sense of plenty. The "10,000 vols" at the "Library of the [Andover] Theological Institution" and the "16000 vols." at the Charleston, South Carolina, social library amazed two visitors. Even the almanacs that some people used as their diaries reinforced such numerating, such as one drug merchant's 1842 *Lowell Almanac*, which reported that the Middlesex Mechanics Association "contains upwards of 2500 volumes. In the cabinet are about 4000 specimens."[41] Americans clearly approached literary institutions with abacus in hand.

This penchant did not extend to the institution's capitalization. Only one diarist or letter writer, a Hartford businessman, appraised a library's financial base, that of New York's Astor Library, which he visited in April 1860. He recorded that it was "Said to have cost about $600,000 [with an] Income [of] about 15,00[0] per annum," but then quickly added, "Free to all." For him, the figures rhetorically emphasized that John Jacob Astor expressly endowed the library for the public as a monument to beneficence more than wealth. This impression is underscored by the fact that similar reduction to the bottom line was sometimes used to judge the success of mass efforts at literary benevolence. One peddling tinsmith attending an 1860 "great Library Festival" in Springfield, Massachusetts, weighed the fundraising results in literary dollars: "got (1200) twelve hundred dollars," he recorded, proud of his city's generous donors; "600, this day," he wrote on the next.[42] People apparently only fixated upon such sums when they yielded a greater social benefit.

Quantitative records of libraries had qualitative counterparts that stressed the human dimension. Patrons might characterize librarians as either "polite, affable, and very pleasant," "very gentlemanly & accomplished," or "old [and] limping"—if indeed they got a chance to meet them at all.[43] Librarians, though not unappreciated, were often invisible to tourists who interacted mainly with the architecture, public exhibits, and abstract numbers of mostly inaccessible volumes. Much of the social life within prestigious libraries was simply not on display to passers-by restricted to certain areas. But unlike famous authors' homes, libraries were not envisioned as shrines of living or once-living celebrities, and so tourists seldom imagined the faces behind funding, collecting, or cataloging. Instead, the vast and rare holdings—and the beneficent social relations of literature they represented—were the main attractions.

LIBRARIANS: FROM SOCIAL SENSE TO SOCIAL SERVICE

However much extensive library collections awed visitors, the allure of many books quickly wore thin for librarians themselves—the more books, the more need for control over holdings. Ungoverned by modern professional standards of cataloging, purchasing, storage, and classification, libraries greatly differed from one another and remained relatively disorderly. Few patrons desired standards anyhow, for they viewed libraries as but extensions of usually haphazard private lending and borrowing. With one's own bookshelves in casual disarray, who needed finer regulation within institutions? Paid librarians, too, awaited professionalization, for, like their unpaid home-based counterparts, they performed sundry tasks that required skillful juggling and often exhausting labor—sometimes added to other occupational roles as teachers, ministers, or officeholders. Both paid and home librarians collected, preserved, arranged, cataloged, retrieved, and circulated printed material. The difference, of course, was that overseeing one's own collections was usually a labor of love (the lending and borrowing testified to a rich social life), whereas professional librarianship was an underpaid job serving mostly clueless strangers or snippy regular patrons.[44] The material deprivations, added to overwork, tension, and emotional strain, all suggest how undervalued paid librarianship was in a society in which nonprofessional literary dissemination was the norm.

Demands upon Librarians

Not surprisingly, the pressures caused many librarians to resign, including Horace Davis, who served only about a year at the San Francisco Mercantile Library Association, or William B. Sewall, who lasted somewhat longer at the Portland Athenaeum. Of course, the position usually provided only part-time employment and, even if it did more than that, the pay was insubstantial. Low salaries only further discouraged longstanding job commitment. For example, Sewall, a businessman from Hallowell, Maine, earned only fifty dollars for his "Salary as Librarian for 1825," at a time of the dollar-a-day workingman's wage. Even at Harvard University's more advanced law library librarians still faced problems inherent in performing an ill-defined role, including a salary that barely supported expenses, let alone a meager diet of bread and water, in one case.[45]

Despite librarianship's drawbacks, there were still people desperate enough to seek the job.[46] One of these was Mellen Chamberlain, then an aspiring law student from a rural New Hampshire family with scant means for funding his education. Hoping to improve his lot in life, he sent his "application for the Librarianship of Harvard Law School" in January 1846, while reading law in Brattleboro, Vermont, and tutoring in Greek and Latin on the side. By October, he was preparing to move to Cambridge, to take his new position, and to attend Simon Greenleaf's and William Kent's lectures at Harvard. By January 1847, he was working in the library under the tutelage of Greenleaf, who had shouldered principal responsibility for making Dane Hall's collection the nation's premier reference resource for law by 1846.[47]

The initial hurdle facing Chamberlain and other neophytes was simply figuring out where the books were and, when they were returned, where they belonged—a real problem for the Harvardian drowning in a collection of over 12,000 items. One of the first things he did was to "Look ... over the Library somewhat ... to understand the arrangement of the books." Absent any standard classification system, he had to master the library's idiosyncratic shelf organization, the incoherence of which resulted from his predecessors' clashing schemes of order and hasty follies of attribution (evidently, the published catalog little helped him). Harvard was not unique in this; many librarians assumed that a book's frontispiece or spine title was enough to determine its place on the shelf. "Very many look no farther than the title page, and hence make as wrong classifications as did the learned librarian who placed Burton's Anatomy of Melancholy among works of Surgery!" Cyrus Bradley complained while searching for books at Dartmouth College to bring home during winter break. Given the degrees of variation in genre attribution, looking for a book was probably more guesswork than science. To make matters worse, many libraries had no standard catalogs unless someone took it upon themselves to write one by hand—a painstaking and time consuming task. William B. Sewall spent about a month "preparing catalogue of Athen. Lib.[rary]."[48] So, without such lists, one could not even be sure what was in the library short of scanning the shelves to decode the organization.

After initiating himself, Chamberlain wore various hats in his role as librarian, including the laborious job of compiling a shelf list catalog. On January 11, 1847, he "took charge of the return books while Mr Stone was employed on the Large Library." Two days later he was knowledgeable enough to retrieve material from the stacks; he reported that he "worked hard in the Library delivering books for the first time under my administration." Settling into the job, he performed different functions, some even on a single day. On one occasion he explained, "I was deeply immersed in business. Making a shelf catalogue & receiving books and closing accounts with students." At any time, illustrious visitors could drop in or demand attention. "Message from the President that he & Dr Walker would come to the Library at half past eleven," he once noted. "They did so & I had the pleasure of some very pleasant conversation with Mr. [Edward] Everett [the president] about books & c." On another day, "Dr. [Joseph Green] Cogswell came out," Chamberlain recorded, "and I talked with him about old pamphlets and catalogues."

In receiving callers he listened to suggestions for acquisitions or accepted donations. When it came to purchasing new books, he probably trudged over to Boston's bookstores, like Little and Brown's and Thomas O.H.P. Burnham's, to order books and pick up bundles. It comes as no surprise that he griped only a month after beginning his job, "These days have done little or nothing more than to work hard in the Library daytime and read evenings. Have hardly stepped out of doors."[49]

The most tiring tasks for him and others who performed library work was fetching or returning books to shelves, rearranging them as new titles came in, and the periodic inspection and inventory of the holdings, which required removing each volume from the shelf, looking it over carefully for mildew or other rot, and, reshelving it. Books, of course, are heavy items and when carried up and down ladders they seem to become all the weightier. Chamberlain faced the added problem that so many law books were huge tomes. "Tired & dusty from handling books all day, shall be pleased when this work is over," he declared at the start of a biannual inspection. The next day the job was done, for a while at least, and he rejoiced, "Worked hard on the Library this morning & finished all that is to be done for six months in the way of arranging books." This feeling was also captured by Elizabeth Dwight Cabot concerning her husband's "examination of the books" at the Boston Athenaeum: "Elliot has been on a ladder at the Athenæum all the week & has gone over every book in it," she remarked with but little sympathy; "Tonight he is what the servants call 'through,' which is jolly, & he feels very much as females do when they have overhauled their closets & piece-bags only he doesn't know it." Indeed, women did know what it felt like to haul books around like clothing and household items, for the task of "arranging" home library books—"no slight job," according to one textile magnate's daughter—was usually theirs. Both housework and paid librarianship connoted similar, essential, and yet devalued services.[50]

Librarianship as Service

While the physical labor of librarianship—whether amateur or professional—was demanding, the occupation, like housewifery, was also emotionally trying. Being sequestered for hours at a time made Chamberlain lonely: "Quite a relief to have some company—students in for books." Yet, conversely, too many demanding patrons could vex librarians. A librarian only known as "X" valued his precious solitude in an essay appropriately entitled "Miseries of a Librarian." People "imagine his 'miseries' to be comprehended in sitting behind a counter, dozing over plays tossing out novels," the disgruntled "X" complained. He corrected this misapprehension: "One of his greatest 'miseries' is the trouble of listening to the idle babble of visitors." He explained, "No one can step into the Library, without boring him with tedious harangues, unmeaning questions, uninteresting descriptions, and somniferous criticisms." If the visitors were not strangers but welcome friends and family, would the "babble" be seen as idle?—perhaps the patrons were only extending the literary sociabilities they engaged in at home. Given their devaluation, librarians would not benefit from heavy foot traffic, for it was but one short step from providing a service to being seen as a servant abused by incessant demands: "It is almost impossible to convince them that such and such books are NOT IN, when they pretend to see them on the shelf." The exasperated librarian continued: "The rogues *will not* be persuaded, and often go out of the shop as snappingly as mudturtles out of their own shells!" "X" went on to identify other job-related interpersonal "miseries," including "the extreme difficulty of collecting the four-pences" or fines, to "the impossibility of suiting the palates of all readers at all times," to "the continual loss and vexation ... from customers' losing and abusing his volumes." All in all, "X" conceded that the duties "render[ed] his life as uncomfortable as that of a short-tailed horse in fly-time."[51] In the world of paid librarianship social sense eroded, as formerly sociable interactions over home-based book borrowing and lending reduced to mere tongue wagging, money exchange, and complaints.

For all its "miseries," however, librarianship, even as voluntary work, could satisfy the desire to be of service while learning valuable skills, especially for people whose labor was undervalued anyway. This might include earnest adolescents; "I took care of the Library books this morning, having been desired to do so by the Librarian," one fourteen-year-old Sunday School student registered, proud of his responsibilities. Librarianship also provided intellectual labor in a time when most people still worked with their hands. This was especially true for women, with limited options beyond schoolteaching for nonmanual occupations. One who left the classroom for the stacks was Maria Mitchell, the famed Nantucket astronomer; she profited by her term as "Librarian of their Athenæum or Lyceum," according to John Park, who once met her, and from the "reading and reflection" that could attend the job, if there were not too many patrons. In that she gave some "direction" to the reading of "the young people in the town," her interventions foreshadowed later librarians' commitment to social service. Librarianship could empower women by providing them with paid employment, time to read, and community influence. For Mitchell, her influence carried vestiges of social sense. "Her visitors in the afternoon were elderly men of leisure, who enjoyed talking with so bright a girl on their favorite hobbies," her biographer noted, adding, "at the library ... , the young girls made her their confidante and went to her for sympathy and advice. The boys, as they grew up, and went away to sea ... made a point, when they returned ..., of coming to tell their experiences to such a sympathetic listener."[52]

For most librarians, however, the job less frequently accommodated social sense than provoked the "miseries" set out by "X." In this regard, paid disseminators like librarians held much in common with paid distributors treated badly at the hands of their prospective customers. Unlike agents' relationship to their customers as but a point in the cash flow between publishers and their market, librarians' relationship to users was that of a node in the circuit of literary dissemination outside of direct sales. Sellers' miseries emerged from their identification with the commercial market of literary dollars, but librarians' miseries were due to providing remunerated service in a society that held it in such contempt that even servants demanded to be called "help." Ironically, then, librarians' meager literary dollars relegated them to a lower status than if they remained unpaid disseminators. Only with the growth of professional librarianship later in the century, as everyday home-based practices gave way to institution-based procedures, would the miseries at least be better compensated, if not entirely alleviated.[53]

TEACHERS: FROM SOCIAL SERVICE TO PROFESSIONALISM

The paltry number of librarians, too small and undifferentiated for the 1850 census even to grant them their own category, paled before those of the largest single type of paid literary disseminators—schoolteachers—of which there were 105,858 at midcentury. Not surprisingly, teachers' professionalization had advanced beyond social service well ahead of librarians'. Teacher training colleges (i.e., "Normal Schools") appeared after 1838, teacher institutes were held regularly, and specialized journals abounded among the many hallmarks of professionalization. An important component of early Normal School training and an expectation of the many yet-untrained teachers was elocution, recitation, reading aloud, and teaching students to do so. Seldom thought of today as paid disseminators of texts, teachers then actually spent much of their classroom time reading printed texts aloud. Oral reading was sometimes the only way a particular book reached students who could not otherwise afford to buy it. Teachers were, in this sense, disseminating middlepersons between publishers and "consumers" (their students, or parents who paid tuition, taxes, or both). Like other folk in the line of fire between the market and the community, teachers often passed through the profession quickly and went on to either marry or seek other employment.[54]

Demands upon Teachers

Nascent professionalization did not help ease demands upon teachers. Though young men like Mellen Chamberlain at some time in their lives taught primary school, the task fell increasingly to women. In fact, it became the job that working unmarried women were most likely to perform, even though they could make higher wages (up to eighty cents a day) in the textile mills. One Maine teacher, for example, reported in 1841 that she was "paid ... $70 for my 20 weeks teaching," which comes out to about fifty-eight cents a day. And the work was far from steady since unpaid vacations and long intersessions punctuated the academic year. Numerous reasons account for the low pay, including, of course, taxpayers' perennial reluctance to fund education, but certainly one was that the schoolroom existed not as a forum for formal adult public sociability, like the lecture hall, but rather as an adjunct to informal socialization in homes and neighborhoods where group reading and fundamental instruction of children were commonplace and without cost. Thus, schoolteachers faced a problem similar to most other literary disseminators: Why pay for what you can get for free? The very value of highly paid lecturers, as we will see, was that they offered expertise that most people lacked, whereas schoolteachers generally provided to children a similar service to that which parents, older siblings, other relatives, or neighbors were capable of giving. Such informal instruction was only supplemented by schools, for even in Massachusetts, the most advanced state educationally, public school students attended only on average 60.6 days in 1840.[55]

As with many disseminators, teachers saw market needs clash with sociability. Poor educational funding meant miserable student-teacher ratios that strained congeniality. "O the trials a teacher has to endure!" moaned one rural Maine schoolteacher charged with seventy students. Attending to the needs of a diverse student body assembled under one roof while fostering a sociable atmosphere was another problem. One teacher, "metamorphosed from 'chief cook & bottle washer,' besides chambermaid & nurse, into pedagogue in 'less than no time,'" tried her best to juggle "teaching six footers the abstruce[*sic*] mysteries of Cube Root, & all the intermediate heights & ages from 23 down to the Abc-darian ..., thro' all the various branches of education that 40 scholars may be supposed to be engaged in." With large classes composed of various age and educational levels, discipline problems erupted, breaking down in-class sociable exchanges. "This constant warfare is crushing, killing me," Charlotte Forten complained after a "hard day at school." As one witness to a classroom stabbing attempt philosophized, "Love of teaching varies as the conduct of the scholars is." Yet teachers, like other disseminators motivated by a higher purpose, regarded their social mission as sacred. "I have felt keenly the responsibility which rests upon me—standing in place of teacher over so many immortal minds," one confessed. Indeed, a desire to "'teach young ideas how to shoot'" in "the old hall of literature," the classroom, motivated many teachers to at least give the vocation a try before inevitably moving on.[56] But as idealistic as they were, teachers understood well the keen difference between dissemination for its own sake versus dissemination as one's employment. For example, reading aloud within homes was usually warmly appreciated, while doing so in the classroom could meet with rebuke, even violence. Unconditional love of literature strained to its breaking point under these circumstances of seeming social chaos.

Paid Oral Dissemination

When schoolteachers and their Sunday school counterparts read aloud to their students on a regular basis, they most often read published works instead of original compositions—these were left primarily to the students. Because teachers, sometimes in lieu of academic texts, read the latest fiction, poetry, or other belles lettres, the line between "reading" (actually, students' listening) for pleasure and studying blurred. Works of these types might as likely be heard read aloud at home. In outlying areas, especially, teachers as paid oral disseminators were—with, perhaps, ministers—the chief agents bringing the greater world of letters to local ears.

It is not surprising, then, that reading aloud and teaching merged in instructors' minds. It was so implicated in pedagogy that one "normalite" bemoaned its excessive practice as detrimental to extemporaneous instruction: "I think it is a fault for a teacher to read much to his class." She concluded rather that the teacher's "intellectual knowledge acquired from books should be so digested and so moulded in his mind that he can give out this knowledge as it originated in himself and had

partaken of his spirit." Normal School instructors nevertheless sometimes insisted that reading aloud facilitated learning rather than
detracted from it. "Mr. Rowe remarked this morning on the importance of a teacher being a good reader," one student noted in her diary
while enrolled in Westfield Normal School. Lexington Normal School
principal Cyrus Pierce emphasized oral reading skills for his teachers;
a student transcribed one of his lessons on reading, which highlighted
elocution and comprehension. "'You can all improve the power,
compass and strength of your voice!'" he enjoined, "'You can be more
articulate in your words, and protract these more.'" No matter how well
said, the words could only come alive if the teacher grasped the author's
meaning: "'If you *do not* understand them, it will beget in you this
habit; that of disliking the author himself, and your interest will gradually decrease; on the other hand if you *do* comprehend the meaning of
the author ..., [he] will become more and [more] interesting to you as
you proceed; it is like a cloudy and a bright sunshiny day; it involves an
important part of mental discipline.'" Learning to be good readers thus
meant excellent comprehension as well as oral communication skills.
Some teachers availed themselves of elocution lectures geared toward
the profession—"illustrations of the manner in which reading in
schools & elsewhere should be conducted," one neophyte attending a
Teacher's Institute called them. But, certainly, students contemplating
careers as teachers got enough experience in the Normal School classroom, where they read aloud daily, if not from the Bible or hymnals,
then from the classics or recent works, including "The Dial Flower"
(Felicia Hemans), "My Soul is Dark" (Lord Byron), "The Negro Boy"
(Leigh Hunt), a lecture "on the geological and Mosiac records" (Hugh
Miller), and texts such as Ebenezer Porter's *Rhetorical Reader*. Of the
latter, one Normalite declared, "I think this an excel[l]ent book to learn
to read well in, but I have got rather tired of it, having read in it so
long."[57] Teachers in training walked a literary road indeed.

Once out of the classroom as pupils and back into the schoolhouse
as teachers, they began socializing their students through reading
instruction. One of the main purposes of reading aloud was to help
students become attentive and active listeners. Thus, at an early age
links were forged between social communication and the printed word
that would characterize adult literary sociabilities. Hence, sluggish
learners were targeted, reprimanded, and drilled. "Joseph Chandler ...
is not attentive to what I read to him, especially in Grammar," his
instructor complained when she began student teaching. "I will read
over something about '*verbs*' for instance," she continued, "and then

ask him what I have been reading about and he knows nothing concerning it." One New Haven teacher similarly read to her class to reinforce listening skills, stimulate thought, and hone retention. "Miss Bradley … read to us a description of the vessel that the Pilgrims came over to American in," a thirteen-year-old student recorded; "It was called the 'May Flower,' and afterwards we wrote as much as we could remember of it." Thus, Bradley and other educators who read aloud could teach composition while giving a lesson in history.[58]

Although it ideally stimulated critical reflection, reading out loud was simply practical—a way of "republishing" rare, borrowed, or expensive texts for common use in the classroom in a time before widespread textbook adoptions. Teachers otherwise had to muddle by with students using different textbooks, so everybody was decidedly not on the same page. Furthermore, oral renditions of the latest research, instructive fiction, or poetry the teacher might have at hand introduced pupils to a wider range of material than most school districts could afford. "[R]ead to the scholars from my Sabbath school book, 'Clinton, a Tale for Boys' they like it," one teacher recorded of a book she may have borrowed from the library. About a boy who falls in with thieves and winds up in reform school, the story probably frightened some unruly pupils into good behavior. Reading aloud texts for these targeted purposes was practical because they could indirectly handle emerging problems unaddressable through a fixed curriculum.[59]

Some texts were so often "orally duplicated" by teachers, however, that the effect was one of "publishing" it in the minds of every student who learned the words by heart. When one teacher read aloud to his class an "extract … from [Robert] Burns," one student remarked that it "seemed as familiar as my own name." It led this wheelwright's daughter to muse upon a former teacher who recited the same poetry too much: "'O wad some power the giftie gie us / To see oursels as ithers see us.'" She wondered, "How many times has … Mr. Allen of the Hancock School repeated that to us?" and imagined her own voice reproduced again and again: "Echo answers. 'How many?'"[60] Texts not only passed from hand to hand in dissemination, but also from teachers' memories to students' ears. The only literary purchase in these series of oral duplications may conceivably have been for the volume containing Robert Burns's 1786 poem, "To a Louse on Seeing One on a Lady's Bonnet at Church." It was the teacher's job, however, like that of many paid oral disseminators, to dispense a literary morsel of social sense: to see ourselves as others see us.

PERFORMATIVE LITERARY DISSEMINATION

While a teacher might render an orally delivered text like Burns's poem in a highly dramatic manner, it was not a requirement of the job, and it might be only one part of it. And students, of course, did not pay the teacher each time he or she read a particular text aloud. By contrast, the period saw a proliferation of another class of oral disseminators: textual performers for a paying public. Textual dissemination occurred at public readings, theatrical events, exhibitions, and lectures, nearly all of which cost audience members the price of admission. Such performances ranged from highly professional to barely amateur. Although some of these could yield substantial dollars, many panorama showmen, public readers, and lecturers, like other literary disseminators, were only sporadically employed. Overall, the livelihoods of amateur performative disseminators were as unstable as that of those who distributed printed material, if not more so. The dynamic between literary dollars and social sense differed somewhat between face-to-face distribution and performative dissemination. The very public nature of performances emphasized the social: an audience collectively heard a text. Furthermore, performances provided food for conversation for weeks on end afterward, and occasioned countless reports in letters to people who could not attend—forms of nonmarket dissemination in and of themselves.[61]

As much they were social, these performance events were literary. Although entertaining, they were not escapist fare; indeed, high literary culture then blended with popular culture. Lectures offered at the lyceum and other institutions by celebrities such as Ralph Waldo Emerson and lesser lights alike were generally not extemporaneous, but rather were orally delivered performances of original literary manuscripts. One audience member for an Emerson lecture recalled, for example, "In the desk stood the lecturer and read his manuscript." Paid lecturers often wrote upon literary themes, including the "Immortality of Shakespeare's works," "The Influence of the Literature of the last and present Centuries," "the life, character & writings of Lord Byron," and even "Lectures and Lecturers."[62] There were also notable speakers, like the aforementioned Fanny Kemble, offering public readings of drama, poetry, novels, and belles lettres. Alongside these were loosely based theatrical dramatizations of literary publications, ranging from Harriet Beecher Stowe's *Uncle Tom's Cabin* to Walter Scott's *Guy Mannering*, to *Cinderella*. Moreover, audiences had to be familiar enough with printed classics to get the humor and references in various literary burlesques. One spoof of Thomas Moore's poem, *Lallah Rookh*, featured an "aquariam ... [and] all sorts of crawling & moving things in it[,] fishes, lobsters ... veritable mermaids, half woman half fish sailing up and down."[63] Panoramic entertainments depicted scenes from literature such as *Uncle Tom's Cabin* or John Bunyan's *Pilgrim's Progress*, as well as places only read about in periodicals or books, such as "the Panorama of Dr Kane" (a visualization of Elisha Kane's popular narratives of Arctic exploration) and "[John] Skirvings Panorama of Fremont's overland Journey to Oregon and California" (based probably on the explorer's book). So-called moving panoramas were paintings on cloth, some allegedly "3 miles long," which were unrolled while a script describing various scenes was recited.[64] All of these performances suggest that ample literary dollars were to be made beyond the printed word.

The richness of this culture of performance meant literature could reach consumers outside of avenues of print distribution. In fact, one could become quite literary without much reading, as can be seen in the case of audience members subject to occupational eyestrain or chronic vision impairment. One literary-minded Boston dressmaker, for example, seldom mentioned books in her diary and account books filled with references to calico, muslin, silk, ribbons, laces, and whale bones. She lavished attention instead on public lectures she often attended with her husband, a distiller, in the evenings after hours of sewing. Able to sit after a long day, with her eyes shut if she wished, she "heard the rev Mr Emerson from Concord deliver a lecture on peace" or "Mr Field lecture on the life & Character of Columbus"—twenty-five lectures in all, occurring about once a week during one winter lecture season. No one would think of her as not "well read." Nor would they of one physician's wife, whose eyes required surgery (one of them of was blind), for she followed the same pattern as the dressmaker: plenty of lectures, panorama, tableaux, and theater, but little reading (see fig. 4.3).[65] The two women's location in a thriving urban performance market, of course, gave them advantages that rural folk did not enjoy. Yet the backcountry was certainly not entirely devoid of literary performances. Indeed, it was a ripe field worked by touring performers, many of them petty amateurs, attracted there because of the lack of competition. These itinerants brought the literary world to small-town America.[66]

Panorama Men

Among these commercial performers to be encountered in country towns were panorama men. For example, in rural Massachusetts, Seth Arnold caught a Mississippi River panorama while attending an 1847

LECTURE ON MATRIMONY.

Fig. 4.3 Although it pokes fun at audience reaction, this cartoon shows that women (some listening with eyes closed) commonly attended lectures, popular forms of disseminated literature. *Source:* "Lecture on Matrimony" *HNMM* 22 (1861): 726. Courtesy of Cornell University Library, Making of America Digital Collection.

antislavery meeting in Middleborough, while up in Conway a schoolboy viewed an *Uncle Tom's Cabin* canvas a little over a year after the book appeared in print—the accompanying script may have been the first time he heard words from the book. Alongside commercial properties were scripts tailored to the local market, which could pander to its supposed ignorance, as in the case of one Bangor exhibition that reportedly tried to pass off a thinly veiled image of Boston's thriving Washington Street for an ancient Babylonian thoroughfare. These shenanigans aside, entrepreneurial traveling exhibitors often brought an omnibus package of knowledge and entertainment to rural folks starved for it. Charles Cobb, in hardscrabble Woodstock, Vermont, saw for nine cents one exhibition that included a cyclorama with dissolving scenes of battles and astronomical phenomenon, along with projected microscopic views of bacteria in waterdrops, all set off by fireworks and music. Cobb was excited, if a bit confused by the showman's script, noting, "The exhibitor said respecting his views of the heavens, that light which comes to us from the sun in the space of 8 minutes—(or seconds, I'm cussed if I can tell which) being almost 12,000,000 miles a minute, was occupied in coming from some planets seen in Lord Rosse's telescope, 225,000,000 YEARS! If 8 minutes is 95,000,000 miles how many miles is 22,000,000 years—!!! According to the bible, that planet is at least 224,990,000 years older than the world!"[67] Panorama men and their fellow exhibitors who orally disseminated something beyond the normal reach of ordinary folk, could pick up a few cents along the way for doing so.

This was no easy go, as the case of a panorama showman in rural Maine makes plain. L. Eaton Emerson from Lewiston Falls described the "Exhibitor[']s Life" as one of continual travel: "Left Lewiston Falls, Me. on the 11th of Setr at 1 O'clock P.M. travelled through Minot (Cor.) Mechanic Falls, Welchville, Norway Village, Harrison Flat, Bridgton Centre, then to Pike School House so called in Fryburg Me. Gave an Exhibition[.] The house was filled to overflowing." The tour continued on to South Chatham, New Hampshire, and back into Hardwick, Maine, for nighttime unrollings in the open air or schoolhouses. Emerson exhibited the "Panorama of California" before "camphene" gaslight, which illuminated the twenty-six scenes, including a "Gaming Saloon," a "Miner Prospecting," a "Grizzly Bear," and the "first great Mail from the States No.g 60 Bags of Letters & 80 Newspapers." The script opened with "Ladies and gentlemen[,] We propose to give you at this time a birds eye view of life in California." It then described all the scenes and alerted viewers that they were seeing for the first time depictions previously described only in print. One showed gold miners at work: "'*Scene Thirteenth.*' ... miners are then obliged to sink from 1 to 12 ft in the *bed* of the stream before they arrive at the rotten granite. ... [T]he gold is found in pockets along the banks of the river, this accounting for the many stories you have read in newspapers of individuals at work upon the bank of a river suddenly obtaining 5,7, & even $12.000 from a small pocket."[68] Night after night, these showmen brought the printed word to life wherever they went.

Life on the go naturally took its toll, and inevitable conflicts with local religious authorities disparaging secular entertainments distressed the exhibitor as well. To mollify potential critics, showmen might seek prior permission from the town's ministers. On one occasion, Emerson recorded that he "Drove to Hardwick, Had a talk with the Ag[en]t. He had no objections if the Teacher had none. So posted off to see the teacher (a minister)[.] He had none, and so we circulated our Bills." When Emerson distributed these advertisements, they revealed that the show would include a presumably blackface public reading of "Black Diamonds," a published minstrel burlesque on lecturers. This infuriated his antislavery hosts: "the 'Black Diamonds' Knocked *him* [the minister] crazy and he came blowing along, like a young Locomotive to see the *Agent.*" The teacher "came up and countermanded *orders*—and refused to let us have the [school]house." Moreover, he "cautioned his pupils against the demoralizing influence of Panorama's in general, & this one of California in particular." Not surprisingly, Emerson "Did not get much of a house," as he calculated his receipts against outlays: "Took $6.50 Expe[nd] 6.50 Paid 37 1/2 cts for Camphene 1/2 a Gallon."[69] Because of the censure, the showman lost community support and, subsequently, money and time, not to mention a half gallon of illumination fluid expended for a small crowd. Such was the price for offending local social sense. The people of Hardwick respected public lecturers and antislavery activists enough to place them before a night's fleeting entertainment lampooning them. Emerson could only pick up stakes in hopes of better luck elsewhere.

Lecturers

Great and commonplace lecturers alike sometimes shared problems with panorama men. Finding a friendly forum for presentation was sometimes difficult, especially for speakers espousing radical causes like abolition. "The orthodox minister refused to let me speak in his church, because I was a son of Mr. Garrison & would be likely to sympathize with my father in his views," abolitionist William Garrison Jr. complained in a letter; "Ludicrous as this was we were forced to look elsewhere & a Mr. Curtis, a reader of the Tribune & a unitarian, offered us a nice little hall of his own." Happily, many lecturers did not have to seek venues because they were invited to deliver before fixed bodies, like lyceum associations and literary clubs. Still, one waggish magazine contributor likened solicitations to hunting lecturers: "wherever they see a lion of fair size and tolerable roar, they seize him by letter, [and] hurry him by steam to the trap." Even invitations could occasion juggling. Before the days of booking agencies, uninvited lecturers often had to solicit for themselves and scope out travel routes that maximized their effort and minimized time and distance between successive engagements. Planning an itinerary provided a good opening for a pitch. "I have been engaged to lecture before several Lyceums in the towns on the River below you," one minister started his query to speak before a rural lyceum for "the usual" ten-dollar fee. "I therefore write to enquire whether the people of Bernardstown could be induced to give a hearing on the 17th?" he continued. "As your town is so near Greenfield & on the railroad," he explained, "it would be more convenient to visit it at the time mentioned than at any other, should my services be in request." Another solution to scattering one's energies was to arrange for courses that allowed the lecturer to stay put for a while.[70]

Constant travel and nightly performances chipped away at lecturers' health, vocal chords, and good humor, afflicting even the most celebrated. Ralph Waldo Emerson "finds it necessary to lecture for a support," one of his friends remarked, "He really has so much to say that he does not need to have it ground out of him." Travel itself required fortitude; one intrepid Massachusetts amateur walked through ten inches of snow from Danvers to Salem to deliver a lecture on reading to a rapt audience. "Wherever, between November and April, there is a snow-drift, you may be sure there is a lecturer in it," one magazinist joked, declaring, "no hod-carrier or mariner earns his money more laboriously and faithfully than a lecturer." Naturally, fatigue was lecturers' constant companion. Sarah P. Remond, an African American abolitionist, was worn down by a string of lectures she squeezed in before leaving for London. "I have lectured very frequently, in fact had more invitations recently that I could fill," she wrote; "Lectured on three successive evenings last week, which was rather too much for me and I am now with my friends … for a little rest, then go to York, to lecture there." Another woman acting as a substitute for a no-show depleted her energy talking for more than an hour before her ladies' group: "It is rather fatiguing, but I do enjoy to use all my feeble endeavours, to advance the all important subject of physiology." Dedication alone could not revive the exhausted lecturer.[71]

What lecturers made for their time and stress depended upon the market. Pay for most lecturers, especially those moved to speak by ideology rather than profit, was insubstantial, simply because so many could speak and were willing to do so for nothing or next to nothing. However, though some lecturers—especially local members of small town lyceums—spoke gratis, wealthier organizations paid their speakers something. Even among spokespersons for highly organized reform associations the rewards varied. Former slave William Craft, a lecturer and subscription representative, was "willing to accept" the goodly sum of "£220 per annum" as London agent for the Massachusetts Anti-Slavery Society in 1860, but offered "to pay all my expenses, such as traveling, getting up meetings &c." Yet his colleague, black abolitionist lecturer Charles Lenox Remond, was "able to earn so little for the past year" (1859) that he could not afford even a few weeks' vacation from a grueling schedule. Payment fluctuated with popular support for such causes, but the market generally favored knowledgeable, entertaining, and accommodating lecturers. As we have seen, ten dollars remained typical as late as 1852 in the countryside, but the going rate for lecturers at city and large town lyceums was constantly inflating. In New England, which had the most advanced system, the fee in the 1830s and 1840s was about twenty-five dollars for a single night—slightly more than a month's wages for laborers—but the amount would double by the late 1850s. An executive board member of the Portland lyceum figured the "average paid [to] lecturers [was] $23.35" per appearance before a hall seating one hundred people. John Park, who served on the

Worcester Lyceum council, suggested the same amount was sumptuous for so few hours of work: "Mr Alexander H. Everett gives the Lyceum a very good lecture on the French Revolution of 1830. I said *gives*—but he has twenty or twenty five dollars for his gift."[72] The difference between a lecture delivered in the spirit of giving and one remunerated with many literary dollars was great indeed. The high pay suggests the degree to which locals craved such performative literary experiences in order to maintain a sense of intellectual community.

"Undoubtedly, a lecture is the most profitable form of literary labor," a magazine essayist pronounced in 1857, while explaining that publishing simply did not pay as much for the author. The essayist went on to calculate that "A lecturer ... will write a discourse of sixty or eighty pages, occupying an hour in the delivery, which he will deliver five evenings in the week for three months; and if he be paid ... fifty dollars every time, his three months' lecturing give him just three thousand dollars. If he publish his manuscript ... how soon would he get three thousand dollars for it?" By contrast, the top magazines then paid only about three-to-five dollars a page, and the chances to make money in book publishing, as we have seen, were even less. Yet only "Hundreds" lectured for top fees, while many thousands appeared in print. Moreover, lecturers who were invited repeatedly enough to hope for that three-thousand dollars numbered between twenty and thirty, or even less.[73]

While lecturing offered the possibility of a literary profession for a few, for the many it resembled the social, amateur, and minor authorship we discussed in chapters 1 and 2. Indeed, some of the authors treated there, like Mellen Chamberlain, Henry W. Cushman, and Eunice Cobb, occasionally tried their hand at lecturing for little or no pay. Charlotte Forten contemplated doing so, but confessed, "I do think reading one's composition, before strangers is a trying task."[74] All lecturers though, even professionals, held some things in common with social authors who disseminated their unpublished writings to known and limited readerships: (1) they had some control over the locales into which their texts would go; (2) they received feedback from audiences, from which they could later tinker with their texts; and (3) they withheld texts from publication, at least for a while. In this latter action, lecturers' motivations differed from social authors' in that the market value of lectures, once published, dropped. Above all, lecturing made social sense because it required extensive face-to-face interactions amid on-the-ground sociabilities surrounding the event. Literary dollars were to be made without sacrificing too much social sense.

CONCLUSION

All literary distributors and disseminators shared similar woes. If they took on lecturing, bookselling, subscription vending, and librarianship out of devotion to literature, they risked disappointment. Lugging around dusty volumes, listening to complaints, sleeping in strangers' homes, and having doors slammed in faces—these were only some of the inevitable problems. Under these conditions literature threatened to become, for those getting it out to the people, a commodity like anything else exchanged in the market. As literary dissemination itself likewise became commodified—assigned a dollar value that hardly compensated for the earnestness with which most people pursued it—it was perceived as merely a job, less a service.

Just as literature for its own sake was imperiled by the marketplace, so too was social sense. Social ties based upon buying and selling literature were often as implausible as a poorly drafted prospectus or a false promise to buy. Sociable conversations with customers easily devolved into suspicious interrogation. Long hours alone in the stacks isolated librarians at times; conversely, they rued time spent in idle chatter with patrons. True, similar disaffections afflicted disseminators outside as well as in the market. Still, relationships expressed through gratis circulation of printed material held social meanings that were not simply apart from monetary considerations, but irreducible to measurable quotas of exchange—the source of Emily Dickinson's "Disgrace of Price" mentioned at the outset of this volume. What was endemic to literary distribution in the marketplace was anathematic to social dissemination outside of it.

Nonetheless, market distribution and paid dissemination, in helping get the books and periodicals out where they might not have otherwise gone, served sociable literary life. Agents brought printed items to the doors of customers seldom visiting bookstores. Librarians increasingly oversaw effective purchasing, cataloging, care, maintenance, and, above all, use of books that may have remained forgotten on shelves. Lecturers and teachers also disseminated by reading aloud to "captive" classes and lyceum patrons, thus introducing them to literature they might not have read on their own, while widening, too, print's potential market. Increased access to literature resulted in it playing a more central role in the construction of everyday social life, say, as literary gifts were exchanged among friends or borrowed books were read aloud in family circles.[75]

Neither fully entrenched within the literary marketplace nor entirely outside of it, petty distributors and paid disseminators represent a wild card in antebellum literary history. They frustrate grand generalizations about its course based on what conventional evidence for distribution (for example, advertisements, best-seller lists, or publishers' shipping invoices) suggests about availability, sales, and, above all, readership. Because these free agents left so few records by contrast, we may never know for sure where the books or periodicals ultimately went. The same may be said, of course, for social disseminators acting outside the market with all the literary clippings, book bundles, "exchanged" papers, and poetic transcriptions they broadcast throughout the land.[76] Together, the two insured that literature did not stay confined to major cities or towns on main transport routes, and so moderated the strong dichotomy between literary metropolis and lagging provinces that characterized other Western nations.[77] Yet here the place of distributors was more crucial than that of social disseminators, whose role, if not one of always resisting the market, was at least one of buffering locally situated social relations of literature from the national market culture that challenged, even threatened, them.[78] Distributors, by contrast, themselves represented the market, and thus also were a wild card in local literary life, which without them might have continued to domesticate the products of the market through social sense. In short, distributors provided an alternate way of viewing literature, as a commodity. In this sense, our consideration of these distributors challenges generalizations about the reading public's practices formulated from conceptions of the supposed integrity of traditional communities unpolluted by market relations, as expressed through national literary distribution. Distributors guaranteed that market transactions over literature could take place just about anywhere. As they enacted monetary exchange relations of literary dollars amid the traditional reciprocities of social sense, they comprised the future while compromising the past.

CONCLUSION
"The Privilege of Going On"

The future of literary production and distribution during and after the Civil War increasingly played out in the marketplace of print, not in the local arena of social relations. This, of course, is not surprising given the widespread socioeconomic transformation of national life. Many changes had been well underway before hostilities began, but the war's dislocations broke down much of literary social sense's vestigial resistance, sacrificed for the national cause. Amid the crisis, socially instrumental general reading for entertainment and edification inevitably seemed escapist. Consequently, patriotic or civic newspaper reading became more valorized, widespread, and intensive than ever.[1] The ensuing postbellum industrial capitalist surge set literary production and distribution in a professional, cash-driven direction. Literature now mostly reached consumers through a profit-based system addressing the widest market regardless of specific local realities and needs. With the age of the full-time, well-paid author and corporate distributor at hand, their amateur counterparts would be measured against the new professional yardstick.

Because today's readers, writers, and publishers are still this postbellum age's children, it is difficult for them to assess the previous one on its own terms. To appreciate fully the tightrope between literary dollars and social sense walked by earlier writers, distributors, and disseminators requires examining the later period of market domination. We thus conclude here by considering professional trends in light of some of our informants' postbellum literary experiences. We compare these and their antebellum roots to those of a few contemporary writers who, though later canonized, shared social authorship and amateur patterns with our informants. We then assay changes in literary distribution and amateurism's fate under the new regime. We conclude by sketching the new authorship system's typology and setting it within emerging divisions between production and consumption. What did they mean for the social relations of literature?

THE PROFESSIONAL TREND

Writing and distributing print materials partook of a massive shift in employment patterns accompanying postbellum economic and cultural consolidation under industrial capitalism. Growing concentrations of wealth and need for specialized technical expertise spawned new professions and redefined older ones. Increasingly, toward century's end, writers' and distributors' former in-and-out patterns of market participation gave way to at least the possibility of steady, long-term employment. Yet the public conception of authorship was influenced, ironically, by the canonization of some writers, like Ralph Waldo Emerson, Henry David Thoreau, and, eventually, Emily Dickinson, whose careers, as we will argue, reflected antebellum social authorship and amateur practices. The three's negotiations of literary dollars with social sense seem almost poignant when set against the actual cutthroat big-business climate of postbellum print distribution we describe at the end of this section. Inasmuch as national corporate marketing enabled professionalization—while making irrelevant the type of social authorship and genteel amateurism then still associated with canonical figures—writers and distributors would come to accept, in one way or another, that social sense, in its antebellum expression, was poorly adapted to the pursuit of postbellum literary dollars.[2]

Postbellum Literary Careers

To be sure, these professionalizing trends did not signal social sense's demise, as will be evident from our consideration of Charlotte Forten, Lucy Larcom, John Townsend Trowbridge, and writers encountered in chapter 1 who either achieved minor author status or who continued to pass in and out of print. Yet, because professionalization was part of a larger socioeconomic transformation, prior patterns of literary sociability would be muted or enlisted to serve the new order. Though Forten (to some extent), Larcom, and Trowbridge could be said to have attained successful literary careers, they stopped short of fully embracing the emerging professional ethic. In this, as we will see, they little differed from their antebellum contemporaries with more limited postwar market engagement. Ambiguity toward literary dollars would remain common both inside and outside the marketplace of print.

Antebellum social sense's incongruity with postbellum literary commercialization can be seen in Lucy Larcom's memoir, *A New England Girlhood*. Published in 1889, it focused upon the time before she established her professional authorial reputation—her childhood and years at the mills; one chapter briefly narrates her Illinois sojourn and return back east. Only on the last few pages did she assess her literary calling with scant mention of her many publications, including those in the *Atlantic Monthly* and her editorial work at *Our Young Folks*. Neither did she appraise her postbellum contributions to the major literary periodicals, *Harper's*, *St. Nicholas*, and the *Independent*, nor her several volumes of poetry and prose. After years of professionalism—from the time she left her full-time teaching position at Wheaton in 1863 to write, to the moment she commanded twenty-five dollars for one poem in an 1870 issue of *Scribner's*, to the days spent completing her memoir—she apologized for her choice: "I did not attempt writing for money until it became a necessity." Some of her diffidence was prescribed rhetoric; women who chose writing over teaching or marriage, as Larcom did, still risked social disapproval. Still, some of her reserve reflected the wisdom of an industry insider who nevertheless maintained the values of an earlier time. Knowing well that an "author" was an elusive projection—a compromise between personal vision and public endorsement of varying amounts over a lifetime—she could never lay claim to the title. Certainly, remuneration, though sufficient, was unstable enough to congest the easy flow of literary dollars due the author's efforts. So, she concluded her memoir with the cautious observation that "Success in writing may mean many different things." She added, "I do not know that I have ever reached it, except in the sense of liking better and better to write, and of finding expression easier." Besides learning how to avoid writer's block, Larcom also discovered how to avoid blockages in public approbation: "It is something to have won the privilege of going on," she confessed.[3] Authorship was an entitlement, and longevity a sign of connecting well with the reading public, and, at the same time, *the key* to success within the marketplace.

While earning the privilege of going on, however, Larcom was slowly relinquishing to modernity the social world in which she grew up. *A New England Girlhood* was an elegiac celebration of the lost world of her childhood in Beverly and Lowell, Massachusetts. Its subtitle, *Outlined from Memory*, confessed that the past was still alive within her mental universe. The book's vibrancy and verisimilitude jogged the recall of readers who themselves had lived through the antebellum era; it likewise validated what young folk heard in the spoken and written memories of their elders. "My audience," Larcom asserted in the preface, "is understood to be composed of girls of all ages, and women who have not forgotten their girlhood." At the same time, its nostalgic tone appealed to those who stubbornly resisted change—especially the diminishment of sociabilities. This partly accounts for her gendered notion of her primary audience, for many northeastern women at least perceived that a loss of sociality had occurred, much to their detriment. Yet her story reached out beyond women to embrace men, too, who would have remembered what women were like in the days of yore, within the traditional moral economy of town life. "Whatever special interest this little narrative of mine may have is due to the social influences under which I was reared," she declared to her readers. Certainly, social sense imbues every page. *A New England Girlhood* often shuns nostalgic self-absorption ("[e]ven an autobiographer has to say 'we' much oftener than 'I'") and instead recalls distinct social relations and social spaces: an aunt who lived "down-stairs in the same house" and who taught her to sew; a sister who "would get up before daylight and run over into the burying-ground"; the "working-girls" in Lowell boardinghouses, "all of us thrown upon our own resources, but thrown much more upon each others' sympathies." Most of all, she recovered the social meaning inherent in everyday objects—furnishings, books, even "shovel and tongs, that it had been my especial task to keep bright." "Nobody can buy the old associations," she asserted in defiance of a growing commercialism that threatened to commodify even memories themselves.[4]

Ironically, her memoir was a monetary success, at least for its publishers. Its first run of fifteen hundred copies sold out within a month of its November 29, 1889, printing and it was reissued from the same plates several times thereafter. So successful was it that other writers designed similar memoirs, including that of Sarah P.E. Hale's son, Edward Everett Hale, whose *A New England Boyhood*, published four years later, gave the male perspective. "If Larcom was becoming old-fashioned," her biographer states, referring to a much larger tradition of postbellum New England nostalgia pieces exemplified by John Greenleaf Whittier's *Snow-Bound* (1866), "she was doing so in the best of company." After about a year out on the market, however, *A New England Girlhood* had yielded only about two hundred dollars for Larcom.[5] She would not live long enough to reap from it the full financial rewards due those who "won the privilege of going on."

Like Larcom, Charlotte Forten won that privilege but to a lesser degree, perhaps, and at a much greater cost, for bigotry and poor health continued to threaten her with defeat. Undaunted, Forten kept herself in the literary public eye during and after the war by publishing in major and minor periodicals while she held various positions that supplemented her income as a writer. In October 1862, after recovering from several bouts of illness, she left for Port Royal to teach the freed-people of South Carolina; while there she published letters on her experiences, originally written to William Lloyd Garrison, in the *Liberator*. The next year, in recognition of her literary attainment, William Wells Brown printed her 1855 graduation poem, "A Parting Hymn," and other pieces in his anthology *The Black Man*. In May 1864, around the time she returned to Philadelphia, her "Life on the Sea Islands" came out in the "premier organ of literary high culture in America," the *Atlantic Monthly*, the editors of which "significantly influenced many authors ... in the formative stages of their careers." John Townsend Trowbridge affirmed, "It was a distinction for a young writer to appear in its pages." It also paid more than most magazines and so helped to establish professional authorship in the United States; Forten may have received fifty dollars. Removing from Philadelphia to Boston, between October 1865 and October 1871 she held the position of secretary of the Teacher's Committee of the New England Branch of the Freedmen's Union Commission, while she wrote for periodicals and translated Émile Erckmann and Alexandre Chatrian's popular 1863 novel, *Madame Thérèse*, published by Scribner's in 1869. This and her two 1872 *Scribner's* articles, "Visit to the Birthplace of Whittier" and "The Queen of the Bees," another Erckmann-Chatrian translation, were career highpoints. After these, however, Forten felt mounting racial prejudice more strongly within the high-stakes periodical world: as *Scribner's* increasingly performed the cultural work of national reconciliation after the war, it discouraged African American contributors. Moreover, Forten's growing determination to rebut racist publications made her less marketable to mainstream magazine editors. With major magazine placements drying up, she found supplemental income as a teacher in Charleston and Washington, D.C. between 1871 and 1873 and as a U.S. Treasury clerk starting in 1873. Still, during this time, she continued to place work in the *Christian Register*, a large Unitarian weekly, and the *Boston Commonwealth*. Altogether, payment for these (and possibly others) probably amounted to less than what she received for her 1872 *Scribner's* article, "Visit to the Birthplace of Whittier."[6]

After she married Reverend Francis Grimké in 1878 and evidently stopped working outside of the home, she had more time to write, but also less need for literary dollars. Just how much she published on her own remains uncertain, but enough manuscripts have been uncovered or otherwise indirectly identified to suggest how prolific, if not profitable, her writing may have been. Perhaps because she finally achieved financial and emotional security, an even greater social sense saturated her ink and flowed through her pen as she addressed contemporary issues. Her December 1885 response in the *Commonwealth* to Gail Hamilton's "Race Prejudice" is but one example; the October 1889 essay "Colored People in New England," published in the *Evangelist*, is another. With literary peeps at author's homes becoming ever more popular by the 1890s, Forten rode the wave, but added a critical edge by peering in "At the Home of Frederick Douglass," the famed black abolitionist. In the manner of Hale and Larcom, she too published a memoir in *New England Magazine* in June 1893; her "Personal Recollections of Whittier" recounted her own life story's interaction with that of the poet's.[7] While conceived with a social sense similar to that seen in Larcom's memoir, it did not place the sectional conflict in the background: Forten's was a constant reminder to readers that slavery, against which both she and Whittier fought, was still very much alive in the "old days."

John Townsend Trowbridge was hardly one to neglect slavery or postbellum racism either, but his reformist spirit only accentuated a more general pursuit of literary dollars. His popular 1857 anti-slavery novel *Neighbor Jackwood*, the first chapters of which were written three years earlier to offset the anguish of finishing *Martin Merrivale*, was dramatized in the same year, successfully staged dramatically in Boston, and thereafter had runs in New York and elsewhere. Periodicals, however, were the mainstay of his professionalism. After placing pieces before and during the war in *Putnam's*, *Harper's*, the *New York Tribune*, and the *Atlantic Monthly*—the latter included him in its first number and published both his celebrated poem, "The Vagabonds," and the popular story, "Coupon Bonds"—Trowbridge became an editor and contributor to Ticknor and Fields' illustrated magazine, *Our Young Folks*, which began in 1865. Soon after, Trowbridge took up Linus Pierpont Stebbins' lucrative offer to tour the war-torn South and collect material for a book; the result was a portrayal of secessionist whites' hardened racism titled, *The South: A Tour of its Battlefields,* some segments of which already appeared as articles in the *Atlantic* and *Our Young Folks*. Although the book sold well by subscription, it "had no advertising, and was hardly heard of at all in the ordinary avenues of the book trade," according to its author.[8] Once again, Trowbridge forfeited greater recognition by publishing, as he did with *Martin Merrivale*, in an as yet unconventional format.

After publishing *The South*, Trowbridge's attentions turned mainly toward editing and writing for periodicals, and reprinting pieces in several of his collections. He became editor-in-chief of *Our Young Folks* in 1870 after wresting the position away from Lucy Larcom who, by some accounts, spent too much time on submissions—her continuance of earlier patterns of social authorship that demanded that every manuscript be given close personal attention could not easily give way to the demands of the market for editorial timeliness and efficiency. Trowbridge could cross this divide and, in doing so, could cut himself enough time away from editorial duties to write prodigiously for the market. True, some of this was easy because he could place pieces in the periodical he edited; his popular "Jack Hazard" stories, for example, first appeared in installments in *Our Young Folks*, along with other pieces and poetry. Yet, all the while his pieces continually appeared in the *Atlantic*, the only other periodical for which the publishers allowed him contractually to write while associated with their *Our Young Folks*. That magazine's demise in 1873 little affected his fortunes, however, for he continued to support himself by writing pieces for well-paying periodicals like *St. Nicholas* and *Youth's Companion* and reprinting a diverse range of his works in book form, or in anthologies and as title pieces in volumes of collections. Trowbridge evidently commanded high royalties in sum from his various productions, for between 1870 and 1909 he published at least forty-one original titles.[9] His 1903 autobiography, *My Own Story*, laid out the social sense of the antebellum literary marketplace, already compromised in the 1840s and 1850s, as we discussed regarding *Martin Merrivale*, but brightened by face-to-face encounters with litterateurs like Ralph Waldo Emerson, Henry Wadsworth Longfellow, James Russell Lowell, and Walt Whitman.

Why did Forten, Larcom, and Trowbridge, among so many other would-be professionals, earn the title of author? Some of the attainment is relative, a "function of discourse." Being included over time in anthologies and encyclopedias, having posthumous editions of their work, and becoming the subject of books, like this one, means that today they may yet still be remembered—if researchers are willing to dig them out from under years of obscurity. Recovery seems especially pertinent to Charlotte Forten Grimké who has benefited by recent scholarly interest in neglected African-American writers. But in her own time, certain factors combined to accord her and the others minor repute rather than the virtual obscurity that befell most of the authors treated in these pages. Greater talent, of course, may have had something to do with it, and so did tenacity. Toughened by years of fighting against the odds for that in which they strongly believed—for Forten, abolition of slavery; for Larcom, independence from marriage; and for Trowbridge, literary respectability beyond hack writing—they were able to withstand deterrents that broke most neophyte writers' wills.[10]

Talent and unusual fortitude aside, all three remained connected to social circles that could assist them—certainly not by vaulting them to the top of the profession, but by providing some leads and break-throughs. For example, longtime family friend John Greenleaf Whittier ushered Forten's *Atlantic Monthly* essays into print; Thomas Went-worth Higginson, with whom she had earlier become acquainted in the Sea Islands, provided the preface to *Madame Thérèse* and placed her manuscript, "One Phase of the Race Question" (which she sent him) in the *Commonwealth*. She even maintained a friendship with Daniel Payne, who spent his winters in Jacksonville, Florida, where she lived for a time. Although her everyday postbellum social circles were not always literary, some of her coteries encouraged her writing while only occasionally leading directly to publication. They centered at first upon her fellow teachers in the Sea Islands and in Boston, then her husband's parishioners in Jacksonville and Washington, literati such as author Anna Julia Haywood Cooper within the national capital's well-to-do African American community, participants in the Monday Night Liter-ary Club there (Frederick Douglass was a member), and her cofound-ers at the National Association of Colored Women.[11]

Facing none of the racial and gender prejudice that Forten endured, Trowbridge freely traveled within more extensive social circles to meet many an editor and publisher, especially Mordecai Manuel Noah, an early mentor in New York. In 1853 Trowbridge met writer Francis Henry Underwood in the countinghouse of his publisher, Phillips Sampson, after which Underwood introduced him to now prominent writer and sometime editor of the *Atlantic Monthly*, James Russell Low-ell; Trowbridge would go on to have a long friendship with Lowell. Thus, it was book tradespeople who populated Trowbridge's greater social universe, and, according to his autobiography, not so much family and neighborhood circles.[12]

While Lucy Larcom always maintained close contact with family members, schoolteachers, and her friends from the mills, if only through correspondence, she, too, grew deeply attached to professional circles within the postbellum industry. After James T. Fields took the editorship of the *Atlantic* in 1861, she was invited to Annie Fields's influential Boston salon, and eventually became a frequent and enthusiastic guest there. All the while Larcom maintained with Whittier a friendly relationship, most evident in her yearly summer outings with him and his circle at Bearcamp in West Ossipee, New Hampshire.[13] She, Forten, and Trowbridge, in savoring the sometimes uneasy blend of sociability and professionalism wherever it emerged, only advantaged themselves and furthered their literary ambitions.

All three were also tractable, adapting to changing market conditions. Most notably, they continued publishing in major magazines, which meant reaching audiences as much as fifty times larger than did the typical novel, printed in an initial run of 2,000. Literary magazines clearly transported many an author along the road toward professionalization, and the farther along they went on this road the more likely they might become highly paid and well known. All three followed at least two of three stages in the ascent of literary magazines that began in the 1850s and continued throughout their lifetimes. All got their start during the first stage, 1840 to 1870, which saw the rise of such magazines that (1) featured short fiction, essays, and poetry, (2) were established by major publishing houses, and (3) were increasingly expected to pay their authors, who were as yet usually unsigned and only occasionally identifiable through mere initials or pseudonyms. Trowbridge took the name "Paul Creyton"; Larcom, "Angelina Abigail"; and Forten, "Lottie." They ventured into the next stage, 1870 to 1890, by appearing in the illustrated monthlies with large distribution among the middle classes, such as *Our Young Folks, Scribner's* (with a circulation of 100,000 by 1881) and *Harper's* (185,000 by the late 1880s), which were likely to name their authors. Escalating prices for serials no doubt drove Trowbridge's "Jack Hazard" yarns in *Our Young Folks* and his other running stories in the *Companion*. While none of the three authors seems to have submitted original pieces to one of the many budding syndicates that attracted the upcoming generation, it is hard to know if their work was pirated by these marketers. By the era of mass circulation, 1890 to 1900, of up to 880,000 subscribers, top magazines (due to reliance upon advertising revenues) became inexpensive and fit for a general public; features included nationally oriented ads, cheaply reproduced photographic illustrations, serialized novels, premiums for new subscribers, romance and action narratives, and "brand name" authors. By this time, all three were nearing the end of their lives, however. Trowbridge seems to have put his energies into his anthologies; Larcom focused upon writing devotional books, but also looked to *New England Magazine* and *Youth's Companion* (with a circulation of half a million by about 1893) when she needed money. Too little is known about Charlotte Forten Grimké's publications for this period beyond her essay on Whittier for *New England Magazine*. More complete lists of publications for all three authors would reveal much more about what may have distinguished major from minor professionals. So, too, would information on their turn toward lecturing for income, and possible participation in James Redpath's lecture circuit, which provided substantial income and publicity for many professional authors.[14] Lecturing helped them "go on" into the twentieth century, but they could not take full advantage of the period's increasing professional opportunities.

If "going on" allowed these three to become minor writers within their own time, how did the majority of people considered in this book, especially the dabblers in chapter 1, fare? Only a few of those besides Forten, Larcom, and Trowbridge who passed in and out of print during the antebellum years and lived beyond them held minor status in the more competitive postbellum market of emerging professionalism. Elizabeth Cary Agassiz, Edward Everett Hale, and Louisa Park Hall were, arguably, already minor lights. Hale would go on a path similar to that of the three aforementioned authors: publication in the *Atlantic Monthly*, numerous minor book projects, and the popular short novel, *Man without a Country* (1865), but unlike Larcom and Trowbridge he wrote as a sideline while retaining a full-time position as a minister. Though she would publish frequently in the *Atlantic Monthly*, writing was only a small part of Agassiz's activities, too, crowded as they were by acting as her husband's assistant and publicist, running a girl's school, and eventually founding and heading what would become Radcliffe College. Hall became a fading light, however, possibly due to her father's discouragements in the 1840s and her duties as a minister's wife; during the remainder of the century, she mainly reprinted work or published short, often privately printed pieces.[15] Caroline Gardiner Cary Curtis and Martha Reade Nash Lamb, would go on to publish several volumes after the Civil War. Lamb, an apparent divorcee, was rare among the group for making a later, independent living as magazinist and editor of the *Magazine of American History* between 1883 and 1892, while Curtis, who remained married, kept more or less quietly within the family fold.[16] A few of the other amateurs published a handful of volumes (often reprints of antebellum works) with mostly private printers or minor publishers, which are little remembered today.[17] Elizabeth Jocelyn, as might be expected, continued to contribute obituaries, but also had some success with her poetry, especially the sixteen-page reprint from the *Berkshire Courier* (1861), *No Sects in Heaven* (advertised as having sold 300,000 copies in London by 1873), and collections of poetry, not all hers, bearing titles that showed slight variations of the poem; it was at best minor renown for little remuneration.[18] Some of the earlier amateurs published only brief printed versions of public addresses. Mary Poor saw her memoir, a 1903 paper titled "Recollections of Brookline" that she read before the Brookline Historical Society, printed in that society's periodical.[19] James A. Healy, installed as Bishop of Portland, Maine, in 1875 had religious addresses and letters printed.[20] Mellen Chamberlain, who went on to become a judge and a librarian of the Boston Public Library, printed several civic-minded lectures.[21] Lesser talents though they may have been, the amateurs who seldom reared their heads in the literary marketplace during the last four decades of the nineteenth century probably chose, as before, to retire from the increasingly harsh realities of publishing rather than being forced out.

Social and Amateur Practices among Canonized Authors

What about the major talents who got their start during the antebellum years and have today remained part of the literary canon? Did Emily Dickinson, Ralph Waldo Emerson, and Henry David Thoreau, for instance, at some time practice "social authorship" or pass in and out of print? Dickinson is the most obvious example of a writer who probably chose to remain a social author rather than one in print. Indeed, she defied the publishing industry by inventing her "own domestic technologies of publication," and thus dramatically maintained the gestures of social authorship, even as the practices were dying. In this sense, her social authorship became one of theatrics, ingeniously radical demonstrations against the doleful impact of the market upon socially inflected literary sensibilities.[22]

Dickinson made a ritual of dissemination as a form of publication. She sent letter poems, sometimes delivered through intermediaries in the manner of social authors, to Susan Gilbert Dickinson, despite the fact that she lived right next door. She also obliterated the line between poetry and correspondence, the traditional carriers of social manuscripts, and went so far as to incorporate the iconography of stamps into the lines of her poems. A more compelling act of defiance was in her epistolary relationships with two editors: Samuel Bowles of the *Springfield Republican*, and Thomas Wentworth Higginson, who was associated with the *Atlantic Monthly*, both of whom respected her reluctance to print the very poems she mailed to them. She, however, knew that her poems were read aloud by Susan Dickinson—a form of traditional social publication the poet probably relished.[23]

Regarding the production of her own work, Emily Dickinson magnified social manuscript formats and implicated them in her art. She thumbed her nose at "fixed" texts by constantly editing her own or inviting others, Susan Dickinson being the most active, to collaborate. In adamantly clinging to manuscript publication, she utilized "certain manuscript features—calligraphic orthography, punctuation, capitalization, and line breaks—[to] help to convey meaning." The letter format also inspired her, but she frequently lapsed into the letter poem, a characteristic blending not uncommon among her contemporaries. Epistolary poem "gifts" in honor of birthdays or other special days or poems on separate sheets enclosed inside letters gave outlet to her creativity. Dickinson also made formalistic use of excerpts—augmenting her own words with published poetry, as antebellum social authors often did. She included common enclosures found in letters—such as newsclippings, dried flowers, ribbons, and stamps—and these often became intrinsic to the text of her letters and poetry. Conversely, her poetry notes sent with gifts mimicked traditional social forms; one sent pinned around a piece of pencil to Bowles (or his wife) not only hints that her correspondent is lazy in replying, it also speaks volumes about handwriting versus print—for example, the sense of handscript being, like a handshake, a necessary gesture of social intercourse, but one easily dispensed with in print. Even the materials Dickinson used for writing—particularly, fine stationery—alluded to everyday scribblings of ordinary social authors. Just as they jotted messages in newspapers (which were cheaper to mail than letters), she, too, composed on a periodical's margin. She also wrote on the back of a shopping list and used old envelopes, reminiscent of correspondence itself, for writing. By writing on the back of a "legal form" or "pharmacy wrapper," Dickinson subverted the printed word with original handscript. Like common folk who sewed their own diaries, commonplace books, or composition pamphlets, she handcrafted her "fascicles," even though blank books were much cheaper during the second half of the nineteenth century than before.[24]

Before her identity as a social poet against the market increasingly solidified in the postbellum years, Dickinson passed in and out of print like any of her antebellum contemporaries. Like them, she was inspired to write by everyday occurrences, social events, and holidays; and also, like her contemporaries, had her creations pirated by well-meaning thieves who found outlets in periodicals that seldom paid for copy. Her first stolen publications were valentines, those socially inspired manuscripts that were typically composed by her contemporaries and mailed or sent via page throughout February to various friends, classmates, family members, and neighbors. Two of these, one written for her sister's beau, wound up in periodicals—one, a college publication, the *Indicator*, and the other a high profile newspaper, the *Springfield Daily Republican*—evidently absent her assent. Her next pirated publication, "Nobody knows this little rose," published in the latter, apparently was sent to a woman as a note accompanying a floral gift. Again, the idea was unexceptional among her contemporaries who, knowing how their recipients valued presentation notes as much as the gift itself, took pains to write something heartfelt. With the outbreak of war, Dickinson reflected her society's obsession with reading and writing about it. Her remaining publications, nearly all originally printed during the Civil War era in the *Springfield Republican*, the *Drum Beat*, the *Round Table*, and the *Brooklyn Daily Union*, were either secretly placed by other people or, in the case of the *Drum Beat*, cajoled from her by patriotic Unionists. With the exception of two more poems printed in 1866 and 1878, she successfully resisted publication until her death in 1886. Ironically, just as her self-constructed image as a social poet had matured, she was becoming something of a curiosity, if not a celebrity—a victim of "the public's vicarious consumption of [female authors'] 'personal lives'" in the latter half of the nineteenth century.[25]

Henry David Thoreau also achieved a modest celebrity in his time, but unlike Dickinson, he, as a "connected critic" of the literary marketplace, actively pursued print publication. Thoreau's earliest efforts at professionalism went well beyond the average amateur's. Although his first publications, first an 1837 obituary in the local *Yeoman's Gazette*, then with the *Dial* in July 1840, were not recompensed, he early on sought out paying venues, and in January 1843 published "A Walk to Wachusett" in the genteel "ladies' magazine" we discussed in chapter 1, the *Boston Miscellany*, which offered its authors high rates. After he moved to Staten Island in May, he visited in New York City "every bookseller[']s or publisher's house," including Harper's, "and discussed their affairs with them," but with little success. While there, he also "tried the Democratic

Review, the New Mirror, and Brother Jonathan," as well as the *Knicker-bocker*, the *Ladies' Companion*, and the *New World*. "My bait will not tempt the rats," he complained to his mother. He did around this time publish with a New York periodical, the *United States Democratic Review*, that on average offered its authors about two dollars per page. A paid author upon his return to Concord in November 1843, he received ten dollars for an essay in the *Dial*, and continued to publish in its pages until its demise in April 1844. Although the next three years were spent writing (only rarely publishing in print), drafting his books, living at Walden Pond, and lecturing, his work would appear again in the popular month-lies. In March and April 1847 he published a signed, lead essay, "Thomas Carlyle and His Works," in *Graham's Magazine*, and in 1848 the serial, "Ktaadn, and the Maine Woods," came out in five installments in the *Union Magazine*. Later acceptances by *Sartain's*, *Putnam's*, and the *Atlantic Monthly* proved that Thoreau could compete for literary dollars with the most popular of authors in the increasingly lucrative marketplace for periodicals.[26]

Like amateur and minor authors who were often shepherded into print by members of their social networks, Thoreau was advantaged by his literary and professional friends' encouragement, advice, praise, and often tireless efforts to publish his work. Ralph Waldo Emerson recommended that his friend Thoreau start his journal, the "quarry and substance of much of his best work." Thoreau's first professional publication—in the premier issue of the *Dial*—was solicited, spon-sored, and virtually thrust upon the reluctant editor, Margaret Fuller, by Emerson. Emerson helped in various other ways—by finding Thoreau paid work outside of publishing, by seeking a publisher for *A Week on the Concord and Merrimack*, and by coordinating with Tho-reau a publicity campaign for it in the United State and England (for example, sending out review copies) once it was brought out by Munroe and Company, which did little to promote its sales. The *Tribune's* Horace Greeley, who Thoreau met in New York, was likewise invaluable, primarily as his informal agent who placed pieces in popu-lar periodicals, wrote dunning letters to editors who were sluggish in paying, and publicized his lectures and printed publications in the pages of his paper.[27]

While Thoreau was in print more regularly than most of his amateur counterparts, like them he hardly earned enough by writing to make a living. Although he managed to place much of his work in paying periodicals, extracting the promised money was often difficult or impossible. Despite badgering by Emerson, Thoreau was evidently never paid as promised for his essay, "A Walk to Wachusett," printed in the short-lived *Boston Miscellany*, which tried to appease him with free copies; the three dollars per page owed him by *Sartain's Union Magazine* for two sketches printed in July and August 1852 also went unpaid by the then financially unstable periodical. Greeley had to wrest payment for his "client" from *Graham's*. Book publishing proved even more risky. Thoreau's first book, *A Week on the Concord and Merrimack*—technically published by Munroe but in reality financed by Thoreau himself, who was expected to pay costs from sales or else reimburse the company—was a monetary disaster. He took 706 of the remaining copies (left from the edition of 1,000) in October 1853 with some debt still owed to Munroe, and sold or otherwise disposed of some of them himself. Recompense for the more successful *Walden*, financed by Ticknor and Fields, who offered a substantial royalty, was nonetheless meager. Throughout much of his life, Thoreau relied upon other sources of income: schoolteaching; caretaking for the Emerson household "in very dangerous prosperity," as he jocularly described it; tutoring; surveying; and involvement with his father's pencil factory. While living in New York, he, like Joshua Harris, even tried to sell periodical subscriptions, with similarly sorry results.[28] For all his nonliterary employment, Thoreau had relatively better luck inside the literary marketplace than many aspiring professionals who printed without pay, who had no entrée to influential circles, who were discouraged from lecturing (namely, women), and who were thus almost wholly dependent on income from other sources.

Although he aimed at reaching a wide reading public through print, Thoreau, like most of his contemporaries, great and ordinary, fashioned personal records and literary pieces with no specific intent to publish them except to a small audience of familiar readers. He wrote academic compositions in his youth for his preceptors, composed for specific readers, and, of course, kept notebooks and journals that became the repository of original poems, ideas, drafts, and excerpts for publications. Some scholars consider his journals, still today not printed in their entirety, his finest production. Social dissemination to other authors and intellectuals further honed his writing. With Emerson and William Ellery Channing, for example, he exchanged poetry and journals. One scholar even likened the then common habit among the transcendentalists (and other of their contemporaries) of exchanging journals to "paying a social call." He read aloud from his unpublished manuscripts and solicited comments from Mary Moody Emerson, while Bronson Alcott heard manuscripts that would become part of *A Week on the Concord and Merrimack*. Besides garnering inspiration through his social networks, Thoreau tapped into everyday events and the nonliterary production they inspired. The logic and language of account books and agricultural recordkeeping, for example, filters through *Walden* as it does through many multifunction antebellum diaries. His poems could originate in ordinary social communication, as did his earliest published ones, which were first written for and about people he knew. A good example is his first book, begun with some penciled, dated notes later copied into his journal; it was about a simple excursion with his brother, and ended as a monumental tribute to him. Even Thoreau's private correspondence, the mainstay of social authorship, could become material for print. Like those of his social-author counterparts, Thoreau's letters were not immune to theft by a well-meaning editor—in his case, Horace Greeley, who pirated one for his *Tribune*.[29] So, though Thoreau's ambitions centripetally went outward in the direction of literary dollars wherever he could find them, he remained intellectually sustained through the social sense of his surrounding circles and their centrifugal literary practices. With a would-be professional's consciousness all too painfully aware of the market's elusive rewards, he thus nevertheless remained, especially at the start of his career, much within the social-authorship fold.

The same generalizations about social authorship that pertain to Thoreau might, to an even greater extent, apply to Ralph Waldo Emerson. Aside from the youthful zeal for academic composition, verse writing, and translation that affected most students, the obvious comparison lies in the extent to which personal records stimulated ideas and acted as wellsprings of inspiration for future publication. Like Thoreau, Emerson assiduously kept journals, called by one scholar "his greatest formal achievement, his true and adequate genre," from which he drew material for lectures and printed pieces. The journals were, in part, collaboratively conceived in that he interwove, in the manner of a conversation, quotations with his own ideas, extracted correspondents' letters and other people's journals into his own, and allowed some intimates within his circles to peruse them, hear them read, and comment upon them. This coterie included Bronson Alcott, Margaret Fuller, and his Aunt Mary Moody Emerson, who first helped him develop his journalizing. He similarly used sociabilities—a dinner party at which he read aloud some verses, for example—to subject his pieces in progress to criticism. Emerson also wrote occasional poetry; one example not published in his lifetime accompanied an 1868 New Year's present to Lidian, his second wife. He especially valued the four-volume anthology he compiled (not intending it for print) from transcripts of his aunt's correspondence, laden with philosophy, literary quotations, and ideational extensions of them, and selections from her spiritual "almanack," which profoundly influenced his language, imagination, intellectual development, and writings. No doubt the rhyming journal he kept with Ellen Tucker Emerson became as precious a memento as her letters, which he allowed good friends to see. Not content to let social manuscripts lie dormant, he attempted to print a volume of his deceased brother Charles's papers and Thoreau's journals. He published pieces of both of his brothers, Charles and Edward, his deceased wife's poetry in the *Dial*, and, of course, Margaret Fuller's *Memoirs*, which liberally combined her published and unpublished writings with personal reflections and other material by members of her circles. In a move that seems undermining of social authorship and at the same time respectful of it, Emerson conceived "Verses of the Portfolio," a department of the *Dial* devoted to poetry written without print as an end.[30] Surely he held in high regard the unpolished style of social manuscripts and their unpretentious sentiments that arose from social sensibilities, even though he himself painstakingly edited his own writing for print by major commercial publishing houses.

Despite his publishing record, Emerson never relinquished the means of social authorship in that his main venue for publishing was not print but the spoken word. His literary professionalism, ironically, was wedded to more traditional oral delivery. He accumulated "seven thick volumes" worth of unprinted sermons and lectures by "the early 1840s" alone in addition to "thousands of pages of journals." As a minister, he was required to write sermons—literary productions in their own right—but only one was published before 1877, "The Lord's Supper," which appeared the previous year. After he left the ministry in 1832, the lecturing he invariably turned to when financially strapped became a primary source of his literary dollars; by the early 1850s he was delivering as many as eighty lectures a year. Although he published more lectures (or permutations of them) than sermons, he sometimes objected to timely newspaper transcriptions that effectively devalued oral publication and delivered, for a few pennies, what would cost a half dollar or more in the lecture hall. Of course, he would get none of the proceeds of the pennies and make more from the half-dollar receipts in one night than he could by placing the piece in most magazines. With the rise of corporate tour management through lecture bureaus and commercial booking agents in the 1860s, the stakes grew even higher, for although the service usually cost 10 percent of the take, the efficiencies gained made it even more profitable so that lecturers might expect to reach audiences of 50,000 within each season—without the former hassle of lecturers making their own connection with sponsoring committees. There is little wonder that Emerson quickly availed himself of these new booking arrangements as soon as they emerged.[31] As much for—and probably more than—the dollars it provided, lecturing made social sense for, unlike print, oral publication was immediate, enacted in real time before a live and often interactive audience.

Because he savored the social remnants of authorship, Emerson devoted much time and effort to promoting, financing, editing, and guiding other authors' work into print. Advancing their professionalism seemed more urgent than getting his own words in print. The world of sponsorship, that liminal space between being in and out of the market altogether, was perhaps more agreeable to Emerson than the world of publishing that fixed his own ideas into typeset words. Besides editing the *Dial* and championing Thoreau, as we have seen, he brought out American editions of Thomas Carlyle's work, and acted as "agent" to him and to Margaret Fuller. Another of his "clients," Jones Very, submitted his *Essays and Poems* to Emerson's significant and "high-handed" editorial changes, and another still, Bronson Alcott, entrusted his arcane manuscript, "'Psyche: or the Breath of Childhood,'" to his friend's editorial eye that spotted six pages' worth of "'verbal inaccuracies.'" While he undoubtedly longed for collaboration, it is clear that Emerson was not among the best of agents regarding marketing strategies. Certainly, the *Dial* would not survive in the competitive periodical market; his advice to Fuller about publishing *Summer on the Lakes in 1843* with Munroe and Company, instead of Little and Brown, who had financed her book, had she followed it would have entailed monetary loss.[32] Emerson, however, volunteered prodigious time and effort, and often money, for unselfish social and literary ends that brought him into the market more than he perhaps would have liked to be.

Emerson thus responded to the market in a way that differed dramatically from Dickinson's subversive disdain and Thoreau's tentative embrace with frequent regenerating recourse back to social authorship. Rather, Emerson aimed to reconfigure the evanescent relations among social, amateur, and professional authorship so that the creativity of the older forms could enrich and enliven the new. In doing this, he had the advantage of his position as a much sought after and well-paid lecturer. Given the high regard and widespread popularity oratory still enjoyed in the antebellum years, his solution, for the moment at least, allowed him to transfer social and amateur authorship practices to a world of face-to-face professional orality, to which the printed word played only a secondary and enhancing role.[33] The solution could not work for long, for market-driven ways of disseminating the printed and spoken word were nigh, and these would help to make the antebellum regime of orality obsolete.[34] Ironically, it would be the many printed editions of his work, culminating in the twelve-volume edition of his oeuvre just after the turn of the century, that would both keep him in the public eye and assure his longstanding place in the American literary canon.[35]

Changes in Literary Distribution

With the Civil War years, the transformation in authorship that made it a career possibility affecting, in different ways, Dickinson, Emerson, Forten, Larcom, Thoreau, and Trowbridge had its distributional counterpart, as literary dissemination informally coursing through social networks was increasingly replaced by professionals selling to customers in the field. Much of this paralleled other industries' vertical and horizontal integration and nationally oriented mass marketing. For print distribution, two interrelated communication systems facilitated product and personnel movements: (1) railroad monopolies, which offered more direct travel without having to change lines, along with through ticketing and baggage handling (and better reliability of postal delivery); and (2) the telegraph, which became a way to coordinate far-flung business enterprises, especially with salespeople in the field. Other innovations were fiduciary, like war-era federal paper money, which spelled the end of bank-specific notes circulating at variable discounts based on distance and the issuing institution's soundness. Obviously, this removed uncertainty in cash transactions on the road. Another development was modern checking, supported by better clearinghouses, by which customers could respond via mail to billing. The structural changes spawned a culture of hard-drinking, card-playing, sharply dressed, and ever affable drummers lounging in rail coaches or hotel saloons across the land. These foot soldiers, as corporate agents, could make a good living and graduate up the management ladder to watch over successive generations of sales personnel.[36]

Corresponding changes in book distribution were most clearly seen in subscription publishing, which came to vie successfully with traditional houses. Its rise started while hostilities yet raged; several "war books," hawked by disabled veterans and issued by but five or so firms proved its profitability. A stream of sure-fire sellers—often reference books on medicine, law, or religion, along with adventure and standard literature (e.g., Shakespeare or Dickens)—followed, as did overly aggressive sales tactics. To remedy this, major publishers in 1870 agreed to guidelines governing agents' conduct. With public confidence assured, orders only continued to grow, so much so that many authors—like Mark Twain—came to rely upon this venue for its relative profitability. Its success can be attributed to active selling, compared with bookstores' passive approach. These agents and those working for emergent wholesalers differed from their antebellum antecedents in relying upon the hard sell, sometimes codified by employers in printed instructions of how to keep one's foot in the slamming door. A book agent working California's Upper Central Valley for *Tom Sawyer* in the late 1870s noted that she abided by the "instructions" of the "guiding pamphlet" that she "had received in connection with my evil outfit from the city furnishing establishment." (She deployed "evil" sarcastically in light of an eavesdropped conversation she had previously reported that condemned female book agency.) Hard selling brought books where no bookstore could, an ideal adaption to the scattered rural market. That California agent, for example, plied her wares among upstart goldfield settlements around Oroville, about 150 miles from her Oakland home base. Agents were now big-city strangers proffering gentility—via ornate coffee-table volumes or giftbooks—to humble homes, not the earlier travelers from neighboring counties who could weave literature into local social relations while veiling the profit motive. "There was nothing at all agreeable to me except the money I received," Twain's erstwhile agent concluded, shortly before leaving her saturated territory for a grueling stint in Solano County.[37]

Subscription books were not the only items sold hard. Textbooks, too, were vigorously pressed upon school boards making immense purchases for entire systems, as public funding increased, school years lengthened, attendance rates went up, curricula expanded, school libraries developed, and high schools became common. Bribery flourished, needless to say, as agents figuratively broke arms across the country to wrest textbook adoptions. Because this was big business, indeed, they were paid well, up to $5,000 a year. With such high stakes came savage undercutting of the competition. In response, during the 1870s the biggest textbook houses joined in limiting the number of traveling agents and reining in their abuses. When this soon failed, high-pressure underselling resumed until 1890, when the majors formed a monopoly, the American Book Company. It did not end the problems, but merely institutionalized them in a way that stabilized business by removing competition.[38] Textbook agents simply became cogs in large bureaucratic wheels.

Impersonality afflicted other areas of book distribution, too. This is not surprising, since the independent local bookstore, with its lively social life, was an endangered species, its habitat chewed up not only by agents but by discounting in department stores that undercut specialized retailers through bulk buying. Department stores themselves, of course, relied upon volume foot traffic that discouraged ongoing sociabilities characteristic of booksellers catering directly to customers' needs. Eagle-eyed floor managers assured against overfamiliarity between patrons and clerks. Yet even less personal was mail-order purchasing, a practice partly originating from department stores filling postal requisitions. From 1879 until 1904, one mail-distribution giant, the American News Company, virtually monopolized sending paperback series via low second-class periodical postage rates. For other types of trade books, publishers cooked up other direct-mail selling schemes, from book clubs organized from afar to appeals through printed advertisements—the latter increasingly taken up by yet another middleman, the ad agent.[39] In short, because the direction of economic change was toward scale, monopoly, and mass marketing, earlier social relations surrounding dissemination disappeared quite rapidly. Books were becoming but consumer items brought into a person's life by either the direct hard sell or the more distant impersonal market.

The case for periodicals was similar. In fact, it was the American News Company itself that also achieved near total control over national periodical distribution, especially to newsstands and other outlets catering to quickly moving customers, as well as in railroad trains and stations. The conglomerate's power was so vast in the outright buying of virtually all copies beyond direct subscription sales that it could make or break emerging periodicals. But even local newspapers felt the weight of the changes, as they began to purchase ready-made copy (sometimes even preprinted "insides" of four-page sheets) from syndicates that relieved them of the burden of locating talent, eliciting stories, editing them, and negotiating payment. The dissemination of professional authors' work had become big business, at the expense of many amateurs and their networks of social authorship.[40]

Dissemination from lecture platforms after the Civil War also followed the corporate path, as lecturing became more highly organized and speakers better and more regularly paid. The key figure in the change was Boston's James Redpath, who in 1868 began his Lyceum Bureau, which would rule the circuit well into the twentieth century. He developed a star system in which notables signed contracts with him to appear at successive venues, thus essentially professionalizing the relationship between booking agency and speaker. The system meshed well with promoting one's career as a writer, so it was not surprising to see luminaries like Henry Ward Beecher and Mark Twain among Redpath's literary stars. These and lesser lights rode the rails under the auspices of lyceum bureaus to even smaller communities, thus linked into an emerging national entertainment system that included not only individuals but traveling companies with stage sets, and even, eventually, the Chautauqua movement, one of the last hold-overs of community-controlled self-edification. All this fell under lecture bureaus' purview, but circus and vaudeville circuits also held in common many traits and some performers. The net effect was that geographically scattered audiences increasingly experienced similar homogenized entertainment products. No longer did communities offer thoughtful invitations to distinguished guests to speak upon topics of local concern. In fact, one 1871 commentator on the Western lecture circuit called its speakers "numbskulls" who "draw to them the rough and uncouth element in every town they visit, and ... shut out all the culture and refinement of the same town."[41] The national market had triumphed.

WHITHER THE AMATEUR?

Just as amateur disseminators receded into the background of larger professionalization, so too did social authors who disseminated their work among their coteries. As we discussed in chapter 1, early-nineteenth-century social authorship could easily evolve into amateur authorship for print surreptitiously, due to piracy, or simply because the author wanted to take the next step. Antebellum amateurism, then, may be seen as a stage on the way to professionalism, as a midway point in the spectrum between social authorship and professionalism, or as a dead end for the talentless or unmotivated. But it also often stood as an end in and of itself, one that kept (at times) private social sense ever flowing into the public sphere, where the resulting printed work might or might not be remunerated. By the late nineteenth century, however, social authorship outside of academic concerns (classroom composition and recitation of original work), was reprivatized, hearkening back to the early modern period when printing opportunities were much rarer than they were in the antebellum United States.[42] Reprivatization meant that writers were increasingly producing for their own self-edification and a much more limited audience that furtively stole glances, or volunteered supportive or critical reads, or accepted written gifts, but that did not itself necessarily engage in writing. Valentines and occasional gift notes, for example, once written by social authors, became mass-produced "greeting cards," purchased by consumers who distributed them to other consumers.[43] Diaries—once handmade, but often commonly manufactured blank books or simple line-a-day pamphlets—now more than ever appeared in personally appealing ornately bound editions, in which discursive entries were encouraged by generous spaces beneath each printed date, while privacy could be secured with lock and key. The diary became increasingly a personal confidante, privy to intimate emotions and reflections, rather than the deliberate social production that previously had been written, at least in part, for other people's scrutiny.[44] Personal letter writing not only diminished with falling telegram prices after the 1860s and the advent of the telephone in 1876, but that which did remain was less likely to have rhetorical literary flourishes, quotations from authors, or literary enclosures.[45] Other, often collaborative literary productions, such as commonplace books and scrapbooks read and admired by antebellum coteries, went into near extinction; as photos became cheaper during and after the Civil War, literary scrapbook keeping was replaced by photograph or stamp collecting—consumer hobbies usually unrelated to literary production (except that collectors filled in blank books)—while the keeping of a commonplace book became "well nigh gone" by the end of the century.[46] Tellingly, many of the scrapbooks that were kept consisted of nonliterary newsclips and commercial prose or images, especially the so-called colorful trade cards that blossomed after the mid-1870s.[47] The mute icon was coming to replace the eloquent word as worth preserving and remembering.

With reprivatization, social dissemination became unnecessary. The habit of reading aloud in homes dwindled, until it became a rare special moment of social devotion hearkening back to an earlier time; more frequently, it was done briefly to convey a striking passage or a practice surrounding putting children to bed or nursing the sick or the infirm.[48] Passing around albums became an end-of-the-school-year ritual at the academic establishment rather than a neighborhood exercise.[49] Public libraries assumed the role of disseminators, which had once been the province of home librarians who voluntarily lent books.[50] Because so many magazines became cheap and nationally oriented (largely due to newsstand distribution and mass-market advertising), there was scarce need to exchange them through the mails; and because the content of many local newspapers became nationalized as well, there was little that would need to be clipped but some news items or personally oriented announcements, like obituaries, which themselves became more informational and less literary.[51]

Due to this reprivatization, the nature of amateurism changed, too. Amateurs, those authors who joined writing groups, practiced, or otherwise honed their skills, now wrote "for the love of it" rather than for supplemental income, professional ends, or propagation of ideas. In this sense they were like social authors who did not print; but bereft of authentic social networks devoted to literary pursuits, they created societies of fellow amateurs.[52] Readers who were once also writers, if only of diaries and letters, could better appreciate published authors' skills and talents, but increasingly, even for amateurs, the mode of reception became much more passive.[53] What published literature did for amateurs became more important than how authors achieved effects—or how those effects might be borrowed and incorporated into one's own heartfelt life narrations and correspondence within social and family circles.[54] With literary interpersonal expression being replaced by models based on the cash nexus, amateurs came to ape published authors' market roles, and that meant having fun with or otherwise manipulating techniques and formulas that sold, not those that furthered communication in the name of social sense. However they might assume the professional guise, outlets for placing their work were diminishing, however. National syndication, particularly, would spell the beginning of the end of local pieces finding their way into town newspapers. In short, as professionals gobbled up more and more of the available work, it disrupted the pathway from unpaid or low-paying local, regional, special interest, and then national (or sectional) publications to paying national ones, which people like Forten, Larcom, and Trowbridge had earlier walked. Not surprisingly, literary amateurism declined so much that it became classed as but one among many competing hobbies—and a minor one at that.[55]

The vast majority of readers would now never think of themselves as writers, nor as sharing with celebrated litterateurs a community of creativity. After all, literature was increasingly one among many alternative entertainment products, including vaudeville, musical theater, melodrama, lectures, blackface minstrelsy and coon-song sheets, player pianos, stereoscopes, comic strips, amusement parks, circuses, spectacles, spectator sports, nightclubs, band concerts, and, eventually, motion pictures, phonographs, and radios. For many readers, the very thought of writing for oneself or for social circles was as outrageous as that of riding a horse through a flaming hoop—it was better to let the hardened professional do it. As readers' sensibility no longer emerged from a base of social authorship and amateurism, but instead from their experiences in choosing among the available (and affordable) media array, they assumed an audience position entailing only a limited commitment that could leave unchallenged deeper faiths and firmer allegiances—the social sense of antebellum years that literature helped to construct and maintain.[56] The new role allowed people from varying backgrounds to come together to achieve a fleeting unity within cultural consumption, without ever bothering to learn how to do the activity or even to inquire how it was done. Part of the enjoyment of reading, say, a best-seller like George du Maurier's *Trilby* (1894) or an issue of a popular ten-center like *Munsey's*, was engaging in a timely nationwide ritual of communalization with other like-minded readers (those unable or unwilling to engage in the literary product, of course, remained much in the shadows or, if not, as points against which to achieve cultural distinction).[57] This was not like the earlier "operational aesthetic" in which audiences were fascinated by the mechanism of hoaxing, but rather like going on an amusement park ride, as a prefabricated set of techniques applied sequentially and aimed at producing effects in the rider.[58] This is not to say that readers responded in lockstep fashion; they could resist, ignore, or misapprehend, and do so selectively within even the same literary work, but—most important for the market—they could respond by either buying or avoiding similar products in the future.[59] How one chose to furnish one's realm of cultural experience based on available options for purchase became the highest form of creative action among audiences in the emerging media marketplace.[60]

The resulting assemblages could produce all manner of diverse personal cultural meanings as before, but what had changed was the mode of engaging the individual objects, and, too, the field from which those objects emerged. Simply put, social authors and literary amateurs read differently than people who were principally consumers of cultural products. It was one reason why late-nineteenth-century reading clubs, themselves in eclipse, played down any creative writing component: to be a reader was a decidedly nonproducing role that was difficult to perform in the presence of a seemingly hypercritical writerly consciousness. Literature either worked or it did not, but there was little point in asking why or how; one just moved on to what did work.

"It gives one a thrill of joy to remember that one has an undoubted right to read the author and omit the interpretation, and to say boldly, 'I like this,' or 'I do not like that,'" one turn-of-the century anticritic observed.[61] Consumer choice reigned supreme.

However, calling consumers' role more passive, while obviously true to some degree, risks turning the change into almost a moral failing on the part of readers. This ignores the overall systemic trend in North America of going from a society largely consisting of producers to one of consumers. In this change, literary production played but a small part, so transformations in reading and authorship, though reflecting the larger trend, can hardly be blamed for it. In many areas of life, the market was mediating cultural interactions more than before through ever-monopolizing systems of specialized production, rationalized output, competitive distribution, and self-conscious consumerism.[62] In fact, one could argue that because of its roots in the traditional moral economy of social sense, postbellum publishing was less adapted as a thoroughly hegemonic force legitimating a market regime than other newer areas of cultural production, at least in terms of sustaining a high profit margin.[63] After all, in 1899 the nation's long-standing premier publishing house, Harpers, went, due to its own fault, into bankruptcy and reorganization, just at the time J.P. Morgan and other financiers were presiding over the formation of immensely profitable national conglomerates through mergers.[64] The failings of Harpers that were endemic to the trade left room enough for experimentation to publicize alternatives to the dominant system, or reforms of it. Thus it may be said that, in small measure, what remained of social sense had morphed into social science in some areas of literary production. But even readers' reception of this was reduced to taking in information from authorized experts, not inquiring into the nature and operational limitations of the social science then practiced.[65] The printed word might inform readers, but readers in the future would seldom inform the printed word, as they had when they could write it, and when amateurs could easily move in and out of print.

Active Amateurs

The professionalization, bureaucratization, and nationalization of publishing that elicited passive literary mass consumption transformed some earlier amateur endeavors in active directions, however. The professional wave coursing through American society redefined amateurism in several spheres where it had once dominated—for example, in sports or in science. As professionalism ever more depended on technical accomplishment, it served a public unable and unwilling to engage in that area of activity. Professionals so successfully legitimated their claims to expertise that they set the norms from which amateurism would be judged. Hereafter, amateurs could choose to internalize those norms or idiosyncratically refuse them, as their pursuits were seen as leisure activities, amenable themselves to the marketplace that would provide, for a price, access to technologies and services.[66]

Consumerization affected even amateur journalism. The practice goes back into the antebellum years, when students handwrote or printed newspapers for a small local readership, including other amateur editors. Commercialization awaited the late 1860s when several companies brought out inexpensive "novelty" hand presses specifically targeting the amateur market—the "dom" (short for amateurdom) was born. The number of publications shot up dramatically and the pace of editorial exchanges increased proportionally, which fostered regular networks of correspondents. Almost immediately "professional"-style trade organizations sprang up, one under the auspices of the prominent New York publisher Scribner's. As with any other trade, annual regional and national conventions followed, out of which emerged in 1876 the National Amateur Press Association, replete with its own permanent bureaucracy. Finally, quondam amateur journalists founded in 1904 an organization called The Fossils to honor earlier "dom" productions. By that time these included not only papers of all sorts, but magazines, books, and even puzzles. Producers only to a degree, amateur journalists were nevertheless identified by manufacturers as consumers reachable through advertising for presses, ink, type, and other printing accouterments.[67]

"Dom" culture was only one focus of marketing to amateurs interested in the press. Tapping into dabbling fans' growing awareness of professional journalism, publishers issued a spate of how-to books bearing titles like *The Ladder of Journalism [and] How to Climb It* or *Hints to Young Editors* (sometimes deemed the first journalism textbook). These were accompanied by insider glimpses like *Secrets of the Sanctum: An Inside View of an Editor's Life*, as well as several journalism histories and biographies of important figures. The trend had organizational expression, too. In that many press clubs then served as meeting points for career journalists, amateurs, and the press-conscious public, they provided not only mutual support for professionals but also "sold" journalism to dues-paying and ticket-buying outsiders through sponsoring lecture series on topics, among other revenue-generating activities. A further cash commitment that amateurs could make was to take the courses in journalistic writing that were slowly springing up (then as now, many enrolled but relatively few went on to pursue careers in such). Some extrainstitutional courses developed, often on a proprietary basis, out of press clubs, but colleges, too, soon ventured offerings of an industrial or literary sort, after calls for the establishment of journalism schools to redress the perceived failings of the nation's presses. Through all these avenues amateurs could learn about editing offices without ever setting foot in one—this, while many professionals themselves continued to start on the ground floor and work their way up.[68]

Somewhat in reaction to instructing amateurs in the technicalities of reportage and other expository prose composition, creative writing courses appeared toward the end of the century. As with journalism, this was accompanied by handbooks or other guides aimed at the amateur, but in fewer numbers. Creative writing instruction, however, differed greatly from courses given in journalism schools: it entered the academy beginning in the 1880s decidedly not as training for professional writing careers, but primarily for self-discovery and personal cultivation in pursuit of education in its broader, humanistic sense. With the literary societies that had flourished at midcentury now in decline, creative writing courses became, perhaps, the best fit for the amateur sensibility. Turn-of-the-century writers' workshops were similar if sometimes less formal in that they often self-consciously rejected academic stultification (even if they kept physically close to campuses), but they seldom in this period openly addressed selling for the market.[69] In these varied ways, amateurs could actively produce literature while purchasing services aimed at them, all with little likelihood that their work would be published. By contrast, the people who authored handbooks, taught classes, or ran workshops were usually professionals.

The professional-amateur spectrum seen in journalism and creative writing played quite differently but no less actively in one area of literary dissemination: librarianship. After all, antebellum librarians were almost all amateurs. Rare pioneers, like Charles Coffin Jewett, advocated professionalization, but rapid library development after the 1850s required hosts of librarians, few of whom could be adequately trained before entering service. The solution to the workforce problem was found in well-educated, middle-class, and usually single women who had few alternate employment options. Staffing needs were so great that employees of both genders could work full-time after (at best) the barest apprenticeships, but part-time and temporary engagement remained common, as did new hires starting work with no preparation at all. Against this reign of amateurs, a professionalization movement, led by a cadre of well-educated, mostly upper-middle-class men, coalesced around standards of classification, cataloging, and conduct. In them was vested enough cultural power to influence local library boards and lower-level librarians, so that the latter became by century's end amateur followers, dabblers in the library "science" touted from above. Yet, the professionalization movement cast them in a leadership role regarding patron needs that led to highly selective acquisition policies. Publishers responded with deep discounts or specialized publications, like expensive finding aids that only institutions would buy. A new market of volume purchasers had been created, centered on librarians who had once been mostly communally rooted conveyancers of books and periodicals between accidental collections and eager patrons.[70] Librarians became consumers of publishers' products to a degree heretofore unimaginable.

To this transformation of amateur literary dissemination in libraries might be added countless, often untraceable similar changes elsewhere. Who knows how many folks took up publishers' offers to sell multiple magazine issues to "clubs" at reduced prices? The contact person acted as subscription agent in holding the group together, but this role hardly went further than that of facilitator of the publisher's outreach. And what of those amateur theatricals that became so common in midcentury middle-class homes and schools? How many participants bought the properties they performed or consulted the various printed guides to amateur staging on the market? These players certainly broadcast literature in a way that stimulated the marketplace for print and, especially, if performed for charity, they might even have sold tickets and engaged in advertising. Newsboys, though they had their start before the war, grew by century's end into a multitude of part-time disseminators who had become enfolded in the metropolitan dailies' corporate marketing schemes. Mass industrialization and commercialization, in short, touched nearly every conceivable form of amateur dissemination.[71]

The New Authorship System

The market, itself, by century's end was served by what would become a modern, hierarchical system of authorship. At the top were literary celebrities of two sometimes overlapping sorts: those famous in the moment for selling alone, like Francis Marion Crawford or Archibald Clavering Gunter (their very unfamiliarity today testifies to their ephemerality, even after their decades-long careers), and those like Henry James or, so it was once thought, William Dean Howells, for their supposedly superior literary quality that predicted some permanence. Needless to say, the former's income from book publication, underscored as it was by the first regular best-seller lists in the 1890s, far overwhelmed the latter's, who had to rely upon periodical placements to make ends meet. Magazine appearances kept them in the public eye, however; it was one form of the publicity that most living prominent American writers increasingly had to undertake by feeding information about themselves to the press. Of course, older luminaries like Charles Dickens or the Schoolroom Poets—William Cullen Bryant, Oliver Wendell Holmes Sr., Henry Wadsworth Longfellow, James Russell Lowell, and John Greenleaf Whittier—sailed along without getting up a wind, but their domain was that of the standard edition, not generally current trade publication. Nor did a few British writers, such as Rudyard Kipling or Robert Louis Stevenson, have to exert themselves much in the United States, for they could sell well while still being deemed literary to such a degree that their very names became virtual trademarks. These celebrities of all sorts represented the horizon of hope for the rising generation, often formally introduced to readers though columns like the *Bookman*'s biographical "New Writers." In the competitive environment of up-and-comers, authorial publicity based on models derived from the literary stars became crucial to landing immediate contracts and long-term success. But in the pages of *Bookman* and the other literary journals and "little magazines" of the 1890s, insurgent voices clamored to be heard, too; these belonged to writers like James Gibbons Huneker, H.L. Mencken, Percival Pollard, and William Marion Reedy, and were variously described as bohemian, aesthete, advanced, avant-garde, or amoralist. Often living unconventional lives or holding opinions offensive to community standards, these authors tried to balance notoriety with aspirations to celebrity; in some cases notoriety got the better of them. These writers could become well-known among a small, like-minded readership for their stance against the stolid authorial personalities Crawford or Howells represented.[72]

However much the celebrities, the wannabes, and the naysayers may have set professional expectations, they made up only a small fraction of the 5,817 Americans claiming (to census takers) in 1900 to being employed as "authors and scientists" (the odd combination itself speaking to the literary emergence of the expert). Of course, many of these may be cases of wishful reporting, but a sizable proportion were eking out a living with their pens. One type was the hack, a freelancer with little talent or hope of further advancement, who wrote for hire or as speculation on a case-by-case basis. These risk takers should be distinguished from workmen (and -women) who played it safe in positions of regular employment that supplied the industry with a steady and predictable stream of words. In so-called literary factories the two sometimes labored in tandem as the workers inside brought the story to the outline stage, after which the outside hack was assigned to finish it quickly for a goodly fee. Publishers of story weeklies, dime novels, or series books were most likely to call upon some combination of hack and workman, but they could show up in just about any area of highly commercialized generic production, from textbooks to reference works, even to the copy created in advertising houses.[73]

Many of the writers who published books and articles in nonfiction genres did so only intermittently, often as part of careers in other professions—especially law, the ministry, medicine, and, increasingly, engineering and higher education. The late nineteenth century, after all, saw the rise of the "expert." Yet because institutional certifications were still in their infancy, one of the only ways to assert one's expertise was through print, where it could be validated or rejected by peer and public. (A related way was on the lecture platform.) The nascent research universities became a congenial home for many of these writers, some of whom, like John Dewey, put part of their efforts into acting the role of "public intellectual." It was a role that would not exclude printed expressions of technical knowledge as progressivism took hold around the turn of the century. Not to be discounted among occasional writers were those who contributed to the period's flourishing labor, immigrant, and minority presses; within these enclaves limited renown could be achieved through the printed word, if not usually through paying writing careers. Another group consisted of some women who continued to write on family-oriented topics within a domestic framework that provided some fundamental financial support; quite different were the many well-educated female pioneers who tried to forge professional careers on par with men and thus undertook similar writing projects as them. These varying groups all shared in having writing for print provide some portion of individual incomes, but hardly all or even most of it for very long. Within the authorship system they were usually but very small stakeholders at the bottom of the hierarchy when compared with the aforementioned full-timers. When they approached the presses, they had to do so on terms set by both the celebrated and petty professionals. If literary dollars had for them anything at all to do with social sense, it was not on the level of the former face-to-face community life, but instead within the context of an increasingly abstract, mechanistic construction of society as somehow distinct from its underlying human relations. This was only underscored by having to act according to professional standards in the marketplace of print.[74]

DESOCIALIZATION WITHIN THE CONSUMPTION-PRODUCTION DICHOTOMY

The move from a widely distributed production-based amateur literary regime with roots in social authorship to one reliant upon masses of consumers and a relative handful of career-oriented producers has usually been inscribed by scholars within a triumphalist narrative. In this story, the late-nineteenth-century marketplace not only made gaining a living from the pen a reality for the lucky or talented few, but, more fundamentally, allowed authors' ever-immanent creative potential to emerge full blown with eager immediacy and ready articulation. The shortcomings of this view are similar to those of neoclassical economists whose work is based on a groundless—if often unvoiced and unexamined—faith in immanent market emergence: that market-oriented behavior is naturalized as an ancient impulse liberated only through the historical development in the postfeudal West of institutions friendly to the transcendental spirit of acquisition. Precapitalist formations are thus seen simply as blockages to the eventual, ultimate, and inevitable liberation of *Homo oeconomicus*'s full human potential, while market regimes correspondingly become the best of all possible worlds because they give vent to deep-seated, omnipresent aspirations that are virtually the same in all times and places. Such an evolutionary hydraulic narrative, when applied to antebellum professional authorship, naturally casts amateurs in the role of victims of unyielding protocapitalist publishers or backward-looking holdovers from a world in which the traditional moral economy of social sense restrained or counterpoised the putatively native will to write for literary dollars. The market would supply the valve to let this thwarted impulse at long last spontaneously spring forth. Accordingly, response to this amateurism varies from heartfelt sympathy for genius unrecognized to dismissive annoyance at writers' perversity for not playing along with the market, but, rather, cramming into their productions distracting local and familial minutiae or enigmatic idiosyncracies. Unsurprisingly, in common parlance, the word *amateur* has become not merely a description of a writer's relation to the marketplace of print, but a negative judgment of quality. An author today, even one not writing for profit, would hardly want to be deemed amateurish or a "mere" amateur.[75]

Literary Dollars' Social Costs

The consequences of professionalization look quite different when such reifications of the immanent literary market are set aside, and one can appreciate the historical complexities of how the changing material base interacted with often subtle but profound reconfigurations of human consciousness. Rather than being able to draw immediately upon some instinctive response to literary dollars' allure, people who had grown up in a time before they felt the fullest impact of industrial capitalism had to encounter, engage, and learn the ins and outs of that emerging market for themselves in light of their prior experiences with amateur production and social authorship. Infusing these experiences, as we have shown, was an ineluctable sense of the social aspects of life, whether of the informal sort, as in the sociabilities of literary coteries, or the formal socialities of writing for familial, benevolent, or other institutional purposes.[76]

With this sense of social authorship and amateurism as a backdrop, making money for writing could at first seem almost like a secondary benefit to furthering or expressing social aims, even for people very much in need, like Charlotte Forten or Lucy Larcom, as was discussed in chapter 2. Forten's first dollar was earned for a romantic thank you poem that might well still have been published had she not chosen to complicate it with a striking, deeply felt criticism of American racism. That addition doomed the poem at national magazines whose audience included slaveholders and their Northern doughfaced supporters. Larcom's blend in *Similitudes, from the Ocean and the Prairie* of religious conservatism with German romanticism could sell just about anywhere, but her free-soil sectionalist gloss closed her off from the vast majority of readers not yet subscribing to that persuasion—and, perhaps, too, from publishers Ticknor and Fields whom, it will be remembered, rejected the volume and had a national marketing strategy that encouraged them to avoid controversy and overt partisanship.[77]

Clearly, for Forten, Larcom, and the other authors we considered at the outset, the attitude necessary for writing for the market at any cost to social sense so that one might be paid well, was not easily acquired. After all, this was the lesson that Trowbridge's Martin Merrivale learned, at great pains, as he abandoned dreams of becoming the richly rewarded great romancer for modestly writing for the good of society, suggesting that the emerging abstractly socially conscious realism he and other midcentury American writers espoused may have been a vestige of earlier concrete social sense that would not be thrown off lightly.[78] Likewise, it was difficult, as we have seen in chapter 3, for people to understand authorial reputations within a framework of market-mediated relations. Rather, as seeming fellow producers, renowned litterateurs were ironically appreciated through leveling, while the financial basis of their careers was blithely ignored. Within prevailing opinion, only an elixir of aesthetic quality, accessible achievement, lucky circumstance, and extensive audiences separated them from common folk adept at the pen. Such widespread producer solidarity could spell only ill for the vanguard of publishers' distributors we discussed in chapter 4, to whom fell the difficult task of bringing literary goods before scattered communities resistant to the logic of literary commodification.[79] Paradoxically, success could only be achieved insofar as these middlemen and -women adapted selling the products of the literary marketplace to local social sense. Overall, whether it be in producing literature for print, beholding the reputations of others who did so, or listening to the ploys of distributors, ordinary Americans did not immediately adapt a market consciousness upon their liberation via literary dollars from the integuments of tradition. That change would come only hesitantly and slowly, with few thoroughly unadulterated market expressions along the way.

Instead, the floodgates were at first opened for social sense to shape, for a time, the very literature being produced under market relations. The moral dilemmas over personal and social relations that stream through midcentury literature are but one residual effect. To this may be added the mountain of reform writing, alongside the many pictures of fading small-town and village everyday life that become ever more regionally specific after the Civil War. It was as if postbellum literature could serve to provide reminders of earlier patterns of human relations in the face of an increasingly desocialized, atomized, and, in some cases, tribalizing society.[80] As social sense itself became an artifact of a system of commodified literature, a mere textual reflection of what it once was in the lifeworld, one naturally wonders how these reflections, through their bloodless inauthenticity, may have themselves helped erode practices of literary sociability and sociality.[81] By the time Larcom published her autobiography *A New England Girlhood* in 1889, the distance had grown so great from antebellum social sense that it demanded an ambitious project of specific memory recovery as untainted as possible by what had become generalized, formulaic nostalgia of the old-oaken-bucket, old-folks-at-home type.[82] Though successful, it was too late, and it was probably too popular for the wrong reasons: the mythologizing of industrious, white, Anglo-Protestant Yankee womanhood in the face of pluralistic threats posed by immigrants from Ireland and Southern and Eastern Europe who were often blamed for labor unrest, and by the Yellow Peril and the Brown Scare, not to mention growing white Northern racism in reaction to the first trickles of African American out-migration from the Jim Crow South and from the "Black Atlantic." The remnants of social sense in the marketplace so geared to nervous, white, middle-class readers, unavoidably took on a self-consciously ethnic (or antiethnic) valence. By the 1890s, even the *Atlantic Monthly*, which had brought before the public socially sensitive pieces by Forten, Larcom, and Trowbridge could publish articles in favor of immigration restriction. What made social sense in print to these readers became socially defensive and, at times, reactionary.[83]

Still, literary traditions, even under full market sway, are seldom thoroughly upturned, due to the long shadows of precedent and influence, so social sense in its attenuated, decommunalized form would remain yet embedded in American writing. Frictions with the market, both the literary one and the system itself, would be not uncommon among writers, even among a few who could arguably sell well because of it. Indeed, in certain periods of social ferment, such as the years before World War I, the 1930s, and the late 1960s, such friction could draw authorial social criticism out from its slumberous latency to become a mainstay of writing practice within the marketplace.[84] However, even in these moments of seeming recovery of social sense, widespread desocialization of readers as individualistically driven consumers tended to undermine the efficacy of such efforts, particularly outside of rare, organic working-class literary constituencies. Still, some measure of conscience, if not always the clearest social consciousness, seems unerasable in American writing.[85]

Canonical Reflections

In light of what became an endemic and fluctuating ambivalence of the literary world toward the market in the wake of diminishing social sense, the work of Emily Dickinson, Ralph Waldo Emerson, and Henry David Thoreau, the canonical writers considered above, invites reexamination, as perhaps do others on the cusp between amateurism and professionalization. Critical estimation of their quality has to some degree depended on their artistic departure from the conventional literature of their times as seen in top magazines and editions from important publishers. (That some unique Americanness has been attributed to canonized writers over those slavishly imitating British models is, of course, also part of the story.) Since none—or, if dubiously including Henry Wadsworth Longfellow, then one—of the canonized writers could be said to be highly successful in the antebellum market, this perception of relative quality itself bespeaks either their ill fit with it or later critics' valorization of this maladaption; perhaps, likely, it was both.[86]

What happens, though, if such canonized work is set against a background not of the aforementioned conventional literature, but of the massive output of other amateurs and social authors who shared this tension with the market? Like this larger group, what canonized authors chose to write about was not always determined by commercial needs or practices, but was done to fulfill social responsibilities to their specific surrounding coterie, often peopled not with just other published writers, but with family and friends as well. It is a mistake, then, to take the anonymous market as the primary audience for this work; it was, rather, the face-to-face relations of the literary circle, with the market playing—if anything at all—a mere supporting role after, perhaps, other different coteries. This fact raises questions concerning the extent to which the primary group or its members may be attributed some measure of credit for the canonical achievement, a case particularly extreme in Mary Moody Emerson's influence upon her famous nephew. If it is inconceivable that he would be the author we know without her, maybe she is a bit of the Emerson we think we know. The existence of key local audiences of producers like her also pushes impersonal intertextual influences more into the background than they have been; what, say, published New York writers, especially self-proclaimed literary nationalists like those of "Young America," were doing perhaps mattered less to Emerson's or Thoreau's writing than small variants within the local intellectual climate of Concord, Massachusetts. It may be an obvious point, but well worth making, for despite gestures toward paying final respects to "the death of the author," American literary criticism has tended to seek after individual genius sitting solitary in the garret, while it has slighted group-inspired creativity, and even belittled the tea drinking and berry picking that accompanied literary sociability. It is certain, too, that the contextual knowledge about that small primary social audience will become ever more crucial as the vast unpublished manuscript oeuvre of Dickinson, Emerson, and Thoreau is more fully assessed by scholars, some of whom argue that it matches or exceeds the quality of much writing of theirs that has already been published. If the role of coteries is kept front and center, as it must be to deal adequately with this material, it promises much insight into common amateur and social authorship practices. This means, too, that the recent trend toward rejecting these canonical authors' works as sources for the study of social history may need to be somewhat reversed. On the other side of the coin, the broader field of amateur and social-author production demands to be fully explored in order to understand why canonical authors may have stood out in their own times and beyond, and what made them unique within their own. They may have been perhaps not particularly well-adjusted to a world of professional authorship, as was the common case, but they may have been amateurs and social authors par excellence. Indeed, in this way, the very terms of our aesthetic appreciation of their work may change. Such a shift in focus, of course, calls for nothing less than a reorientation of antebellum literary study away from a relatively narrow range of publication venues to embrace the immense ocean of print in small-time newspapers and magazines, and the even greater one of literary manuscript production circulated through social networks. The corpus of what may be deemed antebellum American literature would thus expand exponentially.[87]

With this reorientation toward antebellum literary amateurism and social authorship, we may thus come to appreciate the canonized authors all the better, and, possibly, if it encourages further investigation, discover many more amateurs worthy of our close modern attention. Not all talented writers enjoyed "the privilege of going on," after all—nor did many of them want to. Their misgivings—and those of the other writers, readers, and distributors we have discussed in these pages—about the antebellum marketplace of print act as a caution against reifying upon them the drive for literary dollars as a controlling motive. The substantial countervailing force of social sense has been and must not be further ignored. That literary dollars have loomed so disproportionately large in twentieth-century interpretations of mid-nineteenth-century writing is, of course, understandable, since reading and writing for social ends commonly has taken a back seat to doing so for self-actualization. By allowing social sense to complicate our view of antebellum literary production, we can perhaps see how historically contingent our own current literary system is, and how it might be altered in more socially constructive directions. As we rewrite antebellum literary history to counterbalance then hopeful dollars against long-standing sensibilities of what was deemed right and just, maybe through some unimaginable alchemy, we can yet still come to our own collective social senses about the uncharted potentialities of literary life, then and now.

APPENDIX 1

CHARLOTTE FORTEN'S "TO A BELOVED FRIEND; ON RECEIVING A TINY BOUQUET OF WILD FLOWERS FROM THE HILLS OF OUR DEAR NEW ENGLAND"

Through all the warm, bright May-day,
    My weary heart had sighed
For the green hills of the country,
    For the river's cooling tide.

I was weary of the city,
    Weary of the noisy throng,
That through the close and crowded streets
    Went hurrying along.

Weary of stony *pavements*,
    Instead of Nature's *green*—
Of high, thick walls, with only
    Glimpses of sky between.

And I longed to breathe again, love,
    The pure, sweet, Northern air,
To gather on our hill-sides
    The treasures nestling there;

To feel the cooling breezes
   Kiss my flushed and fevered cheek;
To hear their soothing voices
   To my troubled spirit speak.

But while, with earnest longings,
   I thought of them and thee,
Came thy precious little offering—
   Bringing joy and peace to me.

The modest little May-flower,
   The blue-eyed violet,
The bright and graceful columbine,
   In tents of scarlet set.

How thrilled my heart with leasure
   At the welcome sight of these!
As the true heart of a lover,
   When the loved one's face he sees.

Straightway sad thoughts departed,
   And happy memories, then,
Of hill, and vale, and streamlet,
   Came to my heart again.

Thoughts of our pleasant rambles
   On rare and bright May-days;
When blossoms smiled, and robins
   Sang us their sweetest lays

When o'er the green hills roaming,
   We cast aside all care,
And thought alone of Nature,
   The beautiful and fair.

Or when beside Old Ocean
   We stood in silent awe—
And gazed upon the wild waves,
   As they dashed against the shore.

All forms and hues of beauty—
    Of earth, and sea, and skies,
Since the coming of thy flowers,
    Have passed before my eyes.

And I thank thee for these glimpses
    Of my loved and distant home—
When thou and I no longer
    O'er the dear old hills may roam.

I thank thee for these flowers—
    More dear than richest gem;
I shall think of *thee*, beloved one,
    Whene'er I look on *them*.

Source: "Lottie" [Charlotte Forten], "To a Beloved Friend; On Receiving a Tiny Bouquet of Wild Flowers from the Hills of Our Dear New England," *Repository of Religion and Literature and of Science and Art*, July 1858, 89–90; copy in ISL.

APPENDIX 2

LUCY LARCOM'S "MISSISSIPPI AND MISSOURI"

The Mississippi glides down from the romantic regions of the north; from pellucid lakes; from verdant bluffs which at dawn lean against mountains of roseate mist; from islands all gracefully entangled with the foliage of the pawpaw, the cottonwood, and the grape; from shores where the willow twig and the trumpet flower bend to touch the mimic blossom and bough, that reach up to them from the mirrored shore beneath. A pure and a peaceful stream is it, then.

The Missouri rushes from the north-west, the land of many wigwams and unburied tomahawks, bringing sand, earth, and upturned roots from its loose shores and muddy tributaries.

The two rivers meet, as it were, unwillingly. For many miles, a distinct line in the midst of the stream shows their mutual repulsion. But after a time thick, brown flakes are visible upon the transparent waters, and soon both are blended in one dark, powerful river, bearing the hue of the turbid Missouri flood, and the name of the clear Mississippi.

Impetuous as human passion, the great river of the west sweeps onward to the awaiting gulf, and suggests to the thoughtful traveller who is borne upon its bosom the mingling of good and evil in his own nature. How came the strong current within so deeply stained? Shall he name for his fountain head the pure or the foul, or both? And is there any ocean broad and deep enough to absorb from his being the pollutions of earth?

Source: Lucy Larcom, *Similitudes, from the Ocean and the Prairie* (Boston: John P. Jewett / Cleveland: Jewett, Proctor, and Worthington, 1854), 65–66.

APPENDIX 3

EXCERPT FROM JOHN TOWNSEND TROWBRIDGE'S *MARTIN MERRIVALE*

Killings received our author with distinguished patronage.

"I was away when you called on Sanurnay," said he, through his nose; "but I have taken occasion to look over the song and the sketch you left. The song is n't quite as good as the other—do you think it is?" he asked, with a pleasant grimace.

"I thought it was better," replied Martin, modestly.

"O, I don't find fault with it," Killings hastened to say; "though I think it doubtful whether I make use of it," in a discouraging tone. "What—a—that is, how much—did you intend to charge me for it?"

Martin, disheartened and disgusted, answered, that he had no idea of fixing a price on such trifles.

"Sumposing, then, I should say amout fifty cents—"

"Fifty cents for two songs!"

"Two?—ah, yes; but I thought you gave me the first one," said Killings, in a fawning manner. "Well, say a dollar, then,—will that be about the right thing?"

"If that is all the songs are worth to you, I am satisfied," said Martin, with a red, perspiring face. "I leave it all to your generosity."

"I am afraid you are not satisfied," resumed Killings, with an anxious look. "But I will make it all right with you, some time. I shall want to employ you regularly," he added, in a whisper, behind the editor's back, "when the *Portfolio* comes into my hands. The sketch you left is admirably written. You have a decided genius for humorous description."

"I am glad you like it," said Martin, encouraged.

"It's not just what I wanted, however. You don't make your hero quite enough of a wag to make it an omject for me to pay a high price for it. I'll take it of you, though, seeing I engaged it. Will a dollar and a half be a fair price? I'll pay you more for the others, you know; and I shall take a good many of you, promably, in the course of the winter."

"A dollar and a half, did I understand you?" articulated Martin, with a sickening sensation.

"Yes—a dollar and a half; and I'll have it printed in the *Portfolio,* with a complimentary notice of the author," returned the magnanimous Killings, with his pleasant grimace. "That makes two dollars and a half. Can you break an X?"

Martin could not, of course; and Killings, who probably anticipated as much, made the circumstance an excuse for paying him in small change, received at the door of his "Panorama."

Opening a leather pouch, taken from the safe, he counted out forty antiquated fourpences, nearly every one of which was worn smooth, and tendered them to Martin on the crown of his hat. With an expression in which a sense of the ludicrous and a feeling of despondency were blended, the author of the Beggar of Bagdad held his handkerchief; the jingling silver was emptied into it; he tied it up in a little ball, and struck it on his knee, to hear its musical chink; and thus, with sensations he little expected to experience on that great occasion, he carried off his first pecuniary fee earned in the sacred and exalted literary profession.

Source: John Townsend Trowbridge, *Martin Merrivale, His X Mark* (Boston: Phillips, Sampson, 1854), 232–34.

ABBREVIATIONS

Note: for archives from which we cite more than one collection, we give in the notes the collection abbreviation first, followed by a hyphen, then the archive abbreviation. The list does not include every periodical we cite, only those we refer to more than once, excluding those with single-word titles, like the *Liberator.* Finally, a few frequently cited books appear here.

AAB	Archives of the Archdiocese of Boston, Papers of Benedict Joseph Fenwick
AAS	American Antiquarian Society, Worcester, Massachusetts

	JDP	John Davis Papers
	JPBP	Jotham Powers Bigelow Papers
	SFP	Salisbury Family Papers

AHR	*American Historical Review*
AL	*American Literature*
AM	*Atlantic Monthly*
AMECR	*African Methodist Episcopal Church Review*
AQ	*American Quarterly*
AS	*American Studies*
ATHM	American Textile History Museum, Lowell, Massachusetts, Metcalf–Adams Letters
BAL	*Bibliography of American Literature,* ed. Jacob Blanck, 9 vols. (New Haven, Conn.: Yale University Press, 1955–1983)
BC	Boston College, Chesnut Hill, Massachusetts, Moses Adams Papers
BCHS	Beaver County Historical Society, Beaver Falls, Pennsylvania
BH	*Book History*
BHS	Beverly Historical Society and Museum, Beverly, Massachusetts

	EC	Endicott Collection

BM	*Boston Miscellany*
BPL	Boston Public Library Rare Books Department, Boston; all material quoted courtesy of the Trustees of the Boston Public Library
CHC	College of the Holy Cross, Archives and Special Collections, Worcester, Massachusetts
CHDT	Henry David Thoreau, *The Correspondence of Henry David Thoreau*, ed. Walter Harding and Carl Bode (New York: New York University Press, 1958)
CHS	Connecticut Historical Society, Hartford, Connecticut
	JFP Jocelyn Family Papers
	MC McClellan Papers
CIMM	*Century Illustrated Monthly Magazine*
CSL	Connecticut State Library, Hartford
DLB	*Dictionary of Literary Biography* (Detroit: Gale, 1980–)
EEH	*Explorations in Economic History*
EIHC	*Essex Institute Historical Collections*
ELH	*ELH: A Journal of English Literary History*
FOU	*Flag of Our Union*
GPDRC	*Gleason's Pictorial Drawing-Room Companion*
HAM	Frank Luther Mott, *A History of American Magazines*, 5 vols. (Cambridge, Mass.: Harvard University Press, 1957)
HBPUS	John Tebbel, *A History of Book Publishing in the United States*, 4 vols. (New York: Bowker, 1972)
HDTJ	Henry David Thoreau, *Journal*, ed. John C. Broderick and Robert Sattelmeyer, 6 vols. (Princeton, N.J.: Princeton University Press, 1981)
HJR	*Henry James Review*
HL	Houghton Library, Harvard University, Cambridge, Massachusetts, Pickard–Whittier Papers
HLQ	*Huntington Library Quarterly*
HNMM	*Harper's New Monthly Magazine*
HU	Moorland–Spingarn Research Center, Howard University, Washington, D.C., Francis Grimké Papers
HuL	Henry E. Huntington Library, San Marino, California, Literary Manuscripts Collection
ISHL	Illinois State Historical Library, Springfield, Illinois
ISL	Indiana State Library, Indianapolis
JAH	*Journal of American History*

JCFG	Charlote Forten Grimké, *The Journals of Charlotte Forten Grimké*, ed. Brenda Stevenson (New York: Oxford University Press, 1988)
JER	*Journal of the Early Republic*
LED	Emily Dickinson, *Letters of Emily Dickinson*, ed. Thomas H. Johnson, 3 vols. (Cambridge, Mass.: Harvard University Press, 1958)
LHS	Lynn Museum, Lynn, Massachusetts
LJGW	John Greenleaf Whittier, *Letters of John Greenleaf Whittier*, 3 vols., ed. John B. Pickard (Cambridge, Mass.: Harvard University Press, 1975)
LM	*(Boston) Literary Museum* (alternate: *Boston Weekly Museum*)
LMU	Lincoln Memorial University, Harrogate, Tennessee, Cassius Marcellus Clay Papers
LQ	*Library Quarterly*
LR	*Ladies' Repository*
LSML	Harriett Low, *Lights and Shadows of a Macao Life: The Journal of Harriett Low, Travelling Spinster*, ed. Nan Powell Hodges and Arthur William Hummel, 2 vols. (Woodinville, Wash.: History Bank, 2000)
LxHS	Lexington Historical Society, Lexington, Massachusetts
MBEL	Mary Baker Eddy Library for the Betterment of Humanity, Boston, Mary Baker Eddy Collection
MbHS	Marblehead Historical Society, Marblehead, Massachusetts, William B. Adams Papers
MeHS	Maine Historical Society, Portland, Maine

CKNFP	Cargill–Knight–Norcross Family Papers
JEHP	Joshua Edwin Harris Papers

MHS	Massachusetts Historical Society, Boston

AALDAB	Amos A. Lawrence Diaries and Account Books
CFP3	Cary Family Papers III
DDAC	Daniel Dulany Addison Collection
DFCP	D. F. Child Papers
EDP	Everett–Downes Papers
FCL2P	Francis Cabot Lowell II Papers
FCMP	Frank C. Morse Papers
LFP	Lamb Family Papers
LLWP	L. L. Waterhouse Papers

MOS	John Townsend Trowbridge, *My Own Story, with Recollections of Noted Persons* (Boston: Houghton Mifflin, 1903)

NAR	North American Review
NASS	National Anti-Slavery Standard
NCC	Nineteenth-Century Contexts
NE	National Era
NEG	Lucy Larcom, A New England Girlhood, Outlined from Memory (Boston: Houghton Mifflin, 1889)
NEGXY	New England Galaxy
NEHGR	New England Historical and Genealogical Register
NEHGS	New England Historic Genealogical Society, Boston
	HWCC Henry Wyles Cushman Collection
NEM	New England Magazine
NEQ	New England Quarterly
NHHS	New Hampshire Historical Society, Concord, N.H.
NLH	New Literary History
OCHS	Old Colony Historical Society, Taunton, Massachusetts
OM	Overland Monthly and Out West Magazine
PAAS	Proceedings of the American Antiquarian Society
PBSA	Papers of the Bibliographical Society of America
PEM	Phillips Library, Peabody Essex Museum, Salem, Massachusetts
	RFP Rogers Family Papers
	LLP Lucy Larcom Papers
PM	Putnam's Monthly
PMHS	Proceedings of the Massachusetts Historical Society
PPL	Portland Public Library, Portland, Maine
RIHS	Rhode Island Historical Society, Manuscript Division, Providence
	CFP Congdon Family Papers
	DFP Diman Family Papers
	HLFP Herreshoff–Lewis Family Papers
	MMC Miscellaneous Manuscripts Collection
	ZAP Zachariah Allen Papers
RRLSA	The Repository of Religion and Literature and of Science and Art
SA	Scientific American
SAR	Studies in the American Renaissance
SB	Studies in Bibliography
SCHS	South Carolina Historical Society, Charleston, N. R. Middleton Family Correspondence

SL	Schlesinger Library, Radcliffe Institute, Harvard University, Cambridge, Massachusetts	
	AFP	Almy Family Papers
	BHFP	Bradley–Hyde Family Papers
	BriFP	Briggs Family Papers
	BroFP	Browne Family Papers
	CAFP	Chamberlain–Adams Family Papers
	CFP	Cabot Family Papers
	CWHDP	Caroline W. H. Dall Papers
	ECAFP	Elizabeth Cary Agassiz Family Papers
	EGLFP	Ellis Gray Loring Family Papers
	FMQP	Frances Merritt Quick Papers
	HC	Hooker Collection
	HFP	Hodges Family Papers
	PoFP	Poor Family Papers
	RSP	Robinson–Shattuck Papers
	SABRP	Sarah Alden Bradford Ripley Papers
	SEBP	Sarah Ellen Browne Papers
	SFA	Swanton Family Addenda
	SFP	Swanton Family Papers
	SFUP	Swanton Family Unprocessed Papers
SM	*Scribner's Monthly [or Magazine]*	
SSC	Sophia Smith Collection, Smith College, Northampton, Massachusetts	
	BFP	Bodman Family Papers
	GP	Garrison Papers
	HP	Hale Papers
	STPP	Sturgis–Tappan–Prout Papers
SUM	*Sartain's Union Magazine of Literature and Art*	
USDR	*United States Democratic Review*	
UVA	University of Virginia Library, Clifton Waller Barrett Library, Special Collections, Charlottesville, Virginia	
	LLC	Lucy Larcom Collection
	NPWC	Nathaniel Parker Willis Collection
VHS	Vermont Historical Society, Barre, Vermont	
	WCP	William Chamberlain Papers
WHS	Wilton Historical Society, Wilton, Maine	
WMQ	*William and Mary Quarterly*	

NOTES

Introduction

1. Emily Dickinson, "Publication is the auction" (poem 788), in *The Poems of Emily Dickinson*, ed. R.W. Franklin, *Variorum Edition*, 3 vols. (Cambridge, Mass.: Harvard University Press, 1998), 2:742. There are many interpretations of this poem, but Marietta Messmer, *A Vice for Voices: Reading Emily Dickinson's Correspondence* (Amherst: University of Massachusetts Press, 2001), 185–86, comes closest to ours.

2. U.S. Bureau of the Census, introduction, cxxxii, and "Exhibit of the Total Manufactures of the United States ...," 733–42, in *Manufactures of the United States in 1860 ...* (Washington, D.C.: Government Printing Office, 1865). On the boom, see Ronald J. Zboray, *A Fictive People: Antebellum Economic Development and the American Reading Public* (New York: Oxford University Press, 1993).

3. Ronald J. Zboray and Mary Saracino Zboray, "The Boston Book Trades, 1789–1850: A Statistical and Geographical Analysis," in *Entrepreneurs: The Boston Business Community, 1700–1850*, ed. Conrad Edick Wright and Katheryn P. Viens (Boston: Massachusetts Historical Society, 1997), 238, table 17.

4. Ronald J. Zboray and Mary Saracino Zboray, "Books, Reading, and the World of Goods in Antebellum New England," *AQ* 48 (1996): 587–622; Charles Sellers, *The Market Revolution: Jacksonian America, 1815–1846* (New York: Oxford University Press, 1991).

5. One very rough indication of the dropout rate (and the extent of amateurism, as well) can be gleaned from the following: of the 879 Americans publishing original adult-market fiction in book form between 1837 and 1857 (inclusive—2,305, in all) in the United States, 68 percent would not publish another in those two decades, and 15 percent would publish but one more. Only 8 percent published more than four. We compiled these figures from our fiction-title database described in Ronald J. Zboray and Mary Saracino Zboray, "American Fiction Publishing, 1837–1857," paper delivered at the annual conference of the Society for the History of Authorship, Reading, and Publishing, Washington, D.C., July 15, 1994; based on Lyle Wright, *American Fiction: A Contribution toward a Bibliography*, 2 vols., *1774–1850* and *1851–1875* (San Marino, Calif.: Huntington Library, 1969, 1965). To be sure, novels by Americans made up an infinitesimal 1.53 percent of the 150,537 titles that a WorldCat search returns for books published in New York, Philadelphia, or Boston during those same years. (There is some minor duplication in these figures for the exact same book simply cataloged differently by librarians or simultaneously published in two or three of the cities.) How many of these were written by Americans cannot be known due to the plethora of reprints from overseas; see Meredith

L. McGill, *American Literature and the Culture of Reprinting, 1834–1853* (Philadelphia: University of Pennsylvania Press, 2003). However, one contemporary estimated that by 1840 Americans authored about half of all titles published in the United States and that this proportion increased steeply thereafter; see Samuel G. Goodrich, *Recollections of a Lifetime; or Men and Things I Have Seen*, 2 vols. (New York: Miller, Orton, and Mulligan, 1856), 2:388–89.

6. Sarah P.E. Hale to Edward Everett, September 21, 1841, HP-SSC.

7. Two classic top-down studies are by William Charvat: *Literary Publishing in America, 1790–1850* (1959; reprint Amherst: University of Massachusetts Press, 1993); and *Profession of Authorship in America, 1800–1870*, ed. Matthew J. Bruccoli (Columbus: Ohio State University Press, 1968).

8. The relationship between canonical and mass-market writers was based, at least in part, upon shared out-of-market manuscript authorship experiences and hardly-in-the-market amateur ventures. The similar literary conventions showing up in canonical and popular works emerged from these shared experiences as well as from low-to-high literary intertextual influence. That both canonical and popular authors usually felt a tension between literary dollars and social sense is a central theme of our book; we recognize both types of writers' consciousness of the literary market and its conventions, as do David S. Reynolds, *Beneath the American Renaissance: The Subversive Imagination in the Age of Emerson and Melville* (New York: Alfred A. Knopf, 1988) and Sheila Post-Lauria, *Correspondent Colorings: Melville in the Marketplace* (Amherst: University of Massachusetts Press, 1999).

9. Howard Zinn, *A People's History of the United States, 1492–Present* (New York: HarperCollins, 1980), 9–10, 645–46, 649, 658–60; Ray Raphael, *A People's History of the American Revolution: How Common People Shaped the Fight for Independence* (New York: New Press, 2001), 1, 6–8; and Howard Zinn, series preface, in Raphael, *A People's History*, xi. For a consensus-history use of the term, see Page Smith, *The Nation Comes of Age: A People's History of the Antebellum Years*, vol. 4 (New York: McGraw Hill, 1981); his theme of "conflict in the American psyche between the yearning for the re-establishment of the true community and the attractions of competitive individualism"(xii), obviously is similar to ours of social sense and literary dollars, but our approach and ends are materialistic, not idealistic, like his.

10. As is conventional in history-of-the-book scholarship, we use the term *book* to include all forms of imprints, including newspapers and magazines; Robert Darnton, "What is the History of Books?" in *Reading in America: Literature and Social History*, ed. Cathy N. Davidson (Baltimore: Johns Hopkins University Press, 1989), 27; Jonathan Rose and Ezra Greenspan, "An Introduction to Book History," *BH* 1 (1998): ix. Another convention we follow is that a history of the book can be much more than artifact-based (i.e., the book itself), but can extend to the historically and geographically specific processes bringing the artifact into existence and giving it social meaning; D.F. McKenzie, *Bibliography and the Sociology of Texts* (London: British Library, 1986).

11. Compare Hugh Amory and David D. Hall, eds., *A History of the Book in America*, vol. 1, *The Colonial Book in the Atlantic World* (New York: Cambridge University Press, 2000) with, for example, Donald Henry Sheehan, *This Was Publishing: A Chronicle of the Book Trade in the Gilded Age* (Bloomington: Indiana University Press, 1952).

12. Zboray, *A Fictive People*; we refer to "social literary practices" in light of Margaret J.M. Ezell, *Social Authorship and the Advent of Print* (Baltimore: Johns Hopkins University Press, 1999).

13. For example, see Raymond Jackson Wilson, *Figures of Speech: American Writers and the Literary Marketplace from Benjamin Franklin to Emily Dickinson* (New York: Alfred A. Knopf, 1989); Steven Fink, *Prophet in the Marketplace: Thoreau's Development as a Professional Writer* (Princeton, N.J.: Princeton University Press, 1992); Michael

Newbury, *Figuring Authorship in Antebellum America* (Stanford, Calif.: Stanford University Press, 1997); Grantland S. Rice, *The Transformation of Authorship in America* (Chicago: University of Chicago Press, 1997); Terence Whalen, *Edgar Allan Poe and the Masses: The Political Economy of Literature in Antebellum America* (Princeton, N.J.: Princeton University Press, 1999); Kevin J. Hayes, *Poe and the Printed Word* (Cambridge: Cambridge University Press, 2000); and, for a later period, Michael Anesko, *"Friction with the Market": Henry James and the Profession of Authorship* (New York: Oxford University Press, 1986). James L. West III, *American Authors and the Literary Marketplace since 1900* (Philadelphia: University of Pennsylvania Press, 1988) in its systematic coverage in which the "greats" play a background and illustrative role, is an exception.

14. "Amateur Authors and Small Critics," *USDR* 17 (1856), 63. We define amateurs as (1) those seeking printed publication and, if achieving it, doing so only sporadically or for a single short period; (2) those being unable or unwilling to supplement their incomes substantially or to earn a living over the long run through writing; and (3) those eluding canonization. Usually scholars are not interested in amateurism per se. Reynolds's main concern in *Beneath the American Renaissance* is with popular authors' impact upon canonical works; amateurs play but an ancillary role. Women's authorship studies also reveal publishing practices outside the canon; see, for example, Susan Coultrap-McQuin, *Doing Literary Business: American Women Writers in the Nineteenth Century* (Chapel Hill: University of North Carolina Press, 1990), esp. chap. 2; Mary Kelley, *Private Woman, Public Stage: Literary Domesticity in Nineteenth-Century America* (New York: Oxford University Press, 1984); Aleta Fiensod Cane and Susan Alves, eds., *"The Only Efficient Instrument": American Women Writers and the Periodical, 1837–1916* (Iowa City: University of Iowa Press, 2001). Ann Fabian, in *The Unvarnished Truth: Personal Narratives in Nineteenth-Century America* (Berkeley and Los Angeles: University of California Press, 2000), treats some amateur writers' self-narration, but not the surrounding publishing practices in depth. Amateurism also figures in Lawrence Buell's *New England Literary Culture, From Revolution Through Renaissance* (New York: Cambridge University Press, 1986) and Cathy N. Davidson's *Revolution and the Word: The Rise of the Novel in America* (New York: Oxford University Press, 1986).

15. William Charvat confessed in the preface to his *Literary Publishing*, 7, that he had abandoned his work on the "economics of authorship," because "[p]ublishing is relevant to literary history only in so far as it can be shown to be, ultimately, a shaping influence on literature," by which he means, essentially, that deemed to be art. See also his *Profession of Authorship*; Michael Davitt Bell, *Culture, Genre, and Literary Vocation: Selected Essays on American Literature* (Chicago: University of Chicago Press, 2001).

16. David S. Shields, *Oracles of Empire: Poetry, Politics, and Commerce in British America, 1690–1750* (Chicago: University of Chicago Press, 1990). On personal writings as a genre, see William Merrill Decker, *Epistolary Practices: Letter Writing in America before Telecommunications* (Chapel Hill: University of North Carolina Press, 1998); the essays in Rebecca Earle, ed., *Epistolary Selves: Letters and Letter-Writers, 1600–1945* (Aldershot, England: Ashgate, 1999) and in Suzanne L. Bunkers and Cynthia A. Huff, eds., *Inscribing the Daily: Critical Essays on Women's Diaries* (Amherst: University of Massachusetts Press, 1996); Susan Miller, *Assuming the Positions: Cultural Pedagogy and the Politics of Commonplace Writing* (Pittsburgh: University of Pittsburgh Press, 1998); and Elizabeth C. Goldsmith, *Exclusive Conversations: The Art of Interaction in Seventeenth-Century France* (Philadelphia: University of Pennsylvania Press, 1988). For a rare antebellum consideration of the phenomenon in the context of literature, see "Gurth," "Unpublished Literature," *SUM* 10 (1852): 136–38.

17. Ezell, *Social Authorship* esp. chap. 2, 39–40; 142, quote on 121; Harold Love, *Scribal Publication in Seventeenth-Century England* (Oxford: Oxford University Press, 1993); Adam Fox, *Oral and Literate Culture in England 1500–1700* (Oxford: Oxford University Press, 2000); Mary Hobbs, *Early Seventeenth-Century Verse Miscellany Manuscripts* (Aldershot, England: Scolar, 1992).

18. On women as social authors, see Margaret J.M. Ezell, ed., introduction to *The Poems and Prose of Mary, Lady Chudleigh* (New York: Oxford University Press, 1993), xvii–xxxvi; Carla Mulford, ed., introduction to *Only for the Eye of a Friend: The Poems of Annis Boudinot Stockton* (Charlottesville: University Press of Virginia, 1995), 1–57. Susan M. Stabile, *Memory's Daughters: The Material Culture of Remembrance in Eighteenth-Century America* (Ithaca, N.Y.: Cornell University Press, 2004). On sites of social dissemination of belles lettres in British America, see David Shields, *Civil Tongues and Polite Letters in British America* (Chapel Hill: University of North Carolina Press, 1997); idem, "British-American Belles Lettres," in *The Cambridge History of American Literature*, vol. 1, *1590–1820*, ed. Sacvan Bercovitch (Cambridge: Cambridge University Press, 1994), 307–44.

19. See the exchange between Elizabeth Eisenstein and Adrian Johns in "How Revolutionary Was the Print Revolution?" *AHR* 107 (2002): 84–128; Margaret J.M. Ezell and Katherine O'Brien O'Keefe, eds., *Cultural Artifacts and the Production of Meaning: The Page, the Image, and the Body* (Ann Arbor: University of Michigan Press, 1994).

20. Ruth Finnegan, *Literacy and Orality: Studies in the Technology of Communication* (Oxford: Basil Blackwell, 1988). Raymond Williams briefly sketches the ensuing historical phases of cultural production beyond orality in *The Sociology of Culture* (Chicago: University of Chicago Press, 1995), chap. 2; social authorship and amateurism, outside of patronage systems, largely eludes him, however.

21. Elizabeth L. Eisenstein, *The Printing Press as an Agent of Change: Communications and Cultural Transformations in Early-Modern Europe*, 2 vols. (Cambridge: Cambridge University Press, 1979), 1:10–14; Harvey J. Graff, *Legacies of Literacy: Continuities and Contradictions in Western Culture and Society* (Bloomington: Indiana University Press, 1987), 28. Rosamond McKitterick, *Books, Scribes, and Learning in the Frankish Kingdoms, Sixth–Ninth Centuries* (Aldershot, England: Ashgate, 1994).

22. Eisenstein, *Printing Press*, 1: pt. 1; idem, "An Unacknowledged Revolution Revisited," *AHR* 107 (2002): 87–105. On scribal production coexisting with printing, see David McKitterick, *Print, Manuscript, and the Search for Order, 1450–1830* (Cambridge: Cambridge University Press, 2003); William Wallace, "Galileo's Sources: Manuscripts or Printed Works?" in *Print and Culture in the Renaissance: Essays on the Advent of Printing in Europe*, ed. Gerald P. Tyson and Sylvia S. Wagonheim (Newark: University of Delaware Press, 1986), 45–54; Love, *Scribal Publication*.

23. Adrian Johns, *The Nature of the Book: Print and Knowledge in the Making* (Chicago: University of Chicago Press, 1998); Eisenstein, *Printing Press*, 1:11, 46; Adrian Johns, "How to Acknowledge a Revolution," *AHR* 107 (2002): 106–25.

24. Michel Foucault, "What is an Author?" in *Language, Counter-Memory, Practice: Selected Essays and Interviews*, ed. Donald F. Bouchard, trans. Donald F. Bouchard and Sherry Simon (Ithaca, N.Y.: Cornell University Press, 1977), 113–38. For a contretemps, see Robert J. Griffin, "Anonymity and Authorship," *NLH* 30 (1999): 877–95.

25. James Hepburn, *The Author's Empty Purse and the Rise of the Literary Agent* (London: Oxford University Press, 1968), 4–21; Marjorie Plant, *The English Book Trade: An Economic History of the Making and Sale of Books* (London: George Allen and Unwin, 1939), 73–76, 99–100. See also Alexandra Halasz, *The Marketplace of Print: Pamphlets and the Public Sphere in Early Modern England* (Cambridge: Cambridge University Press, 1997).

26. Eisenstein, "An Unacknowledged Revolution Revisited," 96; Plant, *English Book Trade*, 23, 26, 29, 31, 34, and 83.

27. Plant, *English Book Trade*, 27–28, 31, 33, 34, 63, 81, 84, 96, 125–26. On the blurry line between early English newspapers and correspondence, see Paul J. Voss, *Elizabethan News Pamphlets: Shakespeare, Spenser, Marlowe and the Birth of Journalism* (Pittsburgh: Duquesne University Press, 2001), 34–75. Cyprian Blagden, *The Stationer's Company: A History, 1403–1959* (Cambridge, Mass.: Harvard University Press, 1960).

28. Mark Rose, *Authors and Owners: The Invention of Copyright* (Cambridge, Mass.: Harvard University Press, 1993); compare the German case in Martha Woodmansee, *The Author, Art, and the Market: Rereading the History of Aesthetics* (New York: Columbia University Press, 1994), chap. 2. Plant, *English Book Trade*, 117–18. Kevin Pask, *The Emergence of the English Author: Scripting the Life of the Poet in Early Modern England* (Cambridge: Cambridge University Press, 1996); Pat Rogers, *Hacks and Dunces: Pope, Swift, and Grub Street* (London: Methuen, 1980).

29. Lawrence C. Wroth, *The Colonial Printer* (1931; reprint Charlottesville: University Press of Virginia, 1964); Matt B. Jones, "Notes for a Bibliography of Michael Wigglesworth's 'Day of Doom' and 'Meat out of the Eater,'" *PAAS* 39 (1929): 77–84; Isaiah Thomas, *The History of Printing in America*, ed. Marcus McCorison, 2 vols. (1874; reprint New York: Weathervane, 1970), 124; Amory and Hall, *History of the Book*, 516, graph 8a and, for overwhelming domination of imports, 514, graph 7b; Richard D. Brown, *Knowledge Is Power: The Diffusion of Information in Early America, 1700–1865* (New York: Oxford University Press, 1989), 115–16, 158–59.

30. Davidson, *Revolution and the Word*, 16–17; Kenneth Silverman, *A Cultural History of the American Revolution: Painting, Music, Literature, and the Theatre in the Colonies and the United States from the Treaty of Paris to the Inauguration of George Washington, 1763–1789* (New York: T.Y. Crowell, 1976), xv, 82–87.

31. Larzer Ziff, *Writing in the New Nation: Prose, Print, and Politics in the Early United States* (New Haven, Conn.: Yale University Press, 1991), esp. chap. 5; E. Jennifer Monaghan, *A Common Heritage: Noah Webster's Blue-Back Speller* (Hamden, Conn.: Archon, 1983); Martin Bruckner, "Lessons in Geography: Maps, Spellers, and Other Grammars of Nationalism in the Early Republic," *AQ* 51 (1999): 311–43.

32. Cathy N. Davidson, "The Life and Times of Charlotte Temple: The Biography of a Book," in *Reading in America: Literature and Social History*, ed. Cathy N. Davidson (Baltimore: Johns Hopkins University Press, 1989), 157–79; James D. Wallace, *Early Cooper and His Audience* (New York: Columbia University Press, 1986). Compare with Henry A. Pochmann, "Washington Irving: Amateur or Professional?" in *Critical Essays on Washington Irving*, ed. Ralph M. Alderman (Boston: G.K. Hall, 1990), 155–66; Bryce Traister, "The Wandering Bachelor: Irving, Masculinity, and Authorship," *AL* 74 (2002): 111–37. Patricia G. Holland, "Lydia Child as a Nineteenth-Century Professional Author," *SAR* 4 (1981): 157–67.

33. George Rogers Taylor, *The Transportation Revolution, 1815–1860* (New York: Rinehart, 1951); Zboray, *A Fictive People*, chap. 4. Mary Ryan, *Cradle of the Middle Class: The Family in Oneida County, New York, 1790–1865* (Cambridge: Cambridge University Press, 1981); Paul E. Johnson, *A Shopkeeper's Millennium: Society and Revivals in Rochester, New York, 1815–1837* (New York: Hill and Wang, 1978); Lawrance Thompson, "The Printing and Publishing Activities of the American Tract Society from 1825 to 1850," *PBSA* 35 (1941): 81–114.

34. Zboray, *A Fictive People*, 6–7; Ronald J. Zboray, "Literary Enterprise and the Mass Market: Publishers and Business Innovation in Antebellum America," *Essays in Economic and Business History* 10 (1992): 168–82; Michael Hackenberg, ed., *Getting the Books Out: Papers of the Chicago Conference on the Book in Nineteenth-Century America* (Washington, D.C.: Center for the Book, Library of Congress, 1987).

35. James J. Barnes, *Authors, Publishers, and Politicians: The Quest for an Anglo-American Copyright Agreement, 1815–1854* (Columbus: Ohio State University Press, 1974). Goodrich, *Recollections of a Lifetime*, 2:388–89.

36. Ronald Weber, *Hired Pens: Professional Writers in America's Golden Age of Print* (Athens: Ohio University Press, 1997), 13–61.

37. Zboray and Zboray, "Boston Book Trades," 210–67; see 213, fig. 1, and 239, table 18. Kenneth L. Sokoloff, "Was the Transition from the Artisanal Shop to the Small Factory Associated with Gains in Efficiency?" *EEH* 21 (1984): 351–82; Jeremy Atack, "Economies of Scale and Efficiency Gains in the Rise of the Factory in America, 1820–1900," in *Quantity and Quiddity: Essays in U.S. Economic History*, ed. Peter Kilby (Middletown, Conn.: Wesleyan University Press, 1987), 286–335.

38. Making ends meet for these papers was, however, difficult due to subscribers' reluctance to pay up. Thomas C. Leonard, *News for All: America's Coming-of-Age with the Press* (New York: Oxford University Press, 1995), 36–47. On newspaper development, compare Carol Sue Humphrey, *The Press of the Young Republic, 1783–1833* (Westport, Conn.: Greenwood, 1996) with William Huntzicker, *The Popular Press, 1833–1865* (Westport, Conn.: Greenwood, 1999).

39. This and the following four paragraphs rely on Ronald J. Zboray and Mary Saracino Zboray, *Everyday Ideas: Socio-Literary Experience among Antebellum New Englanders* (Knoxville: University of Tennessee Press, forthcoming 2005), chaps. 1–3; Ronald J. Zboray and Mary Saracino Zboray, "Cannonballs and Books: Reading and the Disruption of Social Ties on the New England Homefront," in *The War Was You and Me: Civilians in the American Civil War*, ed. Joan E. Cashin (Princeton, N.J.: Princeton University Press, 2002), 237–43; Ronald J. Zboray and Mary Saracino Zboray, "Reading in Antebellum New England: Literary Gifts," paper delivered at the Visiting Scholar Colloquium Series, Schlesinger Library at Radcliffe College, April 15, 1999; now in the collection of the Schlesinger Library, Radcliffe Institute, Harvard University.

40. Moses Adams, undated, Common Place Book, no. 2, c. 1835, BC.

41. John Durham Peters, *Speaking into the Air: A History of the Idea of Communication* (Chicago: University of Chicago Press, 1999), 165–66.

42. Zboray, *A Fictive People*, 10; James Cephas Derby, *Fifty Years among Books, Authors, and Publishers* (New York: G.W. Carleton, 1884), 185; his figure is for the 1850s. Harrison T. Meserole, "The 'Famous *Boston Post* List': Mid-Nineteenth Century American Bestsellers," *PBSA* 52 (1958): 93–110. The best study on edition size and the various sponsored publications passing through trade publishers' hands remains Warren S. Tryon and William Charvat, eds., *The Cost Books of Ticknor and Fields, and Their Predecessors, 1832–1858* (New York: Bibliographical Society of America, 1949). The rage for poetry is covered in James D. Hart, *The Popular Book: A History of America's Literary Taste* (New York: Oxford University Press, 1950), 125–39; and Frank Luther Mott, *Golden Multitudes: The Story of Best Sellers in the United States* (New York: Macmillan, 1947), 103–14. Ralph Thompson, *American Literary Annuals and Gift Books, 1825–1865* (New York: H.W. Wilson, 1936). J. Albert Robbins, "Fees Paid to Authors by Certain American Periodicals, 1840–1850," *SB* 2 (1949–50): 94–104. *HAM*, 2:21.

43. Mary Noel, *Villains Galore …: The Heyday of the Popular Story Weekly* (New York: Macmillan, 1954), 33; *HAM*, 2:22. Donald R. Adams Jr., "Earnings and Savings in the Early Nineteenth Century," *EEH* 17 (1980): 118–34.

44. Sally McMurry, "Who Read the Agricultural Journals? Evidence From Cheneago County, New York, 1839–1865," *Agricultural History* 63 (1989): 1–18; Albert Lowther Demaree, *The American Agricultural Press, 1819–1860* (New York: Columbia University Press, 1941).

45. Gerald Baldasty, *The Commercialization of News in the Nineteenth Century* (Madison: University of Wisconsin Press, 1992); Kevin G. Barnhurst and John Nerone, *The Form of News: A History* (New York: Guilford, 2001). For a study including treatment of fillers, see Ronald J. Zboray and Mary Saracino Zboray, "Gender Slurs in Boston's Partisan Press During the 1840s," *Journal of American Studies* 34 (2000): 413–46.

46. Zboray and Zboray, "Boston Book Trades," 238, table 17.

47. David Jaffee, "Peddlers of Progress and the Transformation of the Rural North, 1760–1860," *JAH* 78 (1991): 511–35; David Jaffee, "The Village Enlightenment in New England, 1760–1820," *WMQ* 47 (1990): 327–46; Rosalind Remer, "Preachers, Peddlers, and Publishers: Philadelphia's Backcountry Book Trade, 1800–1830," *JER* 14 (1994): 497–522; William J. Gilmore, "Peddlers and the Dissemination of Printed Material in Northern New England, 1780–1840," in *Itinerancy in New England and New York*, ed. Peter Benes (Boston: Boston University, 1986), 76–89; Zboray, *A Fictive People*, 34–54; Ronald J. Zboray, "Technology and the Character of Community Life in Antebellum America: The Role of Story Papers," in *Communication and Change in American Religious History*, ed. Leonard I. Sweet (Grand Rapids, Mich.: William B. Eerdmans, 1993), 185–215, esp. 201; David Paul Nord, "Systematic Benevolence: Religious Publishing and the Marketplace in Early Nineteenth-Century America," in Sweet, *Communication and Change*, 239–69; Mark S. Schantz, "Religious Tracts, Evangelical Reform, and the Market Revolution in Antebellum America," *JER* 17 (1997): 425–67.

48. Donald M. Scott, *From Office to Profession: The New England Ministry, 1750–1850* (Philadelphia: University of Pennsylvania Press, 1978); Christine Ann Fidler, "'Young Limbs of the Law': Law Students, Legal Education, and the Occupational Culture of Attorneys, 1820–1860," Ph.D. diss., University of California–Berkeley, 1996; Ronald J. Zboray and Mary Saracino Zboray, "Home Libraries and the Institutionalization of Everyday Practices among Antebellum New Englanders," *AS* 42 (Fall 2001): 63–86; Anne M. Boylan, *Sunday School: The Formation of an American Institution, 1790–1880* (New Haven, Conn.: Yale University Press, 1988), 48–52.

49. Donald M. Scott, "The Popular Lecture and the Creation of a Public in Mid-Nineteenth-Century America," *JAH* 66 (1980): 791–809; and Mary Kupiec Cayton, "The Making of an American Prophet: Emerson, His Audiences, and the Rise of the Culture Industry in Nineteenth-Century America," *AHR* 92 (1987): 597–620. On tie-ins, see C. Peter Ripley, ed., introduction to *The Black Abolitionist Papers*, 5 vols. (Chapel Hill: University of North Carolina Press, 1985–91), 3:29.

50. *GPDRC*, May 3, 1851, 13.

51. Little attention has been given to the topic. See, however, Zboray and Zboray, "Books, Reading, and the World of Goods."

52. Nan Bowman Albinski, *A Guide to Publishers' Archives in the United States*, http://www.sharpweb.org/albinski.html (accessed October 10, 2004).

53. Lewis P. Simpson, *The Man of Letters in New England and the South: Essays on the History of the Literary Vocation in America* (Baton Rouge: Louisiana State University Press, 1973), esp. 201–28; Mary Ann Wimsatt, "The Professional Author in the South: William Gilmore Simms and Antebellum Literary Publishing," in *The Professions of Authorship: Essays in Honor of Matthew J. Bruccoli*, ed. Richard Layman and Joel Myerson (Columbia: University of South Carolina Press, 1996), 121–34. Philip D. Beidler, *First Books: The Printed Word and Cultural Formation in Early Alabama* (Tuscaloosa: University of Alabama Press, 2000), shows the common case of Southern authors publishing in northern cities, particularly Philadelphia and New York. On economic development in the region, see Winifred Barr Rothenberg, "The Invention of American Capitalism: The Economy of New England in the Federal Period," 69–108, and Peter Temin, "The Industrialization of New England, 1830–1880," 109–52, both

in *Engines of Enterprise: An Economic History of New England*, ed. Peter Temin (Cambridge, Mass.: Harvard University Press, 2000); and William N. Parker, "New England's Early Industrialization: A Sketch," in Kilby, ed., *Quantity and Quiddity*, 17–46.

54. The larger set of documents is described in detail in Ronald J. Zboray and Mary Saracino Zboray, "Transcendentalism in Print: Production, Dissemination, and Common Reception," in *Transient and Permanent: The Transcendentalist Movement and Its Contexts*, ed. Charles Capper and Conrad Edick Wright (Boston: Massachusetts Historical Society, 1999), 314–17. Since then we have added at least twenty more informants to the present volume's research base.

55. On the importance of literary centers, see Charvat, *Literary Publishing*, chap. 1. Contra Charvat's argument about Boston's backwardness, see Zboray and Zboray, "Boston Book Trades," and Ronald J. Zboray, "Literary Enterprise in Antebellum Boston," paper delivered at the Seminar in American Bibliography and Book Trade History, American Antiquarian Society, November 9, 1992; now in the collection of the AAS. According to William J. Gilmore, *Reading Becomes a Necessity of Life: Material and Cultural Life in Rural New England, 1780–1835* (Knoxville: University of Tennessee Press, 1989), literary culture was most likely to follow the inland and riverine routes of the market.

56. Peter R. Knights, *Yankee Destinies: The Lives of Ordinary Nineteenth-Century Bostonians* (Chapel Hill: University of North Carolina Press, 1991), 151–55.

57. The best in-depth analysis of literacy remains William J. Gilmore, "Elementary Literacy on the Eve of the Industrial Revolution, 1760–1830," *PAAS* 98 (1982): 87–178. Zboray, *A Fictive People*, 83, presents the reactions of some travelers to American literacy, while comparative regional rates are discussed in appendix 1, 196–201. On occupational structure and class, see Peter R. Knights, *The Plain People of Boston, 1830–1860: A Study in City Growth* (New York: Oxford University Press, 1971), 144–56; and on the complexities of determining the boundaries of the working class, especially in light of poor farmers, see Karen V. Hansen, *A Very Social Time: Crafting Community in Antebellum New England* (Berkeley and Los Angeles: University of California Press, 1994), 30–35. Women taking up the pen out of desperation figure in Kelley, *Private Woman*, and Buell, *New England Literary Culture*, 382.

58. "Inventory," Coll. 159, JEHP-MeHS.

59. "Death of Mrs. Sarah P. Hale," *Boston Patriot*[?], December 3, 1866; clipping in HP-SSC.

60. William R. Taylor and Christopher Lasch, "Two 'Kindred Spirits': Sorority and Family in New England, 1839–1846," *NEQ* 36 (1963): 23–41.

61. George H. Twiss, "introductory note" to "Journal of Cyrus P. Bradley," *Ohio History*, 15 (1906): 207–14; the portion of Bradley's diary covering the Exeter and Dartmouth years (vols. 8–10) has been transcribed by Herbert Wells Hill, 3 vols., and is available in the Dartmouth College Library. Sketch by Alice Park, Palo Alto, Calif., February 1949, in John Park, diary, BPL. Edward H. Hall, "Reminiscences of Dr. John Park," *PAAS*, new ser., 7 (1892): 69–93. On authors mentioned, see Park, diary, May 13 and July 23, 1850.

62. James R. McGovern, *Yankee Family* (New Orleans: Polyanthos, 1975); Harriet Hyman Alonso, *Growing Up Abolitionist: The Story of the Garrison Children* (Amherst: University of Massachusetts Press, 2002), chap. 7; Albert Sidney Foley, *Bishop Healy, Beloved Outcaste: The Story of a Great Priest Whose Life Has Become a Legend* (New York: Farrar, Straus and Young, 1954).

63. Gladys Gage Rogers, "Seth Shaler Arnold, 1781–1871, Vermonter," *Proceedings of the Vermont Historical Society*, new ser., 7 (1939): 217–45; Henry W. Haynes, "Memoir of Mellen Chamberlain," *PMHS*, 2d ser., 20 (1906): 118–46.

Chapter 1

1. Adams, undated, Common Place Book, No. 2, c. 1835, BC. Hill to Adams, April 22, 1825, transcript in Adams, Common Place Book. Hill's "Oh! That I Had Wings Like a Dove" appeared in *Specimens of American Poetry*, ed. Samuel Kettell, 3 vols. (Boston: S.G. Goodrich, 1829), 3:343–34. Alan Rogers, "A Sailor 'By Necessity': The Life of Moses Adams, 1803–1837," *JER* 11 (1991): 19–50; idem, "'A Dangerous Sport': A Boston Boy's Life at Sea, 1820–1837," *American Neptune* 50 (1990): 211–18.

2. Hill to Adams, April 22, 1825; Frederic S. Hill, *The Harvest Festival; With Other Poems* (Boston: True and Greene, 1826); idem, ed., *The Memorial: A Christmas and New Year's Offering*, 2 vols. (Boston: True and Greene, 1827, 1828); Adams, Common Place Book. Hill's magazine was the *New-England Galaxy* (April 30, 1831–May 11, 1833); his name also appears on several imprints from 1830–31, including a bimonthly serial, *The Amateur*. His plays include *The Six Degrees of Crime: Of Wine, Women, Gambling, Theft, Murder and the Scaffold; A Melodrama in Six Parts* (New York: S. French, c. 1850s); and *The Shoemaker of Toulouse; or, The Avenger of Humble Life, A Drama, in Four Acts* (New York: S. French, 1852). On Hill, see William W. Clapp Jr., *A Record of the Boston Stage* (1853; reprint New York: Benjamin Blom, 1968), 295–96, 340, 404.

3. The number of these would-be, onetime, and sometimes published authors who have ever been noticed by scholars relative to those who have not is very small indeed. Lawrence Buell, *New England Literary Culture from Revolution Through Renaissance* (Cambridge: Cambridge University Press, 1986) does deal with some minor authors; he considers motives for their writing and reflects upon their overall careers, but a detailed look at amateur authorial processes fell outside his scope. Some of the best insight on motivations and detail on getting into print comes from work on women writers; see, for example, Mary Kelley, *Private Woman/Public Stage: Literary Domesticity in Nineteenth-Century America* (New York: Oxford University Press, 1984), and Susan Coultrap-McQuin, *Doing Literary Business: American Women Writers in the Nineteenth Century* (Chapel Hill: University of North Carolina Press, 1990). Though most of these works deal with better known writers, their generalizations often apply equally to lesser known ones. Surveys of women writers of nonfiction include Nina Baym, *American Women Writers and the Work of History, 1790–1860* (New Brunswick, N.J.: Rutgers University Press, 1995), and her *American Women of Letters and the Nineteenth-Century Sciences: Styles of Affiliation* (New Brunswick, N.J.: Rutgers University Press, 2002); Sherry Lee Linkon, ed., *In Her Own Voice: Nineteenth-Century American Women Essayists* (New York: Garland, 1997); and Nicole Tonkovich, *Domesticity with a Difference: The Nonfiction of Catharine Beecher, Sarah J. Hale, Fanny Fern, and Margaret Fuller* (Jackson: University Press of Mississippi, 1997). Nothing comparable exists for marginal writers of the opposite sex; see, however, Philip D. Beidler, *First Books: The Printed Word and Cultural Formation in Early Alabama* (Tuscaloosa: University of Alabama Press, 1999), which treats several of them, as does, of course, David S. Reynolds, *Beneath the American Renaissance: The Subversive Imagination in the Age of Emerson and Melville* (Cambridge: Harvard University Press, 1989); see also Daniel A. Cohen, *Pillars of Salt, Monuments of Grace: New England Crime Literature and the Origins of American Popular Culture, 1674–1860* (New York: Oxford University Press, 1993).

4. Because a few writers, although commercially unsuccessful during their own lifetime, later became canonized by literary scholars, many works on general authorship portray conditions that many of their still-obscure counterparts faced. These works include William Charvat, *The Profession of Authorship in America, 1800–1870*, ed. Matthew J. Bruccoli (Columbus: Ohio State University Press, 1968); Raymond

Jackson Wilson, *Figures of Speech: American Writers and the Literary Marketplace, from Benjamin Franklin to Emily Dickinson* (Baltimore: Johns Hopkins University Press, 1987); Stephen Railton, *Authorship and Audience: Literary Performance in the American Renaissance* (Princeton, N.J.: Princeton University Press, 1991); Michael Newbury, *Figuring Authorship in Antebellum America* (Stanford, Calif.: Stanford University Press, 1997); Michael Davitt Bell, *Culture, Genre, and Literary Vocation: Selected Essays on American Literature* (Chicago: University of Chicago Press, 2001); and idem, "Conditions of Literary Vocation," in *Cambridge History of American Literature*, vol. 2, *1820–1865*, ed. Sacvan Bercovitch and Cyrus R.K. Patell (Cambridge: Cambridge University Press, 1995), 9–123.

5. "Amateur Authors and Small Critics," *USDR* 17 (1845): 63.

6. Shawn Alfrey, *The Sublime of Intense Sociability: Emily Dickinson, H.D., and Gertrude Stein* (Lewisburg, Penn.: Bucknell University Press, 2000), 11, 48–80. Apart from the many considerations of transcendentalist circles that we discuss in the conclusion, coterie studies of authorship in the antebellum United States remain yet rare. See, for example, the analysis in Eliza Clark Richards, "Poetic Attractions: Gender, Celebrity, and Authority in Poe's Circle" (Ph.D. diss., University of Michigan, 1997); Edward L. Widmer, *Young America: The Flowering of Democracy in New York City* (New York: Oxford University Press, 1998); and the battles of the literary elements of that group with others described in Perry Miller, *The Raven and the Whale: The War of Words and Wits in the Era of Poe and Melville* (New York: Harcourt Brace, 1956), esp. 104–34. Nicole Tonkovich, "Writing in Circles: Harriet Beecher Stowe, The Semi-Colon Club, and the Construction of Women's Authorship," in *Nineteenth-Century Women Learn to Write*, ed. Catherine Hobbs (Charlottesville: University Press of Virginia, 1995), 145–75. For eighteenth-century and early-nineteenth-century precedents, see David S. Shields, *Civil Tongues and Polite Letters in British America* (Chapel Hill: University of North Carolina Press, 1997); Alexander Hamilton, *The History of the Ancient and Honorable Tuesday Club*, 3 vols., ed. Robert Micklus (Chapel Hill: University of North Carolina Press, 1990); Leon Howard, *The Connecticut Wits* (Chicago: University of Chicago Press, 1943); Milton Ellis, *Joseph Dennie and His Circle: A Study in American Literature from 1792 to 1812* (1915; reprint New York: AMS, 1971); Nelson Adkins, "James Fenimore Cooper and the Bread and Cheese Club," *Modern Language Notes* 47 (1932): 71–79. By contrast, literary coterie study has become not only common but critically well developed by specialists in European literature. Examples include Margaret J.M. Ezell, *Social Authorship and the Advent of Print* (Baltimore: Johns Hopkins University Press, 1999); Sarah Prescott, "Provincial Networks, Dissenting Connections, and Noble Friends: Elizabeth Singer Rowe and Female Authorship in Early Eighteenth-Century England," *Eighteenth-Century Life* 25 (2001): 29–42; Jeffrey N. Cox, *Poetry and Politics in the Cockney School: Keats, Shelley, Hunt, and Their Circle* (Cambridge: Cambridge University Press, 1998); Kathryn R. King, "Jane Barker, Poetical Recreations, and the Sociable Text," *ELH* 61(1994): 551–70; Elizabeth Colwill, "Epistolary Passions: Friendship and the Literary Public of Constance de Salm, 1767–1845," *Journal of Women's History* 12 (2000): 39–68.

7. On the cry for "more copy" see, for example, Joseph J. Belcher, "Newspaperiana," *HNMM* 33 (1866): 367; review of John G. Whittier, *Literary Recreations and Miscellanies*, *NAR* 79 (1854): 539; and Charles Graham Halpine, "Rime of Ye Seedie Printeere Man," in *Lyrics by the Letter H* (New York: J.C. Derby, 1854), 218–21, in which a publisher-printer confronts a newspaper editor leaving work for a night on the town: "The papeeres must to-morrow out; / To-morrow be on hand, / And you are our chief editeere— / More copy we demand" (219). The phrase "more copy" becomes a running refrain in the poem.

8. Mary Gardner Lowell, February 25, 1844, personal journal, FCL2P-MHS. Regarding *Graham's* circulation in the early 1840s, estimates vary from 25,000 to 40,000; Edgar Allan Poe to Charles Anthon, June 1844, transcribed in George E. Woodberry, "Selections from the Correspondence of Poe," *Century* 48 (1894): 855; *HAM*, 1:552. Louisa Gilman Loring to Ellis Gray Loring and Anna Loring, July 20, 1852, EGLFP-SL. The serialization of Stowe's novel began in *NE*, June 5, 1851, and concluded just over a year later; Susan Geary convincingly argues for the four-hundred-dollar fee over the traditionally cited three-hundred-dollar one in "Mrs. Stowe's Income from the Serial Version of *Uncle Tom's Cabin*," *SB* 29 (1976): 380–82. Harriet Beecher Stowe, *Uncle Tom's Cabin; or, Life among the Lowly* (Boston: John P. Jewett, 1852) appeared on March 20, 1852. According to the report to which Loring seems to be referring, Stowe received "$10,300 as her copy-right premium on three months' sale of the work—we believe the largest sum of money ever received by any author, either American or European, from the sales of a single work in so short a period of time." Boston *Traveller* quoted in *Littell's Living Age*, October 16, 1852, 97. Compare J. Albert Robbins, "Fees Paid to Authors by Certain American Periodicals, 1840–1850," *SB* 2 (1949–50): 94–104. Ellery Sedgwick, "Magazines and the Profession of Authorship in the United States, 1840–1900," *PBSA* 94 (2000): 399–425. Compare this with the largely anonymous (and unpaid) fiction authorship of the early Republic; see Cathy N. Davidson, *Revolution and the Word: The Rise of the Novel in America* (New York: Oxford University Press, 1986), 31–33.

9. "Hamlin" to Ballou, November 5, 1856; Harris to Williams, December 3, 1856; Harris to Ballou, December 10, 1856, letterbook, JEHP-MeHS. Williams was associated with two Boston papers, *Uncle Sam* and *The American Privateersman*. Mary Noel, *Villains Galore…: The Heyday of the Popular Story Weekly* (New York: Macmillan, 1954), 18–20, 27–29. The query to Ballou suggests the scope of Harris's ambitions, for his magazines were among Boston's best paying and most widely circulated; George Everett, "Maturin Murray Ballou," *DLB*, vol. 79, *American Magazine Journalists, 1850-1900*, ed. Sam G. Riley (Detroit, Mich.: Gale, 1989), 43–50; Peter Benson, "Maturin Murray Ballou," 27–34, and "Gleason's Publishing Hall," 137–45, in *Publishers for Mass Entertainment in Nineteenth Century America*, ed. Madeleine B. Stern (Boston: Hall, 1980); and idem, *Imprints on History: Book Publishers and American Frontiers* (Bloomington: Indiana University Press, 1956), 209–18. Frank Luther Mott, who estimates *Waverley's* peak circulation at 50,000, calls the magazine "for half a century the favorite of amateur writers," but his generalization that its editor "threw [its pages] open to the unpaid contributions of schoolgirls and their swains" (*HAM*, 2:41–42) clearly needs revision in light of Harris's case. Apart from the Lowell millwomen (see, especially, Judith A. Ranta, *Women and Children of the Mills: An Annotated Guide to Nineteenth-Century American Textile Factory Literature* [Westport, Conn.: Greenwood, 1999]), little has yet been done on working-class amateurs like Harris. See, however, David S. Reynolds, *George Lippard* (Boston: Twayne, 1982); and idem, *Beneath the American Renaissance*. Not all *Waverley* contributors came from the ranks of amateurs, as can be seen in the case of Florida-born Cuban nationalist writer-in-exile Miguel Teurbe Tolón y de la Guardia, whose poems in English appeared in the magazine, even though he was an editor himself and had penned, among several other works, a steady seller that would continue being reprinted until the next century, *The Elementary Spanish Reader and Translator* (New York: D. Appleton, 1852); Matanzas es La Atenas de Cuba, "Teurbe Tolón y de la Guardia, Miguel," *Portal de Matanzas*, http://www.atenas.inf.cu/todo/poetas/MiguelTeurbe.htm (accessed June 8, 2002); for the context of his coterie, see Rodrigo Lazo, "Filibustering Cuba: *Cecilia Valdés* and a Memory of Nation in the Americas," *AL* 74 (2002): 1–30.

10. Forten, December 13 and 16, 1857, *JCFG*, 271. George Pope Morris's and Nathaniel Parker Willis's *Home Journal* only rarely paid for contributions, so Forten may have

been mistaken in her efforts (*HAM*, 2:352). For secondary sources on Forten as an African American writer, see chapter 2 of the present volume. Sara J. Clarke [Lippincott, aka "Grace Greenwood"] to Milo A. Townsend, July 13, 1844, in *Milo Adams Townsend and Social Movements of the Nineteenth Century*, ed. Peggy Jean Townsend and Charles Walker Townsend III (1994), *Beaver County History*, http://www.bchistory.org/beavercounty/booklengthdocuments/AMilobook/title.html (accessed July 1, 2002), sponsored by BCHS. Gillian Gill, *Mary Baker Eddy* (Reading, Mass.: Perseus, 1998), 52–75. Charles M. Cobb, February 6 and August 8, 1852, and November 6, 1854, journal, transcript, VHS. Woodfern published in story papers like *Waverley* (e.g., September 25, 1852, p. 198 and July 24, 1852, p. 53), and *Yankee Privateer: A Nautical and Literary Journal Devoted to the Interests, Instruction and Amusement of Seamen, and the Public Generally* (e.g., August 14, 1852, p. 4). Her husband was Alonzo Lewis (1794–1861), who produced several volumes of verse and miscellaneous prose. Some sense of what it meant for a self-supporting woman trying to write for money in the antebellum Boston publishing trade can be gotten from Fanny Fern [aka Sara Willis Parton], *Ruth Hall: A Domestic Tale of the Present Time* (New York: Mason Brothers, 1855), but compare with Joyce W. Warren's *Fanny Fern: An Independent Woman* (New Brunswick, N.J.: Rutgers University Press, 1992) to help separate fact from fiction. See also Ann D. Wood [Douglas], "The 'Scribbling Women' and Fanny Fern: Why Women Wrote," *AQ* 23 (1971): 3–24. On the early-nineteenth-century context of such marital splits as Woodfern's, see Norma Basch, *Framing American Divorce from the Revolutionary Generation to the Victorians* (Berkeley and Los Angeles: University of California Press, 1999).

11. Hale to Edward Everett, December 26, 1837, and all her other letters below, HP-SSC. She does not specify her books, but Carter published (or acted as an agent for) several illustrated and unattributed children's books in the period, including *Pictures and Stories, for Children* [in twelve parts] (Boston: T.H. Carter, agent, 1837); *Jack and the Bean-stalk, A New Version* (Boston: T.H. Carter, agent, 1837); and *Grandmamma's Book of Rhymes, for the Nursery* (Boston: T.H. Carter, agent, 1838); Hale to Everett, January 23, 1841. For background on her writing, see Jean Holloway, *Edward Everett Hale: A Biography* (Austin: University of Texas Press, 1956), 52. Gillian Avery, *Behold the Child: American Children and Their Books, 1621–1922* (Baltimore: Johns Hopkins University Press, 1994). She also wrote biographies for Marsh, Capen, Lyon, and Webb's The School Library, Juvenile Series. Her later giftbooks, as she discussed in a letter to Lucretia Everett, March 12, 1842, include *The Annualette: A Christmas and New Year's Gift*, ed. by a Lady (Boston: T.H. Carter, 1842–1845); *The Lady's Annual Register, and Housewife's Memorandum-Book for 1843* (Boston: T.H. Carter, 1841–1842); and *Youth's Keepsake* (Boston: Carter and Hendee, 1843). On the phenomenon, see Ralph Thompson, *American Literary Annuals and Gift Books, 1825–1865* (New York: H.W. Wilson, 1936), and, on her books specifically, 109–10, 162–63. Hale to D.H. Williams, April 27, 1843; *The Token and Atlantic Souvenir, An Offering for Christmas and the New Year* 15 (Boston: D.H. Williams, 1842), discussed in Thompson, 65–73. Kelley, *Private Woman*, esp. chap. 6.

12. Bradley, January 5 and March 18, 1835, school journal, NHHS; *The Literary Gazette*, 2 vols. (Concord, N.H.: D.D. Fisk, August 1, 1834–June 26, 1835); he mentions his tenure as coeditor on December 1, 1834. White to Kiddy King, transcript, October 4, 1842, EGLFP-SL. Lowell's nascent magazine, the *Pioneer* (1843), lasted only three months and left him eighteen hundred dollars in debt (William Edward Simonds, *A Student's History of American Literature* [Boston: Houghton Mifflin, 1909], 256–57); Garrison to William Lloyd Garrison, Sr., October 11, 1858, GP-SSC. Harriet Hyman Alonso, *Growing Up Abolitionist: The Story of the Garrison Children* (Amherst: University of Massachusetts Press, 2002), 145–55.

13. Hale, *A New England Boyhood, And Other Bits of Autobiography* (Boston: Little, Brown, 1900), 338. "Offer Extraordinary," and Reynell Coates, "Preliminary Report of the Committee on Prizes," *SUM* 8 (1851): 144, and 9 (1851): 79–80. Holloway, *Edward Everett Hale, A Biography*; John R. Adams, *Edward Everett Hale* (Boston: Twayne, 1977). John Park, June 18, 1845, April 8, and April 28, 1837, diary, BPL; *New-England Galaxy,* April 7, 1837; Leonard Woods, *An Essay on Native Depravity* (Boston: W. Peirce, 1835). Louisa Park's story appeared in a supplement entitled *Prize Papers* (Boston: Harrington, 1837), 1–16; Louisa Jane Hall, *Miriam, A Dramatic Poem* (Boston: Hilliard, Gray, 1837). Rufus Wilmot Griswold, *The Female Poets of America* (Philadelphia: Henry C. Baird, 1853), 111–12. For examples of competitions, see "The Gipsey," *FOU,* July 17, 1847, 3; *FOU,* December 11, 1847, 3; *FOU,* February 5, 1848, 3; "Unprecedented Announcement!" *FOU,* October 7, 1848, 3; Mrs. Maria B. Pitkin to Rev. John Budd Pitkin, June 23, 1834, HC-SL; *Vital Records of Great Barrington, Massachusetts, to the Year 1850* (Boston: New-England Historic Genealogical Society, 1904), 80. Robert A. Rees and Marjorie Griffin, "William Gilmore Simms and the Family Companion," *SB* 21 (1971): 119. James F. English's "Winning the Culture Game: Prizes, Awards, and the Rules of Art," *NLH* 33 (2002): 109–35, though it discusses recent trends, provides theoretical groundwork for understanding antebellum ones, even if by way of contrast, in light of Pierre Bourdieu's concept of cultural capital; Michele Lamont and Annette Lareau, "Cultural Capital: Allusions, Gaps and Glissandos in Recent Theoretical Developments," *Sociological Theory* 6 (1988): 153–68.

14. Healy, January 15, and March 8 and 15, 1849, diary, CHC; Charles le Gobien, Nicholas Moréchal, and Louis Patouillet, eds. and comps., *Lettres édifiantes et curieuses écrites des missions étrangères,* 34 vols. (Paris: Chez Jean Cusson, 1702–1776). Albert Sidney Foley, *Bishop Healy: Beloved Outcaste* (1954; reprint New York: Arno, 1969); James M. O'Toole, "Passing: Race, Religion, and the Healy Family, 1820–1920," *PMHS* 108 (1996): 1–34, esp. 1–2, 11–17. Baker, October 23, 1829, July 12, 1830, and December 24, 1830, diary, NHHS. *New England Christian Herald* (Boston: Boston Wesleyan Association, 1829–1833). Baker, who would continue to write, teach, and serve as a pastor, became a bishop in 1852. James Wideman Lee, Naphtali Luccock, and James Main Dixon, *The Illustrated History of Methodism: The Story of the Origin and Progress of the Methodist Church* ... (St. Louis: Methodist Magazine Publishing, 1900), 556 and 516 (on *Herald*); W.H. Daniels, *The Illustrated History of Methodism in Great Britain and America* (New York: Methodist Book Concern, 1880), 685–87, 553–54 (on Wilbraham), and 560–61 (on the *Herald*).

15. Henry A. Worcester to Joseph E. Worcester, September 29, 1837, SFP-SL; Oliver Gerrish to Olive Gay Worcester, December 5 and June 28, 1841 and April 25, 1846; see also idem to Rufus Marble Gay, July 7, 1841, transcript, SFP-SL; Henry Aiken Worcester, *Sermons on the Lord's Prayer, To Which Are Added Sermons on Other Subjects* (Boston: O. Clapp, 1837); idem, *The Sabbath* (Boston: Otis Clapp, 1840); Henry N. Flynt and Martha Gandy Fales, *The Heritage Foundation Collection of Silver* ... (Old Deerfield, Mass.: Heritage Foundation, 1968), 16, 225, 267. H.B. Hoskins, "New Jerusalem Church," *The History of Gardiner, Pittston, and West Gardiner, with a Sketch of the Kennebec Indians, and New Plymouth Purchase Comprising Historical Matter from 1602 to 1852,* comp. J.W. Hanson (Gardiner, Me.: William Palmer, 1852); Marguerite Beck Block, *The New Church in the New World: A Study of Swedenborgianism in America* (1932; reprint New York: Octagon Books, 1968), 182, cites Worcester's 1836 *Address on the Subject of Public Festivals, Social Entertainment, Receptions, and Amusements,* to underscore the active Swedenborgian pursuit of "'free social intercourse,'" even against Sabbatarian strictures.

16. Arnold, June 27, 1835; April 21, May 3, 15, and 30, and June 16, 1837, transcripts, journal, VHS; idem, *The Intellectual House-Keeper, A Series of Practical Questions to His Daughters, by a Father; or, Hints to Females on the Necessity of Thought in Connexion with Their Domestic Labors and Duties* (Boston: Russell, Odiorne, 1835); Seth Shaler Arnold and E. Colman, *The Family Choir: A Selection of Hymns Set to Music ...* (New York: Kidder and Wright for the American Tract Society, 1837). Arnold is mentioned frequently in the history of his ancestral home; see F.J. Fairbanks, "Westminster," in *Vermont Historical Gazetteer: A Local History of all the Towns in the State, Civil, Educational, Biographical, Religious and Military*, vol. 5, *The Towns of Windham County*, ed. Abby Maria Hemenway (Brandon, Vt.: Carrie E.H. Page, 1891), 1–76. David Paul Nord, "Free Grace, Free Books, Free Riders: The Economics of Religious Publishing in Early Nineteenth-Century America," *PAAS* 106, pt. 2 (1996): 241–72; Lawrance Thompson, "The Printing and Publishing Activities of the American Tract Society from 1825 to 1850," *PBSA* 35 (1941): 81–114.

17. On Forten's pieces in the *Liberator* and *NAAS*, see Brenda J. Stevenson, "Chronology," in *JCFG*, xxxiv–xxxv. Enoch Hale, December 1841, diary, PEM; *The Daily Herald* (Newburyport, Mass.: Morss and Brewster, June 3, 1834–December 30, 1865). Bradley, January 12 and 16, and October 8, 1835, diary, NHHS; *New-Hampshire Patriot and State Gazette* (Concord, N.H.: Hill and Moore, February 2, 1819–December 31, 1862); *Courier and Enquirer* (Concord, N.H.: Odlin and Chadwick, June 13, 1834–June 3, 1836); the Jackson campaign paper was the *Concord Patriot* (Concord, N.H.: January 13, 1835–March 17, 1835); *New Hampshire Argus and Spectator*, 7 vols. (Newport, N.H.: July 25, 1835–June 10, 1842). William Miles, *The People's Voice: An Annotated Bibliography of American Presidential Campaign Newspapers, 1828–1984* (Westport, Conn.: Greenwood, 1987).

18. David A. Kronick, "The Commerce of Letters: Networks and 'Invisible Colleges' in Seventeenth- and Eighteenth-Century Europe," *LQ* 71 (2001): 28–43.

19. Samuel Haber, *The Quest for Authority and Honor in the American Professions, 1750–1900* (Chicago: University of Chicago Press, 1991), 147–49, 164, 179–80, 185.

20. Blake, March 20 and 29, November 7 and 8, 1851, diary, AAS; idem, "Practical Remarks on Illuminating Gas," *SA*, April 3, 12, and 26, May 3, 10, 17, 24, and 31, June 7, 21, and 28, and July 21, 1851, 230, 238, 254, 262, 270, 278, 286, 294, 302, 318, 326, and 342. Michael Borut, "The *Scientific American* in Nineteenth-Century America" (Ph.D. diss., New York University, 1977); Dirk J. Struik, *Yankee Science in the Making* (1948; reprint Boston: Little, Brown, 1962), 291–444. On the European case, see Wolfgang Schivelbusch, *Disenchanted Night: The Industrialization of Light in the Nineteenth Century*, trans. Angela Davies (Berkeley and Los Angeles: University of California Press, 1988). On another way to achieve acknowledged expertise, see Laura Dassow Walls, "Textbooks and Texts from the Brooks: Inventing Scientific Authority in America," *AQ* 49 (1997): 1–25.

21. Nell to William Lloyd Garrison, September 15, 1851, BPL; Robert P. Smith, "William Cooper Nell: Crusading Black Abolitionist," *Journal of Negro History* 55 (1970): 182–99. See the report of Hopedale's leader, Adin Ballou, *An Exposition of Views Respecting the Principal Facts, Causes and Peculiarities Involved in Spirit Manifestations* (Boston: Bela Marsh, 1852). Poor to Lucy Pierce Hedge, March 4, 1852; on his publication, see Poor to Hedge, March 14, 1854; these and all other manuscripts below by Pierce or Poor family members, PoFP-SL; Thomas Lake Harris, *Epic of the Starry Heaven* (New York: Partridge and Brittan, 1854); idem, *A Lyric of the Morning Land* (New York: Partridge and Brittan, 1854). Herbert W. Schneider and George Lawton, *A Prophet and a Pilgrim: Being the Incredible History of Thomas Lake Harris and Laurence Oliphant, Their Sexual Mysticisms and Utopian Communities* (New York: Columbia University Press, 1942), 10–14; R. Laurence Moore, *In Search of White*

Crows: Spiritualism, Parapsychology, and American Culture (New York: Oxford University Press, 1977), chap. 1; Bret E. Carroll, *Spiritualism in Antebellum America* (Bloomington: Indiana University Press, 1997), 53, 57, 144, 161, and 166.

22. Cobb, January 18, and February 8, 22, 23, and 26, and March 14, 1852; July 6, 1851, journal. I. B. Hartwell to Horace Greeley, January 25, 1852, *New York Weekly Tribune*, February 21, 1852. On the relationship of technology to spirit rapping, see Jeffrey Sconce, *Haunted Media: Electronic Presence from Telegraphy to Television* (Durham, N.C.: Duke University Press, 2000), esp. chap. 1. Hartwell had made a name for himself by establishing a singing band in the wake of the musical explosion that accompanied the 1840 Log Cabin Presidential Campaign; Henry Swan Dana, *A History of Woodstock, Vermont* (Boston: Houghton Mifflin, 1889), 230. The school district was about two-and-a-half miles from the center of town in an area dominated by grain mills and a rake manufactory (70, 81), whereas the one on the green had a long and distinguished past (chap. 11) and had served the town's gentry. On Marenda Bigelow Randall's diehard abolitionism, see her letters to Cassius M. Clay, December 26, 1843 and March 11, 1844, LMU. The latter letter is from the post-Garrisonian, communist, and diet-reformist Community Place in Skaneateles, New York. She is listed under "Practicing Physicians" as a "Rational" practitioner in *The Progressive Annual for 1863; Comprising an Almanac, a Spiritualist Register, and a General Calendar of Reform* (New York: A.J. Davis, 1863).

23. Cobb, April 14 and 28, October 3, August 16 and 28, September 19, and October 22 and 29, 1852, journal. Daniel Webster, Andrew Jackson, and Thomas Jefferson also supposedly spoke through Simmons; see *A.E. Simmons' Communications, From Daniel Webster and Others* (Woodstock, Vt.: For the Medium, 1852). Information about Simmons derives from the "Family Bible Records of Bela F. Simmons [his father] of Woodstock VT, including the records of the Judah and Eliza Hatch family," transcription via Denise Perkins Ready and Debbie Axman, "Windsor County Vermont," *USGenNet*, http://www.usgennet.org/usa/vt/county/windsor/contrib.htm (accessed July 2, 2002). Dana, *History of Woodstock*, 63. The *Spiritual Telegraph*, August 23, and September 6, 1856, noted that Austin "lectures in the trance state as he is impressed by the controlling spiritual influences"; via John B. Buescher, "Ephemera," *Spirithistory.com*, http://www.spirithistory.com/56telegr.html (accessed May 24, 2004). The dead revolutionary propagandist Thomas Paine would later "speak" through Wood in print; see his *The Philosophy of Creation: Unfolding the Laws of the Progressive Development of Nature, and Embracing the Philosophy of Man, Spirit, and the Spirit World* (Boston: B. Marsh, 1854). On the importance of Paine to the spiritualist community, see Carroll, *Spiritualism*, 37, 45, 48, 74, 83.

24. Cobb, October 22, and November 16 and 18, 1852; March 14, 1853; June 8, 1853, journal. The Simmons and Pratt families were neighbors; see Dana, *History of Woodstock*, 63. Austin E. Simmons to L.B. Britain, 1856, extract, in Emma Hardinge Britten, *Modern American Spiritualism: A Twenty Years' Record of the Communion Between the Earth and the World of Spirits* (New York: Britten, 1870), 204, suggests that after a brief eclipse, Spiritualism came back strong in Woodstock by the mid-1850s. Still, Dana is silent on the subject in his town history.

25. John Durham Peters, *Speaking into the Air: A History of the Idea of Communication* (Chicago: University of Chicago Press, 1999), 95–98, probes the relationship of spiritualism and technology.

26. On the background of these in social authorship practices, see Mary Louise Kete, *Sentimental Collaboration: Mourning and Middle-Class Identity in Nineteenth-Century America* (Durham, N.C.: Duke University Press, 2000), pt. 1, 11–49.

27. John Park, September 12, and October 6, 1838; and April 4, 1839, diary. Janice Hume, *Obituaries in American Culture* (Jackson: University Press of Mississippi, 2000).

28. Jocelyn, March 7, 10, 13, and 12, 1847, journal; Frances M. (Jocelyn) Peck, February 23, 1856, diary, both, (and other Jocelyn sister manuscripts below) in JFP-CHS. "Lines on the Death of Julia C. Peck," New Haven *Daily Herald*, March 14, 1847. Ellen Strong Bartlett, "Mrs. Elizabeth H. Jocelyn Cleaveland," *NEM* 44 (1911): 529–39. Peter Fulton, "'No Biography or History Had a Word to Say About It': A Nineteenth-Century Manuscript Newly Discovered" (Ph.D. diss., Duke University, 1999), 24–28; 35–43.

29. Rogers, March 2 and 28, 1851, diary, RFP-PEM; idem, "Genealogical Memoir of the Family of Rev. Nathaniel Rogers of Ipswich, Essex Co., Mass. ...," *NEHGR* 5 (1851): 105–52, 311–30; 12 (1858): 337–42; 13 (1859): 61–69. Cushman, August 9, 1855, private journal, HWCC-NEHGS; idem, *A Historical and Biographical Genealogy of the Cushmans, the Descendants of Robert Cushman, the Puritan, from the Year 1617 to 1855* (Boston: Little, Brown, 1855). His genealogy would be deemed as late as 1898 "the largest and most laborious Genealogy yet in print"; Worthington C. Ford, "American Genealogies," *NAR* 82 (1898): 469–78, quote on 474.

30. Christopher Columbus Baldwin to Fenwick, August 28, 1833, AAB. An original sketch was not included in Benedict Joseph Fenwick, *Memoirs to Serve for the Future: Ecclesiastical History of the Diocess [sic] of Boston*, ed. Joseph M. McCarthy (Yonkers, N.Y.: U.S. Catholic Historical Society, 1978), which is based on Fenwick's very polished yet abortive manuscript (introduction, vii–ix). Fenwick's *Memoir* instead extensively quotes (164–69) the seventh volume of the 1809 Paris edition of *Lettres édifiantes*. Poor to Lucy Pierce Hedge, June 17, 1851; idem, "Memoir of John Pierce, D.D., Communicated by Charles Lowell," *Collections of the Massachusetts Historical Society*, 4th ser., 1 (1852): 277–95. Frederic N. Knapp, *A Biographical Sketch of the Rev. John Pierce, D.D. ...* (Boston: Crosby and Nichols, 1849). The father had left an immense legacy of twenty volumes of memoirs (1788–1849), now at MHS, and published in fragments in *PMHS*, 2d ser., 3 (1886): 41–52; 5 (1888): 167–252; 9 (1893): 110–43; 10 (1894): 392–403; and 19 (1905): 362–89. James R. McGovern, *Yankee Family* (New Orleans: Polyanthos, 1975), 5–7.

31. Ann Fabian, *The Unvarnished Truth: Personal Narratives in Nineteenth-Century America* (Berkeley and Los Angeles: University of California Press, 2000), esp. xii.

32. On postal workers filching mail, see "Editor's Table," *HNMM* 11 (1855): 697–701; on them withholding mail from opposition partisans, see Mathew J. Bowyer, *They Carried the Mail: A Survey of Postal History and Hobbies* (Washington, N.Y.: Robert B. Luce, 1972), 22; this happened despite penalties, as stated in *Laws and Regulations of the Government of the Post Office Department* (Washington, D.C.: C. Alexander, 1852), 21. Davis to Eliza Bancroft Davis, January 4, 1826, JDP-AAS. On the fire, see William C. Allen, *History of the United States Capitol: A Chronicle of Design, Construction, and Politics* (Washington, D.C.: Government Printing Office, 2001), 157–59. Persis Sibley Andrews Black (hereafter, Sibley), August 31, 1851, diary, MeHS; Hale to Everett and Lucretia Everett, September 15, 1847.

33. The estimate of items published by request is based on a Boolean search for records of imprints bearing the phrase *by request* produced in forty-nine American cities in OCLC's *WorldCat* database, run October 24, 2004.

34. Forten, July 25, 1856, *JCFG*, 161; Allen, May 18, 1860, diary, ZAP-RIHS; idem, *Memorial of Roger Williams: Paper Read before the Rhode Island Historical Society, May 18, 1860* (Providence: private printing, 1860), 7. The exhumation is rehearsed in Joel Dorman Steele, *Fourteen Weeks in Chemistry* (Chicago: A.S. Barnes, 1873), 239. "The Tree that Ate Roger Williams," *Parade Magazine*, July 25, 1982. Thaddeus DeWolf, October 25, 1855, diary, NEHGS. Solicitation letters appear in Leona Rostenberg, "Some Anonymous and Pseudonymous Thrillers of Louisa May Alcott," *PBSA* 37 (1943): 139–40.

35. Cobb, November 11, 1856, diary, NEHGS; J.H. Cushman to Henry Wyles Cushman, September 7, 1848, HWCC-NEHGS; Melicent P[arthenia (Skilton)] Beers to Mary [Augusta] Skilton, June 28, 1847, ATHM.

36. William T. Gilbert, October 5, 1860, diary, CHS; James Morris Whiton, *A Handbook of Exercises and Reading Lessons for Beginners in Latin* ... (Boston: James Munroe, 1860); *Methodist Quarterly Review* (New York: G. Lane and P.P. Sanford, 1841–1884). The book never was noticed there. Hale to Edward Everett Hale, May 21, 1843 and May 9, 1843; Nathaniel Ward, *The Simple Cobler of Aggawam in America,* ed. David Pulsifer (1647; reprint Boston: James Munroe, 1843). William Ellery Channing, the Younger, *Poems* (Boston: Charles C. Little and James Brown, 1843). "Every book-man keeps a puffer," according to the "Monthly Literary Record," *USDR* 37 (1856): 428; "Critical Notices," *NEM* 9 (1835): 294. On scholarly accounts of puffery, see William Charvat, "James T. Fields and the Beginnings of Book Promotion," *HLQ* 8 (1944–45): 75–94; Miller, *The Raven,* 137–44.

37. Forten, January 16, 1858, *JCFG,* 278. William Stevens Robinson to Benjamin F. Robinson, March 27, 1844, RSP-SL; Leslie Perrin Wilson, "The Barbed Pen of William Stevens Robinson," *Concord Magazine* 4 (May/June 2001), http://www.concordma.com/magazine/mayjun01/warrington.html (accessed May 29, 2004). Case to Edgarton, June 15, 1839, February 9, 1846, and all subsequent Case cites below, HC-SL; *The Rose of Sharon,* ed. Sarah Carter Edgarton, 19 vols. (Boston: A. Tompkins, 1840). On Edgarton, see Amory Dwight Mayo, *Selections from the Writings of Mrs. Sarah C. Edgarton Mayo* (Boston: A. Tompkins, 1849), 9–125; Ann Douglas, *The Feminization of American Culture* (New York: Alfred A. Knopf, 1977), 72–73, 406–7; the sketch of her in Caroline May, *The American Female Poets: With Biographical and Critical Notices* (New York: Leavitt and Allen Brothers, 1849), 461–65; and the entry for her in the *National Cyclopaedia of American Biography,* 63 vols. (New York: James T. White, 1892–1984), 2:437. She also makes an appearance in Griswold, *Female Poets,* 298–302, as does Case, 306–7. William R. Taylor and Christopher Lasch, "Two 'Kindred Spirits': Sorority and Family in New England, 1839–1846," *NEQ* 36 (1963): 23–41, emphasizes that social purpose for the two women writing dominated over career aspiration, monetary need, and intellectual ambition (27, 31). Buell, *New England Literary Culture,* 387, calls Edgarton a "typical female writer" (see also 379, 494 n. 14, and 495 n. 29). Everett to Sarah P. E. Hale, September 29, 1842, HP-SSC. Holloway, *Edward Everett Hale,* 51, 56–57. *HAM,* 1:718.

38. John Park, August 23 and 31, 1839, diary; Alonzo Hill, *A Discourse on the Life and Character of the Rev. Aaron Bancroft, D.D.* (Worcester: T.W. and J. Butterfield, 1839). Bradley, October 19 and 22, and November 12, 1835, diary; Henry Wood, *Trust in God in Public Commotions* (Concord, N.H.: Elbridge G. Chase, 1835). John King Lord, *A History of Dartmouth College, 1815–1909,* vol. 2 (Concord: Rumford Press, 1913), 248–51, 253.

39. Allen to Edward Kavanaugh, October 17, 1837, AAB; idem, *The History of Norridgewock* ... (Norridgewock, Me.: Edward J. Peet, 1849); idem to John H. Willard, February 22, 1867, WHS. Abigale Bradley Hyde to Sarah Hyde, in Lavius Hyde to Sarah Hyde, May 20, 1852, BHFP-SL; Electa Fidelia Jones, *Stockbridge, Past and Present; or, Records of an Old Mission Station* (Springfield, Mass.: S. Bowles, 1854). Dorothy W. Davids, *Our History: Mohican Nation, Stockbridge-Munsee Band* (Bowler, Wisc.: Stockbridge-Munsee Historical Committee, Arvid E. Miller Memorial Library Museum, Spring 2001), http://www.mohican.com/history/oeh.htm (accessed February 23, 2004). Abigail Pierce to Mary Pierce Poor, October 7, 1848; Peter Clarkin, *Reflections on Revelations* (Boston: the author, 1849).

40. Chamberlain, February 19–March 5, 1848, journal, BPL; Hale to Alexander Hill Everett and Lucretia Everett, January 1, 1847; Hale to Alexander Hill Everett, August 6, 1841 (she is referring to Karoline von Greiner Pichler, "Silent Love; or, Leah and Rachel," *BM* 1 [1842]: 11–23); other of her translations for that magazine include E.T.W. Hoffman, "The King's Bride: A Story Drawn from Nature," *BM* 1 (1842): 156–67, 1 (1842): 218–228; idem, "My Cousin's Corner Window," 1 (1842): 257–64; idem, "Master John Wacht," 2 (1842): 18–27, 2 (1842): 68–77. These translations are suggested in Alexander Hill Everett to Sarah P.E. Hale, May 14, 1842 and July 9, 1842, HP-SSC; and Hale to Everett, April 29, 1842. Hale to Edward Everett, September 21, 1841; *HAM,* 1:718–19. The other magazine besides the *Miscellany* to which she refers is the *Monthly Chronicle*, ed. Nathan Hale (Boston: S.N. Dickinson, 1840–42). On women as translators, see Susan Phinney Conrad, *Perish the Thought: Intellectual Women in Romantic America, 1830–1860* (New York: Oxford University Press, 1976), 186–98. Case to Edgarton, January 20, 1842 and February 23, 1840; Poor to Feroline (Pierce) Fox, December 9, 1849; Cobb, "Youth's Department For the Freeman and Visiter[:] Letter from a Little Girl," March 21, 1855, "Written for the Freeman and Visiter[:] To James in Heaven[,] An Acrostic," diary, NEHGS.

41. Harris, February 12 and 14, and June 21, 1857; August 26, September 25, December 2 and 16, January 31, and October 1, 1860; May 23, 1863; July 18, 1860; and January 29, 1857, journal; see also February 12, 1857. On the complex relationship of laboring and writing, see Nicholas Knowles Bromell, *By the Sweat of the Brow: Literature and Labor in Antebellum America* (Chicago: University of Chicago Press, 1993); Newbury, *Figuring Authorship*, chap. 1. For comparative examples of workingclass poetry, see Peter Oresick and Nicholas Coles, *Working Classics: Poems on Industrial Life* (Urbana: University of Illinois Press, 1990).

42. Blake, January 12, 1851, diary; Forten, December 13, 1857, *JCFG*, 271; Osmon Cleander Baker, June 12, 1830, diary.

43. Edgarton to [Henry] Bacon and [Eliza Ann Munroe] Bacon, c. August-September 1838, and two to unidentified recipients, both 1840, in Mayo, *Selections*, 27–28, 34, 36. Bacon, a Universalist minister in Cambridge at the time, would become editor of the *LR*, to which Edgarton frequently contributed. Eliza Ann Munroe Bacon, *Memoir of Rev. Henry Bacon* (Boston: A. Tompkins, 1857). Douglas, *Feminization*, 80–81.

44. Case to Edgarton, February 23, 1840 and March 25, 1842; Hale to Edward Everett, May 31, 1843. Mary Webster to Briggs, August 5, 1853, BriFP-SL; Stephen M. Lawson, "Seventh Generation (continued): Family of Thaddeus Mason Jr. (580) and Lydia Perry," *Capt. Hugh Mason Genealogy*, via *Kinnexions.com*, http://kinnexions.com/ kinnexions/mason/rr01/rr01_332.htm (accessed June 30, 2002). An editorial note to her poem "Fitchburg," *Bay State Monthly* 2 (1885): 328–30, described her as "the author of the words of the familiar ballad 'Do They Miss Me At Home?' and has, for many years, contributed to leading weeklies and magazines" (328). The song was published anonymously before the war, but only became a hit during it, on both sides. A posthumous volume of hers is entitled *The Lost Ring and Other Poems* (Boston: Houghton Mifflin, 1891).

45. Hale to Edward Everett, September 30, 1842; Eliza Buckminster Lee, trans., *Life of Jean Paul Frederic Richter*, 2 vols. (Boston: C.C. Little and J. Brown, 1842). Waterhouse, October 2 [1839?], journal, LLWP-MHS; "Mrs. H.W." is likely Mrs. Henry Ware Jr. (Mary Lovell Pickard), who moved in Waterhouse's circles, had a large family of six, and had a literary bent constrained by a sense of duty to charitable work; Seth Curtis Beach, *Daughters of the Puritans; A Group of Brief Biographies* (Boston: American Unitarian Association, 1905), 64–65; Edward Brooke Hall, *Memoir of Mary L. Ware, Wife of Henry Ware* (Boston: Crosby, Nichols, 1853), 300–303, 326–27. The phrase "scribbling women" originates in Nathaniel Hawthorne to William

D. Ticknor, January 9, 1855, *Centenary Edition of the Works of Nathaniel Hawthorne*, 22 vols., *The Letters, 1853–1856*, ed. William Charvat, Roy Harvey Pearse, and Claude M. Simpson (Columbus: Ohio University Press, 1962–97), 17:304; James D. Wallace, "Hawthorne and the Scribbling Women Reconsidered," *AL* 62 (1990): 201–22, gives an overview of prior scholars' use of the quote. Kelley, *Private Woman* (esp. chaps. 4 and 11) underscores the phrase's diminution of women's intellectual abilities. Robinson, May 28, 1855, diaries, RSP-SL; she resumed her book publishing with compiling and editing her husband's memorial volume, *"Warrington" Pen-Portraits; A Collection of Personal and Political Reminiscences from 1848 to 1876 …* (Boston: Lee and Shepard, 1877), and would continue with two plays and books on women's suffrage and factory labor, culminating in her *Loom and Spindle: or, Life among the Early Mill Girls* (New York: T.Y. Crowell, 1898). Mary Baker Eddy, scrapbook, c. 1830–60, MBEL. On the widely held sentiments in favor of staying single, see Lee Chambers-Schiller, *Liberty, a Better Husband: Single Women in America, The Generations of 1780–1840* (New Haven, Conn.: Yale University Press, 1984); Zsuzsa Berend, "The Best or None!: Spinsterhood in Nineteenth-Century New England," *Journal of Social History* 33 (2000): 935–57.

46. Bradley, September 5, 1836, diary. Among the works frequently read by these authors were William Paley's *Natural Theology* (1794), Francis Wayland's *Elements of Moral Science* (1835); Daniel Dewar's *Elements of Moral Philosophy* (1826); John Abercrombie's *Inquiries Concerning the Intellectual Powers* (1831). Student life at Bradley's Dartmouth can be discerned in Leon B. Richardson, *History of Dartmouth College*, 2 vols. (Hanover, N.H.: Dartmouth College Publications, 1932); Frederick Chase, *A History of Dartmouth College and the Town of Hanover, New Hampshire*, 2 vols., ed. John K. Lord (Cambridge, Mass.: J. Wilson, 1891–1913). Enoch Hale, December 1841, diary. Samuel G. Drake to David D. Plumer, June 29, 1849, BPL; David L. Greene, "Samuel G. Drake and the Early Years of the *New England Historical and Genealogical Register*, 1847–1861," *NEHGR* 145 (1991): 203–33; Francis J. Bosha, "'A Solitary Man Arrayed in Black': The Society's Samuel Gardner Drake, 1798–1875," *NEHGR* 150 (1996): 299–310. Sibley, December 17, 1848, diary. Rev. George K. Shaw, a proslavery Democrat, edited the *Norway Advertiser*, 7 vols. (Norway, Me.: Ira Berry, 1844–50); Joseph Griffin, ed., *History of the Press of Maine* (Brunswick, Me.: Charles H. Fuller, 1872), 122.

47. Maria B. Pitkin to John B. Pitkin, June 23, 1834. Park, June 24, 1837 and October 22, 1839, diary; Louisa J. Hall, *Joanna of Naples* (Boston: Hilliard, Gray, 1838); Felicia Dorothea Browne Hemans, *The Works of Mrs. Hemans, With a Memoir By Her Sister* [i.e., Harriet Mary Browne Hughes Owen], 7 vols. (Philadelphia: Lea and Blanchard, 1840).

48. Pitkin to John B. Pitkin, June 23, 1834; Case to Edgarton, April 12, 1840; Forten, December 13, 1857, *JCFG*, 271; Jocelyn, March 1, 1839, diary. Louisa May Alcott had a similar veiling incident surrounding her first "paid" story; see Ednah D. Cheney, ed., *Louisa May Alcott: Her Life, Letters, and Journals* (Boston: Roberts, 1889), 68.

49. Park, December 18 and 19, 1838, diary. Louisa Jane Hall thereafter published only a few children's pamphlets, a rare verse or hymn, her sixty-eight page *Memoir of Miss Elizabeth Carter, Illustrating the Union of Learning and Piety* (Boston: T.H. Carter, 1844), and a short sacred drama, *Hannah, The Mother of Samuel, The Prophet and Judge of Israel* (Boston: J. Munroe, 1839). After 1852 (Park's death), she published *The Sheaves of Love: A Fireside Story* (Boston: L.J. Pratt, 1861), and a few short poetry volumes.

50. The copying could occur at various stages along the road to publishing: it could be prior to first submission with no further versions (especially true in periodical publishing) or just before the text went to the printer. The latter was more common in book publishing, but even initial submissions of book-length material might end up

in the printer's hands. At any point beyond the final draft, when a clean, exact transcription that incorporated emendations was made from an authorized manuscript, it was called a "fair copy." There could be several of these made. The specific copy used by the compositor to set the text was a "printer's copy," which was a form of fair copy, and it is oftened considered the most authentic version of an author's intention when combined with his or her later proof corrections. Paul Baedner, "Meaning of Copy-Text," *SB* 22 (1969): 311–18; Philip Gaskell, *A New Introduction to Bibliography: The Classic Manual of Bibliography* (New Castle, Del.: Oak Knoll Press, 1995), 40–42, 292–93. Hale to Edward Everett, September 30, 1850; Holloway, *Edward Everett Hale*, 92. Park, July 31, August 2, and September 26, 1837, diary.

51. "Hamlin" to Maturin Murray Ballou, December 10, 1856; Harris to Moses A. Dow, December 31, 1856, both in Harris, letterbook, JEHP-MeHS; Forten, December 16, 1857 and May 21, 1858, *JCFG*, 271, 311; Clarke to Caroline Atherton Briggs, c. 1849–50, BriFP-SL. On women editors in the period through the lens of Clarke's colleague, see Patricia Okker, *Our Sister Editors: Sarah J. Hale and the Tradition of Nineteenth-Century American Women Editors* (Athens: University of Georgia Press, 1995). Samuel Cram Jackson, copy of letter of recommendation, September 15, 1858, in Daniel Wight to unidentified recipient, December 10, 1858, BriFP-SL; Edwards A. Park, *Memorial of Samuel C. Jackson, D.D.* (Andover, Mass.: Warren F. Draper, 1878), 23–24; on Jackson's frequent services as advisor, see, in this same volume (23), Rev. B[arnas] Sears to Edwards A. Park, August 5, 1878.

52. Case to Edgarton, June 15, 1839. André Bernard, ed., *Rotten Rejections: A Literary Companion* (Wainscot, N.Y.: Pushcart Press, 1990).

53. Forten, June 18, 1858, *JCFG*, 318; idem, "Glimpses of New England," *NASS*, June 19, 1858. Blake, March 29, 1851, diary; *SA*, March 29, 1851, 221. Harris, January 16, February 5, April 10 and 23, February 26 and 14, 1857, journal. Forten, December 18, 1857, *JCFG*, 272. On common pseudonymous practices, see Mark Keller, "Reputable Writers, Phony Names: Identifying Pseudonyms in the Spirit of the Times," *PBSA* 75 (1981): 198–209. Even established authors could receive word via the periodical itself, as the following makes plain: "Articles from Mrs. Sigourney, Rufus Dawes, T.S. Arthur and others, are unavoidably postponed, as well as various literary notices. We crave the indulgence of those contributors whose favors were received too late for the present number"; *BM* 3 (1842): 45.

54. Elizabeth Dwight Cabot to Ellen Twisleton, January 16, 1859, CFP-SL. This may be [Mary Eliot Parkman], *Hymns for Young Children* (Boston: Crosby, Nichols, c. 1859). Lucy Hedge to Mary Pierce Poor, January 6, 1856, PoFP-SL; Ellen Hedge, ed., *Heart Songs: A Book for the Gift-Season* (Boston: Crosby, Nichols, 1856). Hale to Charlotte Everett, October 30, 1843; *The Annualette, A Christmas and New Year's Gift, Edited by a Lady* (Boston: Carter, c. 1843). As James L.W. West, III, "Editorial Theory and the Act of Submission," *PBSA* 83 (1989): 169–85, notes for a later time, submission "is likely to require some compromises," and at times "virtually no control" (169).

55. Park, September 9 and 10, 1839, diary.

56. Poor, December 19, 1850, pocket memorandum; see also November 2, 1849, pocket memorandum. Cobb, February 20, 1856, diary. Robinson, January 8 and 13, 1852, diaries; she also seems to have pored over exchanged papers to find clippings from her husband and assembled them in *Opinions of the Press, 1849: Scrapbook*, microfilm (New York: Readex Microprint, 1972). For general background, see Percy Simpson, *Proof-Reading in the Sixteenth, Seventeenth, and Eighteenth Centuries* (London: Oxford University Press, 1935); on professionals, see Rollo G. Silver, "Mathew Carey's Proofreaders," *SB* 17 (1964): 123–33.

57. Hale to Edward Everett Hale, September 6, [1845?]; Alexander H. Everett, *Critical and Miscellaneous Essays, To Which Are Added a Few Poems* (Boston: J. Munroe,

1845). Pierce to Mary Pierce Poor, May 3, 1847; John Pierce, *Brookline Jubilee: A Discourse Delivered in Brookline, at the Request of Its Inhabitants ...* (Boston: James Munroe, 1847). A.E. and J.E. Worcester to Olive Gay Worcester, May 20, 1855 and December 5, 1858, transcript, SFUP-SL; Joseph E. Worcester, *A Pronouncing, Explanatory, and Synonomous Dictionary of the English Language* (Boston: Hickling, Swan and Brown, 1855); idem, *A Universal and Critical Dictionary of the English Language ...* (Boston: Jenks, Hickling and Swan, 1853). On the Anglophilic dictionary competing with Noah Webster's nationalistic one, see Jonathon Green, *Chasing the Sun: Dictionary-Makers and the Dictionaries They Made* (New York: Henry Holt, 1996), 327–31.

58. Bradley, November 18 and 19, and December 3, 1833, school journal; *Collections of the New Hampshire Historical Society* (Concord, N.H.: Jacob B. Moore, 1824-). Samuel Cabot to Hannah Lowell (Jackson) Cabot, February 13, 1853, AFP-SL; [James Elliot] C[abot], "Another View of Acoustic Architecture," *Dwight's Journal of Music, A Paper of Art and Literature*, February 12, 1853, 145–47. It was a rejoinder to a series of papers on acoustic architecture that recently ran in that journal.

59. Enoch Hale, March 9 and 30, 1841, diary; Park, December 23, 1837, diary; A.E. and J. E. Worcester to Olive Gay Worcester, December 5, 1858; Joseph E. Worcester, *A Pronouncing, Explanatory, and Synonymous Dictionary of the English Language* (Boston: Hickling, Swan and Brewer, 1858). On advertising's importance, see Susan Geary's "The Domestic Novel as a Commercial Commodity: Making a Best Seller in the 1850s," *PBSA* 70 (1976): 365–93.

60. Cushman, August 9, 1855, journal; Harris, February 19, 1857, journal; Hale to Charlotte Brooks Everett, December 28, 1841.

61. Enoch Hale, March 30, 1841, diary.

62. Hale to Edward Everett, April 20, 1840; Case to Edgarton, February 23, 1840. Mellen Chamberlain, February 2 and 1, 1849, journal; compare the development of reporting recounted in Dan Schiller, *Objectivity and the News: The Public and the Rise of Commercial Journalism* (Philadelphia: University of Pennsylvania Press, 1981). Poor to Mary Pierce Poor, March 12, 1849.

63. Worcester to Mary A. Byram, October 14, 1842, SFA-SL; [Sarah P. Worcester], *Charles and Rosa; or, Stories for the Little Children of the New Church* (Boston: Otis Clapp, 1842). Park, April 28, and October 29, 1837, diary; Louisa J. Hall, *Miriam; A Dramatic Poem* (Boston: Hilliard, Gray, 1837). Seth Shaler Arnold, July 16, 1839, journal; East Parish Congregational Church (Westminster, Vt.), *The Confession of Faith, and Covenant of the Congregational Church in Westminster East Parish* (Bellows Falls, Vt.: John W. Moore, 1839).

64. Forten, March 28, 1853, *JCFG*, 132; "To W.L.G. on Reading His 'Chosen Queen,'" *Liberator*, March 16, 1855, [4]. Case to Edgarton, April 12, 1840; Edgarton to Case, and to [Julia H. Kinney Scott], both undated [1840], in Mayo, *Selections*, 38–39, 37–38. Worcester to Mary A. Byram, October 14, 1842, SFA-SL; Lucy Hedge to Mary Pierce Poor, January 6, 1856, PoFP-SL. Hale to Everett, April 29, 1842; Carl Franz van der Velde, *Die Gesandtschaftsreise nach China: Eine Erzählung aus der letzten Hälfte des achtzehnten Jahrhunderts* (Dresden: Arnold, 1825). Kelley, *Private Woman*, notes that women's own "deep inner restraints" generally discouraged them from stepping out of their prescribed sphere into the public world of print and, in these cases, to enjoy their productivity (130, 206).

65. Forten, September 11, 1858, *JCFG*, 338; idem, "Glimpses of New England," *NASS*, June 19, 1858, [4]; "Edwin S. Teller,": [pseud.], "Ha—Ha—Ha," idem, "To Correspondents," "The Boy in Boots," [pseud.], "A Splendid Original Romance, Written Expressly for the Adder, The Hunchback of the Wyoming; or, The Stranger of the Susquehannah," [anon.], "*Belubed Bredren*," *Adder*, March 14, 1849: [1–4], in CHS;

Susan Cianci Salvatore, *Racial Desegregation in Public Education in the U.S.: Theme Study, August 2000* (Washington, D.C.: National Historic Landmarks Survey, U.S. Department of the Interior, National Park Service, National Register, History and Education, 2000), 6. Phillip Sage, March 14, 1849, journal, CHS. At the time, the Whig Sage, a Middletown Customs Collector, was facing ouster from his office by a Democrat, so the town's shipbuilders circulated a petition to the incoming Whig President to retain him; Petition (draft), March 5, 1849, in Philip Sage, Sr., Account book, 1818–1855, CHS. According to the son's diary, the petition, if completed, was unsuccessful, for he reports on July 14, 1849, his discharge from the post.

66. Blake, April 11, 19, and 26, and July 10, 1851, diary; Henry M. Paine, "Magnetism of the Atmosphere," *SA*, April 12, 1851, 234; idem, "Gas Light," *SA*, April 26, 1851, 246–47. Paine controversially claimed to be able to generate gas from water; this was condemned by scientist Joseph Henry as among "the most plausable humbugs"; see *The Papers of Joseph Henry*, vol. 8, *The Smithsonian Years: January 1850–December 1853*, ed. Nathan Reingold (Washington, D.C.: Smithsonian Institution Press, 2002), doc. 139. The editor deemed Blake's articles "the most valuable ever published on the subject in our country, and will be used for reference as standard authority"; *SA*, July 12, 1851, 342.

67. William Willis, July 21, 1855, diary, microfilm, PPL, original in MeHS; *Report of the Committee Appointed by the Board of Aldermen of the City of Portland to Investigate the Causes and Consequences of the Riot …* (Portland: B.D. Peck, 1855); John A. Poor was editor of the Whig triweekly *State of Maine* (Portland, Me.: May and Marble, and J. Edwards, 1853–59). When, in violation of strict liquor laws, rioters descended upon a city-controlled building where a stash of alcohol was stored, militiamen fired upon them. Bradley, January 24, 1835, school journal; *The Abolitionist* (Concord, N.H.: D.D. Fisk and E.G. Eastman, 1835). Hamon to Fenwick, April 6, 1839, AAB; idem, *The Life of Cardinal Cheverus, Archibishop of Bordeaux, and Formerly Bishop of Boston, in Massachusetts* (Boston: J. Munroe, 1839); a new edition would appear in France: *Vie du Cardinal De Cheverus, archevêque de Bordeaux*, 2d. ed. (Paris: Librairie Catholique de Périsse frères).

68. Hale to Alexander Hill Everett, November 29, 1841; Park, May 3, 1837, diary. The best survey of book reviewing discourse remains Nina Baym, *Novels, Readers, and Reviewers: Responses to Fiction in Antebellum America* (Ithaca, N.Y.: Cornell University Press, 1984).

69. *HAM*, 1:505, 511–12. William Charvat, *Literary Publishing in America, 1790–1850* (1959; reprint Amherst: University of Massachusetts Press, 1993), 43–44. Park, December 18, 1838, diary; Samuel G. Goodrich, ed., *The Token and Atlantic Souvenir: A Christmas and New Year's Present* (Boston: Otis, Broaders, 1839). Worcester, December 3, 1845, transcript, SFP-SL; Henry Aiken Worcester, *Sermons on the Lord's Prayer, to Which are Added, Three Sermons on Other Subjects* (Boston: Otis Clapp, 1837). Hale to Edward Everett, October 29, 1838.

70. *NEG*, 270; DeWolf, October 31, 1855, diary; Blake, July 15, 1851, diary.

71. Park, April 8 and 19, May 20, July 18, and September 22, 1837, diary. Though the *New England Galaxy* had long been in existence (1817), it had merged on December 31, 1836 with the *Boston Pearl* (founded 1831) to become the *Boston Pearl and Galaxy* under the shaky editorship and proprietorship of Isaac C. Pray Jr. and Henry F. Harrington; the weekly would last only into November 1838. Pray's reputation was dubious for what Mott called his "piratical tendencies" (*HAM*, 1:356).

72. Child to Ellis Gray Loring, July 11, 1838, EGLFP-SL. On Colman, see Melvin Lord, "Boston Booksellers, 1650–1860," p. 93, Boston Booksellers Records, 1640–1860, AAS. John Tebbel, *HBPUS*, 1:396, discusses the bankruptcy and Longfellow. Colman specialized in juveniles like Lydia Maria Child's *The Little Girl's Own Book* (1838) and

Hannah Farnham Sawyer Lee's popular novels (e.g., *Three Experiments of Living ...*, 1837). Hale to Edward Everett, January 23 and May 30, 1841. Her children's books for the firm were the anonymous *Lives of Vasco Nunez de Balboa, the Discoverer of the Pacific Ocean, Hernando Cortes, the Conqueror of Mexico, and Francisco Pizarro, the Conqueror of Peru* (Boston: Marsh, Capen, Lyon, and Webb, 1840) and *The Lives of Christopher Columbus, the Discoverer of America, and Americus Vespucius, the Florentine, with Engravings* (Boston: Marsh, Capen, Lyon, and Webb, 1840).

73. Enoch Hale, March 30, 1841, diary.

74. Rogers, "A Sailor 'By Necessity,'" 19. Ralph Aderman, "Two Contributors to To-Day: A Boston Literary Journal," *PBSA* 74 (1980): 145–46; Earle Coleman, "Edward Everett Hale: Preacher as Publisher," *PBSA* 46 (1952): 139–50. Twiss, "Introductory Note," 213.

75. Cobb, May 30, 1853, journal. Cobb's diary demonstrates his authorial aspirations, for it is filled with literary projects and even mock manuscript magazines, like his *Vermont Collections* (entry for July 1, 1849, copied into his 1853–1854 journal); however, it also shows, through to its conclusion in November 1862, that he published nothing. The only stand-alone nineteenth-century imprint bearing the name Charles M. Cobb emerged in 1897: *The Gallant Union Soldier Boys*, music by Cobb, lyric by M.A. Everest (Vergennes, Vt.: Vergennes Music), which was intended as a "Song and chorus for Memorial Day and Grand Army Reunions." It might be the same person, but Cobb would have been about sixty-two years old.

Chapter 2

1. Since Forten would not marry Francis Grimké until 1878, we use her maiden name throughout. Forten, May 20, 1858, *JCFG*, 311. Our deepest thanks go to Darrol Pierson (ISL) for locating "To a Beloved Friend" in *RRLSA*, July 1858, 89–90, on the basis of the few clues provided. Because the poem was signed only "Lottie," Pierson is also due credit for linking this poem to another, "The Angel's Visit," which appeared in the same journal with an obituary article on Forten's mother. This verified that "Lottie" was indeed Charlotte Forten's pen name. Charlotte Forten, "The Angel's Visit," *RRLSA*, November 1858, 174–75.

2. There are no full-length scholarly biographies of Charlotte Forten Grimké. Brenda Stevenson's preface (xxvii–xxx) and introduction (3–55) to *JCFG* remain the best biographical overview. There are several standard biographical articles; see, for example, Katharine Rodier, "Charlotte L. Forten," in *DLB*, vol. 239, *American Women Prose Writers, 1820–1870*, ed. Katharine Rodier and Amy E. Hudock (2001), 107–17. Ray Allen Billington's edition of *The Journal of Charlotte Forten: A Free Negro in the Slave Era* (New York: Collier, 1953), contains some serious errors, which are emended in Gloria C. Oden, "The Journal of Charlotte L. Forten: The Salem–Philadelphia Years (1854–1862) Reexamined," *EIHC* 119 (1983): 119–36. On the Civil War years, see Lisa A. Long, "Charlotte Forten's Civil War Journals and the Quest for 'Genius, Beauty, and Deathless Fame,'" *Legacy* 16 (1999): 37–48. Of all of her writings, Forten's journal attracts the greatest attention; see Blyden Jackson, ed., *A History of Afro-American Literature*, vol. 1, *The Long Beginning, 1746–1895* (Baton Rouge: Louisiana State University Press, 1989), 172–75; Jacqueline Jones Royster, *Traces of a Stream: Literacy and Social Change among African American Women* (Pittsburgh: University of Pittsburgh Press, 2000), 114, 143–52, 242; Janet Carey Eldred and Peter Mortensen, *Imagining Rhetoric: Composing Women of the Early United States* (Pittsburgh: University of Pittsburgh Press, 2002), chap. 7. On her poems and essays, see Joan R. Sherman, *Invisible Poets: Afro-Americans of the Nineteenth Century* (1974; reprint Urbana: University of Illinois Press, 1989), 88–96; Carla Peterson, *"Doers of the Word"*:

African-American Women Speakers and Writers in the North (1830–1880) (New York: Oxford University Press, 1995), 180–83, and idem, "Reconstructing the Nation: Frances Harper, Charlotte Forten, and the Racial Politics of Periodical Publication," *PAAS* 107, pt. 2 (1998): 301–34. See also Peterson's "Frances Harper, Charlotte Forten, and African-American Literary Reconstruction," in *Challenging Boundaries: Gender and Periodization*, ed. Joyce W. Warren and Margaret Dickie (Athens: University of Georgia Press, 2000), 36–91; William Wells Brown, *The Black Man* (New York: Thomas Hamilton; Boston: R. F. Wallcut, 1863), 190–99; and Elizabeth Rauh Bethel, *The Roots of African-American Identity: Memory and History in Free Antebellum Communities* (New York: St. Martin's Press, 1997), 9–10, 22–23, 142, 170, and 183. Bibliographers have yet to compile a thorough Forten checklist, but see Karen M. Davis, "Charlotte Lottie Forten Grimke (1837–1914)," in *African American Authors, 1745–1945: A Bio-Bibliographical Sourcebook*, ed. Emmanuel Nelson (Westport, Conn.: Greenwood, 2000), 199–204; Anna J. Cooper, *Life and Writings of the Grimke Family* (privately printed, 1951); and Sherman, *Invisible Poets*, 215–16.

3. Forten, May 21, June 18, and July 26, 1858, *JCFG*, 311, 318, 326. Stevenson attributes this output to "the less hectic pace of the Purvis household" (introduction to *JCFG*, 35–36). Forten's prior production included "To W.L.G. on Reading His 'Chosen Queen,'" *Liberator*, March 16, 1855, [4], reprinted in *NAAS* March 24, 1855, [1]; "Parting Hymn" was first printed in the March 1855 graduation program; Elizabeth Frazier, "Some Afro-American Women of Mark," *AMECR* 8 (1892): 381–82; Forten, "Parody on 'Red, White and Blue,'" *Boston Massacre, March 5th, 1770: The Day Which History Selects as the Dawn of the American Revolution. . .* , broadside (Boston: E.L. Balch for William C. Nell, 1858), 4, courtesy AAS; and a "Poem" delivered at the Salem Normal School graduation ceremony. Billington, *The Journal of Charlotte Forten*, 248 n. 6, erroneously reports the latter as published in the *Liberator*, August 24 [i.e., 22 or 29], 1856. Stevenson, introduction to *JCFG*, entitles the piece alternately "The Improvement of Colored People" (25, 542 n. 51) or "Poem for Normal School Graduation" (569 n. 68). Peterson, *Doers*, 180, simply refers to an "untitled poem" printed on the same date. There does exist an extract from the *Salem Register* of an entirely different Forten poem from that reprinted in Billington and in Stevenson, but one that fits the description of a graduation exercise; see "A Coloured Teacher and Poet," *NAAS* August 2, 1856, [2]. Charlotte Forten, "Glimpses of New England," *NAAS* June 19, 1858, [4]; idem, "The Two Voices," *NAAS*, January 15, 1859, [4]; idem, "The Wind among the Poplars," *NAAS* April 2, 1859, [4], reprinted in the *Liberator*, May 27, 1859, 84; idem, "The Slave Girl's Prayer," *NAAS* January 14, 1860, [4], reprinted in the *Liberator*, February 3, 1860, 20; idem, "In the Country," *NAAS* September 1, 1860, [4]. Quote about intellect in Peterson, *Doers*, 178; on her illness, see 184; see also Peterson, "Reconstructing the Nation," 319. Stevenson, introduction to *JCFG*, 25–36. Lisa M. Koch, "Bodies as Stage Props: Enacting Hysteria in the Diaries of Charlotte Forten Grimké and Alice James," *Legacy* 15 (1998): 59–64, attributes the stalled output to hysteria. On "Lost Bride," see Stevenson, chronology, *JCFG*, xxxiv; Peterson, *Doers*, 179–80. Largely because "To a Beloved Friend" has remained lost, it has not been fully situated within Forten's oeuvre. Stevenson, chronology, *JCFG*, xxxv, identifies the poem as "Flowers" and discusses it briefly, but does not link it to the *RRLSA*. The magazine has been given scant notice; see, however, Penelope L. Bullock, *The Afro-American Periodical Press, 1838–1909* (Baton Rouge: Louisiana State University Press, 1981), 43–49, 268–69.

4. Lawrence Buell, *New England Literary Culture: From Revolution through Renaissance* (New York: Cambridge University Press, 1986), discusses his criteria for major and minor authors in the appendix (376) and notes that in "a number of ways, they [major authors] are indistinguishable from the larger group" (387). Some major authors' early

careers paralleled minor authors': see, for example, Leona Rostenberg, "Some Anonymous and Pseudonymous Thrillers of Louisa M. Alcott," *PBSA* 37 (1943): 131–40; Eleanor M. Tilton, "'Literary Bantlings': Addenda to the Holmes Bibliography," *PBSA* 51 (1957): 1–18. Reconstructing complete bibliographies of minor authors is difficult because they often published in periodicals that, if they survived at all, often left only scattered runs. Standard sources like *Poole's Index to Periodical Literature* (1882; reprint Gloucester, Mass.: Peter Smith, 1958), offer little help because they track mostly top magazines. Bibliographies of selected stand-alone imprints, however, are described in *BAL*. Other indispensable sources include Lyle H. Wright, *American Fiction, A Contribution Toward a Bibliography*, 2 vols., *1774–1850* and *1851–1875* (San Marino, Calif.: Huntington Library, 1969, 1965) and Brown University Library's *Dictionary Catalog of the Harris Collection of American Poetry and Plays*, 13 vols. (Boston: G.K. Hall, 1972). Elizabeth McHenry, *Forgotten Readers: Recovering the Lost History of African-American Literary Societies (Durham, N.C.: Duke University Press, 2002)*, 87, *130–33, 137–39.*

5. According to Carla Peterson, Forten lacked "a usable past" that would allow her to tap into African American literary conventions; Peterson, *Doers*, 179, 216–17, argues that Forten's works were published primarily in white abolitionist venues where they addressed and reached a largely white audience. But given that "To a Beloved Friend" and "Angel's Visit" appeared in an African American literary journal, that she was asked to become a regular contributor to it, and that she seized the 1858 invitation by black abolitionist William C. Nell to publish the broadside "Parody on 'Red, White and Blue'" for his "Commemorative Festival," it becomes less evident that Forten self-consciously courted primarily a white media and audience in the antebellum years.

6. Joyce W. Warren, *The American Narcissus: Individualism and Women in Nineteenth-Century American Fiction* (New Brunswick, N.J.: Rutgers University Press, 1984).

7. *NEG*, 270; Lucy Larcom, *Similitudes, from the Ocean and the Prairie* (Boston: John P. Jewett / Cleveland: Jewett, Proctor, and Worthington, 1854).

8. Charlotte Forten Grimké, "Personal Recollections of Whittier," *NEM* 14 (1893): 471.

9. John Townsend Trowbridge, *Martin Merrivale, His X Mark* (Boston: Phillips, Sampson, 1854).

10. Forten, poem excerpt in "A Coloured Teacher and Poet"; idem, "Parody," 4; Bethel, *Roots of African-American Identity*, 22. Forten, December 13 and 16, 1858, *JCFG*, 271. *HAM*, 2:354.

11. Background on the Forten-Smith relationship appears in Oden, "Journal of Charlotte L. Forten," 125–27; Stevenson, introduction to *JCFG*, 18; Forten, April 6, 17, and 27, 1858, *JCFG*, 299, 301–2, 304.

12. Forten, April 5 and 26, May 6, 9, and 25, and September 12, 1857; January 30, 1858; June 4, 1857; and February 4, 8, 15, 16, 19, and 23, 1858, *JCFG*, 208, 214, 217–18, 220–21, 256–57, 283, 224–25, 284–88; Horatio Smith, "Hymn to the Flowers," in *The Poetical Works of Horatio Smith* (London: Henry Colbourn, 1846), 8–10. Ronald J. Zboray and Mary Saracino Zboray, "Transcendentalism in Print: Production, Dissemination, and Common Reception," in *Transient and Permanent: The Transcendentalist Movement and Its Contexts*, ed. Charles Capper and Conrad Edick Wright (Boston: Massachusetts Historical Society, 1999), 310–81.

13. Forten, April 1 and March 29, 1858; June 17 and 23, 1857, *JCFG*, 296–97, 230, 232; Stevenson, introduction to *JCFG*, 22–23.

14. Forten, April 30 and May 1, 1858, *JCFG*, 306–7. Sarah Josepha Buell Hale, *Flora's Interpreter; or, The American Book of Flowers and Sentiments* (Boston: T.H. Webb, c. 1833), 46, 218. John H. Young, comp., *Our Deportment; or, The Manners, Conduct and Dress of the Most Refined Society ...* (Detroit: F.B. Dickerson, 1881), 412. If Smith relied only upon flowers available, it might be simply coincidental that this specific

mix so ideally fit the situation. Still, the language of flowers was so well known that it is unlikely that the symbolism eluded either sender or recipient. On Maying, see chapter 8 of Nathaniel Hawthorne, *The Blithedale Romance*, 2 vols. (Boston: Ticknor, Reed, and Fields, 1852).

15. Forten, May 2 and 3, 1858, *JCFG*, 307. Ronald J. Zboray and Mary Saracino Zboray, "Reading in Antebellum New England: Literary Gifts," paper delivered at the Visiting Scholars Colloquium, Schlesinger Library, Radcliffe Institute, Harvard University, April 16, 1999; Eric Leigh Schmidt, "Practices of Exchange: From Market Culture to Gift Economy in the Interpretation of American Religion," in *Lived Religion in America*, ed. David D. Hall (Princeton, N.J.: Princeton University Press, 1997), 69–91; Allison Kyle Leopold, *Allison Kyle Leopold's Victorian Keepsakes: Select Expressions of Affectionate Regard from the Romantic Nineteenth Century* (New York: Doubleday, 1991). Ronald J. Zboray and Mary Saracino Zboray, *Everyday Ideas: Socio-Literary Experience among Antebellum New Englanders* (Knoxville: University of Tennessee Press, forthcoming, 2005), chap. 3. George Shephard Burleigh, *The Maniac, and Other Poems* (Philadelphia: Moore, 1849). Sherman, *Invisible Poets*, xx–xxi, notes the similarities between antebellum white and black poetry. Charlotte Forten [Grimké], "List of books read from Dec. 1854 to Jan 1, 1857," HU, Box 40–45. Mary Kelley, "Reading Women/Women Reading: The Making of Learned Women in Antebellum America," *JAH* 83 (1996): 401–24, 409–10, 416.

16. Another possible interpretation is that she and Smith typically spoke the language of "Signifyin(g)" among white Salem society, and this is reflected in the poem. Studies of "signifyin(g)" point to the layers of often indeterminate meanings in African American poetry and other genres that can easily escape white audiences. Henry Louis Gates Jr., *The Signifying Monkey: A Theory of African-American Literary Criticism* (New York: Oxford University Press, 1988). On the "Flower-Fairies' Reception" as an "allegory," see Peterson, *Doers*, 223.

17. To underscore Forten's attitude to the two cities compare, for example, Emma Jones Lapsansky, "'Since They Got Those Separate Churches': Afro-Americans and Racism in Jacksonianism Philadelphia," *AQ* 32 (1980): 54–78, with James Oliver Horton and Lois E. Horton, *Black Bostonians: Family Life and Community Struggle in the Antebellum North* (New York: Holmes and Meier, 1999), chap. 6. On African American writers' rhetoric about cities, see Yoshinobu Hakutani and Robert Butler, eds., *The City in African-American Literature* (Madison, N.J.: Fairleigh Dickinson University Press, 1995). On the country/city dichotomy, see Raymond Williams, *The Country and the City* (1973; reprint London: Hogarth Press, 1993), 302; Ronald J. Zboray and Mary Saracino Zboray, "The Mysteries of New England: Eugène Sue's American 'Imitators,'" 1844," *NCC* 22 (2000): 457–92.

18. "Leisure" in the stanza's first line may either be a misprint of the word *pleasure* or it may be intentional; the latter seems plausible. The rhyming of the words *pleasure* and *leisure* in African American poetry can denote a contrast of idleness with work—or slaveholder with slave, as in George Moses Horton's poem, "To the Fourth": "To take the world's attention / The sound of victory won; / The labor is at leisure, / 'Tis pain turned into pleasure." The labor/pain at leisure is, of course, slave labor abolished. George Moses Horton, *Naked Genius* (Raleigh, N.C.: Southern Field and Fireside, 1865), 108; Joan R. Sherman, ed., *The Black Bard of North Carolina: George Moses Horton and His Poetry* (Chapel Hill: University of North Carolina Press, 1997), 42, locates in his writing a work/leisure theme. Wordplay upon *pleasure* appears throughout Daniel A. Payne's *The Pleasures* (Baltimore: Sherwood, 1850). Forten uses the word *leisure* in much the same way. The liberating bouquet turns her pain into (p)leasure. To achieve this doubling, Forten intentionally (mis)spells it; the reader's eye automatically fills in the missing "p." The space in kerning left by the printer

removes all doubt that *leisure* has been misspelled. Cleanly broken letters are rare; usually some trace remains, but here there is none (we thank ISL's Darrol Pierson for checking the sole surviving issue for breakage). The relative lack of printing errors (indicating tight proofreading) makes it being a random mistake remote, especially since it occurs in such a potentially meaningful place. African American writers' traditional associations of the leisure/pleasure dyad with its opposite—slavery and pain—suggest that Forten is concerned as much with future emancipation as with her own personal experiences with bigotry.

19. Lawrence W. Levine, "Slave Songs and Slave Consciousness: An Exploration in Neglected Sources," in *Anonymous Americans: Explorations in Nineteenth-Century Social History*, ed. Tamara K. Hareven (Englewood Cliffs, N.J.: Prentice-Hall, 1971), 90–130.

20. *Christian Recorder of the African Methodist Episcopal Church* (Philadelphia: Book Committee of the African Methodist Episcopal Church, 1852–1856). A.W. Wayman, "A Short Synopsis of the Baltimore and Philadelphia Conferences," *RRLSA*, July 1858, 70. Alexander A. Payne, *Recollections of Seventy Years* (1888; reprint New York: Arno, 1968), 139; Bullock, *Afro-American Periodical Press*, 44–46; Daniel Alexander Payne, *A History of the African Methodist Episcopal Church* ... (Philadelphia: Book Concern of the A.M.E. Church, 1922), 44. Forten, May 14, 1858, *JCFG*, 310.

21. Alexander Hill Everett to Sarah P.E. Hale, September 29, 1842, SSC-HP.

22. Stevenson, introduction to *JCFG*, 14; Lisa A. Long, "Charlotte Forten's Civil War Journals and the Quest for 'Genius, Beauty, and Deathless Fame,'" *Legacy* 16 (1999): 37–48; Buell, *New England Literary Culture*, 382. On her writing for money, see Forten, December 13, 1858, *JCFG*, 271. Mary Kelley, *Private Woman, Public Stage: Literary Domesticity in Nineteenth-Century America* (New York: Oxford University Press, 1984); Susan Coultrap-McQuin, *Doing Literary Business: American Women Writers in the Nineteenth Century* (Chapel Hill: University of North Carolina Press, 1990). Peterson, *Doers*, 150. Bullock, *Afro-American Periodical Press*, 4. Donald Franklin Joyce, *Gatekeepers of Black Culture: Black-Owned Book Publishing in the United States, 1817–1981* (Westport, Conn.: Greenwood, 1983), 11; Jackson, *History of Afro-American Literature*, 125; Frankie Hutton, *The Early Black Press in America, 1827–1860* (Westport, Conn.: Greenwood, 1993), xiv. Michael Sokolow, "'New Guinea at One End, and a View of the Alms-House at the Other': The Decline of Black Salem, 1850–1920," *NEQ* 71 (1998): 213–15. Forten, May 21, 1858; July 25, 1856; February 7, 1858, *JCFG*, 311, 161, 284–85, 311; Galyle T. Tate, "How Antebellum Black Communities Became Mobilized: The Role of Church, Benevolent Society, and Press," *National Political Science Review* 4 (1993): 16–29.

23. Forten, May 16, 1858, *JCFG*, 310. Bullock, *Afro-American Periodical Press*, 44; Stevenson, chronology, *JCFG*, xxxv; Peterson, "Reconstructing the Nation," 319. None of the scattered numbers that may have been issued between March 4, 1856 (vol. 3, no. 39) and the first number of the new series in January 1861 have survived. Augustus H. Able III, *The Holdings of Mother Bethel African Methodist Episcopal Church Historical Museum in Manuscript and Print*, microfilm, ed. F. Leonard Williams and Harvey L. Wilson (Philadelphia: Mother Bethel African Methodist Episcopal Church, c. 1973), 8. Gilbert Anthony Williams, *The Christian Recorder, Newspaper of the African Methodist Episcopal Church: History of a Forum for Ideas, 1854–1902* (Jefferson, N.C.: McFarland, 1996), 17–18. Payne, *Recollections*, 138; Bullock, *Afro-American Periodical Press*, 43–48; Josephus Roosevelt Coan, *Daniel Alexander Payne: Christian Educator* (Philadelphia: A.M.E. Book Concern, 1935), 97.

24. Payne, *The Pleasures*, 7–23, 27, and 30. Idem, "Mrs. Mary Virginia Forten," *RRLSA*, November 1858, 172–74. Coan, *Daniel Alexander Payne*, 58; Payne, *Recollections*, 72–74, 51–52. A slightly different version of the first two quotes appeared in Daniel

A. Payne, "The Triumphant End of Mrs. Mary Virginia Forten," *Colored American*, August 29, 1840, 3.

25. Payne, "Mrs. Mary Virginia Forten," 174.

26. *Ibid.* Forten, May 21 and June 18, 1858, *JCFG*, 311, 318–19. Forten, however, was skeptical of spiritualism; see August 16, 1854 and January 16, 1858, *JCFG*, 96, 278. Idem, "The Angel's Visit," 174–75.

27. Forten, July 26 and December 2, 1858, *JCFG*, 326, 350. Payne, "Mrs. Mary Virginia Forten," 174.

28. Payne, "Mrs. Mary Virginia Forten," 174. Bullock, *Afro-American Periodical Press*, 44. Forten, "Life on the Sea Islands," *AM*, May–June 1864, 587–96, 666–76; Emile Erckmann and Alexandre Chatrian, *Madame Thérèse; or, The Volunteers of '92*, trans. Charlotte Forten (New York: Scribner's, 1869). Compare, for example, Van Wyck Brooks, *The Flowering of New England, 1815–1865* (New York: E.P. Dutton, 1936) with his *New England: Indian Summer, 1865–1915* (New York: E.P. Dutton, 1940). As Buell notes, "compensation for literary journalism would triple between 1860 and 1880" (*New England Literary Culture*, 57).

29. William Wells Brown, *The Black Man* (1863; reprint New York: Arno, 1969), 199; Forten, "To a Beloved Friend," 89. Brown would later include Forten among his group of "Representative Men and Women," in *The Rising Son; or, The Antecedents and Advancement of the Colored Race* (1874; reprint Miami: Mnemosyne, 1969), 475–76. On Forten's postbellum publications, see Peterson, "Reconstructing the Nation," 319–31.

30. Shirley Marchalonis, *The Worlds of Lucy Larcom, 1824–1893* (Athens: University of Georgia Press, 1989), 1. For a brief general background, see idem, "Lucy Larcom," *DLB*, vol. 221, *American Women Prose Writers, 1870–1920*, ed. Sharon M. Harris (2000), 246–252; Beverly G. Merrick, "Lucy Larcom," *DLB*, vol. 243, *The American Renaissance in New England*, 4th ser., ed. Wesley T. Mott (2001), 233–39. For essays on Larcom by her acquaintances, see Susan Hayes Ward, ed., *The Rushlight: Special Number in Memory of Lucy Larcom* (Boston: G.H. Ellis, 1894). For bibliography, see Susan Alves, "Lucy Larcom (1824–1893)," in *Nineteenth-Century American Women Writers: A Bio-Bibliographical Critical Sourcebook*, ed. Denise D. Knight and Emmanuel Nelson (Westport, Conn.: Greenwood, 1997), 292–97; and Shirley Marchalonis, "Lucy Larcom (1824–1893)," *Legacy* 5 (1988): 45–52. On payments by the various periodicals mentioned, see *HAM*, 1:505–06; Ellery Sedgwick, *The Atlantic Monthly 1857–1909: Yankee Humanism at High Tide and Ebb* (Amherst: University of Massachusetts Press, 1994), 46–75; *NEG*, 270. On Larcom's periodical publications, see Marchalonis, *Worlds*, 62, 110–11, 15–16, 130, 137, 95–6, 109, 115–18, 87, 113, 130, and 132.

31. Larcom to [Ann Danforth Spaulding], May 15, 1854, and all letters between the two below, LLC-UVA. Idem to [John Greenleaf Whittier], December 9, 1853, quoted by permission of HL. On the important relationship between Larcom and Whittier, see Shirley Marchalonis, "A Model for Mentors?: Lucy Larcom and John Greenleaf Whittier," in *Patrons and Protégées: Gender, Friendship and Writing in Nineteenth-Century America*, ed. idem (New Brunswick, N.J.: Rutgers University Press, 1988), 94–121.

32. *NEG*, 11, 127–28, 159, 170–75; Marchalonis, *Worlds*, 30 and 35. See Harriet H. Robinson, *Loom and Spindle; or, Life among the Early Mill Girls* (Kailua: University of Hawaii Press, 1976), 99–109.

33. Emeline [Larcom] to Lois Barrett Larcom, September 16, 1841, in "The Mill Letters of Emeline Larcom, 1840–1842," ed. Thomas Dublin, *EIHC* 127 (1991): 232. *NEG*, 209–13, 221. Judith A. Ranta, *Women and Children of the Mills: An Annotated Guide to Nineteenth-Century American Textile Factory Literature* (Westport, Conn.:

Greenwood, 1999), 43–55, and, on the magazine that first published Larcom, 52–53; see also Jeannine Dobbs, "America's First All Women's Magazine," *NEGXY* 19 (1977): 44–48. Much, of course, has been written on Lowell mill women's literary activities. See, for example, Susan Alves, "Lowell's Female Factory Workers, Poetic Voice, and the Periodical," in *"The Only Efficient Instrument": American Women Writers and the Periodical, 1837–1916*, ed. Aleta Feinsod Cane and Susan Alves (Ames: University of Iowa Press, 2001), 149–64; Benita Eisler, introduction to *The Lowell Offering: Writings By New England Mill Women (1840–1845)*, ed. idem (Philadelphia: Lippincott, 1977), 13–41.

34. Marchalonis, *Worlds*, 41–44, 48, 50–55, 77; *NEG*, 217; Marchalonis, *Worlds*, 62, 48–50; Larcom to [Ann Danforth Spaulding], September 23, 1853. On the out-migration, see Lois Kimball Mathews Rosenberry, *The Expansion of New England; The Spread of New England Settlement and Institutions to the Mississippi River, 1620–1865* (Boston: Houghton Mifflin, 1909). Larcom left at an opportune moment when Illinois' 1845 education law favored broad competency across subjects characterizing the curriculum in the progressive Massachusetts schools she attended; few native westerners had this, thus causing a shortage of qualified teachers. John Williston Cook, *Educational History of Illinois: Growth and Progress in Educational Affairs of the State from the Earliest Day to the Present* (Chicago: Henry O. Shepard, 1912), 45, 544, 546. Compare Larcom's experiences with those treated in Polly Welts Kaufman, *Women Teachers on the Frontier* (New Haven, Conn.: Yale University Press, 1984).

35. Marchalonis, *Worlds*, chaps. 3–4; Larcom, *NEG*, 17. Easterners' difficulties in living out West were treated in several popular contemporary books, especially those of Caroline Kirkland; Lori Merish, "'The Hand of Refined Taste' in the Frontier Landscape: Caroline Kirkland's *A New Home, Who'll Follow?* and the Feminization of American Consumerism," *AQ* 45 (1993): 485–523. However, east-west discourse took on a new flavor in the early 1850s, as nationalism mixed with antislavery, "free soilism," and nativism to stage the Republican Party's emergence. Eric Foner, *Free Soil, Free Labor, Free Men: The Ideology of the Republican Party before the Civil War* (New York: Oxford University Press, 1970). Larcom's *Similitudes* also were similar to that period's literary sketches; Kristie Hamilton, *America's Sketchbook: The Cultural Life of a Nineteenth-Century Literary Genre* (Athens: Ohio University Press, 1998), 138, 143.

36. *NEG*, 241–42, 219. The tensions identified in this paragraph are evident throughout Larcom's correspondence with Henry S. Spaulding, particularly October 3, 1850; February 14, 1851; and February 4, 3 April, and March 20, 1852, ISHL. Susanna Egan, "'Self'-Conscious History: American Autobiography After the Civil War," in *American Autobiography: Retrospect and Prospect*, ed. Paul John Eakin (Madison: University of Wisconsin Press, 1991), 70–94; Eagan notes Larcom's continuing attention to "local flora and fauna" as a "resource for her American writing" (81). Lessing and Herder followed a similar path for nationalistic ends; see Mary M. Colum, *From these Roots: The Ideas That Have Made Modern Literature* (Port Washington, N.Y.: Kennikat, 1937), 23, 39, 43. Compare any of Larcom's similitudes with Johann Gottfried Herder's fable, "The Sun and the Wind," *Projekt Gutenberg: Deutschland*, http://gutenberg.spiegel.de/herder.fabeln/sonnwind.htm (accessed June 21, 2002), or his narration, "The Eternal Burden" at the same source and date, http://gutenberg.spiegel.de/herder/erzaehlg/ewigbuer.htm. On the overlay of nature and moralism in Herder's fables, see Karl Hillebrand in "Herder," *NAR* 116 (1873): 389–425, esp. 406. Friedrich Wilhelm Krummacher, *Elijah, The Tishbite* (New York: American Tract Society, 1838); on his parables, see "Rev. Dr. F.W. Krummacher," *LR* 4 (1869): 446–47. Marchalonis, *Worlds*, chaps. 3 and 4; on her later translations of three poems by Herder, Lessing, and Jean Paul Richter in *Arthur's Home Magazine* in 1854,

see 87. For context on Richter, see Edward Vere Brewer, *The New England Interest in Jean Paul Friedrich Richter* (Berkeley and Los Angeles: University of California Press, 1943). Larcom's symbolic strategy of working through her ambivalence concerning marriage is considered in Zsuzsa Berend, "'The Best or None!': Spinsterhood in Nineteenth-Century New England," *Journal of Social History* 33 (2000): 935–57.

37. Larcom, *Similitudes*, 94.
38. Marchalonis, *Worlds*, 41–42. Alves, "Lowell's Female Factory Workers," 158, discusses Larcom's "The River," written for the *Offering*, about nature and human destiny. On earlier writers' nationalistic uses of American rivers, see John D. Seelye, *Beautiful Machine: Rivers and the Republican Plan, 1755–1825* (New York: Oxford University Press, 1991), and on the symbolism of the Mississippi and Missouri as the east-west dividing line, 193. Whittier's sense of literary nationalism, localism, and moralism was compatible with Larcom's; Edwin Harrison Cady and Harry Hayden Clark, eds., *Whittier on Writers and Writing: The Uncollected Critical Writings of John Greenleaf Whittier* (Syracuse, N.Y.: Syracuse University Press, 1950), 2–96.
39. Marchalonis, *Worlds*, 86. Whittier sponsored many women; Joseph M. Ernest Jr., "Whittier and the 'Feminine Fifties,'" *AL* 28 (1956): 184–96. Annie Fields, "Whittier: Notes on His Life and of His Friendships," *HNMM* 86 (1893): 341, dubs him "the foster-father of Lucy Larcom's children of the brain." It is unclear whether "Bring Back My Flowers" was conceived during Larcom's Lowell days; *NEG*, 218–19; according to Daniel Dulany Addison, *Lucy Larcom: Life, Letters, and Diary* (Boston: Houghton Mifflin, 1895), 16, she kept a prose sketchbook. John B. Pickard, "The Liberty Party 1844–1845," *LJGW*, 1:621. *NEG*, 254–55; Marchalonis, *Worlds*, 38–39. Lucy Larcom, "The Burning Prairie," *NE*, May 25, 1848, 83. Marchalonis, *Worlds*, 49. J[ohn] G[reenleaf] W[hittier], "The New England Offering," *NE*, September 23, 1847, 2; idem, "The New England Offering . . . ," *NE*, August 3, 1848, 123. Rufus Wilmot Griswold, *The Female Poets of America* (Philadelphia: Henry C. Baird, 1853), 360–61. Marchalonis, *Worlds*, 50; *NEG*, 224. A reviewer of Griswold in the *USDR* 24 (1849): 232, like Larcom, objected to the lack of selectivity: "Looking at the index, one is aghast at the numbers of the Female Poets." Marchalonis, *Worlds*, 49–50, cites the reprinting of "A Schoolmistress's First Day," *NE*, July 13, 1848, 109. On Griswold, see Shirley Marchalonis, "Lucy Larcom," *DLB*, vol. 221, *American Women Prose Writers, 1870–1920*, ed. Sharon M. Harris (2000), 246–52. John Peter Nathaniel Austin, "The Literary Compilation in America: 1820–1850" (Ph.D. diss., Columbia University, 2001), pt. 1.
40. Marchalonis, *Worlds*, 79–81 and 86. Whittier to Larcom, July 28, 1853, in *LJGW*, 2:222; see also Whittier to James Thomas Fields, July 8, 1853, 2:221.
41. Whittier to Fields, July 8, 1853, in *LJGW*, 2:221–22. The best work on Fields and his firm remains Warren S. Tyron, *Parnassus Corner: A Life of James T. Fields, Publisher to the Victorians* (Boston: Houghton Mifflin, 1963); see also Annie Fields, *James T. Fields, Biographical Notes and Personal Sketches . . .* (Boston: Houghton Mifflin, 1881); and Michael Winship, *American Literary Publishing in the Mid-Nineteenth Century: The Business of Ticknor and Fields* (Cambridge: Cambridge University Press, 1995). John Greenleaf Whittier's publications with the firm include *Old Portraits and Modern Sketches* (1850); *The Chapel of the Hermits, and Other Poems* (1852); *Lays of My Home and Other Poems* (1843); *Leaves from Margaret Smith's Journal in the Province of Massachusetts Bay, 1678–9* (1849); and *Songs of Labor, and Other Poems* (1851). On the German vogue, see: Henry A. Pochmann, *German Culture in America: Philosophical and Literary Influences, 1600–1900* (Madison: University of Wisconsin Press, 1957), 327–41; Scott Holland Goodnight, "German Literature in American Magazines Prior to 1846," *Bulletin of the University of Wisconsin*, no. 188 (1907): 1–264, esp. 43–55, 106; Martin Henry Haertel, "German Literature in American

Magazines, 1846 to 1880," *Bulletin of the University of Wisconsin*, no. 263: 1–188; and Lillie Vinal Hathaway, *German Literature of the Mid-Nineteenth Century in England and America* (Boston: Chapman and Grimes, 1935), 9; Stanley M. Vogel, *German Literary Influences on the American Transcendentalists* (New Haven, Conn.: Yale University Press, 1955), 167, notes the scarcity of German-language books in Boston as late as the 1840s. Vogel exemplifies the characteristic scholarly overemphasis upon the German-transcendentalist connection over other types.

42. On Jewett, see Lynne P. Shackelford and Everett C. Wilkie Jr., "John P. Jewett and Company," *DLB*, vol. 49, *American Literary Publishing Houses, 1638–1899*, ed. Peter Dzwonkoski, 2 pts. (1986) pt. 1:226; Susan S. Williams, "'Promoting an Extensive Sale': The Production and Reception of *The Lamplighter*," *NEQ* 69 (1996): 179–200; Philip M. Fragasso, "John P. Jewett: The Unsung Hero of *Uncle Tom's Cabin*," *NEGXY* 20 (1978): 22–29; Susan Geary, "Harriet Beecher Stowe, John P. Jewett, and Author-Publisher Relations in 1853," *SAR* 1 (1977): 345–67; idem, "Scribbling Women: Essays on Literary History and Popular Literature in the 1850's" (Ph.D. diss., Brown University, 1976). On the children's book market, see Gillian Avery, *Behold the Child: American Children and Their Books, 1621–1922* (Baltimore: Johns Hopkins University Press, 1994), 65–152; on this literature's profitability, see Gail Schmunk Murray, *American Children's Literature and the Construction of Childhood* (New York: Twayne, 1998), 53. *Similitudes* could aid parents' moral lessons; see Anne Scott MacLeod, *American Childhood: Essays on Children's Literature of the Nineteenth and Twentieth Centuries* (Athens: University of Georgia Press, 1994), 87–111. Caroline Maria Hewins reported in "The History of American Children's Books," *AM* 61 (1888): 126, "Between 1840 and 1850, a German influence was felt in children's books." John H. Amory made his name with works like *The Young Rover* (Boston: James B. Dow, 1836); and *Alnomuc: or, The Golden Rule: A Tale of the Sea* (Boston: Weeks, Jordan / New York: John S. Taylor, 1837). Joseph Banvard published *Who Is God?* (Boston: Massachusetts Sabbath School Society, 1839, copy at AAS), before Jewett brought out his naturalist "Library Series," for children. *BAL*, 5:299. Whittier to Larcom, July 28, 1853, in *LJGW*, 2:222–23.

43. Whittier to Larcom, July 28, 1853; Whittier to Fields, July 8, 1853, *LJGW*, 2:222; Larcom, *Similitudes*, 6. Quote from Marchalonis, *Worlds*, 80, 172–73; Addison, *Lucy Larcom*, 68. Larcom to [Ann Danforth Spaulding], September 23, 1853. Whittier to Larcom, July 28, 1853 in *LJGW*, 2:222. Compare, for example, "The Prairie Violets," *NE*, September 23, 1847, with its revised counterpart in *Similitudes*, 69–70.

44. Whittier to Larcom, September 3, 1853, in *LJGW*, 2:233. *NEG*, 159. Larcom to [Ann Danforth Spaulding], September 23 and November 17, 1853. On distributing Eastern books in the West, see Ronald J. Zboray, *A Fictive People: Antebellum Economic Development and the American Reading Public* (New York: Oxford University Press, 1993), chap. 4; Walter Sutton, *The Western Book Trade: Cincinnati as a Nineteenth-Century Publishing and Book-Trade Center ...* (Columbus: Ohio State University Press for the Ohio Historical Society, 1961); Warren S. Tryon, "Ticknor and Fields' Publications in the Old Northwest," *Mississippi Valley Historical Review* 34 (1947): 589–610. The edition size compared favorably with the five-thousand-copy first run of Harriet Beecher Stowe's *Uncle Tom's Cabin*, which Jewett suspected would sell well because of its *National Era* appearance. It seems likely that Larcom received the same deal as Stowe and Maria Cummins (author of the 1854 novel *The Lamplighter*) or worse—that is, 10 percent after Jewett's initial investments were recouped and the 25 to 33 percent discount to retailers was figured in. By this standard, if Larcom made fifty dollars, she would be doing well. Geary, "Harriet Beecher Stowe," 351–52; Williams, "'Promoting an Extensive Sale,'" 186.

45. Lucy Larcom to [Ann Danforth Spaulding], November 17, 1853. Russell Duino, "The Cleveland Book Trade, 1819–1912: Leading Firms and Outstanding Men" (Ph.D. diss., University of Pittsburgh, 1981), 58–60. Lyman Beecher, *Sermons, Delivered on Various Occasions* (Boston: John P. Jewett / Cleveland: Jewett, Proctor, and Worthington, 1852); idem, *Lectures on Political Atheism and Kindred Subjects …* (Boston: John P. Jewett / Cleveland: Jewett, Proctor, and Worthington, 1852). Vincent Harding, *A Certain Magnificence: Lyman Beecher and the Transformation of American Protestantism, 1775–1863* (Brooklyn, N.Y.: Carlson, 1991). The first modern use of the term "benevolent empire" apparently was in Gilbert H. Barnes, *The Antislavery Impulse, 1830–1844* (1933; reprint New York: Harcourt, Brace, and World, 1964), 18.

46. Larcom to [Ann Danforth Spaulding], November 17, 1853. Whittier to Lucy Larcom, November 28, [1853], in *LJGW*, 2:240–41. Larcom to [Spaulding], November 17, 1853. The bibliographical description here relies upon *BAL*, 5:299.

47. Harriet Beecher Stowe, *Uncle Tom's Cabin; or, Life Among the Lowly, Illustrated Edition, Complete in One Volume* (Boston: John P. Jewett / Cleveland: Jewett, Proctor, and Worthington, 1853). The same firm illustrated Daniel Wise's *Minnie Brown, or, The Gentle Girl* (Boston: G.C. Rand, 1853) and Wise's ensuing series, along with Jacob Abbott's *Rollo in Europe* series (e.g., *Rollo on the Atlantic* [Boston: W.J. Reynolds, 1853]); Carl Jefferson Weber, *A Bibliography of Jacob Abbott …* (Waterville, Me.: Colby College Press, 1948); John B. Boles, "Jacob Abbott and the Rollo Books: New England Culture for Children," *Journal of Popular Culture* 4 (1972): 507–28. Lucy Larcom to [Spaulding], November 17, 1853.

48. Whittier to [Lucy Larcom, November 28, c. 1852], DDAC-MHS. Pickard, *LJGW* (2:240) dates it November 28, 1853. "Literary Notices," *NE*, November 10, 1853, 178; J[ohn] G[reenleaf] W[hittier], "New Books," *NE*, September 29, 1853, 154; see also review of December 22, 1853, reprinted in *LJGW*, 2:241 n. 1. Larcom, "Blessed Be Nothing," *NE*, November 17, 1853, 184; "The Indian Summer," *NE*, November 24, 1853, 187; "True Heart-Throbs," *NE*, December 1, 1853, 189.

49. Larcom to [Ann Danforth Spaulding], May 15, 1854 and November 17, 1853; Marchalonis, *Worlds*, 87. Ralph Thompson, *American Literary Annuals and Gift Books, 1825–1865* (New York: H.W. Wilson, 1936). In an 1840s New York City bookstore inventory, gift book prices averaged about sixty-six cents, whereas juvenile titles averaged at twenty-one cents; Zboray, *A Fictive People*, 145, table 8; however, a scan of Orville Roorbach, *Bibliotheca Americana: Catalogue of American Publications …* (New York: P. Smith, 1939), suggests a higher range for the most popular titles. For example, Emily Percival's *The Souvenir Gallery: An Illustrated Gift Book for All Seasons …* (Boston: Phillips, Sampson, 1851) was six dollars, while William Buell Sprague's *Women of the Old and New Testament; A Series of Portraits* (New York: D. Appleton / Philadelphia: George S. Appleton, 1850) started at ten (Roorbach, *Bibliotecha Americana*, 513 and 592). Apparently, the number of gift books produced for the season previous to *Similitudes* was unusually low; "Editorial Notes: Literature," *PM* 1 (1853), 230.

50. Whittier to [Lucy Larcom], [May] 14, [1854?], DDAC-MHS. Marchalonis, *Worlds*, 274 n. 20, believes that an undated manuscript at MHS may be the beginnings of this novel (and, on writing, see 88–89). Larcom to [Spaulding], September 16, 1854. Whittier to Larcom, [October] 15, 1854, DDAC-MHS. Larcom to [John Greenleaf Whittier], January 1, 1855, LLP-PEM. J[ohn] G[reenleaf] W[hittier], "The Era's Contributors," *NE*, February 1, 1855, [2]. Larcom to Mrs. S.A. Spaulding, February 16, 1855. Larcom to Whittier, February 22, 1855, in *LJGW*, 2:274 n. 1. Whittier to Larcom, March 2, 1855, in *LJGW*, 2:274. These unhappy teaching years are treated in Paul C. Helmreich, "Lucy Larcom at Wheaton," *NEQ* 63 (1990): 109–20.

51. *BAL*, 5:299. Marchalonis, *Worlds*, 118. *HBPUS*, 1:428–9. Lucy Larcom, *Lottie's Thought-Book* (Philadelphia: American Sunday-School Union, 1858); idem, *Ships in the Mist, and Other Stories* (Boston: Hoyt, 1860); idem, *Leila among the Mountains* (Boston: Hoyt, 1861). Little is known about Hoyt; see David Dzwonkoski, "Henry Hoyt," in Dzwonkoski, *American Literary Publishing Houses*, pt. 1:218. *NEG*, 272. Marchalonis, *Worlds*, 139 and 156. Mary Kathleen Geissler, "The Social Meaning of Women's Literacy in Nineteenth-Century America" (Ph.D. diss., University of Southern California, 1986), argues that Larcom denied having a career due to ambiguities over gendered literacy. R. Gordon Kelly discusses Larcom, her coeditor Trowbridge, and *Our Young Folks* within the "institutional matrix" of publishing in his *Mother Was a Lady: Self and Society in Selected American Children's Periodicals, 1865–1890* (Westport, Conn.: Greenwood, 1974), 19–24. Marchalonis, *Worlds*, 154–56, 166, 182–83, 188.

52. The best source on story papers remains Mary Noel, *Villains Galore … The Heyday of the Popular Story Weekly* (New York: Macmillan, 1954); on circulation figures, see 33. See also Ronald J. Zboray, "Technology and the Character of Community Life in Antebellum America: The Role of Story Papers," in *Communication and Change in American Religious History*, ed. Leonard I. Sweet (Grand Rapids, Mich.: William B. Eerdmans, 1993), 185–215; Michael Denning, *Mechanic Accents: Dime Novels and Working-Class Culture in America* (London: Verso, 1987). Some individual firms are covered in Madeleine B. Stern, ed., *Publishers for Mass Entertainment in Nineteenth Century America* (Boston: G.K. Hall, 1980), and some writers in David S. Reynolds, *Beneath the American Renaissance: The Subversive Imagination in the Age of Emerson and Melville* (New York: Alfred A. Knopf, 1988) and Daniel A. Cohen, *Pillars of Salt, Monuments of Grace: New England Crime Literature and the Origins of American Popular Culture, 1674–1860* (New York: Oxford University Press, 1993). Many contemporary Philadelphia and New York papers specialized in reprinting cheap European novels. By contrast, the Boston story paper publishers were responsible for about half of the original American-authored fiction titles published in the three cities during the later 1840s; see Ronald J. Zboray and Mary Saracino Zboray, "American Fiction Publishing, 1837–1857," paper delivered at the annual conference of the Society for the History of Authorship, Reading, and Publishing, Washington, D.C., July 15, 1994; based on Wright, *American Fiction*. Essays on some firms appear in Dzwonkoski's *American Literary Publishing Houses*: Joseph J. Hinchliffe and Philip B. Dematteis, "F. Gleason's Publishing Hall/M.M. Ballou," pt. 1:176–78; Timothy D. Murray, "Jones's Publishing House," pt. 1:231; Earl R. Taylor, "Star Spangled Banner Office," pt. 2:432; Deborah G. Gorman, "Williams Brothers …" [and other iterations], 2:493–94. Story paper readerships may be as much as ten times greater than circulation figures due to informal, out-of-market dissemination; *GPDRC* May 3, 1851, 13. Frederick Gleason published *FOU* (1846) and about half a dozen other weeklies, including *GPDRC*, (1851). The Williams brothers began their *Uncle Sam* in 1841, the *Yankee* in 1843, the *Weekly Omnibus* in 1847, and the *Flag of the Free* in 1848. Justin Jones was the publisher of the *Star Spangled Banner* (1846) and several other papers before he sold out to Street and Smith in 1859.

53. *MOS*, 46–47, 52–56; Trowbridge emphasized that he was born on a farm, not in a village, and that the nearest settlement was Spencerport within the town of Ogden (11–12). For further background, see David E.E. Sloane, "John Townsend Trowbridge," *DLB*, vol. 202, *Nineteenth-Century American Fiction Writers*, ed. Kent P. Ljungquist (1999), 271–78; Rufus A. Coleman, "Trowbridge and Clemens," *Modern Language Quarterly* 9 (1948): 232–46; idem, "Trowbridge and Shillaber," *NEQ* 20 (1947): 232–46; and idem, "Trowbridge and Whitman," *PMLA* 63 (1948): 262–73. For contemporary assessments, see John Burroughs, "J.T. Trowbridge," *SM* 9 (1874): 32–36; William Dean Howells, "Editor's Easy Chair—III," *HNMM* 108 (1904): 481–82. Context on the scene

of Trowbridge's childhood must be pieced together from several sources, including Paul E. Johnson, *A Shopkeeper's Millennium: Society and Revivals in Rochester, New York, 1815–1837* (New York: Hill and Wang, 1978); Whitney R. Cross, *The Burned-Over District: The Social and Intellectual History of Enthusiastic Religion in Western New York, 1800–1850* (Ithaca, N.Y.: Cornell University Press, 1950). On the *Rochester Republican*, see W. H. McIntosh, *History of Monroe County, New York* … (Philadelphia: Everts, Ensign and Everts, 1877), 134. Spencerport, being an agricultural canal town without manufacturing, fits the model of Cross, *Burned-Over District*, 55–77, and affirmed by Johnson, *Shopkeeper's Millennium*, 137, which maintained that revivalism had little sway outside factory towns, so it is not surprising that Trowbridge was cool to the evangelicalism of what he disdainfully called "imported revivalists" (*MOS*, 30). This section of the chapter is based loosely upon Ronald J. Zboray's "A Glimpse of Cheap Publishers in Antebellum Boston: John Townsend Trowbridge's *Martin Merrivale: His 'X' Mark*," *Dime Novel Round-Up* 60 (1991): 78–83, with permission.

54. On the type of farm life Trowbridge encountered in Illinois on his 1845–47 sojourn with his sister Elizabeth Venilia Greene and her husband Daniel Moon Greene, see David E. Schob, *Hired Hands and Plowboys: Farm Labor in the Midwest, 1815–60* (Urbana: University of Illinois Press, 1975), esp. 234–49. Jonathan D. Sarna, *Jacksonian Jew: The Two Worlds of Mordecai Noah* (New York: Holmes and Meier, 1980), chap. 7. Evert A. Duyckinck, *Cyclopaedia of American Literature*, 2 vols. (New York: T.E. Zell, 1875), 2:902. *MOS*, 132, 135–36.

55. *MOS*, 157–58, 179, 192, 132, 149–53, 150. His early contributions to the Boston cheap fiction trade include Paul Creyton, "The Gamester," *Union Jack*, September 30, 1848, [2]. "To Our Correspondents," *FOU*, December 16, 1848, [3]; see also "To Our Correspondents," *FOU*, April 28 and May 26, 1849. Gleason probably was the silent partner because in 1849 he brought out several of Trowbridge's short pieces in pamphlet form. Other of his pamphlets of the period included *Paul Creyton's Great Romance!!! Kate, The Accomplice; or, the Preacher and the Burglar: Story of Real Life in the Metropolis* (Boston: Star Spangled Banner Office, 1849); and *Lucy Dawson; or, The Bandits of the Prairie, A Romance of the Far West, Being a Tale of Crime and Daring, Founded on Facts* (Boston: George H. Williams, 1850). Paul Creyton [i.e., Trowbridge] to Charles [Graham Halpine], December 23, 1852—this item is reproduced by permission of the HuL. On this letter's colorful recipient, see William Hanchett, *Irish: Charles G. Halpine in Civil War America* (Syracuse, N.Y.: Syracuse University Press, 1970), 5.

56. Kelly, *Mother Was A Lady*, 22. Trowbridge, June 1, 3, 8, and 23, July 2, September 20, and December 8, 1853; January 5, 1854; August 2, 1853; January [i.e., October due to his "misuse" of a pocket diary with printed dates] 25 and 28, [1853], diary, BPL. Idem, *The Deserted Family; or, Wanderings of an Outcast* (Boston: L.P. Crown / Philadelphia: J.W. Bradley, 1853); idem, *Burrcliff, Its Sunshine and Its Clouds* (Boston: Phillips, Sampson, 1853); *MOS*, 203–4; *BAL*, 5:314–15; on *Brighthope's* pricing, see advertisement in Maturin M. Ballou, *History of Cuba; or, Notes of a Traveller in the Tropics* (Boston: Phillips, Sampson, 1854), [234]. Basic facts about the firm are covered in Elizabeth Ann Peck, "Phillips, Sampson and Company," in Dzwonkoski, *American Literary Publishing Houses*, pt. 2:364–65. On the children's market, see Sarah A. Wadsworth, "Louisa May Alcott, William T. Adams, and the Rise of Gender-Specific Series Books," *Lion and the Unicorn* 25 (2001): 17–46. On Trowbridge's earlier health problems, see B[enjamin] P[enhallow] Shillaber to Charles [Graham Halpine], May 17, 1853, HuL. *MOS*, 202.

57. *MOS*, 193, 203; Trowbridge, January 27[?], February 4 and 6, March 19 and 23, and April 8, 1854, diary. This may be author "Ellen Louise" Chandler Moulton who first came to Boston in 1853 to submit her portfolio to editors, one of whom she married

(William U. Moulton); Ellen Louise Chandler Moulton, *The Poems and Sonnets of Louise Chandler Moulton* (Boston: Roberts Brothers, 1889); Lilian Whiting, *Louise Chandler Moulton, Poet and Friend* (Boston: Little, Brown, 1910). *MOS*, 188–89. Mihai H. Handrea, "Books in Part and the Number Trade," in *Book Selling and Book Buying: Aspects of the Nineteenth-Century British and North American Book Trade*, ed. Richard G. Landon (Chicago: American Library Association, 1978), 34–51.

58. *MOS*, 205.

59. "John Townsend Trowbridge, Esq.," *Ballou's Pictorial Drawing Room Companion*, April 25, 1857, 268.

60. *MOS*, 193.

61. Parenthetical page references hereafter are to the first edition cited above (see note 9), in its apparent first issuance as three chapter numbers, subsequently sewn together. Geary, "Harriet Beecher Stowe," 346–47, mentions a forerunner to this and other scenes of Martin approaching publishers, "The Author's Tragedy; or, The Perfidious Publisher," *Broadway Journal*, April 1845.

62. Ossian E. Dodge, "We are Growing Very Old, Kate," arranged by L. Louis, *LM*, October 13, 1852, 336; idem, "Mary O'Shane: A Ballad," *LM*, June 12, 1852, 16. On panoramas, see Stephan Oettermann, *The Panorama: History of a Mass Medium*, trans. Deborah Lucas Schneider (New York: Zone, 1997), and other sources cited in chapter 4 of the present volume. *MOS*, 164.

63. "Ossian E. Dodge," *LM*, May 12, 1849, 380; "Ossian E. Dodge, Vocalist," *LM*, October 27, 1849, 153. Eunice H. Cobb, diary, July 3, [1853], NEHGS. On the daughter's death, see entry for June 25, 1853. Douglass, "Mr. Ossian E. Dodge," *North Star*, October 19, 1849. Ossian E. Dodge, *Biographical, Historical and Incidental Sketch of Ossian E. Dodge* (Boston: Wright and Potter, c. 1860s), i–iv; Earl R. Hoover, "Important People or Events of the Western Reserve Too Long Overlooked, No. 2, Ossian Euclid Dodge," *Western Reserve Historical Society News* 27 (1973): 1–5; Philip D. Jordan, "Ossian Euclid Dodge: Eccentric Troubadour," *Historian* 31 (1969): 194–210.

64. On puff writing, see William Charvat, "James T. Fields and the Beginnings of Book Promotion," *HLQ* 8 (1944–45): 82–94. The practice was so prevalent that it was spoofed in the press; see "Important Publication Expected," *Vanity Fair*, March 24, 1860, 203, which targets the *Home Journal's* editor Nathaniel Parker Willis as skilled "in the elegant art of concealed puffery." Another magazine critic moaned that "too often the case, impartial criticism has been lost in indiscriminating puffery"; see Charles Nordhoff, "Concerning Authors," *LR* 16 (1856): 536. Charlene Avallone, "Calculations for Popularity: Melville's Pierre and Holden's Dollar Magazine," *Nineteenth-Century Literature* 43 (1988): 85, 108. Herman Melville savagely satirizes puffs and obsequious fan letters in book 17 of *Pierre; or, The Ambiguities* (New York: Harper, 1852). On book reviewing discourse, see Nina Baym, *Novels, Readers, and Reviewers: Responses to Fiction in Antebellum America* (Ithaca, N.Y.: Cornell University Press, 1984).

65. This underscores paper money's erasure of the personal, as discussed in David M. Henkin, *City Reading: Written Words and Public Spaces in Antebellum New York* (New York: Columbia University Press, 1998), chap. 6. The term *tenspot* was in use as early as 1848, according to Robert L. Chapman, *Dictionary of American Slang*, 3d. ed. (New York: HarperCollins, 1995), 554.

66. Paul Creyton to [Charles Graham Halpine], April 30, [1854?]; this item is reproduced by permission of the HuL; Trowbridge, diary, May 7, 1854. Although Trowbridge used the word *number* in his diary to mean a pamphlet of thirty-six pages (or three chapters), in this entry he probably intended "number 15" to mean chapter 15, for he would write the rest of the book, chapters 16–32, over a period of three months—roughly the amount of time it took him to write the first fifteen chapters.

67. *MOS*, 165.

68. *MOS*, 66, 67.

69. Compare Edgar Allan Poe, Review of Nathaniel Hawthorne, *Twice-Told Tales*, *Graham's Magazine*, May 1842, 298–300. Andrew Levy, *The Culture and Commerce of the American Short Story* (Cambridge: Cambridge University Press, 1993), chap. 1.

70. William Dean Howells, "Pernicious Fiction," *HNMM* 74 (1887): 824–26.

71. Trowbridge, August 24 and September 1, 1854, Diary; *MOS*, 205.

72. Margaret's disciplining through love is similar to that discussed in Richard H. Brodhead's *Cultures of Letters: Scenes of Reading and Writing in Nineteenth-Century America* (Chicago: University of Chicago Press, 1993), chap. 1. Herman Melville, *The Confidence Man: His Masquerade* (New York: Dix, Edwards, 1857), 5.

73. *MOS*, 462, 459. Compare Richard F. Teichgraeber III, *Sublime Thoughts/Penny Wisdom: Situating Emerson and Thoreau in the American Market* (Baltimore: Johns Hopkins University Press, 1995), esp. 267–74.

74. *NEG*, 272.

75. Larcom to Whittier, quoted in Addison, *Lucy Larcom*, 68. Compare Marchalonis, *Worlds*, 80, which posits that Larcom "remained a little in love with him all her life."

76. Forten, May 11, 1856, *JCFG*, 156.

77. S[amuel] T[aylor] Coleridge to William Blackwood, February 24, [1826], in Eric W. Nye, "Coleridge and the Publishers: Twelve New Manuscripts," *Modern Philology* 87 (1989): 65.

Chapter 3

1. Larcom to Robinson, December 16, 1854, and all subsequent letters or diary entries by either below, RSP-SL.

2. A handful of works treat general aspects of literary celebrity; see, for example, Leo Braudy, *The Frenzy of Renown: Fame and Its History* (New York: Oxford University Press, 1986); and, especially, Susan Barerra Fay, "A Modest Celebrity: Literary Reputation and the Marketplace in Antebellum America" (Ph.D. diss., George Washington University, 1992). Scott Casper, *Constructing American Lives: Biography and Culture in Nineteenth-Century America* (Chapel Hill: University of North Carolina Press, 1999), touches upon literary celebrity. For contemporary views, see Charles Sumner, *Fame and Glory: An Address before the Literary Societies of Amherst College* ... (Boston: W.D. Ticknor, 1847), and *Homes of American Authors* (New York: George P. Putnam, 1853). George P. Putnam, "Leaves from a Publisher's Letter-Book," *PM* 14 (1869): 467–74; the "homes" book is discussed on 468–70.

3. Scholars have considered specific celebrated American authors; see, for example, Thomas N. Baker, *Sentiment and Celebrity: Nathaniel Parker Willis and the Trials of Literary Fame* (New York: Oxford University Press, 1999); Eliza Clark Richards, "Poetic Attractions: Gender, Celebrity, and Authority in Poe's Circle" (Ph.D. diss., University of Michigan, 1997); Loring E. Hart, "The Beginnings of Longfellow's Fame," *NEQ* 36 (1963): 63–76; Mary G. De-Jong, "Her Fair Fame: The Reputation of Frances Sargent Osgood," *SAR* 10 (1987), 265–83; Howard N. Meyer, "Higginson, Thoreau, and the Equation of Fame," *Thoreau Journal Quarterly* 11 (1979): 5–11; and James M. Farrell, "John Adams's Autobiography: The Ciceronian Paradigm and the Quest for Fame," *NEQ* 62 (1989): 505–28. On European writers, see James Philip Carroll, "From Erasmus to Klopstock: Fame and the Republic of Letters" (Ph.D. diss., University of Washington, 1992); Kevin Andrew Dalton, "Middle Class Celebrity and the Public Sphere: John Wilkes, Olaudah Equiano, Walter Scott, and Charles Dickens" (Ph.D. diss., University of Virginia, 1994); Joel Pace, "Wordsworth in America: Publication, Reception, and Literary Influences" (Ph.D. diss., University of Oxford,

1999); Linda H. Peterson, "'No Finger Posts—No Guides': Victorian Women Writers and the Paths to Fame," in *A Struggle for Fame*, ed. Susan P. Casteras and Linda H. Peterson (New Haven, Conn.: Yale University Press, 1994), 35–47; Charles Dantler Albergotti, "Byron, Hemans, and the Reviewers: Two Routes to Fame" (Ph.D. diss., University of South Carolina, 1995); Lisa Marie Wilson, "Pen Names: Marketing Authorship in a 'Romantic Age of Personality,' 1780–1830" (Ph.D. diss., State University of New York–Buffalo, 1999); and Keith C. Odom, "Jane Austen's Rise to Fame," *Conference of College Teachers of English Studies* 54 (1989): 47–52. A broader interpretation of authorial impact appears in Carol McGuirk, "Haunted by Authority," in *Robert Burns and Cultural Authority*, ed. Robert Crawford (Iowa City: University of Iowa Press, 1997), 136–58.

4. This suggests a deviation from the transhistorical Western European tension between Roman civic fame or public glory and its Judeo-Christian challenge of inner worth and private devotion before the eyes of God, which is set out in Braudy, *Frenzy of Renown*. Such a dichotomy might have been moderated by legacies of the seventeenth-century Puritan interplay of *exemplum fidei* within a soteriological approach to Christian ethical action upon the worldly stage in a progressive historical drama of social and personal salvation. See Sacvan Bercovitch, *The Puritan Origins of the American Self* (New Haven, Conn.: Yale University Press, 1975). If this be true, the view of twentieth-century declension from an earlier time when public and private were much more separated needs revision; Richard Schickel, *Intimate Strangers: The Culture of Celebrity* (Garden City, N.Y.: Doubleday, 1985). One key distinction between early-nineteenth-century celebrity and its twentieth-century counterpart is that the later period, with its increasing professionalization, saw specific yet significant property interests attached to image maintenance and control. Michael Madow, "Private Ownership of Public Image: Popular Culture and Publicity Rights," *California Law Review* 81 (1993): 125–240. For the argument that turn-of-the-century professionalization accounts for the nature of twentieth century celebrity, see Charles Leonard Ponce de Leon, *Self-Exposure: Human-Interest Journalism and the Emergence of Celebrity in America, 1890–1940* (Chapel Hill: University of North Carolina Press, 2002).

5. As a trade courtesy, editors mailed copies of their paper to their counterparts elsewhere in the faith that recipients would respond in kind, all in the understanding that the copy could be freely "borrowed" with, at best, a credit line to the original donor; Ronald J. Zboray, *A Fictive People: Antebellum Economic Development and the American Reading Public* (New York: Oxford University Press, 1993), 119–21.

6. Don Avery Winslow, July 3, 1860, diary, AAS; Abby Clark Stimson, July 23, 1850, diary, DFP-RIHS; Healy, June 14, 1849, diary, CHC; Charles F. Low, January 12, 1857, diary, BPL; Eddy, scrapbook, c. 1830–60, MBEL. Studies of author obituaries remain on the frontier of reception history; see August A. Imholtz Jr. and Charles Lovett, eds., *In Memoriam: Charles Lutwidge Dodgson, 1832–1898: Obituaries of Lewis Carroll and Related Pieces* (New York: Lewis Carroll Society of North America, 1998). For general consideration of obituaries, see Janice Hume, *Obituaries in American Culture* (Jackson: University Press of Mississippi, 2000). Harriet Martineau pioneered a more-down-to-earth obituary style that, like our informants, did not memorialize through hero worship; see Barbara Garlick, "'The True Principle of Biographical Delineation': Harriet Martineau's 'Biographical Sketches' in the *Daily News*," in *Victorian Journalism: Exotic and Domestic*, ed. idem and Margaret Harris (Queensland, Australia: University of Queensland Press, 1998), 46–61. On *Lalla Rookh*'s popularity, see Grace Warren Landrum, "Notes on the Reading of the Old South," *AL* 3 (1931): 69. On its appeal, see Susan B. Taylor, "Irish Odalisques and Other Seductive Figures: Thomas Moore's Lalla Rookh," in *The Containment and Re-Deployment of English*

India, November 2000, http://www.rc.umd.edu/praxis/containment/taylor/taylor.html (accessed April 20, 2004).

7. Christopher Keith, August 30, 1857, diary, MMC-RIHS; Thomas Dick's most popular book was *Philosophy of a Future State* (Philadelphia: Hogan and Thompson, 1827). On Sue, see Ronald J. Zboray and Mary Saracino Zboray, "The Mysteries of New England: Eugène Sue's American 'Imitators,' 1844," *NCC* 22 (2000): 457–92. Katherine Bigelow Lawrence Jr., March 1, 1852, journal, transcript, LFP-MHS. Harriet Low, March 5, 1833, *LSML*, 1:518–19. Bradley, November 10 and 12, 1832, school journal, NHHS; Aurilla Moffitt, April 5, 1845, journal, OCHS. Sandra Tomc, "An Idle Industry: Nathaniel Parker Willis and the Workings of Literary Leisure," *AQ* 49 (1997): 780–805; Baker, *Sentiment and Celebrity*, 122; a long tribute to Mary Willis appeared in "Editor's Table," *The Lady's Book* [i.e., *Godey's*] 30 (1845): 279, followed the next month by mourning verses, L.A.S.W., "Glen Mary," *The Lady's Book* [i.e., *Godey's*] 31 (1845): 32. Henry Augustine Beers, *Nathaniel Parker Willis* (Boston: Houghton Mifflin, 1885), 276.

8. Susan D. Tucker, May 11, 1855, journal, VHS; *Vergennes Citizen*, 6 vols. (Vergennes: Henry G. Judd, 1855–60), began publication on that date. Jocelyn, August 7, 1839, diary, JFP-CHS; William Thompson Bacon's books included *The Idle Man, A Miscellaneous Assemblage …* (New Haven, Conn.: n.p., 1835) and *Poems* (1837; reprint New Haven, Conn.: Benjamin and William Noyes / Boston: C.C. Little, 1839). Healy, March 1, 1849, diary; F.W.J. Hemmings, *Alexandre Dumas, The King of Romance* (New York: Scribner's, 1979), 154–55; Dumas was in the midst of a postrevolutionary economic slide that would last from 1848 until his bankruptcy in 1852. Joseph Lye, December 23, 1822, "A Diary of my daily occupations," transcript, LHS; Joseph T. Buckingham, *Personal Memoirs and Recollections of Editorial Life*, 2 vols. (Boston: Ticknor and Fields, 1853), 1:107–110; *Maffit's Trial; or, Buckingham Acquitted on a Charge of Slander against the Character of John N. Maffit …* (New York: C.N. Baldwin, 1831); *A Correct Statement and Review of the Trial of Joseph T. Buckingham for an Alleged Libel on the Rev. John Maffit …* (Boston: William S. Spear, 1822); Stimson, January 4, 1853, diary. On Thackeray's reception, see Richard Clark Tobias, "American Criticism of Thackeray 1848–1855," *Nineteenth-Century Fiction* 8 (1953): 53–65. Samuel May Jr., to John Bishop Estlin, June 5, 1849, BPL.

9. Elizabeth Pierce to Lucy (Tappan) Pierce and John Pierce, January 6, 1843, and all manuscripts by Pierce or Poor family members below, PoFP-SL. John Webster Morris, *Memoirs of the Life and Writings of the Rev. Andrew Fuller*, ed. Rufus Babcock (Boston: Lincoln and Edmands, 1830); on why the Congregationalist Pierce might be attracted to the Baptist, see Pope Alexander Duncan, "Influence of Andrew Fuller on Calvinism" (Ph.D. diss., Southern Baptist Theological Seminary, 1917). On the metaphor of book or author as friend, see Wayne C. Booth, *The Company We Keep: An Ethics of Fiction* (Berkeley and Los Angeles: University of California Press, 1988), chap. 6.

10. The one-third estimate derives from Ronald J. Zboray and Mary Saracino Zboray, *Everyday Ideas: Socio-Literary Experience among Antebellum New Englanders* (Knoxville: University of Tennessee Press, forthcoming, 2005); about a sixth of the books charged out of the New-York Society Library between 1847 and 1849 were biographies, strictly defined; Zboray, *A Fictive People*, 163, table 15. On the popularity of the genre, see Casper, *Constructing American Lives*.

11. John Gibson Lockhart, *Memoirs of the Life of Sir Walter Scott, bart.*, 7 vols. (Edinburgh: R. Cadell / Boston: Otis, Broaders, 1837–38); Daniel F. Child [and Mary D. Child], April 26, 1841, diary, DFCP-MHS; Rufus Gay to Olive Gay Worcester, February 19, 1838, SFP-SL; Mellen Chamberlain, November 28, 1843, diary, BPL. Scott's American impact can be glimpsed in George Harrison Orians, "The Influence

of Sir Walter Scott Upon America and American Literature before 1860" (Ph.D. diss., University of Illinois, 1927); Emily Bishop Todd, "The Transatlantic Context: Walter Scott and Nineteenth-Century American Literary History" (Ph.D. diss., University of Minnesota, 2000). On the rage for literary biography during what Samuel Taylor Coleridge dubbed the "Age of Personality," see Francis L. Hart, "Boswell and the Romantics: A Chapter in the History of Biographical Theory," *ELH* 27 (1960): 45–65. For a wider discussion, see David Ellis, *Literary Lives: Biography and the Search for Understanding* (New York: Routledge, 2000).

12. William Lloyd Garrison Jr. to William Lloyd Garrison Sr., August 3, 1860, GP-SSC; Osmon Cleander Baker, February 9, 1832, diary, NHHS.

13. S.W. Goddard to [Annie DeWolf Middleton], June 9, 1852, SCHS; Sarah [L. Chamberlain] to Jane [E.] Shedd, November 28, 1839, WCP-VHS; James Gillman, *The Life of Samuel Taylor Coleridge*, vol. 1 (London: W. Pickering, 1838); Bradley, November 3, 1835, diary, NHHS; Washington Irving, *Abbotsford and Newstead Abbey* (Philadelphia: Carey, Lea, and Blanchard, 1835); Martha Osborne Barrett, August 13, 1854, diary, PEM; William Henry Channing, *Memoir of William Ellery Channing …*, 3 vols. (Boston: William Crosby and H.P. Nichols, 1848). Casper, *Constructing American Lives* discusses the applications for their own lives that readers found with biographical information in hand; see chap. 2.

14. J. Reynolds Hixon, October 25, and September 14, 1836, diary, OCHS; on anti-Catholicism, see Jenny Franchot, *Roads to Rome: The Antebellum Protestant Encounter with Catholicism* (Berkeley and Los Angeles: University of California Press, 1993), chap. 5. Benjamin Waterhouse, quoted in Louisa Lee Waterhouse, October 1, 1839, journal, LLWP-MHS. Waterhouse's ambivalence was a common enough reaction. Lodwick Hartley, "The Dying Soldier and Love-Lorn Virgin: Notes on Sterne's Early Reception in America," in *The Winged Skull*, ed. Arthur H. Cash and John M. Stedmond (Kent, Ohio: Kent State University Press, 1971), 159–69; idem, "*The North American Review* on Laurence Sterne: A Document in a Literary Reputation," *AL* 44 (1972): 299–306.

15. Harriet Low, April 13, 1831; April 15, 1833, *LSML*, 1:217, 2:537–38; Forten, June 14, 1854, *JCFG*, 71; Thomas Moore, *Life of Lord Byron, with His Letters and Journals*, 6 vols. (Boston: Little, Brown, 1853); John R. Congdon, October 23, 1851, journal, and all his other items below, CFP-RIHS; the book to which he refers may have been John Mitford, *The Private Life of Lord Byron, Comprising His Voluptuous Amours, Secret Intrigues, and Close Connection with Various Ladies of Rank and Fame …* (London: H. Smith, 1836); William Hoyt, February 1, 1851, journal, BPL; R.C. Dallas, *Recollections of the Life of Lord Byron, from the Year 1808 to the End of 1814 …* (Philadelphia: A. Small, and H.C. Carey and I. Lea, 1825). Work on Byron's celebrity tends to focus on his American reception; see Frank Lane, "Byron's Reputation in America, 1810–1860" (M.A. thesis, Duke University, 1941); William Ellery Leonard, *Byron and Byronism in America* (1907; reprint New York: Gordian, 1965). On British reception, see Andrew Elfenbein, *Byron and the Victorians* (Cambridge: Cambridge University Press, 1995); Ghislaine McDayter, "Conjuring Byron: Byromania, Literary Commodification, and the Birth of Celebrity," in *Byromania: Portraits of the Artist in Nineteenth and Twentieth-Century Culture*, ed. Frances Wilson (New York: St. Martin's, 1997), 43–62; and, within his circles, James Soderholm, *Fantasy, Forgery, and the Byron Legend* (Lexington: University of Kentucky Press, 1996).

16. Frances Merritt [Quick], November 5, 1858, diary, FMQP-SL; she refers to Basil Montagu, *The Life of Francis Bacon, Lord Chancellor of England* (London: W. Pickering, 1834), and the subject's 1621 dubious conviction and dismissal from court for accepting bribes. Park, December 6, 1838, diary, BPL; Chamberlain, February 27, 1844, diary. Forten, February 7, 1857, *JCFG*, 190; Martha Griffith Browne, *Autobiography of a Female Slave* (New York: Redfield, 1857); she and her book receive rare consideration

in Joseph Franklin Lockard, "'Writing Race' in Nineteenth-Century American Literature" (Ph.D. diss., University of California at Berkeley, 2000), chap. 6.

17. Barrett, March 15, 1855, diary. On Barrett, see Karen V. Hansen, *A Very Social Time: Crafting Community in Antebellum New England* (Berkeley and Los Angeles: University of California Press, 1994), 4–6, 8, 21–22, 39–40, 60–61, 79, 89, 145–46, 158, 162, 168. Jean-Maire Seillan, *Lectures de Corinne; ou, L'Italie de Germaine de Staël* (Nice: Université de Nice-Sophia Antipolis, 2000). Ripley to George F. Simmons, February 23 entry in February 20, 1848, SABRP-SL; Isaac Webb, September 25, 1841, journal, and his other manuscripts below, MC-CHS; Elizabeth Dwight Cabot to Ellen Twisleton, March 4, 1860, and all her other letters below, CFP-SL; Florence Nightingale, *Notes on Nursing: What It Is, and What It Is Not* (Philadelphia: Lippincott, 1859). Case to Edgarton, December 15 [c. 1842], HC-SL. Edgarton herself inspired appreciative fans; see Catherine E. Kelly, *In The New England Fashion: Reshaping Women's Lives in the Nineteenth Century* (Ithaca, N.Y.: Cornell University Press, 1999), 149. Elizabeth Oakes Prince Smith, "The Western Captive; or, The Times of Tecumseh," *New World* 2, extra ser., no. 27–28 (1842): 1–39. Mary Pierce to Henry Varnum Poor, August 7, 1840; Mary Howitt, *Birds and Flowers, and Other Country Things* (Boston: Weeks, Jordan, 1839). William Kelly Bartlett, December 17, 1837, journal, NHHS; Nathaniel Hawthorne, "Night Sketches, Beneath an Umbrella," in *Token and Atlantic Souvenir: A Christmas and New Year's Present*, ed. Samuel G. Goodrich (Boston: American Stationers' Company, 1838), 81–89.

18. Hale to Edward Everett Hale, February 25, 1846, and the rest of her letters below, HP-SSC; she probably refers to Ida Gräfin Hahn-Hahn, *Clelia Conti* (Berlin: Duncker, 1846). The author was a divorcée with several lovers who sired illegitimate children with her; see Christiane Schulzki-Haddouti, "Identität und Wahrnehmung bei Ida von Hahn-Hahn und Ida Pfeiffer anhand ihrer Orientberichte" (Diplomarbeit im Studiengang Kulturpädagogik an der Universität Hildesheim, 1995). Harriet Low, June 28, 1833, *LSML*, 2:572; Frances Trollope, *The Refugee in America: A Novel*, 3 vols. (London: Whittaker, Treacher, 1832). Tucker, July 18, 1852, diary; Elizabeth Oakes Smith, *Woman and Her Needs* (New York: Fowler and Wells, 1851), might be her reference.

19. Mary Gardner Lowell, March 4, 1844, diary, FCL2P-MHS; Charles Dickens, *A Christmas Carol in Prose, Being a Ghost Story of Christmas* (New York: Harper and Brothers, 1844). Wright to Martha Coffin Wright, March 2, 1861, and all letters by her below, GP-SSC; Thomas Carlyle, *Oliver Cromwell's Letters and Speeches*, 2 vols. (New York: Harper and Brothers, 1851). Bradley, October 3, 1836, diary; Francis Wayland, *Occasional Discourses, Including Several Never Before Published* (Boston: James Loring, 1833). Poor to Henry Varnum Poor, July 27, 1839; Johann Peter Eckermann, *Conversations with Goethe in the Last Years of His Life*, trans. Margaret Fuller (Boston: Hilliard, Gray, 1834).

20. Charlotte Brooks Everett, June 22, 1846, journal, 1846, EDP-MHS; Anne Marsh-Caldwell, *Emilia Wyndham* (New York: Harper and Brothers, 1846). James Amsted Brown, February 23, 1858, journal, VHS; Washington Irving, *Life of George Washington*, 5 vols. (New York: Putnam, 1856–1859). Henry Varnum Poor to Mary Pierce Poor, January 26, [1840], PoFP-SL; Charles Dickens, *Life and Adventures of Nicholas Nickleby* (Boston: H.P. Nichols, 1838).

21. Patricia Meyer Spacks, *Gossip* (New York: Knopf, 1985), especially on authorial biography, chap. 5; Hansen, *A Very Social Time*, chap. 5. Melanie Tebbutt, *Women's Talk? A Social History of "Gossip" in Working-Class Neighbourhoods, 1880–1960* (Aldershot, England: Scolar, 1995), 2–6, and chap. 1; Ned Schantz, "Jamesian Gossip and the Seductive Politics of Interest," *HJR* 22 (2001): 10–23.

22. On the distinction between the two types of information, see Ralph L. Rosnow and Gary Alan Fine, *Rumor and Gossip: The Social Psychology of Hearsay* (New York:

Elsevier, 1976), chaps. 2, 4, and 6. On a novelistic treatment of information flow through different immediate and mediated discourses, see Jan B. Gordon, "Gossip, Diary, Letter, Text: Anne Bronte's Narrative Tenant and the Problematic of the Gothic Sequel," *ELH* 51 (1984): 719–45.

23. Hannah Lowell Jackson to Sarah (Jackson) Russell, January 1838, transcript, AFP-SL; Louisa J. Hall, *Joanna of Naples* (Boston: Hilliard, Gray, 1838). Elizabeth Pierce to "my beloved sister," May 17, [1854?]; Maria Susanna Cummins, *The Lamplighter* (Boston: John P. Jewett, 1854).

24. Mary Pierce to John Pierce and Lucy (Tappan) Pierce, June 27 entry in letter begun on and dated June 19, 1837; Harriet Martineau, *Society in America*, 2 vols. (New York: Saunders and Otley, 1837). Sarah Browne to Sarah Ellen Browne Jr., in Alice Browne to Sarah Ellen Browne Jr., March 29, 1857, SEBP-SL; Fanny Kemble, *A Year of Consolation*, 2 vols. (New York: Wiley and Putnam, 1847); Catherine Clinton, *Fanny Kemble's Civil Wars* (New York: Simon and Schuster, 2000). Elizabeth Dwight Cabot to Ellen Twisleton, September 4, 1854.

25. Agassiz to Mrs. Thomas Cary, March 11, 1851[?], and Cary to Elizabeth Cary Agassiz, April 15, 1857, ECAFP-SL. Brontë had met Thackeray in December 1849; see Elizabeth Cleghorn Gaskell, *The Life of Charlotte Brontë*, 2 vols. (New York: D. Appleton, 1857), vol. 2, chap. 18. See also Toni Louise Oplt, "Charlotte Brontë," in *DLB*, vol. 159, *British Short-Fiction Writers, 1800–1880*, ed. John R. Greenfield (1996), 37–38. Nathan Kilbourn Abbott, October 11, 1859, diary, NHHS. (Sigourney was 69 at the time.)

26. Lamb, "Formative Influences," *Forum*, March 1891, 53; Ellen Wright to Martha Coffin Wright, March 8, 1861.

27. Poor to Pierce, February 10, 1840, and Pierce to Poor, February 14, 1840; Nathaniel Hawthorne, *Twice-Told Tales* (Boston: American Stationery Company / John B. Russell, 1837).

28. Forten, March 23, 1858, JCFG, 295; Larcom to Robinson, April 25, 1855; Chamberlain, February 21, 1847, journal; Brougham's inclusion in George Gilfillan, *A Gallery of Literary Portraits* (Edinburgh: W. Tait, 1845), reflects the high regard of him as a man of letters.

29. For example, see George W. Curtis, H. T. Tuckerman, and G. W. Greene, *Homes of American Authors; Comprising Anecdotical, Personal, and Descriptive Sketches, by Various Writers* (New York: G. P. Putnam, 1853); "Sunnyside, The Home of Washington Irving," *HNMM* 14 (1856): 3–21, illustration on 3. Forten, June 13, 1854, JCFG, 70.

30. Unidentified traveler, Loch Lomond, Scotland, to Hannah Rantoul, August 21, 1859, EC-BHS; Isaac Webb, March 17, 1842, journal; Issac Webb to Professor Holdich, December 21, 1840; Issac Webb to Professor Holdich, November 23, 1841; Bernardin de Saint-Pierre, *Paul and Virginia*, trans. Helen Maria Williams (New York: Evert Duyckinck, 1805), frequently republished in the United States; Marie de Rabutin-Chantal, Marquise de Sévigné, *Letters from the Marchionness de Sévigné to her Daughter the Countess de Grignan*, 7 vols. (London: J. Sewell, 1801). Frederick Lathrop Gleason, August 23, and October 15, 1860, journal, CHS. Mary Grosvenor Salisbury, June 9 and 26, and July 24, 1848, diary of European trips, SFP-AAS; Walter Scott, *Kenilworth; A Romance* (Edinburgh: A. Constable, 1821). Gleason, July 16, 1860, journal; Nat Simpkins, May 8, [1846], diary, BHS. William W. Stowe, *Going Abroad: European Travel in Nineteenth-Century American Culture* (Princeton: Princeton University Press, 1994), chap. 3; he writes, "The traveling class was a reading class, and travel was seen as a preeminently literary activity" (13).

31. Tucker, July 1, 1853, journal; Emmeline Ober, August 17, 1849, diary, BHS; Chamberlain, September 30, 1856, diary; Sylvester Judd, *Margaret: A Tale of the Real and*

Ideal, Blight and Bloom ... (Boston: Jordan and Wiley, 1845); Abbott, October 3 and [8], 1859, diary.

32. Mary Grosvenor Salisbury, June 10, 1848, diary of European trips; Robinson (with William Stevens Robinson), August 26, 1856, diaries.

33. Forten, May 29, 1857, *JCFG*, 222; Park, November 28, 1838, diary.

34. Philip B. Kunhardt Jr., Philip B. Kunhardt III, and Peter W. Kunhardt, *P.T. Barnum: America's Greatest Showman* (New York: Alfred A. Knopf, 1995), 61–62; Rev. J.M. Jephson, *Shakeaspeare [sic]: His Birthplace, Home, and Grave* ... (London: Lovell, Reeve, 1864), 43; William Tappan to Ellen Tappan, October 29, 1855, STPP-SSC. On later literary souvenir hunting, see "The Editor," "Nebulae," *Galaxy* 12 (1871): 593.

35. John R. Congdon, July 8, 1844, private journal; Mary Grosvenor Salisbury, September 22, 1848, diary of European trips; Sarah I. McClellan Webb, June 13, 1849, diary; Nancy Hoard Lincoln Salisbury, May 4, 1852, diary, SFP-AAS. On tourism and other cemetery outings, see Stanley French, "The Cemetery as Cultural Institution: The Establishment of Mount Auburn and the 'Rural Cemetery' Movement," *AQ* 26 (1974): 37–59.

36. Abbott, October 9, 1851, diary; Chandler Eastman Potter, *Mysteries of Manchester* (Manchester, N.H.: J.P. Emery, 1844). Moffitt, March 28, 1844, personal journal; a contemporary who had seen Willis in the flesh described him as "the most unintellectual, unpoetical looking person imaginable" (Sophia Seymour to Clarissa Seymour, [1837], NPWC-UVA). Wright to Martha Coffin Wright, February 23, 1861; on Kemble and Sedgwick's schoolgirls, see John C. Furnas, *Fanny Kemble: Leading Lady of the Nineteenth-Century Stage* (New York: Dial, 1982), 357–58; Bradley, January 6, 1835, diary. Charles Colbert, *A Measure of Perfection: Phrenology and the Fine Arts in America* (Chapel Hill: University of North Carolina Press, 1997).

37. Chamberlain, December 15, 1846, journal, BPL; Forten, July 10, 1854, *JCFG*, 84; Larcom to Harriet Hanson Robinson, January 15, 1859; for a review of the portraits by Samuel W. Rowse and Charles A. Barry, see *AM* 3 (1859): 653–54; Park, November 27, 1839, diary; Caroline Barrett White, September 3, 1849, diary, AAS.

38. Forten, July 6, 1854, *JCFG*, 82. Creamer published *Eleanor; or, Life without Love* (Boston: J. French, 1850); and *Delia's Doctors; or, A Glance behind the Scenes* (New York: Fowler and Wells, 1852).

39. K.A. Wilson to Joshua Lawrence Chamberlain, March 30, 1856, CAFP-SL; Rogers, September 22, 1851, diary, RFP-PEM; he had read Nathaniel Hawthorne's *The Scarlet Letter, A Romance* (Boston: Ticknor, Reed and Fields, 1850) on March 17 and 19, 1850; Ellen Wright to Martha Coffin Wright, November 4, 1860. "Margie F." was the seventeen-year-old daughter of Margaret Fuller's brother, William Henry.

40. Selina Cranch Bond, April 6, 1846, a daily journal, MHS; Caroline Gardiner Cary Curtis, February 26, 1859, diary, 1859, CFP3-MHS; Poor, May 4, 1858, account book, vol. 26; Robinson, May 31, 1855, diaries; see also May 23, 1855, for an Emerson visit; Robinson's encounter with the parrot is mentioned in Lucy Larcom to Robinson, July 24, 1857.

41. Forten, August 10, 1857, *JCFG*, 246–47. On visiting, see Cameron Lynne Macdonald and Karen V. Hansen, "Sociability and Gendered Spheres: Visiting Patterns in Nineteenth-Century New England," *Social Science History* 25 (2001): 535–61; Hansen, *A Very Social Time*, chap. 4.

42. Katherine Bigelow Lawrence Jr., November 21, 1849; September 23, and April 9, 1852; and December 10, 1851, journal, transcripts. Lady Georgiana Fullerton, *Ellen Middleton, A Tale* (New York: D. Appleton, 1849); *Grantley Manor, A Tale* (New York: D. Appleton, 1848). Tupper's works include *Proverbial Philosophy* (New York: Baker, 1849), *Crock of Gold, A Rural Novel* (New York: Wiley and Putnam, 1845), and "The Anglo-Saxon Race" (1850)—a racist watershed, according to Kwame Anthony Appiah, "Race," in *Critical Terms for Literary Study*, ed. Frank Lentricchia and

Thomas McLaughlin (Chicago: University of Chicago Press, 1995), 276. Elizabeth Dwight Cabot to Elizabeth Eliot, May 27, 1856.

43. Abraham Joseph Warner, February 19, 1851, diary, CHS; *The Whig Almanac and United States Register* (New York: Greeley and McElrath, 1843–1855). Clarissa W. Williamson, August 1842, added entry in William Durkee Williamson, album and diary, BPL; on similar events, see Edward Everett Hale, *A New England Boyhood* (New York: Cassell, 1893), 262.

44. Park, October 30, 1851, diary; Helen Aldrich de Kroyft, *A Place in Thy Memory* (New York: J.F. Trow, 1850), is discussed in James Emmett Ryan, "The Blind Authoress of New York: Helen De Kroyft and the Uses of Disability in Antebellum America," *AQ* 51 (1999): 385–418; Chamberlain, August 4, 1845, diary.

45. Child to John Child, December 11, 1847, copy in Child, diary, 1847; Andrew Jackson Davis, *The Principles of Nature, Her Divine Revelations, and a Voice to Mankind* (Boston: Banner of Light, 1847); Forten, June 17, 1857, *JCFG*, 229. Chamberlain, October 19, 1844, diary. Phelps's books include *Botany for Beginners ...* (Hartford: F.J. Huntington, 1834); *Chemistry for Beginners* (Hartford: F.J. Huntington, 1834); *The Female Student; or, Lectures to Young Ladies on Female Education* (New York: Leavitt, Lord / Boston: Crocker and Brewster, 1836); and the novel *Ida Norman; or, Trials and Their Uses*, 2 vols. (New York: Sheldon, Lamport and Blakeman, 1854); see Simona Badilescu, "Chemistry for Beginners: Women Authors and Illustrators of Early Chemistry Textbooks," *Chemical Educator* 6 (2001): 114–20; and Nina Baym, *American Women of Letters and the Nineteenth-Century Sciences: Styles of Affiliation* (New Brunswick, N.J.: Rutgers University Press, 2002), chap. 2. Carson Dana Benton, April 30, 1855, diary, CSL. Truth frequently visited reform communities; see Nell Irvin Painter, "Difference, Slavery, and Memory: Sojourner Truth in Feminist Abolitionism," in *The Abolitionist Sisterhood: Women's Political Culture in Antebellum America*, ed. Jean Fagan Yellin and John C. Van Horne (Ithaca, N.Y.: Cornell University Press, 1994), 150; idem, "Representing Truth: Sojourner Truth's Knowing and Becoming Known," *JAH* 81 (1994): 461–92; idem, *Sojourner Truth: A Life, A Symbol* (New York: W.W. Norton, 1996), chaps. 10 and 15–16. Olive Gilbert, *Narrative of Sojourner Truth, A Northern Slave, Emancipated from Bodily Servitude by the State of New York, in 1828* (Boston: printed for the author, 1850). Etta M. Madden, *Bodies of Life: Shaker Literature and Literacies* (Westport, Conn.: Greenwood, 1998).

46. Moffitt, June 15, 1844, personal journal. She met him again at lectures on June 18 and 19, 1844, prior to his return to England; John B. Gough, *An Autobiography* (New York: Gough, 1845); W. Carlos Martyn, *John B. Gough, The Apostle of Cold Water* (New York: Funk and Wagnalls, 1893). Julius Catlin, February 11, 1840, CHS; Lilian Handlin, *George Bancroft, The Intellectual as Democrat* (New York: Harper and Row, 1984), chap. 7; Russel Blaine Nye, *George Bancroft, Brahmin Rebel* (New York: Alfred A. Knopf, 1944); on his conversational weaknesses, see Ronald J. Zboray and Mary Saracino Zboray, "Whig Women, Politics, and Culture in the Campaign of 1840: Three Perspectives from Massachusetts," *JER* 17 (1997): 290.

47. Willis, November 20, 1850, diary, microfilm, PPL, original in MeHS; Park, September 16, January 18, 19, and 20, 1850, diary. Stewart Marsh Ellis, *The Solitary Horseman; or, The Life and Adventures of G.P.R. James* (Kensington, England: Cayme Press, 1922). A contemporary account roasted him: "Mr. James has come among us as a lecturer—-to pick up . . . a few greasy pork-besmeared and corn-fed Cis-Atlantic dollars"; "Mr. George Payne Rainsford James' Poems on America," *American Whig Review* 12 (1850): 402–5. On Kemble's readings, see Catherine Clinton, *Fanny Kemble's Civil Wars* (New York: Simon and Schuster, 2000), 144–46; Fanny Kemble Wister, *Fanny, The American Kemble: Her Journals and Unpublished Letters* (Tallahassee, Fla.: South Pass, 1972), 207–8.

48. Stanley Fish, *Is There a Text in this Class? The Authority of Interpretive Communities* (Cambridge, Mass.: Harvard University Press, 1980), 171–73. Wright to Martha Coffin Wright, December 7, 1860; and February 23, 1861; idem to Eliza [Wright Osborne], December 19, 1860; idem to Martha Coffin Wright, January 10, 1861. On Kemble in the local context, see Richard Birdsall, "Berkshire's Golden Age," *AQ* 8 (1956): 328–55.

49. Wright to "My dear sister," January 12, 1861; idem to Martha Coffin Wright [January 1, 1861?], fragment. Wright later, on February 23, 1861, reported to her mother that Kemble dubbed "'Woman['] s Rights' twaddle!!!" Clinton, *Fanny Kemble's Civil Wars*, 60, 87, 128, 135, 268, treats the relationship with Sedgwick. On Kemble's relationship to feminism, see Furnas, *Fanny Kemble*, 350–51.

50. Quote from Sarah P.E. Hale to Edward Everett, May 15, 1842, HP-SSC. Charles Dickens's visits to the United States have received much attention. It began in earnest with his 1842 visit, with accounts of the balls given in his honor, such as W. Crosby and Company's *Report of the Dinner Given to Charles Dickens in Boston*, followed shortly after by Thomas Hood's "Boz in America," *New Monthly Magazine* 66 (1842). Dickens's visit to Boston even resulted that year in a spoof, *Quozziana*, by Samuel Kettell. A year later Thomas G. Cary published a *Letter to a Lady in France* rebutting Dickens's *American Notes*. Late-nineteenth-century reminiscences include George W. Putnam, "Four Months with Charles Dickens," *AM* 26 (1870): 476–82, 591–99; and M.A. De Wolfe's edition of Annie Fields, *Memories of a Hostess: A Chronicle of Eminent Friendships ...* (Boston: Atlantic Monthly Press, 1922), chap. 4. A representative list of twentieth-century treatments includes, chronologically, William Glyde Wilkins, *Charles Dickens in America* (London: Chapman and Hall, 1911); Edward F. Payne, *Dickens Days in Boston: A Record of Daily Events* (Boston: Houghton, Mifflin, 1927); N.C. Peyrouton, "Some Boston Abolitionists on Boz," *Dickensian* 60 (1964): 20–26; Michael Slater, *Dickens on America and the Americans* (Austin: University of Texas Press, 1979); Sidney Phil Moss, *Charles Dickens' Quarrel with America* (Troy, N.Y.: Whitston, 1984); Jerome Meckier, "Dickens Discovers America, Dickens Discovers Dickens: The First Visit Reconsidered," *Modern Language Review* 79 (1984): 266–77; idem, *Innocent Abroad: Charles Dickens's American Engagements* (Lexington: University of Kentucky Press, 1990); Nigel Gearing, *Dickens in America* (London: Oberon, 1998); Sidney Phil Moss, *American Episodes Involving Charles Dickens* (Troy, N.Y.: Whitston, 1999), 3–85; Anny Sadrin, ed., *Dickens, Europe, and New Worlds* (Houndmills, England: St. Martin's Press, 1999); James C. Simmons, *Star-Spangled Eden: Nineteenth-Century America through the Eyes of Dickens, Wilde, Frances Trollope, Frank Harris, and other British Travelers* (New York: Carroll and Graf, 2000), 95–131; Jeremy Tambling, *Lost in the American City: Dickens, James, and Kafka* (New York: Palgrave, 2001), 1–47. None of these authors, however, surveyed extant letters and diaries of ordinary Americans from the period of Dickens's tour.

51. Hale to Edward Everett, January 31, 1842; Park, February 6, 1842, diary.

52. Mary Elizabeth Fiske, February 14, 1842, diary, LxHS; Payne, *Dickens Days*, 45–49. Charlotte Henrietta Pettibone, December 15, 1841; February 17 and 19, 1842, diary, CHS; Olive Gay Worcester to Rufus Marble Gay, February 18, 1842, SFP-SL; Joseph M. Field, "The Wery Last Obserwation of Weller Senior," quoted in Payne, *Dickens Days*, 106. "Henry" to Mary Pierce Poor, [February 8], 1842, postscript in Lucy (Tappan) Pierce to Mary Pierce Poor, [c. late January or early February 1842]; Lucretia Anne [Peabody] Everett to Sarah P.E. Hale, March 3, 1842, HP-SSC.

53. Hale to Edward Everett, January 31, 1842. Pettibone, February 19, 1842, diary; Payne, *Dickens Days*, 16; Hale to Everett, January 31, 1842; Park, February 5, 1842, diary; Payne, *Dickens Days*, 93-94; Albert Gallatin Browne to Sarah Smith (Cox) Browne,

April 16, 1842, BroFP-SL; Charles Dickens, *American Notes* (1842; reprint Gloucester, Mass.: Peter Smith, 1968), 77.

54. B.H. to Caroline A. Briggs, postscript, in Rebecca Briggs to Caroline A. Briggs, January 25, 1842, BriFP-SL. Squeers appears in *Nicholas Nickleby*, as does the senior Mrs. Nickleby; Charley Bates is in *Oliver Twist*. Hale to Alexander Hill Everett, February 16, 1842; and Alexander Hill Everett to Sarah Hale Jr., c. February 1842, HP-SSC. Bruce A. Ronda, *Letters of Elizabeth Palmer Peabody, American Renaissance Woman* (Middletown, Conn.: Wesleyan University Press, 1984). On the event, see idem, *Elizabeth Palmer Peabody: A Reformer on Her Own Terms* (Cambridge, Mass.: Harvard University Press, 1999), 208.

55. Hale to Edward Everett, January 31, 1842; idem to Alexander Hill Everett, February 16, 1842; idem to Edward Everett, January 31, 1842; Annie De Wolf to "My Dearest Aunt," in February 1842, in Alicia Hopton Middleton, "A Family Record," in *Life in Carolina and New England during the Nineteenth Century*, ed. idem (Bristol, R.I.: D.B. Updike, 1929), 54–55; Annie Lawrence, January 27, 1842, diary, LFP-MHS. Colbert, *A Measure of Perfection*; Lucy Hartley, *Physiognomy and the Meaning of Expression in Nineteenth-Century Culture* (Cambridge: Cambridge University Press, 2001).

56. Albert Gallatin Browne to Sarah Smith (Cox) Browne, April 16, 1842; Park, February 6, 5, and 7, 1842, diary; Park to Mrs. Jeremiah Lee, February 27, 1842, in his diary.

57. Sarah P.E. Hale to Edward Everett, May 15, 1842.

58. Poor to Feroline (Pierce) Fox, April 17, 1842; Amos A. Lawrence, November 9, 1842, diary, AALDAB-MHS; Charles Dickens, *American Notes for General Circulation* (New York: Harper and Brothers, 1842); Park, November 9, 1842, diary; Case to Edgarton, December 15 [c. 1842]; Wright to Martha Coffin Wright, January 10 and 30, 1861. The reception was almost immediately timed with the book's first appearance in Boston. Peter S. Bracher, "The Early American Editions of *American Notes*: Their Priority and Circulation," *PBSA* 69 (1975): 365–76, esp. 367.

59. Hale to Nathan Hale Sr., and Edward Everett Hale, January 22, 1844; Charles Dickens, *A Christmas Carol, in Prose, Being a Ghost Story of Christmas* (London: Chapman, 1843); Annie Chamberlain Keene to Frances Adams Chamberlain, mid-May 1857, CAFP-SL; Charles Dickens, *The Personal History and Experience of David Copperfield, the Younger* (New York: G.P. Putnam, 1850); Katherine Bigelow Lawrence Jr., February 24, 1851, journal; Charles Dickens, *Pictures from Italy* (New York: W. H. Colyer, 1846); Barrett, [August 20, 1859?], diary; Charles Dickens, *Hard Times* (New York: T.L. McElrath, 1854); Child, March 22, 1844, diary; Susan King to Ellis Gray Loring [undated, 1851], EGLFP-SL.

60. Lawrence H. Houtchens, "Charles Dickens and International Copyright," *AL* 13 (1941): 18–28. Even at the Great Boz dinner Dickens had to phrase his plea in sociable terms: "I would rather have the affectionate regard of my fellow-men than I would have heaps and mines of gold"; quoted in Payne, *Dickens Days*, 101.

Chapter 4

1. Harris, July 11, and May 16, 1856, journal, JEHP-MeHS.

2. On the tension between traditional social relations and market-oriented ones, see Karl Polanyi, *The Great Transformation* (1944; reprint Boston: Beacon, 1957); Maurice Godelier, *Transitions et subordinations au capitalisme* (Paris: Editions de la Maison des sciences de l'homme, 1999); Immanuel Maurice Wallerstein, *Historical Capitalism* (London: Verso, 1983); idem, *The Second Era of Great Expansion of the Capitalist World-Economy, 1730–1840* (San Diego: Academic, 1989); Allan Kulikoff, "The Transition to Capitalism in Rural America," *WMQ* 46 (1989): 120–44; Christopher

Clark, *The Roots of Rural Capitalism: Western Massachusetts, 1780–1860* (Ithaca, N.Y.: Cornell University Press, 1990).

3. Harris, July 11, 1856, journal. For a how-to book for agents, see J. Walter Stoops, *The Art of Canvassing; or, The Experience of a Practical Canvasser* (New York: printed for the author, 1857). Issues of distribution are covered in Richard D. Brown, *Knowledge Is Power: The Diffusion of Information in Early America, 1700–1865* (New York: Oxford University Press, 1989); Ronald J. Zboray, *A Fictive People: Antebellum Economic Development and the American Reading Public* (New York: Oxford University Press, 1993); Anne C. Rose, *Voices of the Marketplace: American Thought and Culture, 1830–1860* (New York: Twayne, 1995), xxi–xxiii, and chaps. 3–5. Scholarship on market-oriented distribution far outweighs that on marginal distributors. The emphasis has been upon a few economically successful entrepreneurs who heralded future developments, not the many obscure or failing distributors. On sources available for studying both, see Ronald J. Zboray and Mary Saracino Zboray, *A Handbook for the Study of Book History in the United States* (Washington, D.C.: Library of Congress, 2000), 51–57. On failure due to delinquent subscribers, see Thomas C. Leonard's *News for All: America's Coming-of-Age with the Press* (New York: Oxford University Press, 1995), 36–47.

4. On performed sermons and on ministers as textual performers, see Teresa Toulose, *The Art of Prophesying: New England Sermons and the Shaping of Belief* (Athens: University of Georgia Press, 1987), 7–8, 11–12, 85–88, 91–93; and Donald M. Scott, *From Office to Profession: The New England Ministry, 1750–1850* (Philadelphia: University of Pennsylvania Press, 1978).

5. Leonard, *News for All*, 118–24. Ronald J. Zboray and Mary Saracino Zboray, *Everyday Ideas: Socio-Literary Experience among Antebellum New Englanders* (Knoxville: University of Tennessee Press, 2005), pt. 2; idem, "Reading and Everyday Life in Antebellum Boston: The Diary of Daniel F. and Mary D. Child," *Libraries and Culture* 32 (1997): 291.

6. Harris, July 11, 1856, journal; Arnold, July 17, 1847, journal, transcript, VHS; *The African Repository and Colonial Journal* (Washington, D.C.: American Colonization Society, 1825–92); John Patton to Caroline W.H. Dall, undated, CWHDP-SL; John Park, December 12, 1840, diary, BPL; Chamberlain, October 8, 1846, journal, BPL; Park, March 28, 1849, diary. Agents linking authors to publishers were still rare; see Thomas L. McHaney, "An Early Nineteenth Century Literary Agent: James Lawson of New York," *PBSA* 64 (1970): 177–92; James and Patience Barnes, "Thomas Aspinwall: First Transatlantic Literary Agent," *PBSA* 78 (1984): 321–31. Sources on itinerant selling usually mention print distribution; see, for example, David Jaffee, "Peddlers of Progress and the Transformation of the Rural North, 1760–1860," *JAH* 78 (1991): 511–35, and his "The Village Enlightenment in New England, 1760–1820," *WMQ* 47 (1990): 327–46. On petty retailers, see Lewis Atherton, *The Pioneer Merchant in Mid-America* (Columbia: University of Missouri Press, 1939); idem, "Itinerant Merchandising in the Antebellum South," *Bulletin of the Business Historical Society* 19 (1945): 35–59; and idem, *The Southern Country Store* (Baton Rouge: Louisiana State University Press, 1949). Penrose Scull and Prescott C. Fuller, *From Peddlers to Merchant Princes: A History of Selling in America* (Chicago: Follett, 1967).

7. Edward Everett to Edward Everett Hale, April 10, 1850, HP-SSC. Oliver William Bourn Peabody, Samuel Weller Singer, Charles Symmons, and John Payne Collier, eds., *The Dramatic Works of William Shakspeare …*, 8 vols. (Boston: Phillips, Sampson, 1850–51). Sarah Jocelyn, November 14, 1840, diary, and other Jocelyn sister manuscripts below, JFP-CHS; John Park, June 12, 1841, diary. On postbellum subscription production, see Marjorie Stafford, "Subscription Book Publishing in the United States, 1865–1930" (Urbana: University of Illinois Press, 1943) and Frank Elbert Compton, *Subscription Books* (New York: New York Public Library, 1939),

105–43. On sales work, see Michael Hackenberg, "Hawking Subscription Books in 1870," *PBSA* 78 (1984): 137–53; and Keith Arbour, "Book Canvassers, Mark Twain, and Hamlet's Ghost," *PBSA* 93 (1999): 5–37. See also William Stevens Powell, "Patrons of the Press," *North Carolina Historical Review* 39 (1962): 423–99; and Amy M. Thomas, "'There is Nothing So Effective as a Personal Canvass': Revaluing Nineteenth-Century American Subscription Books," *BH* 1 (1998): 140–55. *"Agents Wanted"*: *Subscription Publishing in America*, http://www.library.upenn.edu/exhibits/rbm/agents/index.html, (accessed April 27, 2004).

8. Weeks, Jordan, and Co. to Cyrus Farnham, c. 1840, and subsequent correspondence between them below, HC-SL; Harris, May 21, 1856, journal. Keith Arbour, *Canvassing Books, Sample Books, and Subscription Publishers' Ephemera 1833–1951 in the Collection of Michael Zinman* (Ardsley, N.Y.: Haydn Foundation for the Cultural Arts, 1996), introduces the reader to a rare and wide-ranging collection at the University of Pennsylvania that contains specimens; the Harry Ransom Research Center at the University of Texas, Austin, also has a collection of publishers' dummies, or "blads."

9. Samuel Gardiner Drake to David D. Plumer, July 12, 1833, and all Drake–Plumer correpondence hereafter, BPL; Samuel Gardiner Drake, *The Book of the Indians of North America* ... (Boston: Josiah Drake, 1833); Maureen Konkle, "Indian Literacy, U.S. Colonialism, and Literary Criticism," *AL* 69 (1997): 482 n. 23; Philip Gould, "Reinventing Benjamin Church: Virtue, Citizenship and the History of King Philip's War in Early National America," *JER* 16 (1996): 645–57. "Prospectus of the '*Whip and Spur*'" (Newport, N.H.: Carleton and Harvey, July 24, 1844), in Henry Wyles Cushman, subscriptions, 1844, HWCC-NEHGS; A.E. and J.E. Worcester to Olive Gay Worcester, December 5, 1858, SFUP-SL. Practices described in this paragraph did not change much after the Civil War; see Hackenberg, "Hawking Subscription Books."

10. Weeks, Jordan, to Cyrus Farnham, c. 1840.

11. Drake to Plumer, May 8, 1827; Benjamin Church, *The History of Philip's War, Commonly Called the Great Indian War of 1675 and 1676*, ed. Samuel G. Drake, 2d. ed. (Boston: J.H.A. Frost, 1827). Arnold, July 12 and 28, 1847, journal.

12. Harris, May 16, 1856, journal; Weeks, Jordan, to Farnham, c. 1840. Drake to Plumer, July 12, 1833.

13. Drake to Plumer, June 9, 1827. Sylvanus Cobb, May 16, 1836, journal, BPL.

14. Benson, May 5, 1837, memoranda, NHHS. Harris, June 16, 1856, journal; Molly Winger Berger, "The Modern Hotel in America: 1829–1929" (Ph.D. diss., Case Western Reserve University, 1997), chaps. 2 and 3. Benson, April 28, May 28, 23, 9, 12, and 21, and June 2, 1837, memoranda. *Sunday School Advocate* (New York: Sunday School Union of the Methodist Episcopal Church, 1841–1921).

15. Arnold, July 7, 14, and 8, 1847, journal; Harris, July 11, June 21, and August 21, 1856, journal.

16. Weeks, Jordan to Farnham, c. 1840; The *Ladies' Magazine* had recently been absorbed by *Godey's Lady's Book* (Philadelphia: L.A. Godey, 1840–58); Drake to Plumer, July 12, 1833.

17. Arnold, January 1 and 29, 1848, December 11, 13, and 14, 1847, journal; Justin Edwards, *The Temperance Manual* (New York: American Tract Society, [1847?]). On colporteurs selling material, see T.S. Arthur, "The Colporteur," *GPDRC*, September 10, 1853, 174.

18. Paul Atwood Gibson, December 12, 1852, pocket memorandum, NHHS; Samuel Maunder's *The History of the World*, 2 vols. (New York: Henry Bill, 1852) was sold only by subscription; Harris, May 10, April 11, and June 12, 1856, journal; the copy paper is discussed in MeHS's collection finding aid; Arnold, October 14, 1847, journal; Abraham Kohn, c. February 15, 1843, "A Jewish Peddler's Diary," ed. Abram Vossen Goodman, in *Critical Studies in American Jewish History: Selected Articles from*

American Jewish Archives, 3 vols. (Cincinnati: American Jewish Archives, 1971), 1:59, 70. "Most general peddlers probably carried imprints," writes William J. Gilmore in "Peddlers and the Dissemination of Printed Material in Northern New England, 1780–1840," in *Itinerancy in New England and New York*, ed. Peter Benes (Boston: Boston University, 1986), 80.

19. William T. Gilbert, January 13, 1860, diary, CHS. On bartering, see Susan Geib, "'Changing Works': Agriculture and Society in Brookfield, Mass., 1785–1820" (Ph.D. diss., Boston University, 1981). Arnold, May 5, 1849, and February 24, 1853, journal; *Maps of the Missions of the American Board of Commissioners for Foreign Missions, September, 1849* (Boston: American Board of Commissioners for Foreign Missions, 1849). Roswell Chamberlain Smith, *Geography on the Productive System, for Schools, Academies, and Families* (New York: Paine and Burgess, 1847); idem, *Smith's Atlas: Designed to Accompany the Geography* (New York: Cady and Burgess, 1850); idem, *Smith's First Book in Geography: An Introductory Geography Designed for Children* (1846; reprint New York: Cady and Burgess, 1850); Elijah H. Burritt, *The Geography of the Heavens: and Class Book of Astronomy Accompanied by a Celestial Atlas*, rev. and corr. by O.M. Mitchel (New York: Huntington and Savage, 1848); Ormsby MacKnight Mitchel, *Atlas Designed to Illustrate Mitchel's Edition of the Geography of the Heavens ...* (New York: Huntington and Savage, 1849). Orville A. Roorbach, *Bibliotheca Americana; Catalogue of American Publications ...* (1852; reprint New York: P. Smith, 1939), gives the then-current list prices of the Smith's geography and atlas at eighty-four cents, the primary at thirty-eight cents, and Mitchel's at one dollar and twenty-five cents (596, 371).

20. May to Richard D. Webb, September 11, 1855, BPL; he refers to Boston's *National Anti-Slavery Bazaar*, New York's *National Anti-Slavery Standard*, Boston's *The Liberator*, Lisbon, Ohio's *Anti-Slavery Bugle*, and Providence's women's rights periodical, *Una*.

21. Arnold, May 15, and June 16, 1837, October 26 and 31, 1835, and January 18, 1836, journal; Seth S. Arnold and E. Colman, *The Family Choir: A Selection of Hymns Set to Music ...* (Boston: Kidder and Wright, 1837); Arnold, *The Intellectual House-Keeper ...* (Boston: Russell, Odiorne, 1835). Ann Fabian, *The Unvarnished Truth: Personal Narratives in Nineteenth-Century America* (Berkeley and Los Angeles: University of California Press, 2000).

22. Park, December 12, 1840, diary; John James Audubon, *The Birds of America*, 7 vols. (New York: J.J. Audubon / Philadelphia: J.B. Chevalier, 1840–44); a twenty-page prospectus for the book is in the Case Western Reserve University Library. The original double elephant folio edition measured about 38 by 26 inches. *HBPUS*, 1:239. Everett to Edward E. Hale, January 6, 1846, HP-SSC; idem, *Critical and Miscellaneous Essays, To Which are Added a Few Poems*, 2 vols. (Boston: J. Monroe, 1845–46).

23. See, for example, George E. Littlefield, October 15, 1840, auction sales, BPL; William B. Adams, sale at auction room, January 3, 1835, MbHS; Willis, November 20, 1845, diary; Park, January 3 and 6, 1842, diary; he refers to the *Globe*, published in Washington, D.C.; Sarah I. McClellan Webb, September 1 and 2, 1848, diary, MC-CHS; Zachariah Allen, October 2, 1858, diary, ZAP-RIHS; idem, *Philosophy of the Mechanics of Nature, and the Source and Modes of Action of Natural Motive Power* (New York: Appleton, 1852). Michael H. Harris, "'Books! Books! Books!!!': The Estate Auction as a Source of Books in Frontier Southern Indiana (1800–1850)," *Proof* 5 (1977): 15–26.

24. Harriet Hanson Robinson (with William Stevens Robinson), February 12, 1852, diaries, RSP-SL; Moses Adams III, retrospective of 1819, common place book, no. 2, c. 1835, BC. Joseph T. Buckingham, *Personal Memoirs and Recollections of Editorial Life*, 2 vols. (Boston: Ticknor, Reed, and Fields, 1852), 1:23; there were many versions of Joseph Addison's tragedy available; on its cultural importance, see Julie K. Ellison,

Cato's Tears and the Making of Anglo-American Emotion (Chicago: University of Chicago Press, 1999).

25. Frederick Lathrop Gleason, February 16, 1859, journal, CHS.

26. For a Vermont music teacher who sold books as a sideline—thirty-six in a single winter—see Don Avery Winslow, January 1, 1861, diary and account book, AAS. J.D.B. DeBow, *Seventh Census of the United States: 1850* (Washington, D.C.: Robert Armstrong, 1853), lxviii; Ronald J. Zboray and Mary Saracino Zboray, "The Boston Book Trades, 1789–1850: A Statistical and Geographical Analysis," in *Entrepreneurs: The Boston Business Community, 1700–1850*, ed. Conrad Edick Wright and Katheryn P. Viens (Boston: Massachusetts Historical Society, 1997), 238, table 17; J. Reynolds Hixon, December 11 and 28, 1838, diary, OCHS; U.S. Bureau of the Census, 1850 Census, Population Schedules for Massachusetts, in *Family Archive CD #307 Census Microfilm Records: Massachusetts, 1850, From the National Archives* (Novato, Calif.: Brøderbund, 1998), disk 2, Hampden County, section 2, Census Microfilm Roll 319, p. 33.

27. Armsby, April 18, and March 3, 1853, diary, AAS; William Hoyt, August 7, 1851, journal, BPL; see also August 9, 1851. On a successful book dealer, see Wyman W. Parker, "Henry Stevens Sweeps the States," *PBSA* 52 (1958): 249–61.

28. In Boston in 1832, for example, only the dry-goods industry and the metal trades accounted for higher percentages of overall capitalization; Zboray and Zboray, "Boston Book Trades," 216, table 1.

29. Even primers offered guides to the factories; Jacob Abbott, *The Harper Establishment; or, How the Story Books are Made* (New York: Harpers, 1855). For a later adult "tour," see A.H. Guernsey, "Making the Magazine," *HNMM* 32 (1865): 1–31. Abraham Joseph Warner, February 19, 1851, diary, CHS.

30. Pierce to Lucy (Tappan) Pierce and John Pierce, December 15, 1843, PoFP-SL.

31. Augustus Dodge Rogers, December 28, 1849, RFP-PEM; Park, December 11, 1850, diary; Cyrus Parker Bradley, March 28, 1835, school journal, NHHS. On interior scenes in antebellum bookstores (as opposed to only their business aspects): Wallace J. Bonk, *Michigan's First Bookstore: A Study of the Books Sold in the Detroit Book Store, 1817–1828* (Ann Arbor: University of Michigan Press, 1957); David Marshall Stewart, "William T. Berry and His Fabulous Bookstore," *Tennessee Historical Quarterly* 37 (1978): 36–48; and Zboray, *A Fictive People*, chap. 10, on the organization of stock. The Old Corner Bookstore in Boston generated several antiquarian accounts, but the best scholarly view remains Warren S. Tryon, *Parnassus Corner: A Life of James T. Fields, Publisher to the Victorians* (Boston: Houghton Mifflin, 1963). See also Madeleine B. Stern, "Elizabeth Peabody's Foreign Library," *American Transcendental Quarterly* 20 (1973): 5–12. Lucy (Pierce) Hedge to Mary Pierce Poor, November 30, 1847, PoFP-SL; Samuel May, Jr. to John Bishop Estlin, December 19, 1845, BPL; Park, March 21, 1840, diary; John Wesley Hanson to Harriet Jane Hanson, 1846, RSP-SL; Samuel May, Jr. to John Bishop Estlin, September 5, 1848, BPL.

32. Mary Mudge, February 2, 1854, high school common-place book, SL; Gibson, April 9, 1857, pocket diary, NHHS; William Allen Butler, *Nothing to Wear: An Episode in City Life* (New York: Rudd and Carleton, 1857) was reprinted in several periodicals. Gleason, November 29, 1859, journal; Edward G. Parker, *Reminiscences of Rufus Choate, The Great American Advocate* (New York: Mason Brothers, 1860). Sarah Edes, October 16, 1852, diary, AAS.

33. Chamberlain, August 19, 1843, diary and commonplace book; November 16, 1847, journal, BPL; Rogers, December 22, 1846; November 22 and 29, 1849; April 12, 1847; and January 22, 1850, diary, RFP-PEM; Chamberlain, January 9, 1847, journal.

34. Rogers, March 23, 1847, diary. Benjamin Peirce, "Notice of the Computations of Mr. Sears Walker," *Proceedings of the American Academy of Sciences* 1 (1846–48): 57–68; Dirk J. Struik, *Yankee Science in the Making* (1948; reprint Boston: Little, Brown, 1962), 415–17. Rogers, December 1, 1849, diary. On the range of people noting the Parkman-Webster story, see Ronald J. Zboray and Mary Saracino Zboray, "'Shocking News!': A Historical Ethnography of Early Nineteenth-Century Newspaper Readers' Ritual Response to Tragedy," paper delivered at the Cultural Studies Association Convention, Pittsburgh, June 7, 2003, 8–10; Simon Schama, *Dead Certainties (Unwarranted Speculations)* (New York: Alfred A. Knopf, 1991), pt. 2. Dahlia [i.e., Margaret Fuller], "Chat in Boston Bookstores," *Boston Quarterly Review* 3 (1840): 323–31.

35. Bradley, May 25, 1835, diary, NHHS; H.M. Brackenridge, *History of the Late War, between the United States and Great Britain* (Baltimore: Joseph Cushing, 1817); Mason Locke Weems, *A History, of the Life and Death, Virtues and Exploits of General George Washington …* (Georgetown, D.C.: printed for the author, 1800).

36. Agnes F. Herreshoff, February 12, 1841, diary, HLFP-RIHS; Bradley, December 1, 1833, school journal; Anna Loring to Ellis Gray Loring, May 13, [1851], EGLFP-SL.

37. Katherine Bigelow Lawrence, Jr. October 10, 1851, and October 11, 1849, journal, transcript, LFP-MHS; she probably refers to Henry Stevens, the American bibliographer in Europe; Wyman W. Parker, *Henry Stevens of Vermont: American Rare Book Dealer in London, 1845–1886* (Amsterdam: N. Israel, 1963). William Willis, February 16, 1859, diary, microfilm, PPL, original in MeHS; Adolf Growoll, "Charles B. Norton," *Publishers' Weekly,* February 7, 1891, 262–63.

38. On the Atheneum, a social library that contained many rare imports, see William Willis, *The History of Portland, from 1632 to 1864 …,* 2d ed. (1831; reprint Portland: Bailey and Noyes, 1865), 748–49. Baker, June 12, 1832, diary, NHHS; Arnold, July 29, 1852, journal; Sibley, February 11, 1841, diary, MeHS.

39. Asa Hinckley, September 16, 1833, diary, CHS; Mellen Chamberlain, February 17, 1848, journal; Ellen Wright to Martha Coffin Wright, October 1860, GP-SSC. Samuel May Jr. to John Bishop Estlin, September 30, 1847, BPL. Charlotte Henrietta Pettibone, March 25, 1842, diary, CHS. Annie Bigelow Lawrence, June 7, 1843, diary, LFP-MHS. Park, August 1, 1848, diary; Olive Gay Worcester, September 7, 1838, journal, SFP-SL; on the purity of the Worcester air, see Annie Bigelow Lawrence, June 7, 1843, diary; Amos A. Lawrence, September 23, 1842, diary, AALDAB-MHS. On great libraries, see Walter Muir Whitehill, *Boston Public Library: A Centennial History* (Cambridge, Mass.: Harvard University Press, 1956); Theophilus Parsons, *The Influence and History of the Boston Athenaeum from 1807 to 1907* (Boston: Boston Athenaeum, 1907); Phyllis Dain, *The New York Public Library: A History of Its Founding and Early Years* (New York: New York Public Library, 1972); Jane Lancaster, *Inquire Within: A Social History of the Providence Athenaeum since 1753* (Providence: Providence Athenaeum, 2003); and James Conaway, *America's Library: The Story of the Library of Congress, 1800–2000* (New Haven, Conn.: Yale University Press, 2000).

40. Park, November 3, 1847, diary. K. Lawrence, June 24, 1850, journal; Frances Berdan and Patricia Rieff Anawalt, eds., *The Essential Codex Mendoza* (Berkeley and Los Angeles: University of California Press, 1997). A. Lawrence, September 23, 1842, diary; Pettibone, March 25, 1842, diary. Bradley, December 1, 1833, school journal; Louis Leonard Tucker, *The Massachusetts Historical Society: A Bicentennial History, 1791–1991* (Boston: Massachusetts Historical Society, 1995), 43–44, 104.

41. Carroll Norcross, March 3, 1852, diary, CKNFP-MeHS. Henry Wyles Cushman, September 3, 1835, every day book, HWCC-NEHGS; Annie Bigelow Lawrence [Rotch], April 6, 1841, diary; George H. Carleton, diary, 1842, BPL, in *The Lowell Almanac, and Pocket Memorandum, for 1842* (Lowell: A. Upton, 1842).

42. Gleason, April 19, 1860, diary; Dain, *New York Public Library*, 3–10. Jotham Powers Bigelow, February 14 and 15, 1860, pocket diary, JPBP-AAS; in 1857 the local Young Men's Literary Association and the Springfield Institute had combined into the City Library Association, which sought subscriptions to help fund a free library in the City Hall. Springfield Library, "History of the Library and Museums," http://www.springfieldlibrary.org/history.html, (accessed April 23, 2004).

43. Norcross, March 18, 1852, diary; Sibley, June 24, 1849, diary; Bradley, June 11, 1835, diary.

44. Ronald J. Zboray and Mary Saracino Zboray, "Home Libraries and the Institutionalization of Everyday Practices among Antebellum New Englanders," *AS* 42 (2001): 63–86.

45. John E. Bennett, "New England Influences in California," *NEM* 23 (1898): 688–708, and "Hon. Horace Davis," *OM* 29 (1897): 670. Sewall, expenses, December 15, 1825, diary, AAS. The Providence Athenaeum librarian's pay was only fifty dollars a year in the early 1830s; Lancaster, *Inquire Within*, 40, but see also 51–52 and 84. Mellen Chamberlain, February 20, 1847, journal, BPL.

46. Studies of the late-nineteenth-century emergence of librarianship in the United States abound, although often the period under consideration here is considered the dark ages before professionalization. Consequently, antebellum coverage is scanty beyond that found in Zboray and Zboray, "Home Libraries," and two classics, Sidney Herbert Ditzion's *Arsenals of a Democratic Culture: A Social History of the American Public Library Movement in New England and the Middle States from 1850 to 1900* (Chicago: American Library Association, 1947) and Jesse Hauk Shera's *Foundations of the Public Library: The Origins of the Public Library Movement in New England, 1692–1855* (Chicago: University of Chicago Press, 1949).

47. Chamberlain, n.d. January, and October 5, 1846, diary. George B. Chase, *Tribute to Mellen Chamberlain* … (Boston: Massachusetts Historical Society, 1900); Henry W. Haynes, *Memoir of Mellen Chamberlain* (Cambridge, Mass.: John Wilson and Son, 1906). Harvard Law School, History of Harvard Law School Library, http://www.lawlharvard.edu/library/about/history/special_history.php (accessed October 20, 2004).

48. Alfred Chandler Potter, *The Library of Harvard University: Descriptive and Historical Notes*, 4th ed. (Cambridge, Mass.: Harvard Univeristy Press, 1934), 159. Chamberlain, January 6 and 7, 1847, diary; Harvard Law School Library, *A Catalogue of the Law Library of Harvard University* …, 4th ed. (Cambridge, Mass.: Metcalf, 1846). Cyrus Parker Bradley, November 17, 1835, diary, NHHS; Robert Burton, *The Anatomy of Melancholy* (1621); U.S. Department of the Interior, Bureau of Education, *Public Libraries in the United States of America, Their History, Condition, and Management, Special Report*, pt. 1 (Washington, D.C.: Government Printing Office, 1876), 98–99; John King Lord, *A History of Dartmouth College, 1815–1909*, vol. 2 (Concord, N.H.: Rumford Press, 1913), 529. Sewall, January 7 and February 2, 1832, diary. Works on classification or their designers, include Charles Coffin Jewett, *The Age of Jewett: Charles Coffin Jewett and American Librarianship, 1841–1868*, ed. Michael H. Harris (Littleton, Colo.: Libraries Unlimited, 1975); Leo LaMontagne, *American Library Classification* … (Hamden, Conn.: Shoe String, 1961); and Zboray, *A Fictive People*, appendix 2.

49. Chamberlain, January 11 and 13, 1847, January 3, 1848, January 16, April 22, June 5, 15, and 19, February 16, 1847, journal.

50. Chamberlain, January 20 and 21, 1847, diary. Cabot to Ellen Twisleton, May 13 and 19, 1860, CFP-SL; Rotch, July 6, 1839, diary, LFP-MHS.

51. Chamberlain, February 1, 1847, journal; "X," "Miseries of a Librarian," *New England Galaxy*, September 17, 1824. 1. A range of smaller institutions or business enterprises similar to those of this wry observer have been treated in David Kaser, *A Book for a Sixpence: The Circulating Library in America* (Pittsburgh: Beta Phi Mu, 1980); Thomas Augst, "The Business of Reading in Nineteenth-Century America," *AQ* 50 (1998):

267–305; William D. Boyd, "Books for Young Businessmen: Mercantile Libraries, 1800–1865" (Ph.D. diss., Indiana University, 1975); and Sidney Ditzion, "Mechanics and Mercantile Libraries," *LQ* 10 (1940): 547–77 and Robert A. Gross, "Much Instruction from Little Reading: Books and Libraries in Thoreau's Concord," *PAAS* 97, pt. 1 (1987): 129–88.

52. James Whittier, August 22, 1830, diary, AAS; Park to Louisa Park Hall, January 22, 1846, transcript in Park, February 5, 1846, diary. Henry Albers, ed., *Maria Mitchell: A Life in Journals and Letters* (Clinton Corners, N.Y.: College Avenue Press, 2001); Phebe Mitchell Kendall, comp., *Maria Mitchell: Life, Letters, and Journals* (Boston: Lee and Shepard, 1896), 10–11.

53. Daniel E. Sutherland, *Americans and Their Servants: Domestic Service in the United States from 1800 to 1920* (Baton Rouge: Louisiana State University Press, 1981), 47–48; Faye E. Dudden, *Serving Women: Household Service in Nineteenth-Century America* (Middletown, Conn.: Wesleyan University Press, 1983), 4–5, 18, 23. Zboray and Zboray, "Home Libraries"; Howard W. Winger, *American Library History: 1876–1976* (Urbana: University of Illinois Graduate School of Library Science, 1976); Sidney L. Jackson, Eleanor B. Herling, and E.J. Josey, eds., *A Century of Service: Librarianship in the United States and Canada* (Chicago: American Library Association, 1976); Wayne A. Wiegand, *The Politics of an Emerging Profession: The American Library Association, 1876–1917* (New York: Greenwood, 1986).

54. Lawrence Cremin, *American Education: The National Experience, 1783–1876* (New York: Harper and Row, 1979), 182, table 2; Carl Kaestle, *Pillars of the Republic: Common Schools and American Society, 1780–1860* (New York: Hill and Wang, 1983), 124–35. On teacher training efforts, see Jurgen Herbst, *And Sadly Teach: Teacher Education and Professionalization in American Culture* (Madison: University of Wisconsin Press, 1989), chap. 3. On the importance of training student listening skills in relationship to reading, see Mitford M. Mathews, *Teaching to Read: Historically Considered* (Chicago: University of Chicago Press, 1966), 70.

55. Sibley, October 23, 1841, diary. Men might be paid more for the task, but often were not; see Almon Benson, January 5, 1837, memoranda. More specific institutional studies include Donald H. Parkerson and Jo Ann Parkerson, *The Emergence of the Common School in the U.S. Countryside* (Lewiston, N.Y.: E. Mellen, 1998); Lee Soltow and Edward Stevens, *The Rise of Literacy and the Common School in the United States: A Socioeconomic Analysis to 1870* (Chicago: University of Chicago Press, 1981). The school attendance average is from Carl F. Kaestle and Maris A. Vinovskis, eds., *Education and Social Change in Nineteenth-Century Massachusetts* (Cambridge: Cambridge University Press, 1980), 39. On even lower attendance of groups other than white native males, see Cremin, *American Education*, 397.

56. Norcross, December 2, 1851, diary; Sibley, February 16, 1841, diary; Forten, September 18, 1857, *JCFG*, 257; Frank C. Morse, January 4, 1855 and January 14, 1856, FCMP-MHS. Caroline Barrett White, May 15, 1849, diary; Sibley, February 16, 1841, diary, AAS.

57. Frances Merritt, October 8, 1857, diary, FMQP-SL; Martha Osborne Barrett, February 16, 1849, diary, PEM; Susan Johnson, April 3, 1841, journal, LxHS; Caroline Barrett White, October 7, 1850, diary; for a reading exercise involving a hymn book, see Barrett, October 20, 1848, diary; Johnson, March 1 and 27, and June 2, 1841, journal; Leigh Hunt, "The Negro Boy," in *Juvenalia; or, A Collection of Poems* (London: J. Whiting, 1803), 53–54; Merritt, June 27, 1854, diary; Hugh Miller, *The Two Records: The Mosaic and the Geological* ... (Boston: Gould and Lincoln, 1854); Clarissa Harrington, November 14, 1840, daily journal, LxHS. Johnson, June 4, 1842, journal; Ebenezer Porter, *Rhetorical Reader*, 116th ed. (New York: Dayton and Saxton, 1842). Instructional readers contained texts of secular litterateurs, Cremin, *American Education*, 392; Jean Ferguson Carr, Stephen L. Carr, and Lucille M. Schultz, *Archives*

of Instruction: Rhetorics, Readers, and Composition Books in the Nineteenth-Century United States (Lincoln: University of Nebraska Press, forthcoming).

58. Johnson, June 10, 1841, journal; Frances M. Jocelyn, March 1, 1839, diary.

59. Mudge, April 21, 1854, common-place book; Walter Aimwell, *Clinton; or, Boy-life in the Country* (Boston: Gould and Lincoln, 1853).

60. Helen M. Warner, October 22, 1851, Diary, NEHGS.

61. Zboray and Zboray, "Reading and Everyday Life," 285–323; idem, *Everyday Ideas*, chap. 10.

62. Lawrence W. Levine, *Highbrow/Lowbrow: The Emergence of Cultural Hierarchy in America* (Cambridge, Mass.: Harvard University Press, 1988); "Editor's Easy Chair," *HNMM* 30 (1865): 395. Francis Bennett, February 1, 1854, diary, AAS; John Park, November 7, 1839, diary; Almon Benson, October 27, 1836, memoranda, NHHS; Stephen Salisbury III, November 15, 1854, diary, SFP-AAS.

63. Gerald Kahan, "Fanny Kemble Reads Shakespeare: Her First American Tour, 1849–50," *Theatre Survey* 24 (1983): 77–98. The most widely performed Uncle Tom adaptation was George L. Aiken, *Uncle Tom's Cabin; or, Life Among the Lowly: A Domestic Drama in Six Acts* (New York: S. French, 1852); Daniel Terry, *Guy Mannering; or, The Gipsy's Prophecy; A Musical Play in Three Acts …* (New York: Samuel French, c. 1849); Albert Smith and Tom Taylor, *Cinderella* (London: Lyceum Theatre, 1845). S.E. Hodges to Katharine Craddoc Hodges, March 15, 1860, HFP-SL; William Brougham, *Lalla Rookh; or, The Princess, the Peri, and the Troubadour* (New York: S. French, c. 1857). Walter J. Meserve, *Heralds of Promise: The Drama of the American People During the Age of Jackson, 1829–1849* (New York: Greenwood, 1986); Bruce A. McConachie, *Melodramatic Formations: American Theatre and Society, 1820–1870* (Iowa City: University of Iowa Press, 1992). Richard Butsch, *The Making of American Audiences: From Stage to Television, 1750–1990* (Cambridge: Cambridge University Press, 2000), chap. 5.

64. Rufus Marble Gay to Olive Gay Worcester, January 4, 1849, SFP-SL; Charles F. Low, August 12, 1857, diary, BPL. Elisha Kent Kane, *The U.S. Grinnell Expedition in Search of Sir John Franklin: A Personal Narrative* (New York: Harper and Brothers, 1853). Daniel F. Child and Mary D. Child, October 2, 1849, diary, DFCP-MHS; John Skirving, *Skirving's Panorama of Fremont's Overland Journey to Oregon and California …* (Boston: private printing, 1849).

65. Mary Ann Laughton, March 13, February 7, 1838 and "Expenses of 1839" in diary, PEM; Mary Crowninshield Mifflin, July 15, 1842, diary, BPL. Howard M. Wach, "Expansive Intellect and Moral Agency: Public Culture in Antebellum Boston," *PMHS* 107 (1995): 30–56; Struik, *Yankee Science in the Making*, chap. 6.

66. On other itinerants beyond panorama men and lecturers, see Peter Benes, "Itinerant Entertainers in New England and New York, 1687–1830," in Benes, ed., *Itinerancy*, 112–30.

67. Arnold, May 26, 1847, journal; Edward Cushman Bodman to Luther Bodman Jr. and Philena (Hawks) Bodman, July 8, 1854, BFP-SSC; Mary Pierce to John Pierce and Lucy (Tappan) Pierce, entry for May 9 in May 3, 1838, PoFP-SL; Charles M. Cobb, February 23, 1853, journal, transcript, VHS.

68. L.E. Emerson, September 1855, diary, MeHS; the script is described as "The Property of Dr. L.E. Emerson, Proprietor of the Grand Moving Mirror of CALIFORNIA[;]or— *California as it was & as it is!!*, Printed by those eminent Artists, T[homas] H. Badger & Fred[erick Thomas] Somerby of Boston[,] Mass[.,] Present Co. Emerson & Griffin[,] Lewiston Falls, Maine[,] May 1855." Panoramas are best understood in an international context; studies of them include Richard D. Altick, *The Shows of London* (Cambridge, Mass.: Belknap Press, 1978); Stephan Oettermann, *The Panorama: A History of a Mass Medium* (New York: Zone, 1997); Bernard Comment, *The Painted Panorama*

(New York: Harry N. Abrams, 2000), esp. 55–65. For another panorama that toured mid-nineteenth-century rural Maine, see Tom Hardiman, "The Panorama's Progress: The History of Kyle and Dallas's Moving Panorama of Pilgrim's Progress," in *The Grand Moving Panorama of Pilgrim's Progress*, exhibition catalog (Montclair, N.J.: Montclair Art Museum, 1999).

69. Emerson, October 22, 1855, diary. Julius Caesar Hannibal, *Black Diamonds; or, Humor, Satire, and Sentiment, Treated Scientifically in a Series of Burlesque Lectures, Darkly Colored* (New York: A. Ranney, 1855).

70. Garrison to Wendell Garrison, March 25, 1861, GP-SSC; "Lectures and Lecturers," *PM* 9 (1857): 317; Warren Burton to Henry Wyles Cushman, November 16, 1852, HWCC-NEHGS. On public lecturers and lyceum speakers, see Carl David Mead, *Yankee Eloquence in the Middle West: The Ohio Lyceum, 1850–1870* (East Lansing, Mich.: Michigan State College Press, 1951); Carl Bode, *The American Lyceum, Town Meeting of the Mind* (New York: Oxford University Press, 1956); Donald M. Scott, "The Popular Lecture and the Creation of a Public in Mid-Nineteenth-Century America," *JAH* 66 (1980): 791–809; and Mary Kupiec Cayton, "The Making of an American Prophet: Emerson, His Audiences, and the Rise of the Culture Industry in Nineteenth-Century America," *AHR* 92 (1987): 597–620. On the many varieties of lecturers and their venues, see Donald M. Scott, "Itinerant Lecturers and Lecturing in New England, 1800–1850," in Benes, ed., *Itinerancy*, 65–75. The prevalence of lecturing among amateur writers treated is noted in "Amateur Authors and Small Critics," *USDR* 17 (1856): 63.

71. Ellis Gray Loring to Anna Loring, December 22, 1851, EGLFP-SL; "Lectures and Lecturers," 319; Chamberlain, February 28, 1844, journal; Remond to "Mrs. Chapman," October 6, 1859, BPL; Eunice Hale Wait Cobb, diary, January 10, 1855, NEHGS.

72. Craft to Samuel May Jr., July 17, 1860, BPL; Remond to Samuel May Jr. July 21, 1859, BPL; "Lectures and Lecturers," 318–19; Willis, April 4, 1849, diary; Park, December 28, 1837, diary. Primary source material on black abolitionist lecturers can be found throughout *The Black Abolitionist Papers*, ed. C. Peter Ripley, 5 vols. (Chapel Hill: University of North Carolina Press, 1985–92).

73. "Lectures and Lecturers," 318–19; Ellery Sedgwick, "Magazines and the Profession of Authorship in the United States, 1840–1900," *PBSA* 94 (2000): 404–5.

74. Forten, July 28, 1854, *JCFG*, 91.

75. Ronald J. Zboray and Mary Saracino Zboray, "Books, Reading, and the World of Goods in Antebellum New England," *AQ* 48 (1996): 587–622.

76. Zboray and Zboray, *Everyday Ideas*, pt. 2.

77. Deep and widespread hegemonic penetration of printed literature and other cultural products occurred earlier in the United States than in other city-country literary systems of former British colonies. Raymond Williams, *The Country and the City* (New York: Oxford University Press, 1975); Gerald MacLean, Donna Landry, and Joseph P. Ward, eds., *The Country and the City Revisited: England and the Politics of Culture, 1550–1850* (New York: Cambridge University Press, 1999); Harold Adams Innis, *Empire and Communications* (Toronto: University of Toronto Press, 1972); Compare Lawrence Buell, "Melville and the Question of American Decolonization," *AL* 64 (1992): 215–37.

78. Zboray and Zboray, "Books, Reading," 604–6.

Conclusion

1. Ronald J. Zboray and Mary Saracino Zboray, "Cannonballs and Books: Reading and the Disruption of Social Ties on the New England Home Front," in *The War Was You and Me: Civilians in the American Civil War*, ed. Joan E. Cashin (Princeton, N.J.:

Princeton University Press, 2002), 237–61. On the war as a cultural and literary watershed, see Louis Menand, *The Metaphysical Club: A Story of Ideas in America* (New York: Farrar, Straus and Giroux, 2001), x, chap. 3, 73–77, 146–47.

2. Alan Trachtenberg, *The Incorporation of America: Culture and Society in the Gilded Age* (New York: Hill and Wang, 1982). Compare James L.W. West III, *American Authors and the Literary Marketplace since 1900* (Philadelphia: University of Pennsylvania Press, 1988), chap. 1.

3. *NEG,* 272–74 and chap. 12; Shirley Marchalonis, *The Worlds of Lucy Larcom, 1824–1893* (Athens: University of Georgia Press, 1989), 137, 145–57, 164, 177–78, 180–81, 204, 212–13, 223. For Larcom's poetical works, see *BAL* 5:303–5, 308, 310. *NEG,* 271–72.

4. Caroline Wells Healy Dall, *"Alongside," Being Notes Suggested by "A New England Boyhood" of Doctor Edward Everett Hale* … (Boston: Thomas Todd, 1900), 75; Sarah Deutsch, *Women and the City: Gender, Space, and Power in Boston, 1870–1940* (New York: Oxford University Press, 2000); Timothy P. Duffy, "The Gender of Letters: Charles Eliot Norton and the Decline of the Amateur Intellectual Tradition," *NEQ* 69 (1996): 91–109. *NEG,* 5, 8, 6, 29, 85, 179, 149, 150. Jessica Lewis, "'Poetry Experienced': Lucy Larcom's Poetic Dwelling in *A New England Girlhood," Legacy* 18 (2001): 190, notes a similar social value.

5. Marchalonis, *Worlds,* 251–52, 241; on the first print run, see *BAL,* 5:312. Edward Everett Hale, *A New England Boyhood* (Boston: Little, Brown, 1893); Dall, *"Alongside"*; William E. Bridges, "Warm Hearth, Cold World: Social Perspectives on the Household Poets," *AQ* 21 (1969): 776–77.

6. Brenda Stevenson, introduction to *JCFG,* 36–37, 48, 593 n. 72. William Wells Brown, "Charlotte L. Forten," in *The Black Man, His Antecedents, His Genius, and His Achievements* (New York: Thomas Hamilton / Boston: R.F. Wallcut, 1863), 190–99; Richard H. Brodhead, *Cultures of Letters: Scenes of Reading and Writing in Nineteenth-Century America* (Chicago: University of Chicago Press, 1993), chap. 3, and p. 79; Ellery Sedgwick, *The Atlantic Monthly, 1857–1909: Yankee Humanism at High Tide and Ebb* (Amherst: University of Massachusetts Press, 1994), 2. *MOS,* 250. John Greenleaf Whittier to James Thomas Fields, December 25, 1863, in *LJGW,* 3:55. Ellery Sedgwick, "Magazines and the Profession of Authorship in the United States, 1840–1900," *PBSA* 94 (2000): 399–425; Civil War inflation raised the former five-dollar going rate; higher status writers made more (404–5). *HAM,* 3:13. Forten may have received as much as ten percent in royalties on book sales. Postbellum royalties were not only the rule, but increasingly substantial. Donald Sheehan, *This Was Publishing: A Chronicle of the Book Trade in the Gilded Age* (Bloomington: Indiana University Press, 1952), 88, and on ongoing rates with *Harper's,* 90 and 94. Brenda Stevenson, chronology and introduction to *JCFG,* xxxviii, 49. Charlotte L. Forten, "Waiting for the Verdict," *NASS,* February 22, 1868. *Atlantic, Scribner's,* and *Harper's* paid ten dollars per 1,000 words around this time; see Sedgwick, "Magazines," 409–10. *HAM,* 3:14. Charlotte L. Forten, "A Visit to the Birthplace of Whittier" and "The Queen of the Bees," *SM* 4 (1872): 581–83, and 738–42; and, in the *Christian Register,* "The Flower Fairies' Reception," August 8, 1874; "Letter," June 20 and 27, 1876; "The Centennial Exposition," July 22, July 29, and August 5, 1876; Idem, "Mr. Savage's Sermon: 'The Problem of the Hour,'" *Commonwealth,* December 23, 1876; see Carla L. Peterson, "Reconstructing the Nation: Frances Harper, Charlotte Forten, and the Racial Politics of Periodical Publication," *PAAS* 107, pt. 2 (1998): 322, 329–32. Stevenson, introduction to *JCFG,* 50–51.

7. Stevenson could date most of Forten's manuscripts at HU, but evidently could not always determine their publication (introduction to *JCFG,* 53–54, 547 n. 147). Many of Forten's pieces are reproduced in Anna J. Cooper, ed., *The Life and Writings of*

Charlotte Forten Grimke (privately printed, 1951), 20–150. Katharine Rodier, "Charlotte L. Forten," *DLB*, vol. 239, *American Women Prose Writers, 1820–1870*, ed. Katharine Rodier and Amy E. Hudock (2001), 116–117, believes that many publications are undiscovered. Forten sent "One Phase of the Race Question" to Thomas Wentworth Higginson (December 14, 1885, *JCFG*, 519). See also Stevenson, *JCFG*, 607 n. 8. Forten's husband recalled her "Reminiscences of the South" was published in the *New York Independent*. The manuscript on "Colored People in New England," was sent to the *Evangelist* in October 1889; see Rodier, "Charlotte L. Forten," 115–16. Stevenson dates "At the Home of Frederick Douglass" around the 1890s in her chronology for *JCFG*, xxxix, 607 n.11. The article appears in Anna J. Cooper, *Life and Writings*, 56–61. An example of "author peeps" is *Little Journeys to the Homes of American Authors*, ed. Elbert Hubbard (New York: G.P. Putnam's Sons, 1896); Charlotte Forten Grimke, "Personal Recollections of Whittier," *NEM* 14 (1893): 468–76.

8. *MOS*, 226, 231–33; John Townsend Trowbridge, *Neighbor Jackwood: A Domestic Drama in Five Acts* (New York: S. French, 1857). *MOS*, 159, 318. John Townsend Trowbridge, "The Vagabonds," *AM* 11 (1863): 321–22; John Townsend Trowbridge, "Coupon Bonds," *AM* 16 (1865): 257–72, 399–411. John Townsend Trowbridge, *The South: A Tour of Its Battlefields and Ruined Cities ...* (Hartford, Conn.: Stebbins, 1866). *MOS*, 255, 269–70, quote on 316.

9. Marchalonis, *Worlds*, 182, 188–89; *MOS*, 327. John Townsend Trowbridge, *Jack Hazard and His Fortunes* (Boston: Osgood, 1871); idem, *A Chance for Himself, or Jack Hazard and His Treasure* (Boston: Osgood, 1872). David E.E. Sloane, "John Townsend Trowbridge," *DLB*, vol. 202, *Nineteenth-Century American Fiction Writers*, ed. Kent P. Ljungquist (1999), 271–78. Michael R. Little, "Trowbridge, John Townsend," *American National Biography*, ed. John A. Garraty and Mark C. Carnes, 24 vols. (New York: Oxford University Press, 1999), 21: 849–51.

10. Michel Foucault, "What Is an Author?" in *Language, Counter-Memory, Practice: Selected Essays and Interviews*, ed. Donald F. Bouchard, trans. Donald F. Bouchard and Sherry Simon (Ithaca, N.Y.: Cornell University Press, 1977), 113–38, 124. For a similar point about obscurity, see Joan R. Sherman, introduction to *Invisible Poets: Afro-Americans of the Nineteenth Century*, 2d ed. (Urbana: University of Illinois Press, 1989), xv–xvi; Elizabeth McHenry, *Forgotten Readers: Recovering the Lost History of African-American Literary Societies* (Durham, N.C.: Duke University Press, 2002), 194–95. Katherine Davis Tillman, "Afro-American Poets and Their Verse," *AMECR* 14 (1898): 426.

11. Rodier, "Charlotte L. Forten," 113–14; "Charlotte L(ottie) Forten Grimke," *Contemporary Authors* (Detroit, Mich.: Gale, 2001). Stevenson, introduction to *JCFG*, 41. On the placement of "One Phase," see December 14, 1885, *JCFG*, 519. On the literary club mentioned here, see Dorothy Sterling, ed., *We Are Your Sisters: Black Women in the Nineteenth Century* (New York: W.W. Norton, 1984), 430–31. S. Elizabeth Frazier, "Some Afro-American Women of Mark," *AMECR* 8 (1892): 382.

12. *MOS*, 234–42. Jonathan D. Sarna, *Jacksonian Jew: The Two Worlds of Mordecai Noah* (New York: Holmes and Meier, 1981), 51.

13. Marchalonis, *Worlds*, 166–67, 163; Rita K. Gollins, *Annie Adams Fields: Woman of Letters* (Amherst: University of Massachusetts Press, 2002), chap. 9.

14. Sedgwick, "Magazines," 399–425; Marchalonis, *Worlds*, 49, 253, 196, 214, 256. Robert J. Griffin, "Anonymity and Authorship," *NLH* 30 (1999): 877–95. The *Atlantic Monthly* issued names in the index. Charles A. Johanningsmeier, *Fiction and the American Literary Marketplace: The Role of Newspaper Syndicates, 1860–1900* (Cambridge: Cambridge University Press, 1997), esp. chap. 4. *MOS*, 456, mentions a

"Western lecturing tour." Larcom lectured before schools and women's groups, at Fields's behest; see Marchalonis, *Worlds*, 214. *HAM*, 4:16.

15. Hale's major writings are covered in John R. Adams, *Edward Everett Hale* (Boston: Twayne, 1977). Linda S. Bergmann, "Widows, Hacks, and Biographers: The Voice of Professionalism in Elizabeth Agassiz's *Louis Agassiz: His Life and Correspondence*," *A/B: Autobiography Studies* 12 (1997): 1–21; Nina Baym, *American Women of Letters and the Nineteenth-Century Sciences: Styles of Affiliation* (New Brunswick, N.J.: Rutgers University Press, 2002), chap. 6. Louisa Jane Park Hall's postbellum publications include *Sonnets, Stanzas and a Crescendo Composition* (London: Remington, 1884); *My Body to My Soul* (Providence: privately printed, n.d.); *Verses* (Cambridge, Mass.: privately printed, 1892); and *Bessie Burton, The Little Cripple* (London: Society for Promoting Christian Knowledge, n.d.).

16. Because many informants who became authors after 1861 were better discussed in chapters 3 and 4, we do not limit the names to those who appeared in chapter 1. Curtis's postbellum works include *The Love of a Lifetime* (Boston: Cupples, Upham, 1884); *From Madge to Margaret* (Boston: Lee and Shepard / New York: C.T. Dillingham, 1880). Lamb, "Formative Influences," *Forum* 11 (1891): 50–58; her writings range from *History of the City of New York: Its Origin, Rise, and Progress* (New York: A.S. Barnes, c. 1870s) to *Spicy: A Novel* (New York: D. Appleton, 1873).

17. We searched for these authors' works online in *Poole's Plus: A Digital Index of the Nineteeenth Century*, the two *Making of America* sites at Cornell University and the University of Michigan, and OCLC's *WorldCat*. Osmon C. Baker, *The Last Witness; or, The Dying Sayings of Eminent Christians and of Noted Infidels* (1853; reprint New York: Phillips and Hunt / Cincinnati: Walden and Stowe, 1870); idem, *A Guide-Book in the Administration of the Discipline of the Methodist Episcopal Church* (1855; reprint New York: Phillips and Hunt, 1884); idem, *Manly Elements in the Ministry: A Discourse Delivered to the Graduating Class of the Methodist General Biblical Institute* ... (Boston: J.P. Magee, 1867). Sarah Cary Becker with Federico Mora, *Spanish Idioms with Their English Equivalents Embracing Nearly Ten Thousand Phrases* (Boston: Ginn, c. 1886). Sylvanus Cobb, *Autobiography of the First Forty-One Years of the Life of Sylvanus Cobb, D.D.* (Boston: Universalist Publishing House, 1867). Samuel Gardner Drake with Samuel G. Bishop, *Eulogium on the Death of George Washington* (Roxbury, Mass.: W. Elliot Woodward, 1866). Amos A. Lawrence, *Settlement of Utah; Report of a Committee* (Boston: n.p., 1886). William C. Nell, *Farewell to the Liberator* (Boston: privately printed, 1863). Harriet H. Robinson, *Loom and Spindle; or, Life Among the Early Mill Girls* (New York: T.Y. Crowell, 1898). The output of Stephen Salisbury includes "Notes on Mitla" (coauthored with others), *PAAS* 2 (1883): 82–100, his *A Memorial of Stephen Salisbury of Worcester, Mass.* (Worcester, Mass.: n.p., 1885); and several short pieces on U.S. history and ancient Central American civilizations.

18. Elizabeth H. Jocelyn [Cleaveland], *In Memoriam: Mrs. Eliza Shipman Brown, Obiit. [sic] July 8th, 1866* (New Hartford: privately printed, 1866); idem, *No Sects in Heaven* (New York: Clark, Austin, Maynard, 1861).

19. Mary Weld [*sic*] Pierce Poor, *Recollections of Brookline* (Brookline, Mass.: Brookline Historical Society, 1903). Henry Varnum Poor launched a successful journal and published several related short pieces, including *Influence of the Railroads of the United States in the Creation of Its Commerce and Wealth* (New York: Journeymen Printers' Co-operative Association, 1869).

20. James Augustine Healy, *Why Have I a Religion?* (n.p.: privately printed, 1887); idem, *Pastoral Letter* (Portland, Me.: Diocese of Portland, 1876); idem, *An Address to the Catholics of Maine on the Occasion of the Centennial Inauguration of George Washington as First President of the United States* (Portland, Maine: privately printed, 1889).

21. Some of his works are "Samuel Maverick's Palisade House of 1630" (*PMHS*, January 1885, reprint Cambridge, Mass.: J. Wilson, 1885); *John Adams, The Statesman of the American Revolution with Other Essays and Addresses, Historical and Literary* (Boston: Houghton, Mifflin, 1899), 476; *Landscape in Life and In Poetry* (Concord, N.H.: Republican Press Association, 1886); *Josiah Quincy, the Great Mayor ...* (Boston: Massachusetts Society for Promoting Good Citizenship, 1889); *The Constitutional Relations of the American Colonies to the English Government at the Commencement of the American Revolution ...* (New York: Knickerbocker Press, 1888).

22. The debate continues about whether Dickinson could not or would not publish. Most recent scholarship avers that she did not want her poems in print; see Jerome J. McGann, "Composition as Explanation (of Modern and Postmodern Poetries)," in *Cultural Artifacts and the Production of Meaning: The Page, the Image, and the Body*, ed. Margaret J.M. Ezell and Katherine O'Brien O'Keeffe (Ann Arbor: University of Michigan Press, 1994), 101–38; Elizabeth A. Petrino, *Emily Dickinson and Her Contemporaries: Women's Verse in America, 1820–1885* (Hanover, N.H.: University Press of New England, 1998); Marietta Messmer, *A Vice for Voices: Reading Emily Dickinson's Correspondence* (Amherst: University of Massachusetts Press, 2001), 184–89; Domhnall Mitchell, *Emily Dickinson: Monarch of Perception* (Amherst: University of Massachusetts Press, 2000); Ellen Louise Hart and Martha Nell Smith, *Open Me Carefully: Emily Dickinson's Intimate Letters to Susan Huntington Dickinson* (Ashfield, Mass.: Paris Press, 1998); Martha Nell Smith, *Rowing in Eden: Rereading Emily Dickinson* (Austin: University of Texas Press, 1992); Karen Dandurand, "Dickinson and the Public," in *Dickinson and Audience*, ed. Martin Orzeck and Robert Weisbuch (Ann Arbor: University of Michigan Press, 1996), 273. Alfred Habegger, *My Wars are Laid Away in Books: The Life of Emily Dickinson* (New York: Random House, 2001). A similar view of Dickinson as defiant is propounded by Jeanne Holland, "Scraps, Stamps, and Cutouts: Emily Dickinson's Domestic Technologies of Publication," in Ezell and O'Keeffe, eds., *Cultural Artifacts*, 139–81, quote on 141. Diana Fuss notes Dickinson's "sense of the theatrical" in "Interior Chambers: The Emily Dickinson Homestead," *differences* 10 (1998): 1–46, quote on 21. On her anticommercial stance, see William G. Rowland Jr., *Literature and the Marketplace: Romantic Writers and Their Audiences in Great Britain and the United States* (Lincoln: University of Nebraska Press, 1996), 179.

23. Hart and Smith, *Open Me Carefully*, xxvii. Messmer, *Vice for Voices*; Holland, "Scraps, Stamps," 139–81. Karen Dandurand, "Another Dickinson Poem Published in Her Lifetime," *AL* 54 (1982): 434–37, effectively argues that Bowles would have wanted to publish more of Dickinson's poems after 1858; on Higginson, see David Higgins, *Portrait of Emily Dickinson: The Poet and Her Prose* (New Brunswick, N.J.: Rutgers University Press, 1967), 130–36. Smith, *Rowing in Eden*, 213. Hart and Smith, *Open Me Carefully*, 226.

24. "Fixity" is described by Elizabeth Eisenstein in her *Printing Press as an Agent of Change*, vol. 1, *Communications and Cultural Transformations in Early-Modern Europe* (Cambridge: Cambridge University Press, 1979), 113–26. Hart and Smith, *Open Me Carefully*, xxiii. For examples of literary gifts, see *LED*, 2:373 (no. 232) and 2:628 (no. 575). Smith, *Rowing in Eden*, 52; Holland, "Scraps, Stamps," 149–50. On enclosures, see *LED*, 2:334 (no. 188, violet); 2:338 (no. 192, rosebud); 2:451 (no. 316, clipping); 2:492–93 (no. 369, recipe); 2:569 (no. 480, flower); on gift notes or gift note-poems, 2:429 (no. 287) and 2:485 (no. 358); see also Hart and Smith, *Open Me Carefully*, 176; and on ribbon, 82 and 87; on pencil, see Higgins, *Portrait of Emily Dickinson*, 118. Thomas H. Johnson, "Establishing a Text: The Emily Dickinson Papers," *SB* 5 (1952–53): 30. For a shopping list, see Hart and Smith, *Open Me Carefully*, 176. Ralph W. Franklin, ed., *The Manuscript Books of Emily Dickinson*, 2 vols.

(Cambridge, Mass.: Harvard University Press, 1981). Messmer, *Vice for Voices*, 20, observes, "She not only *adopts* a wide range of fictional personae, she also *speaks* in and through a multiplicity of 'borrowed' or appropriated voices that enter her texts primarily in the form of quotations." Dickinson quotes "from her own and other texts as well as other discursive gestures such as newspaper clippings or flowers." Holland, "Stamps, Scraps," 140–41. Marta L. Werner, *Emily Dickinson's Open Folios: Scenes of Reading, Surfaces of Writing* (Ann Arbor: University of Michigan Press, 1995), 292. Dorothy Huff Oberhaus, *Emily Dickinson's Fascicles: Method and Meaning* (University Park: Pennsylvania State University Press, 1995).

25. Habegger, *My Wars*, 232–38, 246 n. 1. *Indicator* 2 (February 1850): 223–24; Emily Dickinson, "'Sic transit gloria mundi,'" titled "A Valentine," *Springfield Daily Republican*, February 20, 1852; see Dandurand, "Dickinson and the Public," 273. Emily Dickinson, "Nobody Knows this Little Rose," titled "To Mrs____, with a Rose," *Springfield Daily Republican*, August 2, 1858. Habegger, *My Wars*, 389. On Dickinson's habit of sending flowers, see Petrino, *Emily Dickinson*, 143. Dandurand, "Another Dickinson Poem," 434–37. Zboray and Zboray, "Cannonballs and Books." Karen Dandurand, "New Dickinson Civil War Publications," *AL* 56 (1984): 17–27. Idem, "Dickinson and the Public," 274, 268–73; Brodhead, *Cultures of Letters*, 70. On her "public persona *as* a private poet," see Fuss, "Interior Chambers," 32.

26. On Thoreau as a "connected critic," see Richard F. Teichgraeber III, *Sublime Thoughts/Penny Wisdom: Situating Emerson and Thoreau in the American Market* (Baltimore: Johns Hopkins University Press, 1995), xi–xii, and *passim*. John C. Broderick, "Historical Introduction," in *HDTJ*, 1:602. On the *Dial*, see Robert D. Richardson Jr., *Henry Thoreau: A Life of the Mind* (Berkeley and Los Angeles: University of California Press, 1986), 131; Steven Fink, *Prophet in the Marketplace: Thoreau's Development as a Professional Writer* (Princeton, N.J.: Princeton University Press, 1992), 78–80, 95–8; *HAM*, 1:510. Charles R. Anderson, "Thoreau and The Dial: The Apprentice Years," in *Essays Mostly on Periodical Publishing in America: A Collection in Honor of Clarence Gohdes*, ed. James Woodress (Durham, N.C.: Duke University Press, 1973), 92–120. Quotes are H.D. Thoreau to Mrs. John Thoreau, August 29, 1843, H.D. Thoreau to Ralph Waldo Emerson, September 14, 1843, and H.D. Thoreau to Mrs. John Thoreau, October 1, 1843, *CHDT*, 135, 139, 141. Henry D. Thoreau, "The Landlord," *USDR* 13 (1843): 427–30; idem, "Paradise (to Be) Regained," *USDR* 13 (1843): 451–63. On pay, see *HAM*, 1:505. According to Fink, *Prophet*, 112, Thoreau was probably "paid no more than forty dollars for both essays." Thoreau claimed it "can only afford half or quarter pay"; see H.D. Thoreau to Mrs. John Thoreau, October 1, 1843. Thoreau was paid ten dollars for an essay in the January 1844 issue; see Fink, *Prophet*, 126, on the *Dial*, 128, and on continuing magazine placements, 138, 152–53, 157, 259, and 274. Another mid-1840s publication was a letter in the *Liberator*, March 28, 1845.

27. Richardson, *Henry Thoreau*, 7, 74–75, 80, 93; *CHDT*, 43, 73; Fink, *Prophet*, 136, 146–47, 242, 138, 152–57, 192–93, 202, and 259; Richardson, *Henry Thoreau*, 185, 195, 313.

28. Fink, *Prophet*, 64, 78–80, 259, 152; on agreement with Munroe, 199; on remaindered copies, 252; and on debt, 252. Ralph Waldo Emerson to H.D. Thoreau, July 20, 1843, *CHDT*, 126; Raymond Adams, "The Bibliographical History of Thoreau's *A Week on the Concord and Merrimack Rivers*," *PBSA* 43 (1949): 39–47. Fink, *Prophet*, 264–65. Richardson, *Henry Thoreau*, 5–6, 204, 228, 131. *CHDT*, 41, 73; Henry D. Thoreau to Isaiah T. Williams, September 8, 1841, and Henry D. Thoreau to Ralph Waldo Emerson, September 14, 1843, *CHDT*, 53, 139.

29. Richardson, *Henry Thoreau*, 13, 39, 74, 83; "Sic Vita," for Lucy Jackson Brown, is discussed in *CHDT*, 33; "letter-poem" transcribed from his journal and sent to Helen

Thoreau, May 23, 1843, in *CHDT*, 108; Richardson, *Henry Thoreau*, on verse, 39, 47, 48; on journals, 7, 134. Lawrence Rosenwald, *Emerson and the Art of the Diary* (New York: Oxford University Press, 1988), 24; Sharon Cameron, *Writing Nature: Henry Thoreau's Journal* (Chicago: University of Chicago Press, 1985); Perry Miller, *Consciousness in Concord; the Text of Thoreau's Hitherto "Lost Journal," 1840–1841* (Boston: Houghton Mifflin, 1958). On exchange, see Richardson, *Henry Thoreau*, 74; John C. Broderick, "General Introduction," in *HDTJ*, 1:579; quote from Rosenwald, *Emerson and the Art*, 77; on Mary Moody Emerson, see Richardson, *Henry Thoreau*, 252; on Alcott, Adams, "Bibliographical History," 41–42. On bookkeeping, see Teichgraeber, *Sublime Thoughts*, 60; Ronald J. Zboray, *A Fictive People: Antebellum Economic Development and the American Reading Public* (New York: Oxford University Press, 1993), 124. "Sic Vita" later appeared in the *Dial*. Henry D. Thoreau, June 21, 1840, "Copied from pencil," *HDTJ*, 1:134–38; *CHDT*, 31. Fink, *Prophet*, 155.

30. Robert D. Richardson Jr., *Emerson: The Mind on Fire* (Berkeley and Los Angeles: University of California Press, 1995), 7–11, 29, 176. John McAleer, *Ralph Waldo Emerson: Days of Encounter* (Boston: Little, Brown, 1984), 44–45, 47. Rosenwald, *Emerson and the Art*, xii, 24. McAleer, *Ralph Waldo Emerson*, 5, 33. Rosenwald, *Emerson and the Art*, 125, 77, 9; Barry A. Carlson, "Emerson, Friendship, and the Problem of Alcott's 'Psyche,'" in *Emersonian Circles: Essays in Honor of Joel Myerson*, ed. Wesley T. Mott and Robert R. Burkholder (Rochester, N.Y.: University of Rochester Press, 1997), 115–25, esp. 118. Phyllis Cole, *Mary Moody Emerson and the Origins of Transcendentalism: A Family History* (New York: Oxford University Press, 1998), 164; Rosenwald, *Emerson and the Art*, 35. McAleer, *Ralph Waldo Emerson*, 6. Richardson, *Emerson*, 558–59. Robert D. Richardson Jr., "Emerson as Editor," in Mott and Burkholder, *Emersonian Circles*, 105–13; Richardson, *Emerson*, 379. Cole, *Mary Moody Emerson*, 9–10, 167–70, 204; Richardson, *Emerson*, 23–25, 98, 121, 336. Idem, "Emerson as Editor," 107–110.

31. Quotes from Richardson, "Emerson as Editor," 112. McAleer, *Ralph Waldo Emerson*, 121; the sermon appears in Octavius Brooks Frothingham, *Transcendentalism in New England: A History* (New York: G.P. Putnam, 1876), 363–80. "Textual Introduction" to *The Complete Sermons of Ralph Waldo Emerson*, ed. Albert J. von Frank, 4 vols. (Columbia: University of Missouri Press, 1989), 1:33–34. Richardson, *Emerson*, 418–19, 257, 523. Peter Cherches, "Star Course: Popular Lectures and the Marketing of Celebrity in Nineteenth-Century America" (Ph.D. diss., New York University, 1997), 49–50, 58, 87; Donald M. Scott, "The Profession that Vanished: Public Lecturing in Mid-Nineteenth Century America," in *Professions and Professional Ideologies in America* (Chapel Hill: University of North Carolina Press, 1983), 12–28. Richardson, *Emerson*, 419.

32. Richardson, *Emerson*, 218, 316, 319, 445; idem, "Emerson as Editor," 106; Kenneth Marc Harris, *Carlyle and Emerson: Their Long Debate* (Cambridge, Mass.: Harvard University Press, 1978), 46 and passim; on Fuller, see Fink, *Prophet*, 211–212. Jones Very, *Essays and Poems* (Boston: C.C. Little and James Brown, 1839). Richardson, *Emerson*, 318; quote characterizing Emerson's editing from Richardson, "Emerson as Editor," 108. Carlson, "Emerson, Friendship," 115–25, 119–20. Sarah Margaret Fuller, *Summer on the Lakes in 1843* (Boston: C.C. Little and James Brown / New York: C. S. Francis, 1844). Compare Emerson's opposite advice to Christopher Pearse Cranch discussed in Francis B. Dedmond, "'Croaking at Booksellers': An Unpublished Emerson Letter," *AL* 49 (1977): 415–17. Emerson was cash conscious, of course, as his meticulous account books attest, and indeed this itself would lead him to see the profitability of lecturing over book publication; Joel Myerson, "Ralph Waldo Emerson's Income from His Books," *The Professions of Authorship: Essays in Honor of Matthew J. Bruccoli*, ed. Richard Layman and Joel Myerson (Columbia: University of South Carolina Press, 1996), 135–49, 136.

33. Mary Kupiec Cayton, "The Making of an American Prophet: Emerson, His Audiences, and the Rise of the Culture Industry in Nineteenth-Century America," *AHR* 92 (1987): 597–620. Kenneth Cmiel, *Democratic Eloquence: The Fight over Popular Speech in Nineteenth-Century America* (New York: William Morrow, 1990).

34. Gregory Clark and S. Michael Halloran, eds., introduction to *Oratorical Culture in Nineteenth-Century America: Transformations in the Theory and Practice of Rhetoric* (Carbondale: Southern Illinois University Press, 1993).

35. On the canonization process, see Joseph M. Thomas, "Late Emerson: *Selected Poems* and the 'Emerson Factory,'" *ELH* 65 (1998): 971–94.

36. Alfred D. Chandler Jr., *The Visible Hand: The Managerial Revolution in American Business* (Cambridge, Mass.: Harvard University Press, 1977); Benjamin Klebaner, *American Commercial Banking: A History* (Boston: Twayne, 1990), 78–79; Richard S. Tedlow, *New and Improved: The Story of Mass Marketing in America* (1990; Boston: Harvard Business School Press, 1996), xvii–xxx. Timothy B. Spears, *100 Years on the Road: The Traveling Salesman in American Culture* (New Haven, Conn.: Yale University Press, 1995), chaps. 2–5.

37. *HPBUS*, 2:515–34, 106; Frank Elbert Compton, *Subscription Books* (New York: Typophiles, 1943); Marjorie Stafford, *Subscription Book Publishing in the United States, 1865–1930* (Urbana: University of Illinois Press, 1943); Ebenezer Hannaford, *Success in Canvassing: A Manual of Practical Hints and Instructions …* (San Francisco: Occidental, 1884); Michael Hackenberg, "Hawking Subscription Books in 1870: A Salesman's Prospectus from Western Pennsylvania," *PBSA* 78 (1984): 137–53. Alice Fahs, "The Market Value of Memory: Popular War Histories and the Northern Literary Marketplace, 1861–1868," *BH* 1 (1998): 107–39, and Amy M. Thomas, "'There Is Nothing So Effective as a Personal Canvass': Revaluing Nineteenth-Century American Subscription Books," *BH* 1 (1998): 140–55. Keith Arbour, "Book Canvassers, Mark Twain, and Hamlet's Ghost," *PBSA* 93 (1999): 5–37. Though Eliza Fenwick, *Facts, By a Woman* (Oakland: Pacific Press Publishing House, 1881), mixes fact and fiction, its detailed account of agency seems most realistic (see quotes on 38). Before publishers provided how-to guides to agents, they had to devise their own scripts: "I thought how I should best introduce myself and business, and framed a speech, but would forget it at second rehearsal," an antebellum female book agent wrote to a co-worker; "I studied an appearance by which I should … pleasingly solicit subscriptions for my books." Charlotte Hosmer to Jane Mendell, undated, in Jane Mendell and Charlotte Hosmer, *Notes of Travel and Life* (New York: Published for the Authors, 1854), 13.

38. *HBPUS*, 2:559–87; Sheehan, *This Was Publishing*, chaps. 2 and 7; Chandler, *Visible Hand*, 324–26.

39. *HBPUS*, 2:111–12; Susan Porter Benson, *Counter Cultures: Saleswomen, Managers, and Customers in American Department Stores* (Urbana: University of Illinois Press, 1988), chap. 1; Lydia Cushman Schurman, "Those Famous American Periodicals: The Bible, the *Odyssey* and *Paradise Lost*; or, The Great Second-Class Mail Swindle," *Publishing History* 40 (1996): 33–52; Richard B. Kielbowicz, "Mere Merchandise or Vessels of Culture?: Books in the Mail, 1792–1942," *PBSA* 82 (1988): 169–200; Richard Ohmann, *Selling Culture: Magazines, Markets, and Class at the Turn of the Century* (London: Verso, 1996), 94–106.

40. Sidney A. Sherman, "Advertising in the United States," *Publications of the American Statistical Association* 7 (1900): 1–44, esp. 27–28; *HAM*, 3:8; Johanningsmeier, *Fiction*, 20.

41. Charles Francis Horner, *The Life of James Redpath and the Development of the Modern Lyceum* (New York: Barse and Hopkins, 1926); Robert A. McCown, "Records of the Redpath Chautauqua," *Books at Iowa* 19 (1973): 8–16, 18–19; John E. Tapia, *Circuit Chautauqua: From Rural Education to Popular Entertainment in Early Twentieth*

Century America (Jefferson, N.C.: McFarland, 1997), 14–19; Joseph E. Gould, *The Chautauqua Movement: An Episode in the Continuing American Revolution* (Albany: State University of New York Press, 1972), chap. 1. Olive Logan, *The Mimic World, and Public Exhibitions: Their History, Their Morals, and Effects* (Philadelphia: New World, 1871), 454–55.

42. On privatism, see Lyn H. Lofland, *The Public Realm: Exploring the City's Quintessential Social Territory* (Hawthorne, N.Y.: Aldine de Gruyter, 1998), chap. 6, but compare Karen V. Hansen, *A Very Social Time: Crafting Community in Antebellum New England* (Berkeley and Los Angeles: University of California Press, 1995).

43. Manufactured Valentines with preprinted verses inside appeared after 1866; Frank Staff, *The Valentine and Its Origins* (New York: Praeger, 1969), 92–98, 112; American Christmas cards emerged even later; George Buday, *The History of the Christmas Card* (London: Rockliff, 1954), 52, 76–80.

44. Molly McCarthy, "A Pocketful of Days: Pocket Diaries and Daily Record Keeping among Nineteenth-Century New England Women," *NEQ* 73 (2000): 274–96. On "nonliterary" diaries, see P.A.M. Taylor, "Routines of Upper-Class Life in Boston, 1887–1919: Two Women Diarists," *PMHS* 108 (1996): 123–52. Marilyn Ferris Motz, "Folk Expression of Time and Place: Nineteenth-Century Midwestern Rural Diaries," *Journal of American Folklore* 100 (1987): 131–47.

45. Claude S. Fischer, *America Calling: A Social History of the Telephone to 1940* (Berkeley and Los Angeles: University of California Press, 1992), 182–88, traces the change from written to telephoned invitations. Norvin Green, "Are Telegraph Rates Too High?" *NAR* 149 (1889): 571. Though predominantly business-oriented, telegrams increasingly substituted for commonfolk's urgent life-and-death letters. On marriage by telegraph, see Carolyn Marvin, *When Old Technologies Were New: Thinking About Electric Communication in the Late Nineteenth Century* (New York: Oxford University Press, 1988); Mark Twain, "Loves of Alonzo Fitz Clarence and Rosannah Ethelton," *AM* 41 (1878): 320–30. "Letter-Writing not a Lost Art," *Century* 55 (1897): 314, discerned a "new epistolary standard"—of "a strict adherence to topics of personal knowledge addressed to a personal interest"—replacing an earlier taste for more general, news-filled, and literary letters.

46. James Davie Butler, *Commonplace Books: Why and How Kept …* (Hartford, Conn.: Barnard's Journal of Education, 1887), 11. Steven M. Gelber, *Hobbies: Leisure and the Culture of Work in America* (New York: Columbia University Press, 1999), 59–192. On the emergence of photography albums and stamp collecting, see idem, "Free Market Metaphor: The Historical Dynamics of Stamp Collecting," *Comparative Studies in Society and History* 34 (1992): 742–69; Zboray and Zboray, "Cannonballs and Books," 245–46; Alan Trachtenberg, *Reading American Photographs: Images as History, Mathew Brady to Walker Evans* (New York: Hill and Wang, 1989), 82–89. George A. Jackson, "The Future of New England," *NEM* 9 (1891): 671, felt compelled to remind readers that albums were not exclusively for photographs, but had once been farmgirls' literary products and, eventually, family heirlooms.

47. Ellen Gruber Garvey, *The Adman in the Parlor: Magazines and the Gendering of Consumer Culture, 1880s to 1910* (New York: Oxford University Press, 1996), chap. 1. Dawn M. Schmitz, "The Humble Handmaid of Commerce: Chromolithographic Advertising and the Development of Consumer Culture, 1876–1900" (Ph.D. diss., University of Pittsburgh, 2004).

48. On reading aloud, see Ronald J. Zboray and Mary Saracino Zboray, "Reading and Everyday Life in Antebellum Boston: The Diary of Daniel F. and Mary D. Child," *Libraries and Culture* 32 (1997): 285–323. On scholarly reading preferably being silent, see Charles Dudley Warner, "The Novel and the Common School," *AM* 65 (1890): 728. On reading passages aloud, see "East and West," *OM* 1 (1883): 325. The

first American bedtime story books (as designated in their titles) appeared only in 1858–1859 when John D. Felter's three-volume *Stories for Bedtime* were published by the Massachusetts Sabbath School Society in Boston; Louise Chandler Moulton's successful *Bed-Time Stories* (Boston: Roberts Brothers, 1873) set the standard. On bedtime-story practice, see "Books for Young People," *AM* 47 (1881): 124. Mabel Gardiner Bell, "The Subtle Art of Speech-Reading," *AM* 75 (1895), 171, suggests that reading took place in sickrooms, despite enjoinders against it in Florence Nightingale's *Notes on Nursing: What It Is, and What It Is Not* (New York: Appleton, 1860), 44–58.

49. On schools and albums, see Oliver Wendell Holmes, "One Hundred Days in Europe," *AM* 59 (1887): 541. On albums featuring only signatures, see Alice L. Bates, "Autograph Albums of the 1860s," *Manuscripts* 50 (1998): 269–79; Alexander P. Clark, "'Princeton Memories with a Golden Sheen': Student Autograph Albums of the Nineteenth Century," *Princeton University Library Chronicle* 47 (1986): 301–16. Now rare album verses became very short and of dubious originality because they may have been cribbed from verse writers like *Seven Hundred Album Verses* (New York: J.S. Ogilvie, 1884); the book was offered "as an aid to many thousands who ... have not known what to write" in albums; "New Publications," *Manufacturer and Builder* 16 (1884): 215.

50. Compare, for example, Ronald J. Zboray and Mary Saracino Zboray, "Home Libraries and the Institutionalization of Everyday Practices Among Antebellum New Englanders," *American Studies* 42 (2001): 63–86, with Rosemary Ruhig Du Mont, *Reform and Reaction: The Big City Public Library in American Life* (Westport, Conn.: Greenwood, 1977). For studies of small town practices, see Christine Pawley, *Reading on the Middle Border: The Culture of Print in Late Nineteenth-Century Osage, Iowa* (Amherst, Mass.: University of Massachusetts Press, 2001); Deanna B. Marcum, *Good Books in a Country Home: The Public Library as Cultural Force in Hagerstown, Maryland, 1878–1920* (Westport, Conn.: Greenwood, 1994).

51. *HAM*, 4:1–75. News content nationalized largely due to the rise of news agencies, like the Associated Press, which took advantage of the emerging telegraph system; Menahem Blondheim, *News Over the Wires: The Telegraph and the Flow of Public Information in America, 1844–1897* (Cambridge, Mass.: Harvard University Press, 1994), 96–188; Richard A. Schwarzlose, *The Nation's Newsbrokers*, 2 vols. (Evanston, Ill.: Northwestern University Press, 1990), vol. 1. For the bigger picture of changing professional standards, see Hazel Dicken-Garcia, *Journalistic Standards in Nineteenth-Century America* (Madison: University of Wisconsin Press, 1989), 51–62, 89–96. Janice Hume, *Obituaries in American Culture* (Jackson: University Press of Mississippi, 2000).

52. Wayne C. Booth, *For the Love of It: Amateuring and Its Rivals* (Chicago: University of Chicago Press, 1999). The turn-of-the-century decline of these societies is traced in Kolan Thomas Morelock, "Literary Societies, Dramatic Clubs, and Community Culture: A Study of Lexington Intellectual Life During the Gilded Age and Progressive Era" (Ph.D. diss., University of Kentucky, 1999), 7; Thomas S. Harding, *College Literary Societies: Their Contribution to Higher Education in the United States, 1815–1876* (New York: Pageant Press International, 1971), 318. The rise of passive nonliterary commercial amusements and sport spectatorship coincided with the literary lapse and helps explains it, but so do amateur athletics, particularly on college campuses. On passive appreciation, see Lafcadio Hearn, "Note upon the Abuse and Use of Literary Societies," in *Life and Literature*, ed. idem (New York: Dodd, Mead, 1917), 69–76, esp. 74.

53. Daniel H. Borus, *Writing Realism: Howells, James, and Norris in the Mass Market* (Chapel Hill: University of North Carolina Press, 1989), chap. 5. On the different nature of amateur production and reception, see Naomi Lebowitz, *The Philosophy of*

Literary Amateurism (Columbia: University of Missouri Press, 1994), chaps. 1 and 5. Molly Abel Travis, *Reading Cultures: The Construction of Readers in the Twentieth Century* (Carbondale: Southern Illinois University Press, 1998), chap. 1.

54. Much reading advice followed a passive emotionally centered transmission model; see, for example, "Teaching the Spirit of Literature," *AM* 78 (1896): 414, 418. Compare Cheryl Fallon Giuliano, "The Writing Connection: Composing the Learner's Classroom," *Pedagogy* 1 (2001): 387–98, esp. 389.

55. Classic scenes of mock professionalization can be found in chapters 2 and 10 of Louisa May Alcott, *Little Women; or, Meg, Jo, Beth, and Amy* (Boston: Roberts Brothers, 1869). On newspaper syndicates, see Johanningsmeier, *Fiction*; Elmo Scott Watson, *A History of Newspaper Syndicates in the United States, 1865–1935* (Chicago: Watson, 1936), esp. chaps. 1–6. Robert Grants, "The Art of Living, VI, The Use of Time," *SM* 17 (1895): 763, situates the book habitué among "the amateur photographer . . . [and] observer of birds."

56. The need for preselection troubled the course of private-associational book clubs; see Grants, "The Art of Living," 762. K.M. Bishop, "The Ideal Club," *OM* 2 (1883): 632–36; Julia C.R. Dorr, "Culture in a New England Village," *CIMM* 26 (1883): 155–56; "Village Society in Winter," *SM* 15 (1877): 276. More formal clubs are treated in Adolf Growoll, *American Book Clubs: Their Beginnings and History, and a Bibliography of Their Publications* (New York: Dodd, Mead, 1897). For an example of a book-club selection advice manual, see Augusta Harriet (Garrigue) Leypoldt, *List of Books for Girls and Women and Their Clubs* (Boston: American Library Association Publishing Section, 1895).

57. Emily Jenkins, "Trilby: Fads, Photographers, and 'Over-Perfect Feet,'" *BH* 1 (1998): 221–67, esp. 247–50. Matthew Schneirov, *The Dream of a New Social Order: Popular Magazines in America, 1893–1914* (New York: Columbia University Press, 1994), 75–102, assigns mass market magazines an instrumental role in hegemonic construction. On ritual versus transmission in media consumption, see James W. Carey, *Communication as Culture: Essays on Media and Society* (Boston: Unwin Hyman, 1989), 13–36; Pierre Bourdieu, *Distinction: A Social Critique of the Judgement of Taste*, trans. Richard Nice (Cambridge, Mass.: Harvard University Press, 1984). On buying books because they are bestsellers, see Laura J. Miller, "The Best-Seller List as Marketing Tool and Historical Fiction," *BH* 3 (2000): 286–304.

58. Neil Harris, *Humbug: The Art of P.T. Barnum* (Chicago: University of Chicago Press, 1973), 59–89. Regarding ride-style literary properties, see the discussions on shop window design and L. Frank Baum's writing in William R. Leach, *Land of Desire: Merchants, Power, and the Rise of a New American Culture* (New York: Pantheon, 1993).

59. On late nineteenth-century reader resistance, see Barbara Sicherman, "Sense and Sensibility: A Case Study of Women's Reading in Late-Victorian America," in *Reading in America: Literature and Social History*, ed. Cathy N. Davidson (Baltimore: Johns Hopkins University Press, 1989), 201–25.

60. Similarly, domestic goods were then used for identity construction; Regina Lee Blaszczyk, *Imagining Consumers: Design and Innovation from Wedgwood to Corning* (Baltimore: Johns Hopkins University Press, 2000), 355.

61. Patricia Lehan Gregory, "Women's Experience of Reading in St. Louis Book Clubs" (Ph.D. diss., Saint Louis University, 2001); Martha Baker Dunn, "A Plea for the Shiftless Reader," *AM* 85 (1900): 131.

62. Chandler, *Visible Hand*; Philip Scranton, *Endless Novelty: Specialty Production and American Industrialization, 1865–1925* (Princeton, N.J.: Princeton University Press, 1997); Susan Strasser, *Satisfaction Guaranteed: The Making of the American Mass Market* (Washington, D.C.: Smithsonian Institution Press, 1995).

63. John Tebbel, *HBPUS*, 2:12, points out that "while publishing had accounted for 1 percent of American manufacturing wealth in 1850, it constituted less than .25 percent in 1914." The increasing involvement of publishing (and authorship) in big-business issues can be discerned in Walter Benn Michaels, *The Gold Standard and the Logic of Naturalism: American Literature at the Turn of the Century* (Berkeley and Los Angeles: University of California Press, 1987).

64. Chandler, *Visible Hand*, 75–78, discusses the mergers; Tebbel, *HBPUS*, 2:10–12, argues against the idea that publishers in the period were captains of industry on par with monopolists, a point which is seconded in Sheehan, *This Was Publishing*, chap. 1.

65. On the rise of scientifically inflected, expert-oriented literature, see Martha Banta, *Taylored Lives: Narrative Productions in the Age of Taylor, Veblen, and Ford* (Chicago: University of Chicago Press, 1993).

66. Robert A. Stebbins, *Amateurs, Professionals, and Serious Leisure* (Montreal: McGill-Queen's University Press, 1992), 8–9; idem, *Amateurs: On the Margin Between Work and Leisure* (Beverly Hills, Calif.: Sage, 1979). On the defeminization attendant upon professionalization, see Duffy, "Gender of Letters." As the new professional context of authorship—which had been, in Gramscian terms, only emergent in the antebellum years—later became dominant, amateurism and coterie writing was "largely incorporated" into the new hegemonic order rather than residually expressing historically contingent countermarket social authorship dating from the early modern period; Antonio Gramsci, *Selections from the Prison Notebooks of Antonio Gramsci*, ed. and trans. Quintin Hoare and Geoffrey Nowell-Smith (New York: International, 1971). Raymond Williams, *Marxism and Literature* (Oxford: Oxford University Press, 1977), chap. 8, distinguishes between the residual in "alternative or even oppositional relation to the dominant culture," from that "wholly or largely incorporated into it" (122). In this scheme, it would be wrong to consider, say, Metaphysical Club members as social authors, for their parapublishing literary activities were circumscribed by authorial professionalization; Menand, *Metaphysical Club*, chap. 9.

67. Truman J. Spencer, *The History of Amateur Journalism* (New York: Fossils, 1957), 8–138; Elizabeth Harris, *The Boy and His Press: An Exhibition in the Hall of Graphic Arts, National Museum of American History, Smithsonian Institution, 1992* (Washington, D.C.: Smithsonian Institution, 1992); Ralph Babcock, ed., *Your Thoughts: The Story of Amateur Journalism* (New York: Fossils, 1983); Franklyn Curtiss-Wedge, *Amateur Journalism: The Prince of Hobbies* (n.p.: A.E. Wills and F. Curtiss-Wedge, 1903).

68. Thomas Campbell-Copeland, *The Ladder of Journalism; How to Climb It* (New York: Forman, 1889); *Hints to Young Editors* (New Haven, Conn.: Charles C. Chatfield, 1872). A.F. Hill, *Secrets of the Sanctum: An Inside View of an Editor's Life* (Philadelphia: Claxton, Remsen, and Haffelfinger, 1875). De Forest O'Dell, *The History of Journalism Education in the United States* (New York: Teachers' College, Columbia University, 1935), 19; William H. Freeman, *The Press Club of Chicago; A History with Sketches of other Prominent Press Clubs of the United States* (Chicago: Press Club of Chicago, 1894); Elizabeth V. Burt, "A Bid for Legitimacy: The Woman's Press Club Movement, 1881–1900," *Journalism History* 23 (1997): 72–85; O'Dell, *History of Journalism Education*, 1–53; Katherine H. Adams, *A History of Professional Writing Instruction in American Colleges: Years of Acceptance, Growth, and Doubt* (Dallas: Southern Methodist University Press, 1993), 99–122; Whitlaw Reid, "Schools of Journalism," *SM* 4 (1872): 194–205.

69. Andrew Levy, *The Culture and Commerce of the American Short Story* (Cambridge: Cambridge University Press, 1993), chap. 4; Ronald Weber, *Hired Pens: Professional Writers in America's Golden Age of Print* (Athens: Ohio University Press, 1997), chap. 9; D.G. Meyers, "The Rise of Creative Writing," *Journal of the History of Ideas* 54

(1993): 277–97; idem, *The Elephants Teach: Creative Writing since 1880* (Englewood Cliffs, N.J.: Prentice-Hall, 1996); compare Adams, *History*, 71. Joseph F. Kett, *The Pursuit of Knowledge under Difficulties: From Self Improvement to Adult Education in America, 1750–1990* (Stanford, Calif.: Stanford University Press, 1994), 144–46. Stephen Wilbers, *The Iowa Writers' Workshop: Origins, Emergence and Growth* (Iowa City: University of Iowa Press, 1980), 19–31. Anne Ruggles Gere, *Intimate Practices: Literacy and Cultural Work in U.S. Women's Clubs, 1880–1920* (Urbana: University of Illinois Press, 1997).

70. Michael H. Harris, "Charles Coffin Jewett and American Librarianship," in *The Age of Jewett: Charles Coffin Jewett and American Librarianship, 1841–1868*, ed. idem (Littleton, Colo.: Libraries Unlimited, 1975), 43; Zboray and Zboray, "Home Libraries," 81–82; Charles D. Churchwell, *The Shaping of American Library Education*, ACRL Publications in Librarianship, no. 36 (Chicago: American Library Association, 1975), 2; Dee Garrison, "Women in Librarianship," in *A Century of Service: Librarianship in the United States and Canada*, ed. Sidney L. Jackson, Eleanor B. Herling, and E.J. Josey, eds. (Chicago: American Library Association, 1976), 146–68. Wayne A. Wiegand, *The Politics of an Emerging Profession: The American Library Association, 1876–1917* (Westport, Conn.: Greenwood, 1986). On social control, see Dee Garrison, *Apostles of Culture: The Public Librarian and American Society, 1876–1920* (New York: Free Press, 1979).

71. For an example of a publisher-initiated club, see John Dougall, Witness Office, "Sabbath Reading," *American Missionary* 33 (1879): 63. WorldCat contains nearly one hundred amateur theatrical book titles published between 1865 and 1900, among them, Orville Augustus Roorbach, *A Practical Guide to Private Theatricals* ... (New York: Roorbach, 1881). One charity event was advertised in *Amateur Theatricals, at Ives' Hall, January 7th, 1891, For the Benefit of the South Church Music Fund* (Hartford, Conn.: A.W. Lang, 1891), CHS. On newsboys, see David Nasaw, *Children of the City: At Work and at Play* (New York: Oxford University Press, 1985), 62–87.

72. James D. Hart, *The Popular Book: A History of America's Literary Taste* (New York: Oxford University Press, 1950), 187–97; Borus, *Writing Realism*, chaps. 3 and 5. Olga Antsyferova, "Three Interviews of Henry James: Mastering the Language of Publicity," *HJR* 22 (2001): 81–92. Christopher P. Wilson, *The Labor of Words: Literary Professionalism in the Progressive Era* (Athens: University of Georgia Press, 1985), 79; Susan Coultrap-McQuin, *Doing Literary Business: American Women Writers in the Nineteenth Century* (Chapel Hill: University of North Carolina Press, 1990), 195–99. Examples of writer introductions can be found in *The Bookman: A Literary Journal* 1 (1895): 13, 85, 93, 229, 246, 303, 306–7; see also "Gossip about Authors" in *Book Chat* 3 (1888): 355; and "Authors and Books," *The Book Buyer*, new ser., 5 (1888): 57, 60, 63, 67. Henry F. May, *The End of American Innocence: A Study of the First Years of Our Own Time, 1912–1917* (1959; reprint New York: Columbia University Press, 1992), 193–216. Although Thoreau and some other antebellum writers may seem like this notorious turn-of-the-century group, David S. Reynolds, *Beneath the American Renaissance: The Subversive Imagination in the Age of Emerson and Melville* (New York: Knopf, 1988), 6, wisely reminds us that "the interpretation of the major writers as isolated subversives reifies the existing canon." One would hardly class a "connected critic" like Thoreau (Teichgraeber, *Sublime Thoughts*, xi) with these later writers who used the contemporary celebrity machinery to carve out a market niche.

73. U.S. Census Office, *Twelfth Census of the United States*, vol. 13, *Occupations*, comp. William Chamberlain Hunt (Washington, D.C.: Government Printing Office, 1904), xxxiv, table 3. *HBPUS*, 2:8–9; Michael Denning, *Mechanic Accents: Dime Novels and Working-Class Culture in America* (London: Verso, 1987), chap. 2. On hacks, see John T. Dizer, "Authors Who Wrote Dime Novels and Series Books, 1890–1914," in *Pioneers, Passionate Ladies, and Private Eyes: Dime Novels, Series Books, and*

Paperbacks, ed. Larry E. Sullivan and Lydia Cushman Schurman (New York: Haworth, 1995), 73–85. Depending upon whether they freelanced, most journalists would be classed among hacks or workmen (workwomen, too, of course), but a rare few could attain celebrity status; Brooke Kroeger, *Nellie Bly, Daredevil, Reporter, Feminist* (New York: Times Books, 1994).

74. Robert B. Westbrook, *John Dewey and American Democracy* (Ithaca, N.Y.: Cornell University Press, 1991); Wilson, *Labor*; James Phillip Danky and Wayne A. Wiegand, eds., *Print Culture in a Diverse America* (Urbana: University of Illinois Press, 1998); Jean Pfaelzer, *Parlor Radical: Rebecca Harding Davis and the Origins of Social Realism* (Pittsburgh: University of Pittsburgh Press, 1996), esp. 224–28.

75. Barbara Hochman, "Disappearing Authors and Resentful Readers in Late Nineteenth-Century American Fiction: The Case of Henry James," *ELH* 63 (1996): 177–201. Scholars hailing the rise of professionalization include Borus, *Writing Realism*, 28–29; West, *American Authors*, 9–10; Rowland, *Literature and the Marketplace*, 32–33; Wilson, *Labor*, 1–16; and throughout William Charvat, *The Profession of Authorship in America, 1800–1870* (Columbus: Ohio State University Press, 1968) and idem, *Literary Publishing in America, 1790–1850* (1959; reprint Amherst: University of Massachusetts Press, 1993). Heath Pearson, "*Homo Economicus* Goes Native, 1859–1945: The Rise and Fall of Primitive Economics," *History of Political Economy* 32 (2000): 933–89. Critiques of market immanence include R.J. Holton, *The Transition from Feudalism to Capitalism* (Basingstoke, England: Macmillan, 1985), pt. 1; and Maurice Godelier, *Rationality and Irrationality in Economics* (New York: Monthly Review Press, 1972), xv. Pierre Bourdieu, "Neo-Liberalism: The Utopia (Becoming a Reality) of Unlimited Exploitation," in *Acts of Resistance: Against the Tyranny of the Market*, trans. Richard Nice (New York: New Press, 1998), 94–105. On reconceiving amateurism positively, see Booth, *For the Love of It*.

76. The use of reification here and below lies between the relatively narrow one of Georg Lukács, *History and Class Consciousness: Studies in Marxist Dialectics* (London: Merlin, 1971), 83, and the expansive one in Herbert Marcuse, "The Affirmative Character of Culture," in *Negations: Essays in Critical Theory* (Boston: Beacon, 1968), 116. Against orthodox economism's rigid deductions of consciousness from base, see Raymond Williams, "Base and Superstructure in Marxist Cultural Theory," in *Contemporary Literary Criticism: Literary and Cultural Studies*, ed. Robert Con Davis and Ronald Schleifer, 4th. ed. (New York: Longman, 1998), 490–501.

77. *Doughfaced* refers to Northern politicians with Southern principles; John Russell Bartlett, *Dictionary of Americanisms* ... (New York: Bartlett and Welford, 1848), 397–98. On Ticknor and Fields's regional marketing strategies, see Zboray, *A Fictive People*, 58–59, 65, 67.

78. Recent scholars have pushed back American literary realism by several decades—see, for example, David E. Shi, *Facing Facts: Realism in American Thought and Culture, 1850–1920* (New York: Oxford University Press, 1995)—so that it is not surprising that Trowbridge advocated it in the 1850s. See also Nancy Glazener, *Reading for Realism: The History of a U.S. Literary Institution, 1850–1910* (Durham, N.C.: Duke University Press, 1997).

79. Lawrence Buell, "American Civil War Poetry and the Meaning of Literary Commodification: Whitman, Melville, and Others," in *Reciprocal Influences: Literary Production, Distribution, and Consumption in America*, ed. Steven Fink and Susan S. Williams (Columbus, Ohio: Ohio State University Press, 1999).

80. Da Zheng, *Moral Economy and American Realistic Novels* (New York: Peter Lang, 1996); Brodhead, *Cultures of Letters*, chaps. 5–7; Judith Fetterley and Marjorie Pryse, *Writing Out of Place: Regionalism, Women, and American Literary Culture* (Urbana: University of Illinois Press, 2002).

81. Jürgen Habermas discusses the colonization of the lifeworld throughout *The Theory of Communicative Action*, 2 vols., trans. Thomas McCarthy (Boston: Beacon, 1984, 1987).

82. Kimberly K. Smith, "Mere Nostalgia: Notes on a Progressive Paratheory," *Rhetoric and Public Affairs* 3 (2000): 505–27, argues that nostalgia emerged as a response to industrial massification. Michael G. Kammen, *Mystic Chords of Memory: The Transformation of Tradition in American Culture* (New York: Knopf, 1991), 146–62 and chap. 7.

83. Paul Gilroy, *The Black Atlantic: Modernity and Double Consciousness* (Cambridge, Mass.: Harvard University Press, 1993). Francis A. Walker, "Restriction of Immigration," *AM* 77 (June 1896): 822–29. On the role of that year's presidential election in pushing the magazine rightward, see Sedgwick, *Atlantic Monthly*, 258.

84. The notion of "friction," of course is from Henry James via Michael Anesko, *"Friction with the Market": Henry James and the Profession of Authorship* (New York: Oxford University Press, 1986). On periods of socially conscious writing resurgence, see, for example, May, *End of American Innocence*, pt. 3; Michael Denning, *The Cultural Front: The Laboring of American Culture in the Twentieth Century* (London: Verso, 1998).

85. On the concept and alternative realities of "desocialization" in the West, see Jean Baudrillard, *In the Shadow of the Silent Majorities*, trans. Paul Foss, John Johnston, and Paul Patton (New York: Semiotext[e], 1983), 65–91. On organic working-class intellectuals, see Gramsci, *Selections*, 5–27.

86. Michael Gilmore, *American Romanticism and the Marketplace* (Chicago: University of Chicago Press, 1985), 7. Both Reynolds, *Beneath the American Renaissance*, and Sheila Post-Lauria, *Correspondent Colorings: Melville in the Marketplace* (Amherst: University of Massachusetts Press, 1996), trace the productive relations between popular conventional literature and canonical figures. From 1851 until the Civil War, Herman Melville averaged a miserable $320 per year (including lecture fees); see Charvat, *Profession of Authorship*, 200. Charvat also points out that Emerson "did not have a national audience or national response until the second half of the century" (287). Myerson, "Emerson's Income," 137–38. On "Americanness" and canonization, see Lawrence J. Oliver, "Theodore Roosevelt, Brander Matthews, and the Campaign for Literary Americanism," *AQ* 41 (1989): 93–111; Eric Cheyfitz, "Matthiessen's American Renaissance: Circumscribing the Revolution," *AQ* 41 (1989): 341–61. On canonization in general, see John Guillory, *Cultural Capital: The Problem of Literary Canon Formation* (Chicago: University of Chicago Press, 1993).

87. Cole, *Mary Moody Emerson*; see also the role of Ellen Emerson and James Elliot Cabot discussed in Glen M. Johnson, "Emerson's Essay 'Immortality': The Problem of Authorship," *AL* 56 (1984): 313–30. Edward L. Widmer, *Young America: The Flowering of Democracy in New York City* (New York: Oxford University Press, 1999). Roland Barthes, "The Death of the Author," in *Image, Music, Text*, ed. and trans. Stephen Heath (New York: Hill, 1977). Perry Miller, "Emersonian Genius and the American Democracy," in *Nature's Nation* (Cambridge, Mass.: Belknap Press of Harvard University Press, 1967), 163–74, esp. 165–66; Rowland, *Literature and the Marketplace*, chap. 8. Of course, one of the first berrying criticisms was that of Ralph Waldo Emerson in his eulogy on Thoreau, where he noted that Thoreau, "instead of engineering for all America . . . was the captain of a huckleberry party"; Emerson, *Lectures and Biographical Sketches*, in *The Complete Works of Ralph Waldo Emerson*, ed. Edward E. Emerson, 12 vols. (Boston: Houghton Mifflin, 1903), 10:430. Ronald A. Bosco, "The Expanding Textual Circle of New England Transcendentalism," *Text* 11 (1998): 343–64. Martha Nell Smith, "Dickinson's Manuscripts," in *The Emily Dickinson*

Handbook, ed. Gudrun Grabher, Roland Hagenbüchle, and Cristanne Miller (Amherst: University of Massachusetts Press, 1998), 113–37; Messmer, *Vice for Voices,* esp. 1–26; Daria Donnelly, "The Power to Die: Emily Dickinson's Letters of Consolation," in *Epistolary Selves: Letters and Letter-Writers, 1600–1945,* ed. Rebecca Earle (Brookfield, Vt.: Ashgate, 1999), 134–51.

INDEX

A

Abenakis: biography of missionary to, 14; massacre, 19

Abercrombie, John, 24

Abolitionist, The (Concord, N.H.), 37

abolitionist publications: amateur writing in, 9, 34, 37; complex distribution records, 138; as African American venue, 45, 53

Adams, Moses III, xix, 1, 41, 141

Adder, The (Middletown, Ct.), 34, 35

Addison, Joseph, *Cato, A Tragedy,* 141

Adventures of Tom Sawyer (Twain), sold by subscription, 188

advertisements, 18, 189; aimed at amateur journalists, 195, and at mass market, 192; for amateur theatricals, 197; author advice about, 139; as evidence of distribution, 168; by job printers, 139; magazines financed by, 177; in newspapers, 22; for panorama performances, 163; prior sales as part of, 179; produced by hacks and workmen, 199; for self-published imprints, 9; as signaling publication, 31; and subscription publishing, 175. *See also* celebrity reception; puffery

African American authors: and cities, 246n17; coding of heaven for Northern freedom, 52; criticized for being proslavery, 34; lecturing on abolition, 113–14, 116, 165; and leisure-pleasure dyad, 246–47n18; limited venues for, 43,

53–54, 173–74; recent studies of benefit Forten, 176; Signifyin(g) of, 246n16; literary conventions of in Forten's writing, 245n5; and translations by, 7, 173.

African Americans: in book's informant base, xxvi; elite status of Forten's circles questioned, 54; patronage for black authors from, 44–45, 53–54, 176; as publishers, 44–45, 53–54; racist caricatures of, 34, 36, 91, 163

African Colonization Society, xxviii

African Methodist Episcopal Church; periodicals, 54

African Repository, 131, 132–34, 136, 137

Agassiz, Elizabeth Cary, 100, 178

Agassiz, Louis, 111, 178

agents. *See* book subscription canvassing; periodical subscription canvassing.

Aimwell, Walter, *Clinton,* 159

albums, 191, 282n46, 283n49. *See also* scrapbooks.

Alcott, Bronson, 183, 184; *Psyche,* 186

Alcott, Louisa May, *Little Women,* 284n55

Allen, William, *History of Norridgework* (Me.), 19

Allen, Zachariah: "Memorial of Roger Williams," 16; *Philosophy of the Mechanics of Nature,* 140

almanacs, xvii, 143, xvii. *See also* annuals; periodicals

amateur as derogatory, 200

amateur athletics and active popular literary engagement, 283n52

D

"Dark River, The" (E. Jocelyn), 13
Dartmouth College, 18–19, 148
David Copperfield (Dickens), child named
after character in, 123
Davidson, Cathy N., on authors being
anonymous or unpaid, 231n8
Davis, Horace, 151
Davis, Andrew Jackson, *Principles of
Nature*, 113
Davis, John: 15, 121
Day of Doom, The (Wigglesworth), xvii
"Death of the Author, The" (Barthes), 204
de Kroyft, Helen Aldrich, *A Place in Thy
Memory*, 112–13
Deserted Family (Trowbridge), 73
desocialization, 202–3
Dewar, Daniel, 24
Dewey, John, 199
DeWolfe, Thaddeus, 38
Dial, The: 181, 182, 185, 186
"Dial Flower, The" (Hemans), 158
diaries, xxv, 191
Dick, Thomas, 90
Dickens, Charles, 73, 198; *American Notes
for General Circulation*, 122; autograph
acquired, 121; Boston arrival causes
pandemonium, 118; *A Christmas Carol*,
97, 123; comic song about, 118, 119;
converses with fan, 120, 121; *David
Copperfield*, 123; dinner honoring
reported, 118; and English writers previously visiting, 120; fans dressed up like
fictional characters, 120; *Hard Times*,
123; leveled, xxix, 121–22; livestock
named in honor of, 119; meets Hale,
120; meets Park, 121; naming style of
characters imitated by Trowbridge, 74;
Nicholas Nickleby, 98, 120; *Oliver Twist*,
120; *Pictures from Italy*, 123; piracy of
works by, 124; private
dinner parties, 119; and social sense,
265n60; social sense in party conversation of, 120; social sense in readers' use
of works of, 123; toast noted, 118; tours
the U.S., 89, 117, 118; Shakespeare seen
as equal to for human insight, 98;
subscription sales of works, 188

Dickinson, Emily: as amateur writer, 181;
cash nexus seen as "Disgrace" to the
"Human Spirit," xi; and Civil War-era
transformation of authorship, 187; early
venues of, 181; and epistolary relationships with editors, 180; and fascicles,
180; and letter-poems, 179; market
response of, versus that of Emerson, 186;
multivocality via quoting in works of,
279n24; poems by read aloud, 180;
"Publication is the auction," xi, xiii, xxix,
13, 29, 129, 140, 167; reassessment of in
light of social sense, 203–4; as social
author, xxix, 170, 179–80
Dickinson, Susan Gilbert, 179–80
dictionaries, 17, 30–31, 241n57
*Discourse on the Life and Character of Rev.
Aaron Bancroft* (Alonzo Hill), 18, 29
dissemination, xxix; via abolitionists, 130;
attitudes toward seen in library visits,
147–50; audiences as necessarily social at
literary performances, 160; via colporteurs, xxiii, 130; commodification of,
167; complicates evidence from publisher distribution records, 168; distribution compared with, 124, 127–28;
dramatizations of literary works,
160–61; face-to-face and literary-dollars-
and-social-sense dialectic, 130; gratis
versus remunerated, 127, 130, 167–68;
impelled by social sense to achieve common literary experiences, 124; increasing
public access to literature for social purposes, 167; itinerant performers and
offenses to local social sense, 164; via
librarians, 127; librarianship in faces new
demands in move from gratis to paid,
129; major libraries seen as sites of literary achievements in, 128; via ministers,
128; new forums for in antebellum era,
xix–xx; out-of-market social forms
defined, 127; via panorama exhibitions,
127, 161–64; panorama exhibitors and
social forms of, 129; via panoramas
depicting scenes from literature, 161; via
performance events, 160, 189–90;
through performances before audiences,
xxiii–xxiv, 160–66; performative and
literary-dollars-and-social-sense dialec-

H

Habermas, Jürgen, on colonization of the lifeworld, 288n81
Hahn-Hahn, Ida Gräfin, 97, 260n18
Hale, Alexander, 26
Hale, Edward Everett, 6–7, 114, 172, 178
Hale, Nathan, xxvii
Hale, Nathan Jr., 53
Hale, Sarah P.E., 172: on balancing writing with childcare, 23; and *Boston Miscellany*, 20; Carter's publications of, 23, 39, 232n11; and children's books, 5; Colman's children's books by, 243n72; death of son occasions copying, 26; Dickens encountered and reported upon, 118, 120; and entrees into publishing, 41; on female author's writing nettling husband, 23; German translation deemed dull, 34; gift book sent gratis to contributor, 32; and gift books' quality versus remuneration, 38; Hahn-Hahn criticized, 97; illustrations criticized, 29; motive for writing, xiii; and Panic of 1837, 5; private letter of brother leaked to press, 16; proofreads brother's book, 30; publications, 232n11; on publisher's rumored failure, 39; reviews of her books dismissed as puffs, 37; on rewards from publishing, 40; *Simple Cobler of Aggawam* puff declined, 17; sketch of, xxvii; translations of, 238n40; and typographical errors, 32
Hall, Louisa Park, 7; "Caroline Gray," 38; father campaigns to collect prize money, 39; as father's protegee, xxvii; *Joanna of Naples*, 25, 26, 31, 99; literary prospects defended by gossiper, 99; manuscript of transcribed, 26; *Miriam*, 6, 33; *New England Galaxy and Pearl* awards prize, 6, 38; published work, 239n49, 277n15; reads work aloud, 25; receives contributor's fee, 38 reviews *Works of Mrs. Hemans*, 25;
Halpine, Charles Graham, 72, "Rime of Ye Seedie Printeere Man," 230n7
Hamlin, Hannibal, 4
Hamon, Jean-Marie, *Vie du Cardinal Cheverus*, 37

Handbook of Exercises and Reading Lessons for Beginners in Latin (Whiton), 17
"Hannah Binding Shoes" (Larcom), 45, 57, 69
Hannibal, Julius Caesar, *Black Diamonds*, 163
Hard Times (Dickens), 123
Harper and Brothers, xii, 181, 194
Harper's New Monthly Magazine, 22, 27, 56; author submitting manuscript depicted in, 27; circulation, 177; Larcom's plays down contributions to, 171; as venue for Trowbridge's publications, 174; women lecture-goers depicted in, 162
Harrington, Henry F., 242n71
Harris, Joshua (Edwin): as amateur author, 87; canvassing experiences compared to those of clergymen, 136, and Thoreau, 183; commissions on subscription sales, 134; compositional practices, 21; "Dreamland Bridal," 21; "The Dying Stranger," 28; as example of paid distributors, 127; failure as canvasser, 125; *Flag of Our Union* publishes rejection notice, 72; "A Friend," 32; homesickness while canvassing, 136; "Lines in Hattie Shute's Album," 21; "Lines to J.E.H.," 28; pseudonym ("H. Hamlin"), 4; as publishing outsider, 41; purchases sample papers, 131; reports difficulty of finding lodging, 135; sells recipes and impression paper, 137; sketch of, xxvi–xxvii; social intercourse underscores lack of sales, 126; submits manuscripts, 4, 27; subscription solicitations rebuffed, 130–31; victimized by busy-bodies, 136; "A Vision of Dissolution," 21; *Waverley* publishes notices of submissions' fate, 28; *Waverley* publishes poem, 32; "A Wish &c," 28; "Witches' Sacrament," 21
Harris, Neil, on "operational aesthetic," 193, 284n58
Harris, Thomas Lake, 10
Hartwell, Isaac B., 11, 235n22
Harvard University, 112, 148, 149, 151–52
Hathaway, Anne, 105–6
Hawthorne, Nathaniel, 63, 96–97, 108, 111, 238n45